Pro-Family Politics and
Fringe Parties in Canada

Chris MacKenzie

Pro-Family Politics and Fringe Parties in Canada

UBCPress · Vancouver · Toronto

15   14   13   12   11   10   09   08   07   06   05   5   4   3   2   1

Printed in Canada on acid-free paper

Library and Archives Canada Cataloguing in Publication

MacKenzie, Chris, 1963-
  Pro-family politics and fringe parties in Canada / Chris MacKenzie.

  Includes bibliographical references and index.
  ISBN 0-7748-1096-3 (bound); ISBN 0-7748-1097-1 (pbk.)

  1. Family Coalition Party of British Columbia. 2. Family – Political aspects –
British Columbia – History – 20th Century. 3. British Columbia – Politics and
government – 1991-2001. I. Title.

JL439.A53M35 2005   324.271'094   C2005-900194-1

Canadä

UBC Press gratefully acknowledges the financial support for our publishing
program of the Government of Canada through the Book Publishing Industry
Development Program (BPIDP), and of the Canada Council for the Arts, and the
British Columbia Arts Council.

This book has been published with the help of a grant from the Canadian
Federation for the Humanities and Social Sciences, through the Aid to
Scholarly Publications Programme, using funds provided by the Social
Sciences and Humanities Research Council of Canada, and with the help of
the K.D. Srivastava Fund.

UBC Press
The University of British Columbia
2029 West Mall
Vancouver, BC V6T 1Z2
604-822-5959 / Fax: 604-822-6083
www.ubcpress.ca

Sue

Contents

Acknowledgments

This book could not have been written without the help of numerous people, and I thank you all. Special thanks, though, go to a few individuals who have been pivotal in all this.

My gratitude to Yun-shik Chang for his support and, as I once said to him, for "getting me into this mess," will always be deep. I am also indebted to Brian Elliott and David Schweitzer for their patient support and suggestions. I would also like to thank the editorial and publication staff at UBC Press, in particular Emily Andrew and Darcy Cullen for their help and support.

Thanks and special appreciation also go to all the members of the Family Coalition Party and the Unity Party of British Columbia who were kind enough to grant me their time for interviews. In particular, I am greatly indebted to Kathleen and Mark Toth, founders of the Family Coalition Party, who agreed not only to my studying their organization but were also tremendously helpful in providing information that made this book possible. Similar thanks go also to Heather Stilwell and Brian Zacharias. I was greatly appreciative of their time, honesty, and forthrightness. While they may not agree with everything in the book, I hope they regard it as a reciprocal attempt to be fair and honest.

To my family, especially Christel, my mother-in-law, thank you for everything.

Then there are the two most important people in this project. First, thanks go to Bob Ratner, whose undying enthusiasm and commitment to the intellectual pursuit transcends even a vision of the ideal type. His support, encouragement, and guiding hand were invaluable; everyone should be so fortunate.

It all comes down to one person, though – Sue. All I can write here is thank you.

Chris MacKenzie

Abbreviations

CCF   Co-operative Commonwealth Federation
CCR   Canadian Christian right
CHP   Christian Heritage Party of Canada
FCP   Family Coalition Party of British Columbia
NCR   New Christian Right (United States)
NDP   New Democratic Party of Canada (and of British Columbia)
NSM   New social movement
PFM   Pro-family movement
RPBC Reform Party of BC
SMO   Social movement organization

Pro-Family Politics and
Fringe Parties in Canada

Introduction

The birth of new political parties or social movements is often traced back by the people who form them to a sense of alienation or disenfranchisement from mainstream society and politics. Such organizations revolve around issues – be they gay rights, the environment, the traditional nuclear family, pro-choice, or pro-life – their supporters identify as important concerns that have been ignored by the mainstream and so, by necessity, require a formal political voice.

These parties and movements have their own life cycles and degrees of success. The Green Party has become an international political icon for the environment, human rights, and equality. The Christian Coalition emerged in the United States in the 1990s as a dominant political force for the Christian right and pro-family movement, while the Feminist Party of Canada lived a short, ineffectual life in the early 1980s.

The Family Coalition Party of British Columbia (FCP) rose from the ashes of the Social Credit Party's collapse in 1991 and struggled to promote pro-life and pro-family causes in virtual political obscurity for nearly a decade. In November 2000, the FCP merged with four other conservative parties in the province to form the Unity Party of British Columbia. Through their efforts, those working for the FCP were able to have their pro-life and pro-family principles constitutionalized in this new party. With the emergence of this larger pro-life party, the life cycle of the FCP was completed. This book is about that life cycle and the ideological beliefs that drove it.

Throughout the 1990s, rigorous political mobilization took place in Canada and the United States around pro-family issues. It was a decade of increasing religious conservative activism that became gathered under the umbrella of the pro-family movement (PFM), a social movement with a sweeping agenda. Its activists support a political and social agenda that promotes traditional family values and opposes abortion and euthanasia. There is also support for the return of the single-income patriarchal family, for parental choice and control in education, for reduction of the Keynesian welfare state, and for the expansion of free-market neoconservative economics.

The late Reform Party of Canada was arguably the most populist and well-known Canadian version of this ideology. In Canada's 2000 federal election, Stockwell Day, then leader of Reform's successor party, the Canadian Alliance, came under media fire on several occasions for his religious conservative views on abortion and creationism[1] – attacks that hinted at a realization that Reform/Alliance could become, if it wasn't already, a political sanctuary and voice for religious conservative voters. The party, however, like its Reform predecessor, downplayed its social conservatism and religious morality in favour of a platform endorsing fiscal conservatism and espousing themes of Western alienation and electoral reform. It was an effective strategy. With its sixty-six seats, the Alliance formed the official opposition in Canada, based on what is essentially a Canadian version of America's "caring conservatism" as it appeared in the Reagan administration of the 1980s and has fervently reappeared under the presidency of George W. Bush.

In 2004, Bush was carried to re-election on the shoulders of his natural constituents – Christian evangelicals and pro-family movement supporters. The striking feature of this election is that it was driven not by the usual concerns about the economy or personal security but by concerns about the moral and social fabric of the country. Pro-family evangelicals came out in force and voted for a president who shared their moral opposition to gay rights, abortion, and sex education in schools. This electorate, seen as supporting God, guns, and school prayer, made up almost a quarter of the voters in the election, and they voted overwhelmingly for one of their own and someone whom they believe will work to restore a biblically founded social contract to America.

While this result may suggest novel support for a 1950s style of economic and cultural hegemony, it is in fact the continuation of a long social and political tradition. As recently as 1996 religious conservatives in America were having a dramatic effect on presidential politics. Led by US evangelist Pat Buchanan's Christian Coalition, pro-family religious conservatives got busy that year, targeting not just Ross Perot's small Reform Party but the Grand Old Party itself, along with its Republican presidential nominees.[2]

As in the 2004 election, at issue for them was the future of the traditional nuclear family, one in which the married man earns the income while his wife stays at home caring for their children. For the Christian Coalition, government had become overly intrusive and humanist in its affairs, and activists were expressing visceral opposition to legislation that protected rights for gays and lesbians, access to abortion, and equal employment opportunities for women and that placed heavy tax burdens on families. Pro-family forces argued that these things and more were undermining the sanctity of the traditional family and as such threatening the very future of countries like the United States and Canada.

The pro-family argument is a straightforward one: as the family goes, so goes society. And, from their cultural vista, they saw trouble brewing. Canadian or American, pro-family activists saw the traditional family as under attack and falling into an ever-deepening crisis because of an overly intrusive state and an ever-expanding secular value system.

It is this message that the pro-family movement, primarily through the work of the Christian Coalition in the United States, has been slowly generating support for and translating into political power. By the 1996 presidential campaign, this increase in influence had reached a point where Bob Dole's chief strategist warned that, "without having significant support of the Christian right, a Republican cannot win the nomination or the general election."[3] Clearly, given the results of the 2004 election, this was an accurate conclusion and one that George Bush's chief strategist, Karl Rove, obviously took to heart. And with the electoral blessing he received from his natural constituents, it seems highly probable that Bush will pursue, among other things, a constitutional amendment to protect the traditional definition of marriage as that between a man and a woman.

In its most politically pure form, this pro-family agenda calls for economic and social stability through a program of biblically informed, morally constructed, free-market-driven social policies – the sort of measures seen to be needed in a society beset by an apparent rise in social pathologies such as youth crime, teen pregnancy, and unemployment. Simultaneously, and at its tactically most vulgar, it is an agenda that argues modern society has become selfish, hedonistic, godless, man-hating, and lesbian-loving. Indeed, some Pat Buchanan supporters at the 1996 Republican National Convention could be seen sporting T-shirts that read "Intolerance is a beautiful thing."[4]

In Canada, pro-family forces are nowhere near the juggernaut the Christian Coalition has become in the US. The movement in Canada is currently a composite of scattered organizations, all moving independently towards their common goal but lacking any cohesive political unity. Like their American counterparts, organizations like Campaign Life Coalition, REAL Women of Canada, and the National Citizens Coalition are working towards the pro-family vision: a return of the traditional family to its previous position of social eminence, an end to government funding for abortion services, the promotion of free-market economic policies, and a reduction in government interference in citizens' lives.

Despite their lack of organizational unity, pro-family activists in Canada do feel there is reason to be optimistic. Culturally, this attitude is in part linked to signs that American pro-family groups have had a slow but steadily growing cross-border influence on the movement since the mid-1990s. In British Columbia, the Christian Coalition established itself in the late 1990s, and for more than a decade, Focus on the Family, James Dobson's multimillion-dollar pro-family organization, has been quietly carrying on the promotion of its pro-family message. Politically, religious conservatives find optimism not only in the growth of the Reform/Alliance party, but also in the persistence of other smaller political parties.

A unique feature of the pro-family movement in Canada has been the creation of federal and provincial political parties by pro-family activists. Federally, the Christian Heritage Party was formed in 1987 on an overtly Christian, pro-family platform, while in Ontario (1987) and BC (1991), independent efforts brought the Family Coalition Party to life as a pro-family party discretely espousing a Christian world view. These parties were created with the deliberate intention of providing religious conservatives, as well as pro-family and pro-life supporters, with a political vehicle through which they could directly engage in the political process on behalf of their cause. While such parties toil in virtual obscurity, activists argue that playing the role of the pebble in the political shoe of the country will eventually pay off.

These parties are also a direct product of Canadian political culture. The structural organization of the Canadian parliamentary system concentrates party and political power predominantly in the hands of party leaders and executives, and this can severely limit opportunities for political action within a party. This means that, unlike the more permeable American state, where lobbying efforts by movement activists have a greater number of strategic avenues open to them, Canadian activists have the more onerous challenge of convincing a few party executives and leaders to support their cause. Frequently, this situation results in movement activists being unable to make substantial inroads in the political decision making arenas via existing mainstream parties.

As was the case with the founders of the Green Party in Canada, pro-family activists in this country took matters into their own hands. They resorted to creating their own political parties in an attempt to create a political path down which they could march in an effort to influence an otherwise unresponsive Canadian state. The FCP was exactly this – a party of last resort for long-time pro-family activists who had become frustrated and discouraged by years of work within existing political parties that had produced few tangible successes.

When the Family Coalition Party emerged, it became part of a long tradition in Canadian political history – a tradition that includes the Progressive Party, the Co-operative Commonwealth Federation (later the New Democratic Party), and the Green Party. As minor political players, these organizations stand apart from typical political parties in two important ways. First, they are a clear representation of an aggrieved group of citizens. People who support these parties invariably share a concern over a single or small number of issues they believe are being ignored by the government and other larger political parties. Second, and giving these particular minor parties their most unique feature, their supporters do not have electoral success as a primary goal.

Parties like the FCP are more interested in engaging in political education than in winning political power. The FCP was run by social movement activists, not politicians, and they believed that the key to winning public and legislative support for their agenda was a campaign of broad-based educational awareness. As all social movement supporters are apt to do, the Family Coalition Party sought to effect social change its members viewed as favourable for the betterment of society, and they believed that generating awareness through education was vital to achieving their goals. Concomitantly, they understood that consciousness raising must be accompanied with access to the institutions of political power and the formal mechanisms of government policy decision making. Years of failed efforts to gain such access led the founders of the Family Coalition Party to the conclusion that, in the face of a strong Canadian state, such political opportunities must be constructed and that this demanded the creation of a political party. What resulted was a political hybrid: like other minor parties in Canadian political history, the FCP had the form of a political party but the function of a social movement. It is best understood, in other words, as a party/movement.

The kind of form/function dichotomy exhibited by party/movements such as the FCP creates for them a number of unique challenges and tensions that arise from trying to straddle two political and organizational realities. Mobilizing resources, gaining public recognition and political legitimacy, and developing professional expertise are problems that all social movements and minor parties face. A party/movement, however, must contend with a number of other challenges, including convincing what might be called its natural constituency that form need not dictate function. That is, party/movement activists must convince potential supporters that in spite of having a party form, their organization can effectively engage in activities more commonly associated with social movements.

Despite these challenges, the activists in the FCP were firmly committed to its party/movement nature, which they recognized might never lead them to a legislative seat in the province's capital. Their acceptance of this fact may seem paradoxical, given the FCP's form as a party, but it must be kept in mind that they were working primarily towards achieving social change, not towards acquiring political power for its own sake. Like all party/movement activists, they quite simply were not motivated by dreams of strutting the corridors of legislative power. Rather, they were driven more by a sense of moral obligation and by the status frustration that social conservatives have been perceiving for the past three decades in North America.

As far back as 1964, pioneering neoconservative Daniel Bell observed that, "what the right fears as a whole is the erosion of its own social position" (Bell 1964, 2). In Canada, and particularly in British Columbia, social conservatives have become alarmed at the speed of this erosion. Beginning with the federal decriminalization of abortion and the liberalization of divorce laws in the 1960s, women, minorities, and other historically disenfranchised citizens have won hard-fought battles for their right to enjoy the same full political, legal, and cultural lives that Canadian citizenship is supposed to provide. In British Columbia, the new millennium continued this pattern of growing hegemonic inclusion with legislation that, among other things, permitted gay couples to adopt children and to marry.

For social and religious conservatives, these events are only more evidence of the growing fragility surrounding their historically privileged status. In efforts designed to stem these social currents, pro-family forces like the FCP have undertaken what could be called a mission of reclamation, one that seeks to return BC and Canada to what they believe is its rightful Christian heritage and its respect for life and for family. It is an attempt to stop what they see as the destructive forces of liberal individualism and cultural relativism. In this sense, the FCP was a group of pro-life, pro-family conservatives whose aim was to build consensus and support for their social issues rather than just existing as another right-wing party promising tax cuts and pro-business economics.

Certainly their platform included a belief in the free market, but the FCP was first and foremost a party based on *social*, not economic, reformation. The party in fact never came close to developing a full economic policy. Consensus always existed among the membership that the FCP could readily support or adopt the pro-business economic platforms common to any right-wing party. Instead, they expended their energies on their social movement agenda, because, for them, economic platforms were no good without sound moral principles. The relationship was a simple one for the FCP: to prosper economically, the province needed to first build a moral foundation out of pro-family, pro-life, and other social conservative ideals.

In tackling an analysis of this religious conservative organization, this book has three manifest goals. The first is to document the history of the Family Coalition Party of British Columbia, from the genesis of an idea around a kitchen table in Victoria in 1991 through to its merger with the Reform Party of BC and its re-emergence as the Unity Party of British Columbia. However insignificant small parties like the FCP may appear to be, they do shape the political landscape in which they operate, and evidence of this can be found in the details of their daily struggles. As Chapter 1 shows, this was most certainly true of the FCP.

What else emerges in this chapter is that the Family Coalition was a pro-family organization highly commensurate with the political, social, and economic ideals of the US pro-family movement and other similar movements in Canada. It also becomes clear in this chapter that throughout its life cycle, the FCP experienced a chronic kind of identity crisis. Part social movement, part political party, the organization remained in a perpetual state of stunted development.

The second aim of this book is to trace the ideological roots and beliefs of the pro-family movement. Terms like "pro-family," "pro-life," "New Right," "neoconservative," and "neoliberal" are often associated with groups such as the FCP, but it is frequently unclear how these terms are related. Chapter 2 is about unknotting the various ideological strands that inform the pro-family movement in Canada and the United States and exposing the historical relationship between these strands. The result is the picture of a movement whose belief in the sanctity of the traditional family has deep roots in the conservative tradition of Edmund Burke and is one that is best characterized as Christian, conservative, and involved in battles over a variety of social issues. In both countries, it is also a movement sympathetic to the neoconservative economic policies to which Canada and the US have been subjected for the last two decades or so.

The final goal of this book is to understand the FCP's dual character as social movement and political party, and the unique challenges that face a party/movement in Canada's contemporary political climate. To this end, Chapter 3 analyzes the FCP as a social movement. Although this is not immediately apparent because of its political party form, if one separates its form from its function, the Family Coalition's work can be recognized as that of a social movement. Specifically, it can be understood as related to the new social movements because of its focus on identity and quality-of-life issues, even though the conservative nature of the FCP is the ideological antithesis of an NSM. As the chapter will show, it is best understood as a conservative *resurgence movement* that is attempting to promote social change while at the same time resisting the changes being brought about by the efforts of NSMs such as the ecological, gay, and feminist movements. The pro-family movement industry in British Columbia, which includes the activities, roles, and mobilization efforts of the various national and provincial organizations, is also described in this chapter. Particular attention is paid here to the relationships that exist between these organizations and the Family Coalition Party, as well as the role these organizations see the FCP as playing for the pro-family movement.

Chapter 4 is concerned with the FCP as an institutionalized political party in British Columbia. Regardless of its functional activities as a social movement, the party form of the FCP imposed upon its executives all the constraints and challenges faced by other minor political parties in Canada. This chapter first explores the nature of representative politics in Canada and the chronic crisis of representation that typically besets large mainstream political parties in the country. This failure of cadre parties to satisfactorily represent the issues that concern the country's citizens has given rise to the long history of minor political party activism in Canada and is in very large measure the reason for the existence of parties like the FCP. The challenges faced by the Family Coalition Party are then examined. Like other minor parties, the FCP had a small and scattered constituency, a lack of political expertise, and a narrow-issue focus and it had to wage its campaigns under a majoritarian, first-past-the-post election system that favours large parties or those with strongholds of regional support.

Chapter 5 explores the FCP as a party/movement in the tradition of the Co-operative Commonwealth Federation in Canada and the Green parties in Canada and Germany. Fusing party form with movement function presented the FCP with a series of tensions that it would be forced to deal with if it were to become effective and politically sustainable. Not only did it have to overcome the challenges facing social movements and political parties, it also created for itself a unique set of problems that had to be deftly managed. These compounded and created challenges are discussed, as is the prognosis for party/movements as viable political entities.

The Conclusion revisits these arguments and assesses the Family Coalition Party's decision to merge and become the Unity Party of BC in terms of what risks such a decision poses to its movement principles and to the political viability of this new pro-life party.

1
The Family Coalition Party of British Columbia: A Party of Last Resort

Nineteen ninety-one was a year of some remark for conservative politics in British Columbia. Easter brought the resignation of Social Credit premier William Vander Zalm as he faced conflict-of-interest charges surrounding the sale of his Fantasy Gardens. In addition to that, the autumn provincial election foreshadowed the erosion and splintering of the solid conservative bloc known as Social Credit that had largely dominated BC politics for the past forty years. Hugely dissatisfied with Vander Zalm's administration, the electorate had not only brought the NDP back to power after more than fifteen years, but it had also reintroduced the Liberal Party into the BC political landscape.

For religious conservatives in the province, these political developments were a sword with two particularly sharp edges. On one side, the province had taken a decided shift to the left with the NDP victory, which threatened to create a more difficult political climate in which to foster conservative social and economic policies. On the other side, they had lost both a premier and a political party sympathetic to their concerns over pro-life and pro-family issues. Politically homeless, the staunchest of these Socred refugees sat down at a kitchen table in Victoria and created BC's first pro-life and pro-family political party, the Family Coalition Party of British Columbia (FCP).

Registered in June 1991, the FCP was a socially conservative free-enterprise party founded on two unconditional principles. The first supported a definition of human life as beginning from the moment of conception and ending at the point of natural death. The second espoused support for defining family as that of a legally married man and woman with natural or adopted children. The remainder of the party's policies and mandates were directed towards the legislative support of these principles. These included such proposals as the removal of abortion funding from the medicare fee schedule and the passage of "family-friendly" legislation that would ease the tax burden on working parents and grant greater parental control over a child's education.

It was a platform that attracted a small but extremely dedicated core membership of long-time pro-life and pro-family activists. The founders of the party, Kathleen and Mark Toth, had been active in the pro-life movement for more than twenty-five years. The leader of the party, Heather Stilwell, also had a long history of pro-life activism, as well as having been the past leader of the Christian Heritage Party. Executive board members brought equally long records of involvement in the movement, and the majority of the general membership were active or at the very least held memberships in pro-life or pro-family organizations. In its nine years of existence, the FCP ran candidates in two general elections and six by-elections, earning the respect and admiration if not the electoral support of the pro-life and pro-family community in BC.

In November 2000, the FCP, together with the Reform Party of British Columbia and other minor right-wing parties in the province, merged to form a new conservative provincial party, the Unity Party of British Columbia. Odd as it may seem, this kind of merger was in fact one of the hopes if not goals of the FCP from its inception. While determined to keep the party alive and have their message heard, the Toths and others in the party had always been realistic about how much they could achieve as such a small organization. After nine years of marginal existence, they recognized that the Unity merger was timely. After the 1996 provincial election, the high-water mark for the FCP as a political body, the party had found itself unable to build on whatever momentum it had gained in its first five years. In hindsight, even the results of 1996 came to be viewed by the executive as disappointing. This disappointment and latent frustration was born in no small part from the party's inability to expand its membership base. From 1996 until the merger, this number hovered between eight hundred and one thousand members. The executive saw this as evidence that they were unable to expand the party into a more viable political force because of their lack of expertise and manpower. More skilled and experienced in the area of social movement activism, the FCP executive had difficulty managing the demands of developing into a legitimate mainstream political party. In many ways, this was hardly surprising. Many of those involved with the party, while resolutely committed to it, saw its mandate as primarily educative and regarded electoral success as an essential but secondary goal of the organization.

It is this last point that made the FCP unique among the province's political parties. Its aim was to raise awareness among British Columbians about legislation that the party regarded as harmful to the traditional family and that denigrated respect for human life, and to have such laws changed. Yet the party did not consider winning political power as primary to achieving these ends. In this regard, Bill Vander Zalm, who was instrumental in developing the initial membership base for the party, commented that "they are very different from any other political party that I know, in the sense that they are not running to win an election, but rather see it as an opportunity to obtain the best possible platform for the purpose of debating their beliefs and their views of what is needed in this particular society, meaning BC." They were a party seeking change, not power. Indeed, Mrs. Toth remarked that it "would be nice if we didn't even have to be here," but years of frustrating work within other political parties and in the general pro-family movement had produced few tangible victories and ultimately led them to the last resort of forming a political party.

It was a situation that put them in the company of other party/movements in the history of Canadian politics. Unable to achieve the change they were seeking through traditional social movements or mainstream political parties, the founders of the FCP decided to use the form of a political party to do the work of a social movement. It was a decision that would create some difficult struggles for the party, but one that did ultimately lead to the emergence of the province's newest pro-life party, the Unity Party of British Columbia. It was also a decision forced upon the founders by changes within the Social Credit Party and, ironically, one that made a significant contribution to the final collapse of this once venerable political organization.

Put Out on the Street: Social Credit Goes Secular

When Bill Vander Zalm took over the leadership of the Social Credit Party of BC in 1986 and subsequently became premier, a wave of hope and optimism must have run through the province's pro-life and pro-family ranks. Here was a Catholic premier, not afraid to take a stand openly opposing abortion, leading a free-enterprise party founded on Christian principles.[1] Having known Vander Zalm for over fifteen years, the Toths had offered their support to him should he pursue the Socred leadership, and they joined the party as a result of his acclamation as leader.[2] Heather Stilwell and her husband, along with many other FCP members, had also been active within the Social Credit Party before and during Vander Zalm's time with the party. Whatever initial optimism existed, though, likely turned to frustration for these religious conservatives as they witnessed Vander Zalm politically pilloried for his attempts to remove abortion from the medicare fee schedule, as well as the eventual dismantling of the Christian philosophy of the Social Credit Party.

As the Toths describe it, several pro-life lobbyists attended the 1986 Socred leadership convention in Whistler, BC, and backed Mr. Vander Zalm because of the forthright position he took in opposing abortion in general and specifically the use of public funds to pay for the procedure. In 1988, Premier Vander Zalm attempted to turn this position into Social Credit Party policy by making a proclamation in the provincial legislature that the government would no longer fund abortions on demand. In a lengthy ministerial statement, the premier made his government's position clear:

> The Supreme Court in its judgment made a serious statement of concern when it acknowledged that a fetus – Latin for "baby" – at some point was no longer a part of a woman, but rather an individual human being with its own right to protection. At what point they didn't, couldn't or wouldn't say, but rather said legislators would need to decide this very quickly ... My government takes the position that we can in no way be a party to open abortion on demand. The court has spoken. We cannot stop abortions, but we can speak out on behalf of humanity, on behalf of those babies and in support of morality. Our action is not simply an issue of public moneys used for the funding of a cause but rather one where in a forthright way we also say that society cannot be expected to rectify whatever some individuals may be unhappy with in their lives ... The senseless termination of human life at the slightest whim or notion is simply removing yet another stone from the wall of an already crumbling society ... As far as one's moral values influencing government's decisions, I could never support legislation which I would consider to be immoral ... I cannot be a liar or a hypocrite.[3]

The proclamation was subsequently overturned by the courts because no statute had been passed by the government on which to found the removal of abortion funding from the fee schedule.

For Vander Zalm and many of his supporters, this political debacle alluded to a growing conspiracy within the Socred party to undermine the premier's credibility, as well as generate support for an emergent secular humanist philosophy inside the party.[4] In a 1994 *BC Report* article, Vander Zalm described it this way: "In 1988 the tables turned and the knives came out ... Suffice it to say that leaks from confidential cabinet meetings started to undermine the government's efforts. Only that which some wanted to see in public debate was leaked in distorted fashion ... There was the cabinet decision not to fund abortions through the health plan – which soon turned into a pro-life/pro-choice debate."[5] This adversarial climate within the Social Credit Party came to characterize the next three years of Vander Zalm's premiership, as the rift between the conservative and liberal elements within the party continued to grow.

The rift was not so much a product of Vander Zalm's taking over leadership of the Socreds as it was the result of a change in the party's ideological support base that had begun years before. For example, as political scientist Robert Burkinshaw observes, when Bill Bennett won the 1975 provincial election, "Social Credit was not entirely the same party it had once been. It had added to its former populist constituency (which had largely been centred in the interior and the Fraser Valley) much of the sophisticated urban constituency in the upper-middle-class areas of Vancouver, which in the past had usually supported the provincial Liberal party" (Burkinshaw 1995, 199). As he explained in one of his interviews with me, Vander Zalm believes that the tension created by this change fully emerged only after Bennett stepped down:

It started I guess at the leadership convention at Whistler, where the initial rift between the more liberal and conservative element [sic] came to the fore. It existed during Bill Bennett's time and W.A.C. Bennett's time, but because it was viewed by many long-time Socreds as a sort of Bennett party, no one really dared or bothered to challenge much. That changed following Whistler in 1986, and I guess immediately after the leadership convention the more liberal element began to organize and they became more daring during the heated debates over abortion funding in 1988.

This increased activity by the liberal element of the Socreds was forcing the party's religious conservatives to its fringes as they found maintaining their ideological presence a progressively difficult task. In an attempt to counter this growing influence, Kathleen Toth ran for the Socred candidacy in the 1990 by-election in Oak Bay–Gordon Head to at least give some profile to the pro-life religious conservatives in the party. In the press, this was described as a "nasty battle for the Socred nomination in Oak Bay/Gordon Head between Oak Bay Mayor Susan Brice and conservative Catholic Kathleen Toth."[6] Toth lost the nomination to Brice, but Toth says Brice resigned her nomination before the election because "Brice said my people [Toth's] wouldn't help her in an election and so she believed she couldn't win."[7] Later that year, Toth tried again by running for the nomination in the Victoria–Beacon Hill by-election. In this nomination race, Toth says she "ran into a party machine, like the Republican convention. We ran into balloons, bands, and several ministers there, it was obvious overkill, and that they didn't want me to win."[8] She lost the nomination to Suzanne Hansen, a Beacon Hill alderman. These kinds of situations gave more proof to religious conservatives that they were becoming ever more alienated.

This sense of ebbing security among religious conservative Socreds was further accelerated by a 1990 challenge to the Christianity clause in the party's constitution. This proved to be the crippling blow for Socreds like the Toths, who viewed the removal of the clause as the final surrender to the secular and liberal forces within the party. Vander Zalm viewed the situation this way:

It was a real struggle to keep peace between the liberal and conservative elements within Social Credit. That was my challenge, and I found it to be an impossible one, but for many of the conservative elements with Social Credit, that related particularly to its rather pro-Christian image, because basically Social Credit was born out of the Christian movement many years back. And many that related to its pro-Christian image, they suffered great disappointments during that struggle ... because the more liberal element's first achievement was to, in the name of political correctness, destroy the appearance of the pro-Christian image.

The issue of the Christianity clause came forward at the party's 1989 annual convention when an Orthodox Jewish member walked out of the convention in opposition to the clause and the executive's refusal to withdraw it forthwith. Viewing it as exclusionary to anyone other than Christians, the member was quoted as saying, "let the right wingers go because you're opening up the party to the mainstream, liberals and conservatives. Let's make it what it's supposed to be, a mainstream party. That's what Grace McCarthy envisions ... There's room for all. It's time the fundamentalists took the blinders off. The constitution should be changed to meet the 1990s."[9]

After a year-long review, a constitutional amendment convention was held and the Christianity clause was replaced by one that referred to God but mentioned nothing about Christian principles.[10] Some members, like the Toths, viewed this as a deliberate political strategy by Grace McCarthy to wrestle control of the party away from conservatives and further undermine Premier Vander Zalm's credibility.[11] According to Mrs. Toth, when the initial vote for the change was brought to the floor, the change was defeated, but McCarthy quickly stood up and claimed her vote hadn't been counted. During the delay, a number of her supporters were brought in from the hallway outside and, in a second vote, the change was approved.[12] This proved to be a defining moment for religious conservative politics in the province because it led directly to the formation of the FCP. As Mrs. Toth remarked: "The FCP wouldn't have happened if this hadn't happened."

Vander Zalm's staunchest supporters felt that his leadership had been continually sabotaged by these kinds of tactics from the moment of his surprise victory at the 1986 Whistler leadership convention. Vander Zalm had entered the race at its midpoint after meeting with McCarthy, who was hoping he would draw enough votes away from Bud and Brian Smith to allow her to win. His unexpected victory, though pleasant for religious conservatives like the Toths, nonetheless left several high-profile Socreds disappointed. In an article in *BC Report,* Vander Zalm said:

Grace and her advisers were terribly embittered and refused to follow through on the commitment of support; the knives were quickly drawn by a number of losers ... I believed that for the sake of party unity and the good of our province, I should trust the defeated leadership candidates and some of their handlers or advisers and bring them on side by offering them good, high-profile positions ... These appointees were standing behind me from the first day of picture-taking – a most uncomfortable position, I was to learn shortly after.[13]

The Toths and several FCP members who were Vander Zalm supporters cited this chronic backstabbing of the premier by his cabinet as part of their reason for leaving the Socreds and a source of their disillusionment over party politics in general. Asked whether this had motivated his supporters to leave the Socreds and join the FCP, Vander Zalm replied:

Anyone that sees people in politics to be nice people is probably very far off base. They are not the nicest people in society that find their place in politics. They are often people that are seeking power, influence, position, stature, recognition, all the sorts of qualities that don't necessarily make the type of person one would seek out to be a loyal, true and good friend. So for people to view what happened to me as backstabbing, they are losing sight of the fact that it is not really a nice business with nice people.

The ultimate sabotage of Vander Zalm's leadership, though, proved to be self-inflicted. On 2 April 1991, Conflict of Interest Commissioner Ted Hughes found Vander Zalm guilty of using his position as a public official for personal benefit during his sale of Fantasy Gardens, a business privately owned by the premier and his wife. Less than an hour after these findings were released, Vander Zalm stepped down as premier.[14] For the Toths, this was one more nail in the Socred Party coffin, but their loyalty to Vander Zalm remained firm. In a show of support, they wrote letters to the editor defending the disgraced premier and helped organize an eight-hundred-person rally on the lawn of the legislature just days after Ted Hughes' findings.[15]

The proverbial straw came for the Toths in the subsequent leadership convention when Rita Johnston took over the party and declared it pro-choice. This left the Toths not simply without a party in which to be politically active, but without one for which they could even vote. Mrs. Toth describes it this way: "Rita Johnston, who became the leader, informed everybody the Social Credit Party was now pro-choice, and so we realized we didn't have a party anymore, because it is a position of conscience, it's a disqualifying issue for us. If someone doesn't think there is anything wrong with abortion, then we can't vote for them, and we knew we had no one we could vote for, since the other parties had stated their party positions on the abortion issue and they all had the same position."

The risk posed by alienating religious conservatives was not lost on the new Socred leadership, nor was their importance to the party. Socred executives appealed to members like the Toths to stay the course because they recognized that, "under Vander Zalm, the Socreds rallied strong Christian support for the party the likes of which had not been seen since the early 1970s, when W.A.C. Bennett invoked higher powers in the battle against the godless socialists. Prior to the 1986 election, Vander Zalm's proud declaration of faith drew no fewer than 11 potential Socred candidates from the ranks of serious Christians."[16]

For the Toths, it was a hollow appeal. The party they had actively supported for more than five years had betrayed their friend, denied its Christian foundations, and abandoned any moral concern for prenatal life; it had become secular, humanist, and vulgarly opportunistic. For the true religious conservatives of the province, the road to Damascus no longer wound through the Social Credit Party of BC. In fact, Mrs. Toth may have made a prophetic comment during the debate over the Christianity clause when she said, "The roots of the Social Credit party are Christian ... [when she and her family lived in Alberta] we saw the Social Credit party die in one election, and it was after they removed the Christianity clause."[17]

This is a position the Toths hold today regarding the disintegration of the BC Socred party, although whether the collapse of the Socreds was primarily a result of the party's losing the support of its Christian constituency is a matter of some speculation. Some FCP members' comments concur with the Toths: "The rock-solid base of the party was the Christian element and when that left, there was nothing left for the party. That is why the Social Credit Party collapsed." However, there are those, like Mr. Vander Zalm, who remain doubtful about such a unilateral explanation:

> I think that Social Credit did not have an exposé [sic] on Christian members, but many of the more conservative Christians probably felt more at home with Social Credit, where they could mix and mingle with people of similar minds, than they would with another party. If that one issue alone, because it became so controversial towards the end within Social Credit, had turned off all Christians and caused the collapse of Social Credit and the formation and growth of other parties, then the FCP first of all, and Reform secondly should have been much more the beneficiary of that than they were. I don't think the Christian community is nearly as cohesive as some of the other identifiable communities within society as it affects politics.

Nonetheless, the 1991 general election relegated the Socreds to third-party standing as they won just seven legislative seats, and in 1996 they were virtually wiped off the political map in BC when they failed to win a single seat and received less than 2 percent of the popular vote.[18] Conventions suffered a similar fate. Unlike previous conventions, which were heavily attended, the 1994 convention drew only 254 delegates, and only 1,919 of 36,000 members cast a ballot as Larry Gillanders became the new leader of the nearly defunct party. Ironically, a Socred Women's Auxiliary luncheon honouring Mr. Vander Zalm drew more attention than the actual convention. About the lack of interest in this convention, Vander Zalm said, "There are still an awful lot of people out there that would like to support Social Credit. But they might feel more at home with Reform or Family Coalition, now that the Socreds want to become more like where the Liberals are at."[19]

In 1997, Social Credit executives attempted to revitalize the party through participation in the Enterprise League of British Columbia, which was an attempt to rebuild the province's once solid right-wing bloc by bringing together the numerous conservative parties that emerged after the collapse of Social Credit. One of the last Socred leaders, Ken Endean, even entertained changing the name of the party in an attempt to remedy the problem of the splintered right-wing vote, which many conservatives feel allowed the NDP to win the 1996 general election.[20] Grace McCarthy was another supporter of forming such a bloc – "if that doesn't happen in the next three or four years ... we could repeat history" – and Liberal and Reform party executives began discussions on a merging of the parties.[21]

As for the FCP, Mrs. Toth was invited and attended the initial meeting of the Enterprise League. But these initial merger discussions led nowhere, particularly for the FCP. The party was certainly not opposed to such a coalition. In fact, it would have welcomed one, but only if such a merger included the acceptance of the FCP's two foundational principles. It would be another three years of hard work before this situation would arise in the form of the Unity merger.

"What the Heck, Why Don't We Just Do It?": A New Political Party Is Born

There is a certain odd symmetry between celebrations surrounding Easter and the rise of the FCP. Christian, pro-life sentiments had been killed off in the Social Credit Party once Bill Vander Zalm stepped down and Rita Johnston became interim premier, but they were resurrected soon after Easter 1991, when Kathleen and Mark Toth first sat down at a kitchen table with two relatives and a friend to discuss the potential of forming their own political party.

The initial discussion was largely the product of the Toths' frustration with the tumultuous year they had just experienced with the Socreds and a casual remark made by a relative that they should consider forming their own party. The Toths had heard that a pro-life/pro-family party had formed in Ontario several years earlier for reasons identical to their own plight – with no party supporting a position guaranteeing the inalienable right to life, there was no place to cast their vote. Mrs. Toth remembers:

> Mark and I discussed forming another party, "well we have to have ten thousand signatures, that lets us off the hook." We had no responsibility to do that, because although there may be other people who feel like we do, we felt if we could do something that was within our expertise, we would, but we didn't feel obliged to go to those lengths. When we inquired with BC Elections and found out they only needed five signatures, a non-profit society needed five directors, and that would be the beginning of the political party, we felt we didn't have an excuse not to try and the FCP was formed.

After several initial meetings, inquiries to the Family Coalition Party of Ontario, and working out the specific details required to register and operate a political party in BC, the Toths turned in their Socred memberships and prepared to launch the FCP in British Columbia.

The Toths acknowledge that the sanctity-of-life issue was the primary impetus for the party's formation, but certainly the removal of the Christianity clause from the Socred constitution was nearly as significant. One early member observed, "he [a member at the convention] was the impetus for the FCP because Mark and Kathleen felt so frustrated about the issue of Christian values. Without him, there wouldn't be an FCP." For the Toths, there was an inevitable connection between the two, because, as Mrs. Toth puts it, "with the removal of the Christianity clause, we could see it beginning to disintegrate. We felt if the Christian principles were gone, then it wouldn't be long before the rest of it fell." Mr. Toth views these events more as a catalyst. Having run in Edmonton as a pro-life Liberal during the 1979 federal election and been active trying to pass pro-life legislation within the Alberta Social Credit Party, Mr. Toth believes that their "impetus to form this party was forming all the time, maybe unconsciously." After finding out that the BC Election Act required only five signatures to establish a board of directors for a political party, they decided, "What the heck, why don't we just do it?"

Having no experience in the development and workings of a political party constitution, the Toths approached the executive of the Ontario FCP about the possibility of using theirs as a foundation. The Ontario party executive agreed, on the condition that the Toths use the name Family Coalition Party. The Toths did not care for the name, but, needing the constitution, they agreed, and after some minor modifications they had the FCP's first constitution.[22] To acquire the five signatures necessary to register the party, the Toths attended a pro-life convention and gathered twenty-one signatures for the party's first board of directors. On 25 June 1991, the party was officially registered with Elections BC as the society known as the Family Coalition Party of British Columbia.

In British Columbia, the FCP was, as Mr. Toth describes it, "a new kind of party because of strong pro-life, pro-family principles. To my knowledge, there has never been a party whose main principles are pro-life, pro-family. That may be unpopular, but I believe it will be a torch." Despite the recognition of the unpopularity or political incorrectness of taking an inviolable pro-life stand, the Toths drew a hard line:

> There is always someone within the group who would say, "Maybe we should downgrade the abortion issue" so we could get elected. But the basis of our party was the sanctity of life. We wanted that up front, even if not politically wise [sic]. We also felt strongly that family was suffering and we wanted to have that up front as well. We have to protect the traditional family, male and female. Sometimes families have problems, but the family is the source of humanity, and that is where our greatest problem was derived from, the breakdown of the family.

The Toths did, however, deliberately steer the party away from one contentious issue. There was no mention of Christianity, God, or Christian principles in the party's constitution. As Mr. Toth describes it, they spoke to a number of their friends and advisors, including Mr. Vander Zalm and a number of clergy, but were strongly advised not to "even mention the God thing, just do the Christian thing. Therefore, we didn't mention God in our constitution but based the principles on Judaeo-Christian principles."

It is a strategy that was only marginally successful. While most of the membership agreed it was not overtly Christian like the Christian Heritage Party, they did view it as religious in its guiding principles and membership makeup. The most common response among the membership was that, "it's not a religious party per se but a moral party, and religious people tend to join it." So despite the attempts to deflect and downplay their religious conservative roots, only one viable conclusion can be drawn: the FCP was a religious conservative party whose policies and rhetoric resonated strongly with the pro-family, pro-life Christian right movements in the US and Canada. It was a party that, among other positions, was opposed to abortion, gay rights, and feminism.

Abortion, Euthanasia, and Reproductive Technology

As far as the Toths and the FCP membership were concerned, when the sanctity of life is defended, it becomes the cornerstone upon which every other social issue and government policy naturally builds. Mrs. Toth remarked that when you have addressed the pro-life issue, "when that one is right, the other ones fall into place." Another executive member put it like this: "Number one is to defend the sanctity and right to life. Without life, nothing else matters. It doesn't matter if you get an education, if we deny life, we deny everything."

For the FCP, these kinds of moral issues must be given priority over economic considerations. Bill Stilwell, another long-time FCP member, believes "we can address economic issues just as well as anybody else can, but it is the moral issues that have to be addressed, the fundamental underlying causes of what is happening to our society today, and we try to address those issues and direct them from the perspective of the family. So it started from the pro-life thing and becomes more encompassing." It is not surprising, then, that, in its constitution, the second stated purpose of the FCP was: "2(b) To enact laws and policies which recognize the right to life of every innocent human being from conception to natural death."

For the general membership, this clause is what made the FCP a safe haven for their vote. A great many of the membership admitted to spoiling their ballot or simply not voting during provincial elections because there was no pro-life party that they could support. Deeply committed to their pro-life beliefs, members commonly said things like, "Yeah, I wasted my vote, I admit it. I feel conscience bound not to vote for someone I cannot respect morally or ethically, and so I go in there and I spoil my ballot." It also resulted in a general membership concentrated with long-time pro-life activists. Mrs. Toth herself was national president of Campaign Life Canada (which would later become Campaign Life Coalition) for four years in the late 1970s and early 1980s, and Heather Stilwell was a past national president of Alliance for Life.

The single biggest disappointment for the party, then, became the lack of support it received from the province's pro-life population. Estimates put the pro-life community at roughly twenty-five thousand in BC, but with a membership of less than a thousand, this community clearly did not embrace the FCP in a way that might have been anticipated.

Politically, the FCP constructed its policies and activities to reflect its staunch pro-life position. The health care policy stated that the party would "discontinue government funding of abortions, grants to abortion clinics, condoms and syringe programs, in vitro fertilization, sterilization, fetal transplants, fetal experimentation programs and euthanasia" but "support grants for needy pregnant mothers and their babies, early prenatal counselling about alcohol, drugs and poor nutrition so as to decrease the number of premature births and low birth-weight babies." The FCP also held an "opposition to the replacement of elected hospital boards by government-appointed regional community health boards."[23] Additionally, they supported the implementation of a conscience clause for health care workers that would protect them from penalty should they refuse to perform or assist with a procedure they may find "morally repugnant."[24] The party also publicly opposed the availability of the morning-after pill at regional health units and Bill 48, the so-called bubble zone legislation, which prevents pro-life protesters from coming within fifty metres of what they have termed the "Everywoman's Abortuary."[25]

The most significant activism the FCP engaged in concerning abortion came in the spring of 1992, when the party opposed the million dollars allotted to twenty-eight women's centres in the province by the NDP.[26] It took the form of the party collecting 6,100 signatures in an attempt to force the government to hold a referendum on the public funding of abortion under the new Recall and Initiative Act.[27] Despite being unsuccessful, the party continued to collect upwards of ten thousand signatures with which it intended to mount a future attempt.[28]

When it came to elections, abortion rarely emerged as controversial during campaign activities and all-candidates meetings. For the most part, the FCP appeared to be naturally recognized in the province as the pro-life party, for which it was neither attacked nor supported. During a 1996 all-candidates meeting in the West Vancouver–Capilano riding, for instance, candidate Jim Kelly fielded a question about education from a lady who identified him as a member of the "Right-to-Life Party" even though the topic of abortion never arose during the debate.[29] The 1996 provincial election was one of the few times abortion did become polemical. During the campaign, two candidates deliberately highlighted the party's pro-life position in a potentially confrontational fashion. In the Vancouver–Kensington riding, Mark Toth placed a sign on the lawn of Gianna House, a privately owned home beside the Everywoman's Health Clinic, that read, "Your Taxes Pay for Killing Unborn Babies Next Door. The Family Coalition Party would stop such funding. In Vancouver–Kensington vote for Mark Toth."[30] In the riding of Nelson–Creston, candidate Brian Zacharias had a four-foot by eight-foot sign made for the back of his pickup truck that read, "Elect Brian Zacharias. The Family Coalition Party of BC. Homosexuality and Abortion are against God and Nature. Take a Stand. Love Tells the Truth."

Beyond abortion, the FCP was similar to the broader pro-life movement in its position on euthanasia and reproductive technology, yet more passive about speaking out in opposition to them. In identifying respect for life as the overriding principle of the FCP, Mrs. Toth commented that "it's not only abortion but euthanasia, bioengineering, experimental embryology and that," and the party's website stated that "the Family Coalition Party opposes in-vitro fertilization, artificial insemination, fetal transplants, cloning and other fetal experiment programs, embryo and gamete cryogenesis, surrogate motherhood and abortion." Nonetheless, these topics rarely arose during party meetings and strategy sessions.

While the membership did appear to uniformly oppose euthanasia as it did abortion, this trend did not extend to matters of reproductive technology. There was a certain moral horror reflected in members' comments about some of these technologies, but they showed a range of opinions on its acceptability:

> I'm not quite sure of the full impact of it – frozen embryos in Britain, frozen and destroyed, I don't like that, and manipulating genes is no good but using an artificial way for a man and wife to conceive is good. God has given us the technology to use but we have to use it well and not abuse it.

> I think any of that meddling in procreation is absolutely against God's will and anyone who promotes it or does it, well, unless they change their ways will be condemned to hell. It's just not an acceptable part of our society.

> Bad, bad, it's caused more trouble than anything else.

> I know there are many pro-lifers who feel in vitro's okay to help a couple conceive but I feel medical science has used experimentation in the stream of life to the point that it is creating some kind of monster. It's like some things you think are good because this couple wanted a baby so badly, so it must be good, but at the same time they're doing all that experimenting, treating life as if it were a toy.

These statements betray a conflict for the pro-family membership of the FCP. While they see that such technologies could be used to strengthen the traditional family, members also view them as teetering on a humanist slippery slope they believe is having a devastating effect on the traditional family. The way out of this double bind for the FCP was through restricting abortions. They argue that by doing this, and promoting opportunities for mothers to carry to term, adoption waiting lists would be reduced and couples would not have to resort to using such technologies in order to conceive.

Of the reproductive technologies available for women and couples, though, it is still the birth control pill that is blamed for the greatest amount of damage to the traditional family and traditional social values. As one member put it, when the pill was "one of the up and coming things, STDs spread like wildfire and when women went on the pill they became promiscuous, what feminists called sexually active." This link between reproductive control, feminism, and the threat to the traditional family was a common theme among the membership. As another member commented, these technologies allow "unmarried woman or lesbian couples to have artificial insemination, which is appalling because you are deliberately denying that child a father." All in all, they argue, reproductive technologies have promoted the idea that children are a commodity rather than a gift from God, cheapened the value of life, devalued the role of the traditional family, and helped contribute to the acceptance of homosexuality.

Gay Rights

While reproductive technologies are troubling for them, of more serious concern to the FCP is the threat gay rights pose to the traditional family. The prospect of gay couples adopting children and demanding equal status with married heterosexual couples is viewed with egregious and highly moral disdain. One member saw it as an "illogical statement that you can have gay marriage. They can't produce offspring, it is a falsehood, it is a sham." Such opinions were almost unanimous among FCP members. They come from a deeply rooted belief that homosexuality is unnatural, unhealthy, against God's will, and detrimental to the general social well-being:

> If you're going to accept God's laws, which I feel a civilization that will prosper will do, then homosexuality is against the laws of God and nature and when we ignore those laws it is to our detriment. When the government makes a day of it and fusses over it, gives it special status, then the government is going along a Sodom and Gomorrah path.

> We're all fallen creatures – we inherited certain tendencies and faults or evil inclinations, if you like, and each of us is saddled with those imperfections and one of these is homosexual tendencies. So it's a cross, an imperfection that becomes so powerful and they don't necessarily see what they're doing is wrong. So first of all it's spiritually destructive, then physically destructive, obviously it's AIDS, which is killing the homosexuals.

> I don't see why they should have more rights. They're not producing any kids, quite the opposite, they contribute nothing to the family. I can't think of sodomy doing one bit of good for anyone except satisfying someone's pleasure. If they contributed something it would be different but they contribute nothing.

Characteristic of social conservative thought, though, is the presence of a tension between such vehement opposition to homosexuality and the recognition that the gay community may indeed require some kind of assistance or protection. One member, reflecting on her own reaction to gay rights, said that it "brings up antagonistic, hostile thoughts that are wrong and judgmental. For example, when I think of homosexuals as teachers, dentists, doctors and preparing food I get upset. But they're God's children just like yourself and deserve support, but I don't think they should be singled out for special rights. But I do think they need protection from people like me who may be hostile or judgmental." There were also those who took a far more liberal tack on gay rights, although they correctly observed that they were very much in the minority: "I think the party sees them as helping to destroy the family, but I'm not opposed to gay rights. It is an issue that should be left up to the courts to decide. There's no excuse for violence, for prohibition from teaching and things like that. I don't know if kids should be taught those lifestyles in the school, though. Probably I'm the odd one out here."

All these opinions expose the two main oppositions the FCP held regarding homosexuality. The first is the classification of gays as a special-interest group, a status that grants them apparent preferential treatment under the Human Rights Act, as well as providing them with government funding to promote their cause. This was broadly reflected in one of the party's finance policies, which stated: "The Family Coalition Party opposes grants to special-interest groups." Members saw no reason why this group should receive any social right or privilege beyond the average citizen's. One member commented that, "when it boils down to it, 1 percent, although they'd say more, are homosexual and that blows me away, because for 1 percent the amount of rights and privileges is amazing." Another said, "Gay rights, they're damaging. It's ridiculous to talk about them because they have the same rights as anyone else."

In 1994, the party presented a brief to the BC human rights review opposing the NDP government's proposal to recognize same-sex unions as legally equivalent to heterosexual marriages.[31] Their argument was based on the infertility of the same-sex union and the party's position that marriage, as a legal union between a man and woman, has as its primary purpose the procreation and raising of children. From their position, granting legal status to same-sex couples becomes a special right, because, "homosexual and lesbian couples do not suffer discrimination when society rules they are ineligible to adopt children. They have chosen a lifestyle which makes them ineligible."[32] The party also opposed the human rights amendment acts, Bill 32 and Bill 33, because it was believed that these acts would unduly restrict freedom of speech and thus the party's opportunity to voice a dissenting view about homosexuality, particularly during election times.[33] In this instance, there was a general sentiment within the party that the government had elevated the rights of certain special-interest groups over those of others, particularly religious conservatives, through such protective measures.[34]

The other opposition to gay rights was more serious for the membership because of the grave implications it saw such rights having for traditional families. The right of gays to be parents was stridently reviled by the party. The party's 1996 election brochures stated that, "we oppose: the adoption of infants and children by homosexuals," and in one constituency, a newsletter was distributed that included excerpts from William Gairdner's *War against the Family* under the heading "The Radical Homosexuals' Agenda," which was used to buttress the party's opposition to adoption by gay couples. The party took an active role in attempting to prevent the change in the new Adoption Act that would permit gays to adopt by circulating a petition against it throughout churches in the province.[35] Nonetheless, the act passed and was reported in an FCP newsletter: "The worst has happened by Order in Council! On Feb. 17th we learned that the NDP government has secretly changed the Adoption Act to allow same sex couples the same opportunity as heterosexual couples to adopt children."[36]

Management of the party's position against homosexuality was handled in a number of ways by FCP candidates during general and by-elections. Most made little or no reference to gay rights, although during a local television debate, one candidate did say, "Government increasingly is undermining traditional values. They redefined the family and extended same sex spousal benefits to all prov. Gov. [sic] employees and the NDP also *amended the adoption-act to allow Homosexuals to adopt infants and children* [sic] ... The traditional marriage based family is under attack to a large extent through Gov. policies [sic]" (emphasis in the original).

Two candidates, however, chose a strategy that deliberately highlighted the party's position. Brian Zacharias, the Nelson–Creston candidate, had the previously mentioned four-foot by eight-foot sign proclaiming "Homosexuality and Abortion are against God and Nature." The sign, which he acknowledged was a "very bold statement to make," resulted in a visit from the director of the Canadian Anti-Racist Education and Research Society. Unsure whether the visit was official – the two had known each other for many years – Mr. Zacharias nonetheless assumed someone had registered a complaint against the sign.[37]

John Krell, meanwhile, running in Comox Valley, created a political firestorm and ended up on the front page of the local paper by claiming during an all-candidates meeting at the local high school that homosexuals should be discriminated against.[38] He was quoted in the paper as saying, "Homosexuality should still be discriminated against, the homosexuals need help. You do not help a person by affirming them in their lifestyle. You need to help them get out and there are ways out. Their lifestyle choice is wrong, has always been wrong, will always be wrong. They're not following what The Designer says, and they'll suffer for it. So will we if we legitimize it."[39]

Reportedly, the comment resulted in a sound booing of the candidate by students in the audience, and a scathing local editorial said Krell's statement was "nothing less than promotion of hate."[40] Despite this fervent response, Dr. Krell remained unrepentant, arguing that the only way to restore traditional values in society is to "get the truth out and give them an honest choice"[41] – a position that reflected the FCP's stalwart commitment to restoring traditional family values regardless of how difficult the challenge became.

The Public Education System

The reaction to Dr. Krell's statements at the local high school did not surprise many in the FCP. The party regarded the public schools in BC as one of the prime institutions the state and special-interest groups have used to promote a secular humanist agenda for society. FCP members see traditional family values, as well as parental authority, being undermined and slowly destroyed by a humanist curriculum that indoctrinates students with visions of alternative lifestyles, medical freedom of choice, and selfish liberal attitudes. What they see spawned from this program is a generation of young people with no respect for authority or tradition as they pursue a hedonistic, morally bankrupt path of immediate gratification. A typical membership view of the problem with education today contends that "we can see today the deterioration of the family. Through the education system it's been undermined – the increase in homosexuality, condom machines in the high schools and most of all the trust between the children and the parents. It's very subtle. I had never heard of a counsellor when I was in school. How did we manage without them? The school and counsellors are taking over the role of the family."

This usurpation of familial and parental authority by a public body is what most concerned the FCP members. They viewed it as stripping away parents' natural right and ability to raise their children according to their chosen moral code. Some members blamed this trend not only on the Ministry of Education, but also on the British Columbia Teachers' Federation (BCTF):

> I guess in my opinion one of the biggest things wrong with education in BC is the teachers' federation has got so powerful the tail is wagging the dog. Instead of us telling them what we want, it's the other way round. It's time we got them back into the position of servant, not master.

> One of the foulest and most corrupt unions we have is the BCTF – not teachers, but the BCTF because they are totally run by radical people, the radical element of the teaching profession. I know they have taken a leading role in promoting the destruction of education in BC.

The party's educational policies indicated that the remedy for this eroding educational system lay in returning control to parents by abandoning the practice of block funding and adopting a voucher system: "support for education voucher; ... require accountability of trustees, teachers and bureaucrats to taxpayers and parents; funding for Independent schools be increased to meet public levels without any further government control being imposed" (1992), and "encourage the establishment of parental choice schools" (1994).

In 1992, the party submitted a position paper to the government supporting a voucher system for education funding and recommending that the "government of British Columbia establish a pilot program in several BC school districts where the Voucher/Choice system can be evaluated."[42] The argument was that a voucher system would achieve the objectives of giving parents increased control over their children's education by allowing them to apportion the voucher at a school or in a district of their choice. At one executive meeting, it was noted that the "whole concept of block funding is wrong because it sends the message that someone else is paying the bill and it's left so no one is accountable. We need smaller districts and more [school] board accountability." The necessity of increasing control through such decentralization was remarked on by Heather Stilwell at an all-candidates meeting during the 1996 provincial election:

> I think that we have to take a really big step backwards and ask ourselves what we're doing with education funding in the whole province ... I find, as a parent, the Big Brother attitude [of the government] so distressing. They're going to decide how school boards are going to be run, who's going to be allowed to go on strike, and they're going to make massive sweeping changes through the curriculum, and none of the other parties care about curriculum. They'll talk about economics but not curriculum. There's just been some mammoth changes taking place in the career and personal planning program that are invasive to the family and damaging to our children. This government has done no consulting on it. They've rammed it through without consulting the teachers or the parents. I think it's a disgrace.[43]

The FCP claimed that a voucher system would not only aid in diminishing this centralized control and return it to the local level, but would also achieve a second objective. It would introduce a market dynamic to the system, thereby, it was argued, increasing the quality of public education in BC. Jim Kelly, the 1996 candidate in West Vancouver–Capilano, gave a synopsis of the party's overall view on education funding during an all-candidates meeting when he said, "Throwing money at the system won't help. We need to give parents choice and we need to increase competition in the schools to increase quality."[44]

The second major element of the FCP's education policy was equally important to its membership. As it was posted on the party's website, the

FCP said that "vouchers, Charter schools or other parental choices for educating their children within the public school system should be available
to parents who are taxpayers." The membership's support for this position on home-schooling and the traditional school movement was strong
and active. As early as the 1970s, the Toths had been involved with the
attempt to gain funding from W.A.C. Bennett's government for independent schools in the province.[45] More recently, Heather Stilwell had been
the driving force behind founding the traditional elementary school in
Surrey that opened in 1994 and she was playing a supportive role in the
attempt to get a traditional high school approved for the district.[46] She
also took on the role of chair for the Surrey School Board after winning
a second term on the board – a victory won by running on a platform
of parental choice and fiscal responsibility that garnered her the second-
highest vote total on a conservative-dominated board.[47]

Mrs. Stilwell considers this type of local involvement and activism as
crucial to the overall pro-family movement because it provides activists
with a direct avenue to the decision-making processes that affect what
goes on in the schools. She also sees it as "an absolutely perfect way to
politicize parents. At the Surrey Electors Team meeting, there were a hundred pro-lifers, about twenty-five from the traditional school, parents who
have never done anything politically before but they see now how the
school board affects their life."

Arguably the prime target for the political ire of FCP parents who got
involved this way was the career and personal planning program (CAPP)
component of the education curriculum. Pro-family activists believe that
this program indoctrinates students, inculcating in them an ideology that
legitimates alternative forms of family structures and relativist ideas of sexual orientation and moral conduct. One FCP member commented that,
with CAPP, "you have all kinds of sex-related programs being introduced
which are very anti–traditional family. They are very promiscuous, encouraging programs that don't support the idea of chastity. That a child can
have an abortion without parental knowledge – it's unbelievable the state
would deprive the family of that right."

The concerns about the program begin with what is taught as early as
kindergarten. In the family life education component, one of the desired
learning outcomes for kindergarten and Grade 1 students is the ability to
"identify a variety of models for family organization," an objective viewed
by the FCP as tacitly undermining the rightful supremacy of the traditional
family structure.[48] There was also strong opposition to what the FCP viewed
as an unrightful intrusion into familial privacy under the collecting information component. Here, students are to compile personal information including parents' names, incomes, occupations, and the family's religion
and beliefs. This falls under evaluating and teaching Grade 11 and Grade

12 students how to "use their Student Learning Plans as tools to record, analyze, and evaluate their short-term and long-term education, career, and personal goals."[49] Particularly objectionable to FCP parents was that this information is restricted from parents' scrutiny because the Ministry of Education considers it privileged and to be shared only between the student and the school. Additionally, this component supplies senior students with information on how to "access and use resources that can support their efforts to carry out their plans [and] access services and technological resources that can help them carry out their plans."[50] To the fury of the FCP, this included access to information about abortion and related services, which students can pursue without parental knowledge or permission.[51]

Perhaps the most morally objectionable part of CAPP for the FCP was its teachings on sexuality. In grades 11 and 12, students are to "examine the impact of lifestyle choices on the social, physical, and environmental aspects of their personal lives [and] demonstrate a knowledge of key lifestyle practices associated with the prevention of HIV/AIDS, sexually transmitted diseases, and other communicable diseases."[52] To make such an informed evaluation, students are presented with information on homosexuality, use of birth control, and safe sex practices. One FCP member's view of this is that "a certain amount [of sex education] is necessary, but there is a lot of it that is going beyond what is necessary to know about sex. They go completely overboard in what they teach. For example, that there are different lifestyles, like man/man and woman/woman relations and this sort of stupidity. In other words, the school has lost its sense of morality."

An FCP newsletter distributed during the 1996 provincial election highlighted some specific objections regarding the program when it reported:

> The students in the Grade 10 CAPP (career and personal planning) class at Trail's Lloyd Crowe Secondary School is composed of 15-year-olds. A representative of the AIDS network asked the students to tell him as many vulgarities for sex that they could think of. These he listed on the blackboard. Later he would hand out a multiple choice questionnaire [sic] called "20 questions about life or death ... What kind of lubricants are OK to use with condoms?" ... As class ended, he handed out condoms to all the students and a toll-free number for the Vancouver Gay and Lesbian Centre. What happened at Trail is part of a province-wide trend. In Courtenay, the AIDS Coalition hands out material at Vanier Senior Secondary that included a pamphlet called "a brochure on young men questioning their sexuality" ... and a condom fact sheet that included tips to help the sensation during sex.[53]

It is the graphic nature of these types of discussions, accompanied by what is viewed as the active promotion of homosexuality in the schools, that so disturbed the FCP, because, as one member commented, "the homosexual movement is very hateful. They are not really willing to be like you, they want the regular folks to say it's okay, and they want our children, and as the state gets more and more interfering, it becomes more and more easy to get our children." Officially, the party stated: "It is understandable that there are parents who object to schools promoting homoscxuality simply as an alternate life style ... These parents feel that sexual orientation protected by law infringes upon their innate human right to teach their children how to live moral lives within the framework of their value system. Schools which teach that homosexuality is equally acceptable as heterosexuality are contradicting the lessons taught in the home. This is indeed a violation of parental responsibility."[54] The party in fact supported the position of a group of parents who sought to have the mandatory status of the CAPP program repeated.[55]

Two other issues facing the public education system in BC were also matters of concern to the FCP. The increasing pressure that English as a second language (ESL) students were seen to be placing on the resources of the education system led the party to oppose public funding of ESL classes.[56] There was a general consensus among the membership that the poorest immigrants should receive free ESL training but that the majority of new Canadians are well able to afford the costs associated with language training and as such they should bear this burden and not simply expect state support. Moreover, in the supporting statement to the 1995 resolution on this issue, the party stated that, "in Vancouver, ESL students make up 48 percent of the school population, in Richmond 39 percent of students need ESL. Of the 52.5 percent of kindergarten students who require ESL help, *78 percent were born in Canada*" (emphasis in the original).[57] The inference that the existence of the program itself contributes to a laziness among first-generation immigrants in teaching their children English stems in part from a general conclusion among the membership that people have abrogated personal responsibility for themselves to the state. With fewer government posts to lean on, they believe that people will become more self-reliant and assume a more independent posture.

There was also the BCTF's Resolution 102, which was passed, with a mandate to "create a program to eliminate homophobia and heterosexism within the BC public school system."[58] The affront to the FCP was the same as to a teacher who opposed the resolution during debate: "What we are doing here is teaching that homosexuality is normal, natural and acceptable ... The difficulty in that is that we are teaching a value."[59] The FCP expressed its discontent in a local Coquitlam paper, after which it sent an official letter of dissent to the Coquitlam School Board at the request of several local parents who had read the paper.[60]

Feminism

In the FCP's eyes, whereas the danger of a proliferating homosexual agenda in BC schools and popular society lies in the shift towards accepting aberrant lifestyles and family structures, feminism stalks the heart of a family's cultural character.

The FCP membership saw little value in feminism other than the partial remedying of wage inequities and blatant workplace discrimination. By and large, they argued that feminists, in their attempts to strip away the cultural differences between men and women, have denied the natural capacity and role of women as caregivers and nurturers. They see the result as the devaluation and delegitimation of the roles of mother and homemaker. Members argued that motherhood, like any other job, is a legitimate professional choice for women, and one far more noble and self-sacrificing than entering the general workforce. By denigrating women's natural role in this career, they continue, feminists have hurt not only themselves but all women and families by creating a culture that frowns in disappointment at the stay-at-home mother and valorizes the working woman and alternative family structures.

Feminism has "done a great deal of harm to the family," says one member:

> It has denigrated the influence of fathers. Children need fathers and mothers, and by their movement towards empowering themselves, to have power over themselves and over the male hierarchy, they have damaged the influence of men and women. They have promoted the idea that there is no difference between men and women, and there is a difference between the male and female. When you try and combine those two and say that they are exactly equal, they can do what the other one does, I think it wreaks havoc to the original intent of the creator.

Another member concurs that feminists have "done a lot of harm. They didn't mean to do it, but they did. Basically what they did to the woman who decided to stay home and be a wife and mother, they looked down on her – she was nothing and that's what upset me more than anything."

Like their views on gay rights, the membership's opinion of feminism travels a spectrum from this kind of soft negativism to a more malignant view in which feminism has created for the family

> absolute devastation because they have denied the reality of the role of the nature of women. They want to make men out of women. I think in that regard they have been totally destructive to the family and destructive to children. This is another cause of the destruction of the family and leading to divorces as well [sic]. I know men at work whose wives have got up and out to discover themselves – have a big career, absolutely and

totally destructive to the family, and rather than one of sacrifice and work to raise a family it becomes one of self-centredness, selfishness, pride and wanting to reverse the roles.

At the darkest end, there is a sentiment reminiscent of some in the American Christian right. As one FCP member put it, feminism has "four stages: first is the women's liberation, then there is radical feminism, then lesbianism and then finally witchcraft." And as another member pondered, "lesbians and feminism – I'm sure there's a connection there." Most members compartmentalize their views about feminism, separating its few positive aspects from the predominantly negative effects that "radical feminism" has had on the family. Yet such attempts at normalizing their views fail to cast a large enough shadow to obscure the strong anti-feminist sentiment among FCP members.

Politically, the FCP views feminists as another special-interest group that feeds off government subsidies and grants to promote an anti-family agenda. Comments from members reflected a resentment that "they [feminist groups] get government money, our tax money, sixty-five million dollars a year ... to spread their propaganda." The party went so far as to state a policy goal of eliminating the Ministry of Women's Equality: "Among ministries to be definitely dissolved would be the *WOMEN'S EQUALITY MINISTRY* and *THE MINISTRY OF HUMAN RIGHTS AND MULTICULTURALISM*" (emphasis in the original).[61] Replacing the Ministry of Women's Equality was to be a Ministry of Families, which was to oversee and promote legislation specific to the promotion of the traditional family. Had the party formed a government that met with opposition to the formation of this ministry or development of such legislation, it "would not hesitate to invoke Section #33 (the Override Clause) of the *Charter of Rights and Freedoms* should a Charter challenge be initiated to prevent the enactment of legislation to protect the marriage-based, two parent family."[62] The party took the stance that abating the decay of the family in the face of these humanist movements demanded these kinds of strong legislative actions in spite of what it thought would be vigorous opposition from gays, lesbians, and feminists. As one member noted, "the feminists are very angry with us."

The Crisis of the Family

It is the opinion of the FCP membership that somewhere along the path to material prosperity, the family became subject to a process of social erosion that has left it teetering on the precipice of relativist oblivion. Members of the FCP are unsure precisely when or how this dismantling of society's institutional cornerstone began, but they speak with a unanimous voice in their concern for the future of society if the family, in its traditional, nuclear form, does not have its proper apical status restored.

The displacement of the family and its subsequent ideological dismantling is a product – or, as a good number argue, the cause – of a socio-moral crisis in modern society. It is for some FCP members a crisis of faith, of "people trying to live without God," or, "lacking a sense of the belief in a creator, it is the position of a society that there is no such thing as right or wrong." For others, it is the gradual demise of concern for moral behaviour in a culture that covets monetary wealth: "The sense of being, the purpose to life is gone except to succeed financially," laments one member, while another thinks, "We are without morals, there is no right and wrong, and I blame a great deal of it on the education system." There is a sense also that this is a universal rather than localized problem of liberal attitudes sweeping democratic societies like BC, and that this is but the latest in a long line of social crises for nations with a Christian heritage:

> Everything's kind of global, it's not BC or Canada. A euthanasia law was passed in Australia last week. We have this decline of moral values, the attack on the family, it's all wound together. We can't say the government caused all this, there seems to be a worldwide agenda to destroy moral values with the family under attack. The humanist and materialist philosophy which has slowly taken hold of society, well, since the Second World War material things have become more important than values.

> The state is taking over from the family. The family is losing its place. The state is pitting families against each other, giving rights to one family over another. It's happening all over the world – do everything for people and collect taxes to do it.

> I think it's just a gradual change from one kind of mixed society to another kind of mixed society. Believing in a fall, as Christians do, we tend to sin and it manifests itself in different ways at different points in history. The issues can vary between societies but they are only manifestations of the age-old battle between God and the Devil.

Many simply believe that "the crisis is a complete and absolute fundamental breakdown of the family."

Regardless of whether the dissolution is the cause or effect of the crisis, unanimity exists among the FCP that the family is in crisis and that this has generated the numerous social pathologies witnessed in society today. Citing rising rates of divorce, youth crime, single parenthood, poverty, abortions, and high school dropouts, party members stated a deep belief in a healing process for society that centres on restoring a socio-moral order that celebrates the power of the family rather than the state. Members saw a necessary and intimate relation between the roles of these two institutions, a relation that has come to be disproportionately dominated by government in the past twenty-five years. In reflecting on this, one member said that "society is shaped by the two, a dynamic between families and the power structure, government and what not, and when the family is strong we need little government and get maximum freedom." Another member sees:

> There's a problem with families that we're trying to solve with government social programs. Once upon a time our society was structured on the presumption that people had a family to sustain them and the government would sustain widows and orphans or those who through tragedy had been left without family support. But implicit in this was that the family would sustain them and now that social contract isn't being executed. People are being taught to look for government social programs for their security and they're not being rewarded for their actions in their families.

The challenge for the FCP was to battle the social and psychological forces that created this crisis of state dependency and to beat back the creeping humanist and secular value system that underpins it. To do this, says one member, individuals must begin trying to "abide by some morals and spirituality and do good things for people and not be so swayed by the selfishness that seems to be portrayed by society today." For the FCP, this includes restoring a faith in God such that Christian principles can guide not only personal and family lives, but the life of the public body as a whole. Socially, they continue, this means purveyors of popular culture must begin to reel in the violence, profanity, and promiscuity that they have distributed with such wild abandon through the television and movie theatre. Inventions like the v-chip and implementation of rating systems for television programs and music need to be expanded to increase a parent's capacity to control the external influences that can undermine familial morality. Politically, they argue that the government must be forced to relinquish much of its power over families and education, return it to parents and the local community, and acknowledge the primary importance of the family unit. Commenting on the solution to the crisis families are facing, Heather Stilwell sees that "it is really very simple – to just get back where the family is the overriding unit. Where the state only interferes minimally, and then we get back to you don't get married without a marriage preparation course and you don't get divorced this week because you decided you might like to, and men have to support their children and work towards getting the corporations to pay them a little more so the moms can be home."

All of the policies developed by the FCP, well beyond those discussed here, were founded on this vision of promoting the family and minimizing state interference. Entrenched in its constitution was the party's intent "to enact social, educational and economic laws which recognize the family as the basic unit of society."[63] Their definition of marriage and family was definitive: "*THE FAMILY IS TWO OR MORE INDIVIDUALS RELATED BY BLOOD, MARRIAGE OR ADOPTION. The FCP recognizes the definition of MARRIAGE to mean THE LEGAL UNION OF TWO PEOPLE OF THE OPPOSITE SEX*" (emphasis in the original).[64]

To help ease the financial burdens on this traditional ideal, the party's housing and tax policies were structured to be "family-friendly." The FCP housing policy supported the concept of homesteading and lower mortgage rates for young families trying to acquire property. Their tax policy proposed to "design a provincial tax system to sustain the traditional family as the fundamental unit of society and to sustain good government." The party also committed to lobbying "the federal government to permit the spouses in single-income families to file separate tax returns (income-splitting) to benefit from the lower tax rate." Further, it sought support for "giving the same child-care subsidies to all families with children," a policy aimed at allowing parents to use extended family or friends for child care, rather than being restricted to licensed child care centres.[65]

The area of child care is one the FCP felt had been particularly intruded upon by the state. Parents, it contended, are better able than the government to determine appropriate child care services for their children and should be given this control. In 1992, the party made a presentation to the BC Child Care Regulation review committee recommending that "parents be allowed to choose the child-care facility which best reflects the requirements they decide are important to them when judging quality care ... Some parents prefer to have their children cared for in government licensed and regulated facilities, however there are other parents who prefer more informal arrangements with relatives, friends or nannies caring for their children. *Quality child care* is not synonymous with care in government licensed facilities" (emphasis in the original).[66]

Section 16 of the Infants Act, which provides minors with the opportunity to seek medical treatment without parental knowledge or consent, was also opposed by the party because of its diluting effect on parental authority. On its website, the party stated its support "for the right and responsibility of parents to decide what health care their minor children should receive." Officially, the health care policy of the party stated that, "FCP BC opposes the recent amendments to Section #16 of the Infants' Act," and it was agreed among the executive that, given the opportunity, they would have removed the section from the act.[67]

The party also presented the government with its views on the child protection legislation, with recommendations that, wherever possible, the integrity of the family structure be maintained by using extended family as caregivers for abused children rather than government foster care.[68] Their social services policy "supports legislation ... which recognizes the need to protect the integrity of the family ... Child-care givers should first be sought among immediate family members." The party also advocated pursuing a policy where "the rights of parents to care for their own children and the rights of children to be cared for by members of their immediate or extended family *be protected by legislation*" (emphasis in the original).[69] The Ministry for Children and Families was particularly worrisome for the FCP and other pro-family organizations in the province because it was viewed as having "sweeping powers to intervene in the home and a mandate to screen all parents and families for risk of potential child abuse."[70] The fear was that this bureaucratic monster was a consolidated effort by the state to intrude upon and direct family life while usurping parental rights and responsibilities.

To reduce this type of massive government interference in the lives of families and the economy, the party adopted political and economic positions typical of other neoconservative parties like the BC Liberals and the federal Reform/Alliance. For instance, the FCP recommended "cutting the number of government ministries by at least one-third along with their respective bureaucracies ... The remaining ministries would reduce their staff by at least one-third over 18 months."[71] There was also support for an efficient initiative, referendum and recall act. By simplifying these processes, the FCP believed that the government would be forced to become more responsive to the citizens of the province and less heavy-handed in the implementation of legislation. Finally, the party was a champion of injecting democratic freedom via electoral reform into what it saw as an increasingly dictatorial parliamentary system. In 1994, the party passed a resolution supporting the replacement of the current system with one of mixed member proportional representation.[72]

Accompanying this support for a minimalist state was the party's free-enterprise economic policy. There was unanimous support for "a Constitutional Amendment that would mandate a balanced provincial budget" and the pursuit of an economic strategy similar to the precedents set by Ralph Klein in Alberta, Mike Harris in Ontario, and Gordon Campbell in BC. In discussing the economic imperatives the province must follow if it is to balance its budget, members' comments overwhelmingly supported a platform of neoconservative economics:

> We need a substantial break from what has been going on in the past. I think you see that in a certain degree with the Conservatives in Alberta and Ontario. They made a substantial break, they said we have to get this

thing back in order, and despite how the press tries to report it, they seem to be increasing in popularity all the time because they are making substantial changes that people deep down know have to be made and I think it will start taking over more and more across the country.

We're really going to have to go by the New Zealand example and say we don't want your interference. Drop taxes by 75 percent, cut out welfare, cut out UI [unemployment insurance] after three months and any grants to big corporations and special-interest groups. Forget them, we've got to get the government, the bureaucrats, out of our lives.

These economic positions are hardly novel for a conservative political party, but by dovetailing them with unwavering support for pro-family issues, the FCP resolutely placed themselves on the hard-right edge of the political spectrum, a place where economic and social conservatism become inseparable.

From Conception to Unity: Nine Years of Struggle
In giving political voice to these religious conservative ideals, the Family Coalition Party had a life cycle that began and ended in similar fashion. From its registration in June of 1991, the FCP executive had only four months to make their fledgling party battle-ready for a provincial election. By the time the party had merged to become the Unity Party of BC, there was a scant five months until the 2001 provincial election.

In 1991, with less than a hundred registered members and an executive that had extremely limited knowledge of running a political party, let alone preparing one for a provincial election, the FCP found itself on a steeply graded route to Victoria. After running eight candidates who gathered a collective total of 1,200 votes in this autumn election of 1991, the party barely survived an executive vote to disband. Nonetheless, it did survive, running fourteen candidates in the 1996 general election and subsequent candidates in six by-elections.

As Unity – a political coalition primarily of the FCP and the Reform Party of BC – pro-life and pro-family constituents witnessed their best political performance in recent memory, with Unity taking 3 percent of the popular vote in the 2001 general election. While there are those within Unity who regard this fledgling party as more Reform than FCP in character, with its pro-life, pro-family platform and strong FCP presence, it is clear that Unity has become what the FCP was: British Columbia's party for staunch religious and social conservatives. It is the result that many who were involved with the FCP were hoping for and for years had worked hard to achieve.

As a party/movement, the FCP had constantly battled the image of being a fringe, single-issue party unable to provide well-rounded governmental representation for the people of BC. This was largely a self-generated problem. Using a political party form to do the social movement work of generating public awareness had saddled the FCP with this image, which in turn limited its political attractiveness for the typical voter. Improving this situation was one of the motivations that led the executive to accept an offer to merge under the Unity banner, and the 2001 election results suggest it was a sound strategic decision. With its pro-life and pro-family principles enshrined in Unity's constitution, the FCP had achieved something it had been unable to do by itself: generate a much larger membership base.

Party Membership

In 1991 the party started out with twenty-five members, at its peak in 1997 reached roughly 950, and entered the Unity merger just under 900 strong. As these numbers suggest, membership recruitment was a constant challenge for the FCP, which exhibited a consistent pattern of marginal growth throughout its nine years of existence.

Most memberships were the product of individual conversations between friends or people who attended the same churches or community functions or became acquainted through their involvement with pro-life or pro-family organizations. The 1991 and 1996 provincial elections both boosted the membership total by about a hundred, and Mr. Vander Zalm's speaking engagements in the early 1990s netted roughly 250 new memberships. The party's political activism on various issues also helped raise its profile and generate new memberships. For example, the debate over the BCTF's Resolution 102 and the FCP's letter of opposition to it in a local Coquitlam paper resulted in more than a dozen phone calls to party headquarters and two new memberships.

Nonetheless, recognizing the inherent inadequacy of such situations, a membership committee was struck after the 1996 election to actively pursue membership renewals, as well as to generate a strategy for a general membership drive. Mr. Toth saw this as the paramount initiative of the party after the election: "There has to be a membership drive. There are thousands of people out there who hold the same view and it's a matter of convincing them. It's a matter of having more members so we can accomplish the changes we want in society."

The party knew the equation was a simple one: more memberships meant a greater profile, more money, and the chance for better political fortunes.

Originally, the Toths sought out people in the pro-life community for the party's seed memberships. Mr. Toth acknowledges they "were quite well known in the pro-life area, so we got as many as we know from the pro-life arena to join as we could. Kathleen and I also publish a small Catholic paper called *The Trumpet*. We got a lot of members as well from those that subscribe." Mrs. Toth remembers that they "would attend right-to-life conventions and REAL Women conventions, wherever people would be of like mind, so we could set up an information table with literature."

It became frustratingly apparent to the party, though, that this kind of ideological alignment does not automatically convert into political party support. Governmental viability, vote splitting, vote wasting, and the educational focus of the party all played a role in limiting the pro-life community's formal endorsement of the FCP. Norm Herriott, a long-time FCP executive member, believed pro-life supporters saw the "FCP as just splitting the vote, taking the vote away from people who know how to run the place," and another executive member commented that the pro-life community "treated us like we had leprosy. They've stayed far away, afraid that if they associate with a political party in any way, they will lose their charitable status." The Toths recall one FCP member asking a pro-life priest for permission to distribute some FCP flyers and being told: "We can't split the vote; we all have to vote Liberal." By far the most common response the party heard about the lack of support, however, was that a vote for the FCP was a wasted vote because the party had no chance of victory. In a mildly deprecatory tone, Mr. Toth characterized this denial of support as "apathy, passivity, and then there is the feeling of the wasted-vote syndrome. People use their votes also against some parties."

Nor was the FCP the recipient of an immediate or subsequent huge benefit from the disaffected religious conservative faction of the Social Credit Party. As Mrs. Toth remarked, "it was a real revelation. Some of them were not prepared to leave the Social Credit Party no matter what. Although they were very vocal about the removal of the Christianity clause, they just couldn't bring themselves to leave the party." In fact, several members who became key FCP personnel originally remained Socreds for a substantial period after the Christianity clause was removed. This group remained hopeful that they could still effect change from within a well-established party. The migration finally began when, as one latecomer said, "it became obvious it was never going to succeed, we were never going to succeed in bringing in family values, it was getting to be more and more a nonentity."

Most striking, though, was the large number of FCP members who had never before taken out membership in a political party. This element of the FCP membership had historically soothed their pro-life conscience by either not voting or casting a vote for a pro-life candidate, often regardless of the candidate's party affiliation.

Typically, FCP members voted conservatively. Federally they voted Reform, Christian Heritage, and Progressive Conservative. Provincially they usually supported the Social Credit Party. Their belief in free-enterprise economics fitted well with these parties, but their pro-life and pro-family stance often has not.

As far as being pro-life and pro-family is concerned, they regard them as one and the same. One member puts it this way: "It's a necessary and natural relation. I don't think you can be pro-life and not pro-family and vice versa. Family is basically children, they make the family, and marriage is between a man and woman, and life is what you get from that relationship and children are that life."

It was an overwhelmingly white, Anglo-Saxon, and Catholic membership of Western European descent.[73] Of the interviewees for this book, 95 percent were married, with those who reported being single intending to marry and start families; 86 percent reported having children; and all but one respondent indicated an intention to have children in the future. As a whole, there was an average of 3.63 children per household in the sample, with that average jumping to 4.22 when those without children are excluded. Fifteen respondents indicated having five or more children; eight reported having none. The average age of a party member was fifty-five, with only 17 percent of respondents born after 1960.

The average household income was $40,000 per annum, earned through a distribution of occupations in the public, private, trade, and small business domains, while 46 percent of the respondents worked – or did before retirement – as professionals in the private or public sectors (a roughly even distribution). This group included accountants, teachers, medical service technologists, engineers, computer systems analysts, and banking executives. Of those who identified themselves as self-employed (11 percent), most worked in trades including carpentry, plumbing, heating systems, and general construction. Of the 21 percent of respondents who reported being homemakers, all were female, and this accounted for 44 percent of all female respondents. The remaining respondents included a physician, a lawyer, a dentist, and various semi-professional occupations.

In terms of education, 56 percent of the respondents indicated they either held a university degree (29 percent) or had some post-secondary education (27 percent), while 6 percent of the interviewees had not completed high school and 5 percent were high school graduates without further post-secondary education. Of those interviewed, 18 percent had taken some vocational training in addition to their other educational efforts. Those holding master's or law degrees constituted 12 percent of the interview sample, and 33 percent of respondents reported being retired.

In discussing their upbringing, 80 percent described it as traditional, with two parents of the opposite sex, one or more siblings, and a sufficient amount of love and discipline. Of this group, 75 percent considered their upbringing excellent, while 25 percent reported it as good but with the occasional difficulty. Only 8 percent of total respondents indicated a dysfunctional upbringing, characterized by a chronic problem that beset the family while they were growing up. The majority of those interviewed (59 percent) indicated growing up in a Roman Catholic household, while 12 percent reported that their parents followed no organized religion, 7 percent said they grew up in a non-denominational but Christian home, and the remainder identified some Christian denomination.

With respect to their parents' education, 39 percent of those asked stated that their mothers held only an elementary school education, 12 percent had some high school education, and 33 percent had graduated from high school. In addition, 12 percent of the respondents indicated their mothers held a university degree, while the same percentage indicated their fathers were university graduates. Respondents indicated that 31 percent of their fathers had only an elementary school education, 11 percent had some high school education, and 22 percent had graduated from high school. The occupations of respondents' fathers were broad and included farmers, publicans, steam engineers, landlords, teachers, farm machine and heavy equipment salesmen, janitors, millworkers, longshoremen, accountants, carpenters, a shoemaker, an interior decorator, an electrician, a coal miner, a musician, and an architect. Of those interviewed, 49 percent stated their mother's occupation as a homemaker, while others indicated their mothers to be nurses, teachers, secretaries, cooks, farmers, bookkeepers, dressmakers, musicians, and telegraph operators.

Geographically, the FCP was a predominantly Lower Mainland party, with 50 percent of its membership residing in Lower Mainland electoral ridings (Table 1.1). Only 10 percent of its members lived in ridings traditionally associated with the Fraser Valley Bible belt.[74] The heaviest concentrations of memberships beyond these regions were in the three Prince George ridings, the four Okanagan ridings, the Surrey ridings, and the ridings of North and West Vancouver. The latter were virtually all new memberships, the result of some vigorous recruitment by a core of North Vancouver members just before the 1996 provincial election. The memberships in Prince George and the Okanagan were a direct result of Mr. Vander Zalm's speaking engagements in 1993. The Surrey memberships also reflected the impact of Mr. Vander Zalm's involvement, as well as the name recognition enjoyed by Heather Stilwell.

As previously noted, after the 1996 election, the party attempted to develop a two-part strategy to increase overall party membership. Its first priority was to secure the renewals of those 250-odd memberships that had been taken out in 1993 and were up for renewal in 1997. Second, the party intended to target specific ridings and recruit new members by advertising and by using friends, families, or associates in those areas to solicit memberships.[75] Membership numbers from 1997 until the Unity

Table 1.1

Distribution of the Family Coalition Party membership in BC's 75 electoral districts, 1997, in numerical order

BC electoral district	No. of FCP members	BC electoral district	No. of FCP members
1 Abbotsford	16	40 Peace River North	0
2 Alberni	5	41 Peace River South	0
3 Bulkley Valley–Stikine	7	42 Port Coquitlam	10
4 Burnaby Edmonds	6	43 Port Moody–Burnaby	
5 Burnaby North	6	Mountain	5
6 Burnaby–Willingdon	8	44 Powell River–Sunshine	
7 Cariboo North	5	Coast	13
8 Cariboo South	0	45 Prince George–Mount	
9 Chilliwack	16	Robson	27
10 Columbia River–		46 Prince George North	18
Revelstoke	0	47 Prince George–Omineca	29
11 Comox Valley	15	48 Richmond Centre	4
12 Coquitlam–Maillardville	18	49 Richmond East	0
13 Cowichan–Ladysmith	6	50 Richmond–Steveston	5
14 Delta North	18	51 Rossland–Trail	8
15 Delta South	12	52 Saanich North and	
16 Esquimalt–Metchosin	6	the Islands	11
17 Fort Langley–Aldergrove	12	53 Saanich South	7
18 Kamloops	0	54 Shuswap	0
19 Kamloops–		55 Skeena	8
North Thompson	0	56 Surrey–Cloverdale	44
20 Kootenay	0	57 Surrey–Green Timbers	17
21 Langley	17	58 Surrey–Newton	24
22 Malahat–Juan De Fuca	7	59 Surrey–Whalley	31
23 Maple Ridge–Pitt Meadows	6	60 Surrey–White Rock	23
24 Matsqui	42	61 Vancouver–Burrard	4
25 Mission–Kent	5	62 Vancouver–Fraserview	15
26 Nanaimo	20	63 Vancouver–Hastings	9
27 Nelson–Creston	40	64 Vancouver–Kensington	15
28 New Westminster	5	65 Vancouver–Kingsway	7
29 North Coast	0	66 Vancouver–Langara	13
30 North Island	1	67 Vancouver–Little Mountain	7
31 North Vancouver–Lonsdale	16	68 Vancouver–Mt. Pleasant	9
32 North Vancouver–Seymour	25	69 Vancouver–Point Grey	6
33 Oak Bay–Gordon Head	19	70 Vancouver–Quilchena	12
34 Okanagan–Boundary	8	71 Victoria–Beacon Hill	8
35 Okanagan East	20	72 Victoria–Hillside	3
36 Okanagan–Penticton	8	73 West Vancouver–Capilano	45
37 Okanagan–Vernon	4	74 West Vancouver–Garibaldi	3
38 Okanagan West	43	75 Yale–Lillooet	3
39 Parksville–Qualicum	9	**Total**	**894**

Source: Figures from FCP archival records.

merger in November 2000 indicate that this effort was once again only marginally successful. While there was no significant decrease in official membership, neither was there any dramatic growth.

Party Finances
With such a small membership base, the financial resources of the party were consistently scarce. The $2,500 bank balance at the end of 1996 was the most the party had ever been able to carry over into a new year, and at times it had as little as $150.

The bulk of the party's funds came from its annual general meeting, with its associated luncheon and dinnertime banquet with guest speakers and a silent auction. The remainder was derived from membership dues and general donations. Mrs. Toth summed up the FCP's financial strategy and position by saying, "Every time we send out a newsletter, we send out an appeal for funds. It's amazing that people send money and we've survived from these donations. Usually it's not more than $100. Some people send $100 once a year, some people only send $20. It's been just enough to keep us alive. We certainly don't have any extra money, but we have been able to pay our telephone bills and hold our conventions. Conventions bring in money, because we have auctions and fundraisers at the same time. We do renew our coffers at the conventions." The party benefited from some donations in kind, including help to set up its website, discounts on printing costs, and donated election signs, but in general such help was limited and did little to ease its financial challenges.

To get the party off the ground, Mr. Toth remembered, "a few people put in a few dollars to start the organization. The cost of registration we funded ourselves." Another of the founding members recalled that "the party never had money, it just came in dribs and drabs, people would just give $50 or $60." The shortage of party funds was such that the executive were forced in 1992 to amend the constitution, which called for an independent chartered accountant to annually audit the books. Because the FCP was unable to afford the fees for this service, the constitution was changed to allow "two members at large selected by the Management Committee" who will "provide the AGM with a report."[76] Two fundraising dinners were held in the first year, one of which featured Mr. Vander Zalm as a guest speaker. Mrs. Toth recalled that such events "have helped keep us afloat financially, but only barely."[77]

Relief for the party during these formative years came in the form of a benefactor who in 1992 donated $75 at first, with the proviso that Mr. Vander Zalm become the leader of the party. The Toths initially returned the cheque, unwilling to accept conditional donations, but later accepted the benefactor's help with organizing three speaking engagements featuring Mr. Vander Zalm. To this end, a contribution of over $4,000 was made to the party and all the costs for this tour were covered. This benefactor also funded the party's constituency office in Matsqui in the hopes that Vander Zalm would run as an FCP candidate against Grace McCarthy in 1994 and subsequently take over leadership of the party. After this failed to transpire, the benefactor left the party to become active in the Reform Party of BC. Although the parting occurred on less than amicable terms, the Toths acknowledge that without this help, it is unlikely that the party would have survived.

Throughout the party's life, the executive were always acutely aware of how their financial situation hamstrung them. Before the Unity merger, Norm Herriott stated the situation with succinct urgency by saying: "The pressing issue right now is finances; we've got to have money or we won't go anywhere. You can talk about grassroots all you want but you've still got to have money."

Yet there always seemed to be a general sense of confusion among them about how to generate enough money to push them beyond this hand-to-mouth existence. "Haphazard" was the word offered most frequently by executive members in describing the party's financial resources strategy between conventions. Such a state was due in no small part to the lack of expertise within the party in generating financial support, which in turn was symptomatic of the larger problem surrounding party workers.

Party Personnel
The lack of any paid personnel within the party was indicative of the FCP's austere financial position and restricted capacity for development. In a party, membership recruitment, financial management, policy development, media relations, and administrative duties all require dedicated personnel with some degree of expertise. The limited financial resources of the FCP prevented hiring any professionals to meet these needs and forced the party to draw upon its shallow membership base for interested volunteers – a situation that severely truncated the search for political expertise and placed a heavy emphasis on the aspect of dedicated voluntarism. Without even a small stipend to offer as remuneration, the FCP had to take what help its membership was able to offer. This usually meant work for the party was squeezed in between the hectic demands of raising families and earning livings. Members frequently commented that their lack of political progress relative to those on the left was in good measure a product of having families and prioritizing them over the pursuit of politics.

Among the executive, while there existed what could be thought of as heart, there was nonetheless a lack of commitment to the serious pursuit of political legitimation for the party. Only the Toths and a couple of others demonstrated a consistent dedication to the long-term development of the party and its objectives. Other executive members were for various reasons unable to move beyond a point of interest and intermittent contributions. Time, energy, frustration, family obligations, and professional responsibilities were all identified as factors that limited their work on behalf of the party. Long-term dedication and interest existed but did not translate into a consistent pattern of productive involvement.

With few tangible successes to identify, it seems the arduous process of building a political party weighed down those involved. Members with assigned tasks usually completed them, but often long after the timelines set at executive meetings. It was not unusual for items to be pushed forward two or three meetings because work had not been completed or members had not attended a particular meeting to present their work. Executive meetings also often veered from a set agenda to become a forum for venting frustrations about general social disorder. At one meeting, for instance, a member of the executive asked for input on developmental directions for the party and another member spent his response time commenting exclusively on Singapore's practice of caning and its low crime rate.

This was perceived by the executive as a critical situation for the party. Past president John O'Flynn's comment that there was "no money" reflects a mild sense of resignation that simmered within the executive ranks about this problem: "You get the same old people, the same numbers. You have meetings but you start realizing who your core people are." Another executive member put it in more frustrated terms: "Well, I'll tell you, I'm just about at the end of my leash, and if I don't get them to agree to some serious fundraising, I may just drop out of it because we're not putting our heart in it. We're not giving it all, and if we hope to do anything in four years, we've got to get going right now and put it in high gear."

There was also a small but over the later years growing sentiment that this lack of dedicated involvement extended to their party leader, Heather Stilwell. As one member put it, "we have a leader now who has no damn time for anything. She's running for school board, which is good because she'll get her face out there, but she doesn't have time to be a leader while she's doing that." It was not a situation Mrs. Stilwell denied: "I'll be busy for the next three years [with the school board]. I would rather not have the responsibility of the FCP right now, but if they're willing to have me in a holding position right now, I'm okay with that. Even though there's not a lot going on right now there should be – meetings for policy development every two weeks, public relations, finding out what the government is up to – but I'm not doing any of that."

Some on the executive thought the solution to this problem was a matter of finding the money to create salary positions for a leader and an administrative assistant. Others feared that even this would not help and that, when the Toths were no longer able to continue, the party would collapse for a lack of committed personnel. Mrs. Toth summarizes her concern over this last point this way:

As long as we stay well. If someone gets ill – I am just worried about all that stuff on the computer. I have to find someone who can duplicate what I do. But to get people to admit they have computer skills and that they are willing to do it, it's just another job. Most of us are involved in other things. Everyone can honestly say, "I am so busy I haven't got another minute to do anything more." It's true. Somehow we have to find time, because we've put so much work into it now that we have to spread the jobs a little more.

Yet, tempering this pessimistic outlook was the constant involvement of new party members (though small in number), and the continued involvement and support of those long-term activists. In 1996, for example, the FCP board of directors had twenty-two members, more than at any other time to date, and after the general election, there was a renewed vigour within the executive concerning the preparatory work leading up to the next provincial election. Subcommittees for membership, policy, and fundraising were struck, something that had not happened since 1993. There was also a shift in the age of some key personnel in the party. Darren Lowe (president) and Jim Hessels (deputy leader) had been born after 1955, and Heather Stilwell brought to the party the important image of a mature youthfulness that reflected experience and political wisdom. Of the fourteen candidates who ran in the 1996 election, only three were past retirement and four were younger than forty-five. It was a demographic trend that the party hoped to build on through its post-election membership drive.

Asked how active members were recruited to the party, long-term executives emphasized the important role word of mouth played and the enthusiasm new members brought to the party. As Mrs. Toth remarked, "some people discover the party, and if they have never heard of it before, they become very enthusiastic and we hook them right away, and keep them involved. You can't know who is going to stay and who is going to go." The executive tapped into this initial commitment and gained as much ground with it as they could until the enthusiasm and energy of these members waned. This repeated pattern had the net effect of increasing the membership and party profile slightly, and committing at least a few people to more prolonged activity within the party. Mrs. Toth appears to have accepted this as a fact of members' activism within the party: "I have seen it in the pro-life movement. The people become very enthusiastic, they hear the issues and they think, like wow, they become very enthusiastic. When they run up against people who have other causes they are interested in, it discourages them to the point of no longer continuing. I believe every person you give information to, a little bit remains behind, therefore I don't think it's wasted. It's early burnout that has an effect on the party."

In the 1996 election, one riding on the North Shore was particularly characteristic of what Mrs. Toth has described as these "flurries of activity." After hearing about the party, several North Shore members quickly formed a constituency for West Vancouver–Capilano, generated at least fifty new memberships for the party, nominated a young and highly personable candidate, and received the most uncontroversial media attention of the party's campaign. Typical of the activism within the party, however, was the dejected response to having their candidate receive only 174 votes. Dissatisfied, one of the key organizers in the riding said he would probably have been wiser to support the pro-life Reform candidate. There was even a decision to disband the constituency association until the Toths and Mrs. Stilwell attended the dissolution meeting and convinced riding members to retain it.

At that meeting, one member wanted an answer to a single question: "What we want is a reason as to why we should be involved."

Stripped, this question asks about motivation. Electoral success, favourable public response, large outpourings of membership support – none of these existed to give the party the inspirational boost needed for it to carry on being constantly active. It meant that progress and success had to be defined some other way. Discussing the results of the 1996 election, candidate and executive member Gerhard Herwig saw victory this way: "How do you measure success? I wouldn't want to say we weren't successful. We weren't for the average politician, but I think we could say we were successful. We had several thousand people in fourteen ridings vote for us and we got the message out. And you don't know what the long-term effects will be. We don't know what all our successes are. If you look at our numbers, we weren't successful, but success isn't just about getting elected."

For the core activists within the party, such an evaluation is the product of deep religious and moral commitments. As Mr. Herwig puts it, "most people are motivated by their beliefs. Especially when a party like ours has little chance of success at this point, you must have motivation not linked to success." For Mr. Toth and the rest of the executive, this motivation is "the strong belief in Judaeo-Christian principles," which in turn constituted the core of the answer the Toths offered to the question of involvement. At its foundations, the party existed and carried on for nine years because of its members' faith and the executive's commitment to politicizing their beliefs through the FCP.

This kind of dedication, however, could carry the party only so far. The party needed political expertise in the critical process of policy development. This is not to say the FCP was made up of political neophytes, far from it, but most of their political acumen was a product of their social movement activism. From the pro-life movement and their involvement with Social Credit, the Toths brought to the party a wealth of practical knowledge, perhaps none more important than the understanding that a project like the FCP was one of long-term commitment requiring patience and quiet tenacity. The Stilwells brought an equally substantial body of experience to the party with their involvement as founders of the Christian Heritage Party, their experience in the Social Credit Party, and their work with the pro-life movement. Gerhard Herwig, after years as a constituency association president with Social Credit and active involvement in the pro-life movement, was another knowledgeable resource. Other executives brought similar if not as extensive portfolios of pro-life activism to the party. Yet this was simply not enough when it came to matters of policy development. When members took over various portfolios, they tended to be linked to their occupations and their knowledge to be more practical than formal.

It is little wonder, then, that policy development was identified by the party as critical if the FCP was to present itself as a maturing and capable party to the electorate. For the most part, people were assigned to track a ministry of their interest for the purpose of criticizing government policy. They were also responsible for developing FCP policy in that area. Broader committees were formed to address party policy, but these efforts produced only enough information to enable the party to form a superficial position on most provincial issues.

Part of the problem here was the dry, mundane nature of the work. As past president John O'Flynn remarked, "very few people have a taste for that and you have to have a gift for it." It was a reality repeatedly borne out in such comments by executives as, "With policy development, yeah, I think I got assigned with something, I've forgotten now – shows you how much I've done with it."

In no small measure, such statements reflect the burnout a lot of the executive were experiencing, brought on by the necessity of holding multiple responsibilities and positions. It was a situation everyone knew needed remedying. For instance, in commenting on the time when Mrs. Toth was party president, leader, and secretary, Norm Herriott said "that was absolutely too much for her to handle and that slowed us down." The solution to this was the same as it was for policy development and all of the party's other deficiencies: members. As Mrs. Toth put it, "we need a thousand more members – a pool of resources – people from which to draw. We need people with skills, political skills."

All the board members knew this, but they admitted to a sense of loss as to how achieve it, save for one strategy. They believed that attracting charismatic people with some public name recognition would have drawn the attention of the media, increased public awareness of the party, and in turn increased its membership, financial stability, and political viability. To that end, the party did such things as send letters of recruitment to a few notable past Socreds and seek out well-known pro-family activists to speak at its fundraising dinners. Many of the executives' belief in this strategy came from the contribution their most high-profile member made to the party. When Bill Vander Zalm became involved with the FCP, the party enjoyed its greatest period of public profile and membership growth.

The Value of a Name: The Role of Bill Vander Zalm

After failing to gain the immediate support of the pro-life and pro-family communities in the 1991 election and witnessing months of slow membership growth for the party, the founding members recognized the need to generate a profile. It was decided that a series of fundraising rallies should be held to promote the party and increase its membership. In discussions of keynote speakers who would draw a crowd, Mr. Vander Zalm's name came naturally to mind. Mrs. Toth recalls that, "we reasoned the people who would come out to hear Mr. Vander Zalm would be sympathetic to the FCP, and he made no hesitation about talking about this during his speeches, that this was a very worthwhile cause, that it was badly overdue and we needed to get back to family values. It was a way of getting these people in one place and we could reach them." The ex-premier agreed to speak on behalf of the party, with the proviso that he also be permitted to discuss matters of taxation, initiative, referendum, and recall. Originally, ten rallies were to be planned, but scheduling difficulties reduced this to three.

The rallies were planned for late April and early May 1993 in Prince George, Kelowna, and Surrey. They attracted 250, 300, and 356 people respectively, and from that, over 250 people took out FCP memberships. Constituency associations were subsequently formed in Prince George and Kelowna. The FCP also began to enjoy increased media attention, particularly with the speculation that Mr. Vander Zalm might formally return to politics as an FCP candidate.[78] One founding member recalls receiving a phone call from a veteran television reporter within hours of the rallies being tentatively scheduled, wanting information about the ex-premier's involvement with a group the reporter described as Vander Zalm's "natural constituency."

This was not an incorrect observation. In discussing his motivation for becoming involved with the FCP, Mr. Vander Zalm said, "I could feel at ease and receive some gratification in promoting values and principles not with a view of winning a political election, but just as someone helping to raise the voice about those issues that FCP was associated with and strong on ... I met many of my staunchest supporters, those that rallied behind, particularly in times of trouble ... so that in itself for me was gratifying." His speech in Prince George, although beginning with a commentary on taxation, shifted focus to the dangerous erosion of the traditional family by liberal attitudes and government interference:

There is, however, an even more dangerous, though very, very subtle and persistent attack on the traditional family. We must all assume some blame for this – we're too busy to protest or we're afraid to offend neighbour or friend, or we fear the threat of being categorized as bigots or "intolerates" [sic]. The attacks are usually first brought on by a special-interest group, then encouraged by the left in government and the left in media. It's a subtle persistent attack – which, if allowed to continue, will destroy the strongest unit of traditional society: the family.

The socio-moral and economic affinity between the FCP and its most celebrated member nearly resulted in the ex-premier returning to mainstream politics via the 1994 Matsqui by-election. This by-election was the result of Socred Harry de Jong stepping down to provide a seat for the newly appointed leader of Social Credit, Grace McCarthy. At the urging of the FCP, and in particular the benefactor who financed the FCP rallies, Mr. Vander Zalm gave serious consideration to accepting the party's candidacy before finally declining. Again, the associated media speculation over a battle between Vander Zalm and McCarthy brought the FCP into the political spotlight.

Such benefits would be short lived, however, terminating when Vander Zalm's involvement with the party came to an end and he left to join the Reform Party.[79] Mr. Vander Zalm remembers his involvement with the FCP and the switch to Reform this way:

> I attended several of their [FCP] conventions to help debate some of the issues, and to give my views as to what direction they should take and in what manner in order to be a greater influence in the political community, so I stuck with it for several years. But when the provincial election appeared closer, I felt I should at least for a time associate myself with a political party that would be a greater influence. Even though they didn't have all of that which the FCP stood for, they were a part step, and that of course was the Reform Party.

In actuality, the motivation for this switch appears to have been a drive by the benefactor who had sponsored the Vander Zalm rallies and several other pro-life supporters to nominate Vander Zalm for the Reform leadership. Discouraged by the FCP results in the Matsqui by-election, the benefactor left the party to join Reform and convinced Mr. Vander Zalm that he had equal if not greater support there than in the FCP. This support did not materialize, however, and Mr. Vander Zalm returned to private life until he rejoined Reform as the leader and ran a losing campaign as a Reform candidate in the 1998 Delta South by-election. After that, Vander

Zalm remained in the political background until the Unity merger. Although holding no official position with Unity, he is a member and did play a small but important role in the merger and the first annual general meeting of the new party.

An evaluation of Mr. Vander Zalm's involvement with the FCP clearly shows the benefits, but it was an association not free of cost. Two of the party's founding five were opposed to the ex-premier's involvement because of his politically tainted image. One of these two even left the party – a loss the Toths identified as one of the two major setbacks the party suffered in its nine-year history. The other came as a result of their benefactor leaving to join the Reform Party. In doing so, the benefactor wrote to all of the FCP members who had joined because of the FCP rallies, encouraged them to join Reform, and offered to pay their new membership fees. While no FCP memberships were turned in as a result of this action, several constituency associations were eventually deregistered and there was no significant activism from these areas after that time.

In spite of these setbacks, Vander Zalm's involvement with the FCP was critical to its survival, lending credence to the executive's belief in the need for people with a public profile to be involved with the party. And with the emergence of the Unity Party, the FCP and the ex-premier have once again become politically reacquainted. While it seems unlikely that Vander Zalm will re-enter public political life under this coalition banner, his background involvement with the party may nonetheless play a role in Unity's electoral fortunes, as it did with the FCP's.

Electoral History

The FCP's electoral history began a short four months after the party was formed, but by October 1991 the party had managed to register nine constituency associations and eight candidates to run in the autumn election. In total, a little over 1,200 people voted for the FCP in this election, with John Onderwater's 249 votes the highest number collected by any of the party's candidates (Table 1.2).

Despite the party's being only four months old, these results were discouraging enough for the executive to hold a meeting to vote on the FCP's dissolution. Those in favour of dissolving the party harboured a continued belief that their efforts would be more fruitful if they attempted to work within more established parties to promote family-friendly legislation. The work required to maintain a political party structure was felt to be too great a burden for the meagre rewards that could be obtained under the FCP banner. Those opposed, like the Toths, had abandoned any hope for this form of activism. They argued that pro-family and pro-life issues were being deliberately suppressed because of their controversial nature and politically incorrect language, and that the only avenue left that permitted free speech on these matters was the continuation of the party. The resulting 6–4 vote favoured keeping this avenue of free speech open.

The vote itself was a product of some members' unrequited desire for immediate gratification for their efforts over the months leading up to the election. There had been no expectation of electoral victory, but far greater support from the pro-life community had been anticipated. The Toths were disappointed with the results too, but their years of activism had given them an understanding of the need to define success in small incremental terms. That the party existed and had engaged in a provincial election were heralded in their own right as successes for pro-family forces in the province. Throughout the lifespan of the party, this continued to be an opinion strongly held by the membership.

In May 1994, the party ran candidates in two by-elections and enjoyed what would prove to be its greatest success. About the first by-election, Mrs. Toth stressed in her 1993 leader's report that "we must run a candidate in Quilchena because it will bring issues before the public that are not being discussed by the other parties. It will give the FCP exposure which it needs to become better known. Although our candidate won't win, it will be worthwhile." The campaign by Darren Lowe in Vancouver–Quilchena was a small one, reflected in the scant 89 votes he received, but from the party's viewpoint, it did at least place the Family Coalition Party name on the ballot.

It was in the Matsqui by-election, however, that the FCP's most significant piece of political folklore was created. Leading up to the by-election, there had been rampant media speculation about the return of Mr. Vander

Table 1.2

FCP election results from 1991 provincial general election

Electoral district	Candidate	No. of votes rec'd	% of total[a]
Langley	Barrie Norman	175	0.98
Nanaimo	David Bentley	143	0.68
Delta North	Paul Formby	137	0.66
Oak Bay–Gordon Head	Kathleen Toth	166	0.60
Parksville–Qualicum	Gus Cunningham	161	0.64
Saanich North and the Islands	Tom Aussenegg	90	0.36
Surrey–Cloverdale	John Onderwater	249	1.13
Vancouver–Kensington	John O'Flynn	142	0.82

a Figures are approximate.
Source: Based on FCP records.

Zalm to politics as an FCP candidate.[80] This was of particular interest because it would have created a scenario whereby Vander Zalm would have squared off against Grace McCarthy, who was running for a seat after winning the leadership of the Social Credit Party in late 1993.[81] After Vander Zalm declined to run, Mrs. Toth accepted the nomination. While filing her nomination papers at the Elections BC office, she ran into Mrs. McCarthy and introduced herself. She recalls Mrs. McCarthy then accusing her of telling lies about McCarthy's role in the removal of the Christianity clause from the Social Credit constitution. Mrs. Toth says she reminded McCarthy of her presence at the meeting and the issue was dropped. Although an isolated incident, it reflected the antagonistic relationship between McCarthy and religious conservatives who had left the Socreds.

In a press release before the election, it was reported that: "Social Credit Leader Grace McCarthy admitted Thursday it would be a 'political disaster' if she loses an upcoming byelection."[82] For religious conservative Socreds who joined the FCP, there was tremendous satisfaction when McCarthy lost the by-election by less than 70 votes and Mrs. Toth collected 275 for the FCP (Table 1.3). After the election, Mark Toth recalls Mrs. McCarthy's campaign manager making a passing comment to him to the effect that "I hope you're happy now." Despite the satisfaction this small victory brought, however, Mrs. Toth's focus had been FCP exposure: "We were running to have a presence more than anything else. We felt we had to run to maintain credibility." Nonetheless, there appears to be an inescapable truth to John O'Flynn's comment that "the FCP in a way contributed to the final nail in the Socred coffin because of the Matsqui by-election where Grace McCarthy lost by 30 or 40 votes. I do believe the party was instrumental in sealing the fate of the Socreds."

Table 1.3

FCP by-election results

Electoral district	Candidate	No. of votes rec'd	% of total[a]
Matsqui (1994)	Kathleen Toth	275	2.11
Vancouver– Quilchena (1994)	Darren Lowe	89	0.82
Abbotsford (1995)	Kathleen Toth	194	1.54
Surrey–White Rock (1997)	Jim Hessels	198	1.0
Parksville–Qualicum (1998)	Mary Moreau	94	0.36
Delta South (1999)	Jim Hessels	110	0.6

a Figures are approximate.
Source: Based on FCP records.

For a short time later that year, it appeared as if this might have been the FCP's last political campaign. With Grace McCarthy's defeat, hope for a Social Credit resurgence was lost and the Reform Party of BC (RPBC) began to aggressively recruit Socred supporters in an attempt to become the new right-wing party in the province. Part of this strategy included a formal offer to the FCP from the Reform leadership to merge with the RPBC. As Mrs. Toth recalls, she was approached at a conservative forum with an informal suggestion that a merger would be beneficial to both parties. Later, during the RPBC leadership convention, she was contacted again and asked if the FCP executive would meet formally to discuss a merger. With FCP members seeing no difference between the two parties other than the FCP's two core principles and RPBC's reliance on referendums to determine party policy on social issues, the offer was eagerly accepted. In fact, in anticipation of a merger with another free-enterprise party, the FCP had passed a special policy resolution calling for a mandate to pursue the possibility of forming a coalition with another right-wing party.[83]

Initially, the possibility of a coalition seemed to exist, with RPBC's preliminary agreement to include the FCP's clauses protecting the sanctity of life and the traditional family. However, Mrs. Toth says the Reform executive later withdrew the sanctity-of-life clause and removed the operative phrase "to enact social, educational and economic laws and policies" from the traditional-family clause. After this initial failed attempt to merge with the RPBC, the FCP executive returned to the slow development of the party's public profile and Mrs. Toth ran in the FCP's next by-election, a 1995 campaign in Abbotsford in which she collected 194 votes (Table 1.3)

In preparing the party for its second provincial election, Mrs. Toth sent out a letter to FCP constituency executives that laid out the platform on which the FCP would run:

> There will be a provincial election in the Spring of 1996. Between now and then, we must find the best candidates to speak for the values that marriage-based families believe need protection, values like lower taxes for families with children, parental choice schools, removal of Medicare funded abortions and government support for abortion clinics, repeal of the "bubble-zone" legislation and the Human Rights Act, abolish the Women's Equality Ministry and replace it with a Ministry for the Family, changes to the Adoption Act to prevent same-sex couples from adopting infants and children ... These are only a few issues which the Opposition parties are not anxious to support. Unless our candidates are there to introduce controversial issues like this, they will be deliberately left out of the election campaign ... We must see our participation as a chance to show the voters of BC that returning to traditional family values is the only solution to the chaos and disorder in society.

In May 1996, fifteen candidates ran on this platform, collecting over 4,000 votes throughout the province (Table 1.4). Heather Stilwell's 709 votes was the highest total of any FCP candidate, while Alan Idler's 56 was the lowest. Bill Stilwell's 577 votes was the second-highest total and, as Mr. Stilwell and other members noted, was likely a result of name recognition because of Mrs. Stilwell's community profile. The most pleasant surprise for the party was John Krell's Comox Valley campaign. Registering as a candidate at the last minute, Dr. Krell had only nine days to campaign but, with 398 votes, provided the FCP with its third-highest total. The controversy he created over his remarks during an all-candidates meeting that homosexuals should be discriminated against may have bolstered his support, but this is unclear.[84] Mark Toth's Vancouver–Kensington campaign, which included the deliberately controversial sign beside the Everywoman's Health Clinic reading, "Your Taxes Pay for Killing Unborn Babies Next Door. The Family Coalition Party would stop such funding. In Vancouver–Kensington vote for Mark Toth," resulted in only 119 votes. Meanwhile, in Nelson–Creston, Brian Zacharias received 360 votes on the campaign, in which he parked his pickup truck on Nelson's main street with the aforementioned four-foot by eight-foot sign reading, "The Family Coalition Party of BC. Homosexuality and Abortion are against God and Nature. Take a Stand. Love Tells the Truth."

Table 1.4

FCP election results from 1996 provincial general election

Electoral district	Candidate	No. of votes rec'd	% of total[a]
Langley	Barrie Norman	175	0.98
Comox Valley	John Krell	398	1.31
Fort Langley–Aldergrove	Lila Stanford	316	1.17
Delta South	Jim Hessels	304	1.35
Matsqui	Kathleen Toth	385	1.79
Nanaimo	Vicki Podetz	311	1.35
Nelson–Creston	Brian Zacharias	360	1.84
Oak Bay–Gordon Head	Alan Idler	56	0.19
Surrey–Cloverdale	Heather Stilwell	709	2.38
Surrey–Green Timbers	Gerhard Herwig	255	1.27
Surrey–Newton	Bill Stilwell	577	2.24
Vancouver–Kensington	Mark Toth	119	0.63
Vancouver–Point Grey	Eamonn Rankin	62	0.24
West Vancouver–Capilano	Jim Kelly	174	0.75
Yale–Lillooet	Ed Vanwoudenberg	122	0.74

a Figures are approximate.
Source: Based on FCP records.

Beyond these incidents, candidates ran small, quiet campaigns and spent from $250 to $3,000. Candidates reported funding most of their campaigns themselves, with supplemental money being donated by individual members to the candidates. No financial help was given by the party. Candidates reported that most of the help they received to run the campaigns came from their immediate family or friends. Only four candidates identified volunteers who were supporting the party without personally knowing the candidate. Campaign strategies primarily revolved around the distribution of party flyers, the use of a small number of party signs, and attending all-candidates meetings. More than one candidate remarked that they incorporated the distribution of flyers and election material into their evening walks and daily trips.

This was an image characteristic of the FCP campaign, one in which only Heather Stilwell reported having a genuine interest in running for political office. The other candidates ran out of a sense of obligation or necessity. Several admitted to running out of a sense of familial obligation, and many admitted to not having the time or career interest in being a candidate but said they entered the election because the party needed the exposure and no other viable candidates could be found. Further, beyond the Toths, Stilwells, and Herwig, the candidates were for the most part political neophytes. Six had never before run for any type of political office or been seriously involved with the political process.

As in 1991, there was an overall sense of disappointment with the results of the election, but unlike the case in 1991, candidates and executives maintained some sense of optimism. In a post-election debriefing meeting, only the vote totals and lack of media attention were commonly identified as points of frustration. Recognizing their political handicaps, candidates overwhelmingly believed that the process was a valuable learning experience and that, given more expertise, money, and practical experience, their results could improve dramatically in the next election. Agreement was also unanimous that the presence of the party brought at least some attention to pro-life and pro-family causes during the election and for that reason it was vital that the party continue. Despite what Heather Stilwell described as the "doglike determination" required at times to maintain it, she echoed the feelings of the FCP membership in saying it was "absolutely essential for the political history of this province that we maintain the party, that we maintain a right to speak out."

Despite this post-election optimism, the party was unable to build on its modest showing in 1996 and as a result the last three by-elections in which the FCP ran were reminiscent of its past campaign forays. Of them all (Surrey–White Rock, 1997; Parksville–Qualicum, 1998; Delta South, 1999) the most politically interesting was the last.

In Delta South, FCP deputy leader Jim Hessels ran against Reform candidate Bill Vander Zalm. While Hessels was no threat to Vander Zalm, who finished second to Liberal Val Roddick, Hessels did conclude that Vander Zalm negatively impacted his vote total: "I received less votes when he ran than when I ran in that same riding [in 1996]. They didn't see a lot of difference between myself and Bill Vander Zalm. We were both acknowledged pro-life candidates, we had similar views on balanced budgets, on increasing choice in education through a voucher system – it was a daunting task for me to overcome." The numbers bear him out. In 1996, Hessels took 1.35 percent of the popular vote in the riding (304 votes), whereas in 1999 that total diminished to 0.6 percent (110 votes). More telling, though, are Hessels' comments about the similarity between the two candidates. Only a year later, this similarity between Reform and the FCP would finally result in the merger the FCP had been hoping for, if not expecting, since 1991.

Unity: The Second Coming of the FCP
As the 1990s pressed on, what optimism the FCP had created for itself in 1996 began to wane and the party was forced once again to evaluate its future. Only a few months after the election, Darren Lowe, then president, posed the all-important question to those in attendance at an executive meeting: "Where is the party going?"

It was a question predicated in part on a feeling among some of the executive that the party was wallowing and, as one member put it, the electoral results had actually been "very dismal and depressing." Even the membership drive had been evaluated as wanting. One executive said the party got new memberships slowly – "thirteen last month, but I think it's just the fact that people are so fed up with politics that they hear there's an alternative. But I don't think it's the result of any great effort on our part. Our effort isn't anywhere near good enough."

Although the party was never at risk of disbanding, there was an awareness that unless the challenges facing it were addressed vigorously, the FCP was destined to remain a marginal, largely ineffectual political organization. If the FCP were to develop into a political party capable of wielding social and political power in the province, the executive knew they had to critically re-evaluate its primary goal.

Unanimity existed around the necessity of the organization's political party structure, but there were two strains of thought on its principal function. The first underlined the role the party could play in bringing awareness and information to the public about pro-life and pro-family matters, particularly during election times. It was a role that fostered the image of the party as an educator and haven for free speech on these politically incorrect issues. Additionally, this included using the tactics of persuasion on other political parties to have them adopt the FCP's two core principles and support the enactment of family-friendly legislation. Discussing the overlap between these goals, Mrs. Toth reflects this strategy: "That is the first thing in our constitution, to elect people to the BC legislature. In order to carry out all these things, we need to elect people, but there are other ways to skin a cat. If we can get other parties to see the good things we stand for and we can get it in that way, that's fine."

Others shifted the emphasis more exclusively to the goal of electoral success. By 1997, Mrs. Stilwell had come to see the FCP as "at that point where we are party-oriented. I think the people who are really active right now are really focused on it being a political party" and having the goal of electing someone. In part due to the growing frustration some of executive felt over the party's inability to influence other parties, this became for them its proper function. One board member, commenting on the educational aspect of the party, said, "That's about all we're up to right now, but we have to get serious and do whatever is necessary to get someone elected in the next election. Until we do that we can't have any effect. I know some of the parties are talking about what we are because of the noise we are making, but it's not enough because they'll never do anything about it."

Reflected in these remarks was the dual nature of the FCP as part social movement, part political party. Its members were in pursuit of social change down both avenues and had yet to decide which they would concentrate on. Mr. Toth reflects this duality in his comment that, as much as the FCP was "a political party structurally, it is also a movement because of our main concern." Concomitantly, Mrs. Stilwell saw it as "a political party that is part of a social movement." This duality had prevented party executives from establishing a clearly defined goal for the party, something they understood had to be done if it was to be an effective educative voice for the family or an avenue of political power for those in other pro–family movement organizations.

The party's ideological trajectory was another primary concern for the executive. By 1997, two dominant factions had clearly emerged within the FCP concerning its Christian roots. While not denying a Judaeo-Christian foundation, the Toths had deliberately avoided any open Christian references in the party's constitution or policies for fear of appearing dogmatic and sectarian. About the Christian Heritage Party, for instance, Mrs. Toth said, "Christian Heritage is a religious movement – they have a very strict code of conduct I am nervous about." Another board member said: "The CHP, some people felt it was too much and we should leave it out of the constitution." A majority of the membership supported the tactic of leaving out any constitutional reference to Christianity. They believed that the principles of the party, if presented without an overt Christian ethos, could be attractive to a broad range of the population, including, as one member said, "Sikhs, Muslims, Hindus and Asians," all of whom, it was suggested, have strong beliefs about traditional family values.

Nonetheless, it was recognized within the party that the FCP was walking a thin line. In describing the situation, member John O'Flynn said: "The party has tried to stay away from parties like the CHP which are more openly religious. There is intertwining, but the party has been successful in not following what the CHP does. The FCP has from the beginning tried to keep a distance from that, but not always successfully, because the FCP has been brushed by the media with CHP." Another board member, in describing what the FCP stood for, said, "I hate to say it in this manner, but really it's high moral ground, having strong moral fibre – and hopefully that would be Christian or Judaeo-Christian principles. Everyone wants to steer it away from calling it Christian, but sometimes I think we should just put it out front. There are a lot of Christians out there and we may gain a lot of support."

This ambivalence gained strength from those in the party who felt it should pursue precisely such a tactic. A minority of the membership held this position but among them were Heather and Bill Stilwell, respectively:

> I still think we are going to get down to a disagreement about foundational principles which in my mind are religious and the party is trying very hard not to be religious. I don't mean religious in the sense of talking dogma or official religions, but the bottom-line statement is that these policies have been developed because of this basic kind of understanding that comes from, for example, the Christian religion. When the time comes, there will be a battle and there will be fallout because of it.

> The people who have started the party here have tried to stay away from it and this is going to become a dividing line, I think. They are going to come to the realization that it is going to have to become to a greater degree more like the CHP. That is where my sympathies lie.

Party executives became increasingly aware that this issue, and the challenge of escaping the public perception of the FCP as a single-issue right-to-life party, would have to be met and handled with dispatch if they were to establish a solid image that would effectively prepare the party for future elections.

What these matters really pointed to was a denial of identity by the party's executive and general membership. Their socio-moral positions paralleled the Christian right in the US. Admiration and reverence for Alan Keyes, Pat Buchanan, and the Christian Coalition were often articulated. Members of the FCP were religious conservatives, part of the Canadian

Christian right, yet they deliberately attempted to distance themselves from that political, social, and ideological image. Mrs. Stilwell, for instance, commented that the party should attract "a great mass of folks, ordinary Canadians, because we are talking about the kind of things that ordinary people talk about over the coffee table." It is the kind of statement that reflects one founding member's comment that they "fear the media will label us the religious right."

In the late 1990s, the FCP was being forced to grapple with these two issues not simply for the sake of the party itself, but because of the growing potential for a political coalition among all of the province's conservative parties. After the ingenuous 1994 merger offer from the Reform Party, the FCP was doubtful that they could successfully coalesce but was not dissuaded from trying again. In the autumn of 1997, after Wilf Hanni took over the leadership of Reform, another opportunity seemed to present itself. Hanni was a social conservative espousing many of the same opinions as those held by the FCP. A *Vancouver Sun* profile of the new leader reported:

> While other politicians go through contortions trying to avoid single-issue land mines such as abortion or gay rights, Hanni is happy to offer his opinion ... "The homosexual community," he says, "wants not just acceptance, they want approval. They want us to approve of their lifestyle ... The school system is pushing a homosexual, radical position. I don't think they know they are courting a backlash. What we got upset at is when the government starts legislating rights and privileges for small groups in society, right and privileges not available to others" ... He believes there is widespread support for his party's platform. "The party is still committed to old-fashioned family values," he insists. "We want to educate our children with our own inherited values ... Same-sex couples are not equal to traditional families."[85]

With such a natural ally in Reform, it was hardly surprising that Hanni sat down with some of the FCP executive in late 1997 to discuss a possible merger. As in the past, the FCP was open to merging, as long as its two foundational principles was put into Reform's constitution, and Hanni agreed to bring such a motion to the floor of the Reform convention in 1998. As it was reported to the public, it was a move that once again linked the ideologies of Reform, the FCP, and ex-premier Bill Vander Zalm: "BC Reformers will even consider merging with the Family Coalition Party, an anti-abortion organization founded by friends of former Premier Vander Zalm, at their annual meeting in Prince George this June. At the same time, they will consider adding an overt anti-abortion clause to their constitution."[86]

Once again, though, this proved to be a hollow overture to the FCP. The proposed constitutional amendment never made it to the floor of the Reform convention, and by the summer of 1999, Hanni had written to Reform president Vander Zalm and resigned from the party amidst a climate of divisive infighting and disorganization.

Even had the merger proceeded at this time, there were still some significant reservations being voiced from within the FCP. Whenever discussions around a merger arose, the point was always stressed that the FCP's principles would always be susceptible to those within the new party who would seek to undercut or remove them. In his newsletter message to the general membership, president Darren Lowe expressed this reservation by writing to members:

> I believe we each must ask ourselves, that notwithstanding the addition of these clauses to the Reform Party constitution ... are we certain that the majority of Reform Party candidates in the next provincial election are people who share these values and will actively promote them? Almost all of the Reform Party candidates in the 1996 election either did not share these values or did not want to be seen as sharing them. We should never terminate the Family Coalition Party only to see our core issues relegated to the background.[87]

Lowe's caution was for those who would sacrifice the purity of the FCP's social movement principles for the opportunity to join the political mainstream. Again, the party was confronted with the problem of its dual nature, but by the following spring, there finally seemed reason for optimism.

With a provincial election less than a year away, the conservative parties in the province found themselves in political and organizational disarray. There were no fewer than five political parties trying to claim the right-of-centre political terrain. And, of these, only the Reform Party had any real name recognition but only the FCP had any long-term internal stability and peace. In this situation, the likelihood of a Socred-type party re-emerging by the 2001 election appeared completely illusory. As Heather Stilwell put it, "there was a real vacuum in British Columbia politics, on the right, on the social conservative side, that was definitely not going to be filled by the Liberals." With this motivation, by the spring of 2000, discussions between various party executives had begun and news reports began to emerge about a "unite the right" effort.[88]

Over the course of the summer, leaders, presidents, and other executives from the five conservative parties met on numerous occasions to hammer out the foundational principles for what would become the Unity Party of British Columbia.[89] As Mrs. Toth recalls, it was Heather Stilwell who sensed the potential of this opportunity:

Heather attended a big pro-life dinner last year. Heather and her husband were put at a table with Chris Delaney and Bill Vander Zalm. That is when the overtures were made, you know, "We'd like the Family Coalition Party to consider coming on board with Reform," that sort of thing. Heather came to the next meeting of the executive and she said this looks like an opportunity that we shouldn't pass up, we should explore it because we may not ever have the chance again and if it's possible – she said it's different this time, there was good feeling among the people at the table and she felt they were really sincere and they would welcome us. As a result of that, we decided to go ahead.

Mrs. Stilwell concurred, recalling that, "I got a call from Chris Delaney saying they had people who were interested in doing this thing with all of the smaller right-wing parties, but the initiative definitely came from the Reform Party. But I could immediately see the possibilities of it because I knew Chris personally." As the unification talks proceeded, Stilwell's optimistic vision was being confirmed until the issue of pro-life came up. As she pointed out, "Well, of course the biggest problem was the pro-life issue. All the other stuff just fell into place like cards being shuffled. They worried, of course, at the same time Stockwell Day, you know – you could see that developing and people were scared of the issue." The FCP had tripped over this stumbling block before, and it was certainly prepared to do so again. However, things did prove to be different this time.

The pivotal moment came during a meeting in which the parties were voting on the foundational principles for the unification. Kathleen Toth remembers it this way:

> It was about meeting number four. It came to the fact of our two clauses, those two clauses, and Heather and I simply said, "Well, we can't go any farther, if these two clauses are out, then we're out, and you carry on." So then it was the word "conception" that really bugged them. We had this "from conception to natural death," it's just sort of something we're used to. Well, they just hated this word, and so Bill Vander Zalm said, "Well, what if you say 'protection of life at all stages?'" First of all, Heather and I said no, we can't go with that, and then Bill said, "Well, let's just break for fifteen minutes and just go outside and walk around and have a bit of a breather." Mark [Toth] wasn't at the meeting, Mark was outside and we said, "Guess what they want to do, they want to put 'life at all stages,'" and Mark said, "Well, it's the same thing." We looked at each other and said, "Yeah, you're right." So we had already sort of signified that we weren't going to go with this, so when we went downstairs again, they took a vote and everybody voted for this thing and then it got to Heather and I and we voted for it. Well, we nearly hit the roof because they

thought it had to be a consensus, you see, so then they said no, now we want to change it and it was Bill who said, "Look, you voted, and now the Family Coalition goes along with it, you want to change it. Sorry, you just can't do that," so they had to go along with it.

The divisiveness of including an overtly pro-life clause in the new constitution was immediately visible. Social Credit, the BC Conservatives, and the British Columbia Party all declined to involve themselves with a pro-life party, but nonetheless the foundations for a new pro-life, pro-family party had been laid. In the end, it was only the pro-life clause of the FCP that had proven to be a sticking point. The pro-family clause supporting the traditional definition of marriage was accepted without incident, as were the FCP positions on education, health care, and the economy. The next steps were to give the party a name, a constitution, and a leader and prepare for a spring 2001 election, all in less than a year.

At the Unity Party of British Columbia's founding convention in November 2000, more than three hundred delegates from the five parties attended, and once again the foundational principles for the party were unanimously accepted, with the exception of the pro-life clause. While the clause was ultimately accepted, there was a visible exodus of delegates who did not agree with the pro-life character the new party was taking on. For the FCP's other foundational clause, the one promoting the traditional family, the audience applauded – the only policy read out at the convention to receive such a response. By the end of the day, the FCP had achieved what may in fact have been their only realistic goal. They had coalesced with other social conservatives in the province to form a larger and potentially more viable party in the form of Unity BC.

In February 2001, a leadership convention was held in Kamloops, during which Chris Delaney, former president of the Reform Party, won the leadership and then named Heather Stilwell as deputy leader. Even this highly visible role was only part of a significant FCP presence and influence on Unity at this point. Kathleen Toth became the first vice-president of the party and Brian Zacharias, a long-time FCP executive member from Nelson, became president.

Most significant for the FCP, however, was the Unity constitution, which contained their all-important pro-life and pro-family clauses: "We uphold that the individual is the most important factor in organized society, and has certain inalienable rights, responsibilities and freedoms, including freedom of speech, assembly, religion, association, movement, equality before the law, the right to own private property, and *the right to life which must be respected and preserved at all stages*" (Unity Party of British Columbia, Foundational Principles, Preamble, point 4, emphasis added). To ensure the permanence of this principle – and the other five – the last point in the preamble states, *"This preamble is unalterable at any time"* (Preamble, point 6, emphasis in the original). The pro-family principle protecting and promoting the traditional family and definition of marriage states:

> *The traditional family, individuals related by blood, marriage or adoption is the cornerstone of society. We uphold the definition of marriage as the legal union of two members of the opposite sex. A Unity Government would:* A) Repeal the Definition of Spouse Amendment Act. Constitutionalize the definition of marriage as between a man and a woman ... Amend the Adoption Act so that children may only be adopted into the homes of married couples and stable single people. Constitutionalize Parents' rights and responsibilities for their children. (Unity Party of British Columbia, Foundational Principles, principle 8a, emphasis in the original)

A short ten weeks later, the Unity Party ran on a socially conservative, pro-life, pro-family platform and took 3.3 percent of the vote in the provincial election, a result the FCP could only have dreamt about.

Given the limited amount of preparation time and lack of overall political expertise, this was a respectable result. But even during the election run-up, Unity had begun to exhibit many of the same problems that had beset the FCP. Lack of knowledge, resources, and finances during and after the election stalled the organization. Additionally, several FCP supporters were uncomfortable with what they perceived as a lack of democratic decision-making protocols in the new party. The most dramatic example occurred even before the election and eventually forced Kathleen Toth from the Unity executive.

In large part, it was a product of Mrs. Toth's posting on the old FCP website a message stating, *"THE FAMILY COALITION PARTY HAS A NEW NAME! ... And so, after nearly ten years, instead of dying, the Family Coalition Party has been rejuvenated with the help of many people who have the same hopes and goals. We have a new name, a new logo, and a new web-site, which we hope you will visit to learn more about the people who helped bring this about"* (FCP website, <familyparty.bc.ca>, emphasis in the original). According to Mrs. Toth, this inflamed the animosity between herself and leader Chris Delaney. Up until then, Mrs. Toth had been intimately involved in the Unity website's maintenance and development, but the situation reached a boiling point when her access to the site was cut off. In a letter asking for her resignation, Delaney wrote: "You have taken several actions in the past few weeks which have had a very damaging effect on the reputation of the party, and on our ability to attract candidates and support. Your decision to post a notice on the Family Coalition web site stating that the Family Coalition has a new name, was totally erroneous, misleading and ill-conceived."[90]

It was a situation that didn't sit well with those who had come from the FCP. As one executive member put it, there were those who had "almost had it" and were ready to quit. Regardless, by the time Unity's first annual general meeting came around, in November 2001, most of the executive remained on board. It appeared as if those who could not abide the pro-life preamble had been subdued and some measure of organizational calm had been achieved. As the keynote speaker on the opening evening of the convention, Bill Vander Zalm commented on the kinds of difficulties that Unity and its personnel had been facing:

> Within our party, particularly with a new party – and I've been there, I know how it is – a lot of people come in with new ideas and if you don't immediately accept those new ideas there could be frictions ... There needs to be a fair degree of understanding, on each and every one of our parts. We have to recognize that in a new party oftentimes it's not only difficult because we're searching, because we're trying to find that place where we need to be, but also difficult in the sense that we don't have the resources that the old established parties have ... So I think we need to be very under-standing, we need to recognize that we're building a new party and there will be difficulties initially, and we need to recognize as well that we must bring these people in by not hammering them over the head but convinc-ing them in a very orderly way about what it is we're trying to do and why it is Unity is so important to the province. The Unity Party can be a real grassroots movement, it can be to the province in the next election what Social Credit obviously was to the people when it first came to be during the early '50s when we had the coalition of Conservatives and Liberals.

If Unity is to achieve this lofty goal, Vander Zalm vastly understated the amount of work to be done. Only about eighty people turned out to hear him speak on the Friday evening of the convention, and on Saturday morning that number had dropped to sixty-five. By the afternoon, a head count had to be taken to see if quorum of fifty could be reached. Fifty-six were present at the time. Like the Family Coalition Party, the shadow cab-inet and many on the executive are well intentioned and motivated but generally lacking in political and portfolio topic expertise. Additionally, as Vander Zalm noted, the party lacks financial and other resources, as most small parties do.

For those from the Family Coalition Party, though, a goal had been met and progress had been made. In merging with Reform, they had broad-ened their base, both in terms of sheer membership size and populist potential. In evaluating the parallels, Bill Vander Zalm said, "The Unity Party has picked up on not only the conservative economic and more broadly held social views, but also has picked up on the whole issue of life and personal values, so there are without doubt similarities. The only thing is, I think the Unity Party would be a little softer in how it presents the issues." John Hof, a prominent pro-life activist in the province and the president of Campaign Life Coalition British Columbia, offered a similar appraisal in saying:

> The FCP was singular, when it was first formed it was singular issue, it was family values, and the Unity Party tried to broaden the base, tried to have policy on more than those issues and it was successful in creating its policy. If you read their documentation, it is very, very broad-based in what their policies stand for, very social conservative, very conservative on many issues. It's almost as if the party, because it did have that pro-life, pro-family little element in it, it then became tainted, at least in the public's view. I say it's a better version [of the FCP] but bigger would be quantitative and I don't see the difference in the size. I looked at a list of their candidates and I haven't seen too many candidates who wouldn't be comfortable in the Family Coalition Party – the name changed but the faces seemed to be mostly Family Coalition Party faces.

As much as many from the Reform Party or those within Unity might deny it, the truth is that Unity is the next coming of the FCP – a larger, more broad-based pro-life party. Ideologically, its policies and principles are virtually identical; organizationally, Unity is faced with the same drawbacks and limitations as the FCP; politically, Unity is being regarded, like the FCP, as neoconservative, pro-family, and pro-life. Soon after the merger, the party was being publicly evaluated as a marriage between the FCP and Reform, as anti-abortion, as a minor party that will just fade away, and as the new "pro-life front" for the province.[91] Though not entirely due to the FCP, Unity has even inherited the political dilemma of being identified as a religious, Christian-based party – the problem the FCP never resolved is now a challenge for the Unity executive.

Even before the merger, this coming challenge was foreshadowed. In an opinion piece about Reform's 2000 convention and the potential merger, Vaughn Palmer of the *Vancouver Sun* reported:

> A more sensitive topic involves the role of religion in a movement that has strong undercurrents of Evangelical Christianity ... The evangelical fervor appeared to be in the ascendency on the weekend. One of the more zealous Reformers, party president Delaney, delivered a sermon-in-all-but-name Saturday morning and wound up in quasi-biblical terms, urging party members to "clothe themselves" in the new, resplendent armour of righteousness. His protégé, Justin Goodrich, president of the party's youth wing, had earlier outlined a view that the separation of church and state

was established "to keep the state out of church business, not to keep the church out of state business." He asked, "What drives me?" and provided his own answer: "It's my relationship with Jesus Christ." To which several voices in the audience replied: "Amen, amen."[92]

In similar fashion, at the first annual general meeting, an extra verse that made express references to God and Christianity was added to the singing of the national anthem.

Whether the party is a Christian-based one is something Bill Vander Zalm sees as depending on "how it's presented. Few people ever make reference to the fact that the supremacy of God, for example, is a part of the federal Liberal Party constitution and the constitution of Canada, but with Unity, already the media has made some reference to it that it may be more of a religious party. I think it depends on presentation as to how it's presented and perceived." Akin to the FCP, Unity is faced with the difficult challenge of managing its latent Christianity.

Where Family Coalition and Unity do part company is with respect to their goals. Unlike the FCP, whose goals as a party/movement were public awareness and then electoral success, Unity is a party with a single goal: to win political office. In its decision to unify, the FCP took a step away from its movement principles in its effort to broaden its membership base and increase the political viability of its cause. By doing so, it moved closer to the political mainstream and risked having its foundational principles weakened or even dispatched.

Some from the FCP argue that the principles have already been dismantled. Mark Toth pointed out that 99 percent of the FCP membership approved the merger, but it is the remaining 1 percent who regarded the merger as a sellout of the party's principles. Darren Lowe, past president of the party and someone who was highly regarded by the FCP executive, resigned his membership as a result of the merger. Norm Herriott, another long-term executive member of the FCP, commented at the Unity leadership convention that the "demise of a pro-life party" was being witnessed when an amendment was passed that softened the pro-life position of the new party. A few other committed pro-life FCP members shared the sentiment, feeling that the merger created a very real possibility for not only a watering down of the pro-life language in the constitution but even its elimination. Part of this concern was that, as one FCP executive put it, "there wasn't enough commitment on the part of the leadership," a view elaborated on by another with these comments:

[During the election] Delaney was very awkward when it came to saying anything about what would you do about abortion. There's so many good things you could say about it aside from defunding it – and he didn't know how to talk about it, he just didn't have a clue. So, you know, he wouldn't let people like Kathleen Toth educate him either. You know, she could have been a great help to him and eventually he ended up turfing her right out of the party, practically. I don't know how he did that, because the leader doesn't have the authority to kick out the vice-president. It seems like he insulted her so much she just wouldn't work with him is about how he did it. And that whole thing was because she was trying to look after the pro-life stuff and he thought she was getting too pushy.

The fear for this group is that, like Social Credit before it, the Unity Party will ultimately sacrifice principle as an expedient way to achieve political power.

As a party/movement, Family Coalition trod a thin line for nine years, trying to maintain its movement principles and objectives while also trying to develop as a viable political party. With the Unity merger, the FCP did achieve one of its goals – perhaps its only realistic one – but in doing so took a decided step away from its movement origins. Only time will tell if the decision was wise or if the premonitions of some will come true and the FCP principles will become lost under the Unity banner. This is the fear and the challenge that party/movements face when they come to this inevitable developmental crossroad. The founders of the FCP, in choosing to form a political party to pursue social movement goals, sent their organization towards this destiny back in 1991.

While the FCP may have been a political party, its origins were in the activism of the pro-life movement and its existence depended on the laboured efforts of committed activists who had exhausted all other routes that held out the opportunity for the change they sought. The FCP was a core of activists, not politicians, and their goal was change, not power. It was a movement in party clothes, but this political garb necessarily burdened these activists with the realities of party politics as they tried to resurrect ideological support for the traditional family. They acknowledged that it was certainly not the path of least resistance. As the Toths put it, "preferably the route would not be to have to go and form your own party. It's a last resort."

In evaluating a group like the FCP, it may initially be tempting to simply assume that it would face fewer obstacles in pursuit of its goals than a more social democratic movement, particularly given the Christian and capitalist history of Canada. Yet the upcoming chapters, in which the FCP is analyzed as a social movement, a political party, and then a party/movement, will show that this is not the case. Ultimately, it becomes clear that the challenges the FCP faced were no different than the ones any small political body has to deal with, regardless of that body's ideology. This may seem even more surprising given the deep conservative roots that provided the FCP membership with its strength and motivation. The next chapter will try to untangle these roots and make sense of the various connections between traditional conservative thought, neoconservatism, and the Christian right, all of which the Family Coalition Party and now Unity represent.

2
The Pro-Family Movement: Conservative Roots, New Right Economics, and Religious Ideals

The politics of British Columbia's Family Coalition Party was a historical amalgam resulting from the confluence of various political, nationalistic, and ideological trajectories whose point of intersection emerged under the banner of the pro-family movement. Most readily identified with the activism of the Christian Coalition in the United States, the pro-family movement has nonetheless been active in Canada for some years. The roots of the Canadian movement are embedded in a political tradition of American and British conservative thought that can be traced back to the work of Edmund Burke. As can happen, though, the lineage of political and social ideologies that provide the foundations of a movement often becomes tangled and at times lost with the passage of time as social and economic forces transform old political articulations into new ones. For instance, in liberal democracies such as Canada, the United States, and Britain, the current conservative economic tradition that underpins the pro-family movement is typically referred to as a neoconservative or New Right ideology.

Accurate or not, to simply describe the Family Coalition Party as a pro-family example of this political genre does little to capture the depth of the party's political foundations or the breadth of the socio-cultural milieu from which it draws strength. The purpose of this chapter is to untangle the socio-political legacy of the pro-family movement so the FCP's Canadian variant can be properly understood as a mix of British and American conservative influence, traditional conservative concern for the family, Christian morality, and neoconservative economics.

Finding the first thread in this tangle is a simple matter. It is a virtual axiom that the writings of Edmund Burke constitute the origins of modern conservative thought. With the publication in 1790 of Burke's *Reflections on the Recent Revolution in France,* the foundations were in large part laid for all subsequent versions of conservative thought in the Western world. In opposing the revolution, Burke argued that rapid, dramatic social change could only lead to a society's ruin and that, while change was inevitable, it was best achieved through slow, gentle reformation: "Change ... alters the substance of the objects themselves, and gets rid of all their essential good as well as the accidental evil annexed to them. Change is novelty ... Reform is not a change in the substance or primary modification of the objects, but a direct application of a remedy to the grievance complained of" (quoted in Honderich 1990, 5).

This opposition to change stemmed from Burke's rather Hobbesian view of human nature and his accompanying lack of faith in human reason to improve the social and political institutions that past generations had laboured to produce. Family, church, monarchy, social hierarchy, private property, and representative rather than popular government were for Burke the institutions critical to the emergence of a citizenry's goodness and morality. Political rule founded on such traditional institutions and authorities offered no place for equality of persons in Burke's mind, for there existed a natural deference to those with social standing and breeding. The propertied aristocrats, Burke assumed, were the people vested with the wisdom and knowledge to govern a society's citizens in fair and broad-minded fashion.

Burke's is foremost a political philosophy that places greater value on preserving the extant social order than on elevating individual desires above society's needs: families, not individuals, are the basic units of society; nationalism presides over constituent interests; and continuity and social order are favoured over novel political experience and rampant individualism. This is a philosophical orientation that generates a natural tension between the freedom of the individual and society's demand for social order. As the eminent American conservative scholar Russell Kirk observed, the importance of Burke's work lay in his undertanding that a "tension must be maintained between claims of freedom and claims of order" (1982, 1). This tension is a natural essence of conservatism, something that characterizes its features. These features and their attendant tensions – a seeking of equality and opportunity, a respect for tradition, belief in the merits of gradual social reform, resolute support for the sanctity of private property, and faith in the divine – which Kendall and Carey (1964) summarized as the representation of the masses, are the core around which modern conservatism was born.

Two centuries later, despite varying degrees of historical and cultural metamorphosis, this core remains solid. One of Britain's leading conservative scholars, Roger Scruton, remarks in *The Meaning of Conservatism* that: "Society exists through authority, and the recognition of this authority requires the allegiance to a bond that is not contractual but transcendent, in the manner of the family tie. Such allegiance requires tradition and custom through which to find enactment. But tradition is no static thing. It is the active achievement of continuity; it can be restored, rescued and amended as grace and opportunity allow" (1984, 45). Commenting on private property and the individual's relationship to society's institutions, he continues: "In politics, the conservative attitude seeks above all for government, and regards no citizen as possessed of a natural right that transcends his obligation to be ruled ... any political view which regards the state as protector of society must also demand the continuance of property. Moreover, a view which recognizes a title in custom and usage will find nothing wrong with the inheritance and accumulation of wealth" (ibid., 16).

Having made this safe passage into the modern democratic age, Burke's traditional conservative philosophy has nonetheless undergone reformation to its outer shell. Conservative traditions exist throughout Western Europe as well as in North America, and each exhibit their own cultural and historical peculiarities as they forge ahead through history and the machinations of reform. For the present purpose, what is of most concern for the Canadian context is that the modern (after 1945) conservative age of Britain and the United States share some striking similarities. Although it is American, Robert Nisbet's portrayal of conservatism can serve to characterize the modern ideal in both countries:

> Belief in strong but unobtrusive government; an implicit decentralization of administration that directly followed a historically developed autonomy of all the major institutions – family, local community, church, school, business enterprise, and so on; an instinctive preference for the same institutions as the principal shelters of individuals in time of crisis or need – these rather than offices of the central government; a strong conviction in the superiority of common sense and experience in governmental matters over the kind of rationalist intelligence favored by professors and bureaucrats; and finally, almost uppermost, a skepticism of all social reform and a positive hatred of redistributionist schemes involving taxation, tariff, or currency manipulation, or, for that matter, anything in the way of mandated equality. (1981, 129)

Politically, these ideals meant that through the 1960s, British, American, and Canadian conservatives had a difficult time fitting their agenda to the progressive political and economic cultures of the day. However, by the late 1960s, cracks in these nations' social democratic hegemony began to appear. Through to the 1980s, growing government bureaucracies and intervention, inflation, national deficits, crime, unemployment, divorce rates, single parenthood, and a host of other social issues generated a deep concern among people and provided conservative parties with an opportunity they had been waiting for.

What emerged, particularly in the US, was a longing for a return to the "good old days" as conservative-minded people grew dubious about the impact liberal values were having on their society and neighbourhoods. Looking around, they were witnessing some dramatic social and cultural changes, driven in large part by the activism of various social movements, including those propelled by gays, feminists, and environmentalists. The gains being made by these previously marginalized groups, coupled with such factors as student protests over the Vietnam War, were often popularized as a radical left takeover of America (Girvin 1988b). The result was that conservative politics once again became attractive. Robert Nisbet points out that conservatism came to make sense both economically and socially at this time because its "greatest strength is its possession by historic right of such values as localism, decentralization, family, neighbourhood, mutual aid, and belief in growth of business on the one hand and of religion on the other" (1981, 140). It was a situation that would have pleased Burke – his ideas were becoming increasingly popular in late-twentieth-century America.

Likewise, across the Atlantic, problems similar to those in the United States had befallen Britain (Peele 1988). In a search for solutions, attention was drawn in both countries to the intellectual revival of the right in America and the strategies being proffered as solutions to the social and economic problems that were being blamed on the left. What subsequently developed was a relationship that would closely link the political ideologies of Britain, the United States, and ultimately Canada as a new dawn of conservative thought was ushered in – neoconservatism.

Mugged by Reality: Neoconservatism and the New Right

What becomes quickly apparent about this new variant of the old ideology is that it is far removed from the traditional descriptions offered by conservative scholars such as Michael Oakeshott, who describes conservatism as primarily a disposition, one that centres upon "a propensity to use and enjoy what is available rather than to wish for or to look for something else; to delight in what is present rather than what was or what may be ... there is no mere idolizing of what is past and gone. What is esteemed is the present; and it is esteemed not on account of its connections with a remote antiquity ... but on account of its familiarity" (1997, 87).

The dramatic emergence of neoconservative thought and New Right populism since the late 1970s, however, suggests an attitude far more invasive and tactical than Oakeshott's benign description. Neoconservative intellectuals and New Right activists were interested in change – dramatic change. Through deliberate and substantive policy initiatives, they sought a radical alteration of the economic, state, and civil makeup of liberal democracies like the US and Britain.

For instance, in his critique of conservatism, Ted Honderich (1990) argues that in Britain, Margaret Thatcher's Conservative party vigorously pursued a "politics of alteration" far greater in scope than the British

Labour Party had ever been accused of doing. First and foremost, this politics of alteration became an exercise in economic pragmatics. It was believed that restoring Britain to its former glory demanded a drastic shift away from Keynesianism and towards a new accumulation strategy based on classic liberal free-market principles, in particular those of F.A. Hayek and the Chicago School's Milton Friedman. Burke's ghost lingered; he had been a follower of Adam Smith's belief in the liberating potential of the market (Willetts 1992).

The British experience with neoconservativism was directly connected with the work of an American group that Michael Harrington dubbed the "neoconservatives."[1] This group of notable social scientists and intellectuals, including the likes of Robert Nisbet, Seymour Martin Lipset, Patrick Moynihan, Jeanne Kirkpatrick, Irving Kristol, Daniel Bell, Nathan Glazer, and James Q. Wilson, had defected from their social democratic roots in a move that was to have profound implications for the politics of the right.

As Seymour Martin Lipset (1988) describes it, the neoconservatives' split from the American Socialist Party was due to the New Left's increasingly radical posturing over major social issues such as the Vietnam War. Staunchly nationalistic and anti-Communist, the neoconservatives ultimately found kindred spirits for their foreign policy among Republicans and traditional conservatives. Perhaps surprisingly, though, by most accounts they continued to support Keynesian welfare policies and were initially on the liberal side of social issues (Lipset 1988; Gottfried and Fleming 1988).[2] The "godfather" of neoconservatism, Irving Kristol, claimed that "neo-conservatism is not at all hostile to the idea of a welfare state, but it is critical of the Great Society version of this welfare state ... it is opposed to the paternalistic state" (quoted in Etzioni 1977, 436). This lingering (albeit fading) support of the welfare state notwithstanding, by far the most important role for the neoconservatives was to lend the American right something it had always lacked: intellectual credibility.

Given their intellectual pedigree, another seemingly odd feature of these neoconservatives was their crusade for implementing policy change – they were a group far more interested in being political practitioners than academic ideologues (Dorrien 1993). This shift to the pragmatic was the result of the confluence of a number of issues confronting American society. Secularization, intergenerational shifts in ideological beliefs, the student revolts of the sixties, the New Left critique of America as a fascist state, the failure of Roosevelt's New Deal, and, broadly speaking, the forces of modernization all proved sources of motivation for neoconservatives. While much of their focus lay with the cultural determinants of these issues, the solutions they promoted were largely economic in nature and came to be based on a profound shift towards the principles of the free market. The result was that issues of social and moral concern took a back seat to seeking out remedies for a faltering American economy.

To capture the essence of neoconservativism, Gary Dorrien describes it as "an intellectual movement originated by former leftists that promotes militant anticommunism, capitalist economics, a minimal welfare state, the rule of traditional elites, and a return to traditional cultural values" (1993, 8). This type of description exposes why the label neoliberal more accurately captures the overall ideology of the neoconservatives, and it is in fact a label the neoconservatives themselves prefer (Ashford 1981).

This terminological preference is more than a matter of semantics. It exposes a fundamental political difference between Britain, Canada, and the United States that is rooted in their discrepant social and economic histories. In this regard, Seymour Martin Lipset points out that the United States did not develop as a post-feudal society and as a result has developed an anti-statist, populist, and meritocratic political ideology that more closely resembles European liberalism than conservatism: "Liberalism in its original meaning involves an antistatist philosophy, opposition to mercantilism and the alliance of throne and altar, support for economic and political freedoms, laissez-faire and civil liberties ... equality of opportunity and respect, regardless of status ... Tories have stood for a strong state, an established church, mercantilism, communitarianism, and noblesse oblige – the values of a hierarchical manorial society" (1988, 29). Lipset argues that it is this strong anti-statist sentiment in the US that has prevented the emergence of any serious form of socialism. This stands in opposition to Canada and Britain, both of which have traditionally maintained a more prominent and valued role for the state, and both of which have strong socialist political traditions. It also seems that this difference has in part come to account for the greater support in the US for the Christian right and pro-family movement than it has been able to generate in Canada or Britain.

Dorrien's description also captures the close links that exist for neoconservatives between economic and social policies. Embedded in the notion of "traditional cultural values," for instance, is the importance that neoconservatives place on such mediating structures as family, neighbourhood, church, and voluntary associations. It is these structures, neoconservatives argue, that properly anchor the individual in society, provide the innovative flexibility to respond to changing social and economic conditions, and offer workable starting points for viable public policy. Their concern lies in the erosion of these institutions at the hands of liberal or "socialist" policy makers. From here, the underlying argument and strategy emerges: The social and economic salvation of America depended as much on the restoration of these structures to their past prominence as it did on the revitalization of a laissez-faire economy, but focusing on the economic issues and allowing the social ones to follow in the wake was a more politically viable strategy.

What neoconservatism lacked in this pursuit was broad-based mass appeal – it had simply never developed as a mass or populist phenomenon (Gottfried and Fleming 1988; Habermas 1989). It did, however, share common stock with the emergent political populism known as the New Right. From the late 1970s onwards, neoconservatism gradually became equated with the New Right, a perhaps inevitable trajectory, given their similar ideological dispositions (Dorrien 1993).

There is no clear point in time indicating where the influence of the original neoconservatives began to wane and the popular activism of the New Right began to surge. The isms of Margaret Thatcher and Ronald Reagan have been identified as the high-water marks for neoconservative influence (Girvin 1988b) while simultaneously being equated with projects of the New Right (Honderich 1990). Both appear to be defensible positions, given that these administrations gave prominence to the neoconservatives' policy-driven agenda and also reflected the populist ideas of the New Right.

In attempting to construct a profile of the New Right, scholars have created the image of a conservative political gumbo concerned with a range of issues. Sara Diamond sees the New Right as a fusion of "moral traditionalism, economic libertarianism and militaristic anticommunism" (1995, 179). Gottfried and Fleming claim analysts view it as a "collection of general-purpose political organizations" like the Moral Majority or the National Conservative Political Action Committee (1988, 77). Roger Eatwell (1989), meanwhile, has identified four strains of New Right politics: libertarian, laissez-faire, traditionalist, and mythical.

However it is characterized, when the New Right did emerge in the mid-1970s, what became evident was that, as Sara Diamond puts it, "the 'new' twist for the New Right ... was a budding alliance between seasoned conservative activists and the evangelical Christians who were just starting to awaken politically" (1998, 59). Led by Catholic activists such as Paul Weyrich and Connaught Marshner, and backed financially by corporate magnates such as Joseph Coors,[3] the New Right differed from the neoconservatives in that they "learned how to emphasize themes that are more populist than conservative: the fear and resentment of the Eastern 'establishment,' defense of family and conventional morals, popular control over schools and churches. They also display a greater willingness to use single-issue campaigns, such as the Panama Canal treaty or abortion, as the basis of external fund-raising" (Gottfried and Fleming 1988, 78).

This latest manifestation of conservative politics, while maintaining the core ideals of the Burkean tradition, had become more interested in dramatic change than gradual reform. These conservatives were deliberately activist, strategic, and populist in an approach that defended individualism, the market, and meritocracy. It was an approach that deliberately attempted to tap into the mass support of what Brian Girvin terms "lower status opinion" (1988, 10, 177). Tactically, the New Right openly and vigorously pursued an opposition to the broad category of "new social movements," which included feminism, gay rights, and environmentalism, as well as advocacy on behalf of pro-choice and reproductive technology. Such positions created a natural alliance with traditionalist movements that fell under such banners as pro-family and pro-life.

Arguably, though, the New Right's largest source of support and motivation came from the wellspring of Christian activism that spilled into the political realm throughout the 1980s and 1990s (Gottfried and Fleming 1988). This not only gave conservative politics a renewed populist appeal, but it also put matters of social concern on an equal footing with the economic ones. Social and religious conservatives now had a growing political voice with which to express their opposition to matters such as abortion, feminism, and secular humanism. By emphasizing Christian morality, self-reliance, and good old-fashioned "common-sense" values, the New Right began to generate a vigorous and committed base of supporters.

While the neoconservatives and the New Right find their historical and activist roots in the US, Canada, like Britain, has been carried along on this wave of neoconservative thought. Over the last two decades, various analysts have identified a strain of neoconservatism at federal and provincial levels that has been shaped by Canada's unique historical, political, and social structures (Hatt et al. 1990; Havemann 1986; Ratner and McMullan 1985).

Like other Western liberal democracies, Canada has been increasingly feeling the pressure of a globalizing capitalist system, with its attendant requisites of a minimalist state, unfettered markets, and access to cheap mass labour. In response, federal and provincial governments have adopted, to varying degrees of success, neoconservative agendas. Since the late 1970s, Canada has been travelling down an uneven path to what has been described as its "New Establishment Ideology," with its "New Economic Reality" and strategy of "managing consent" (Marchak 1985; Havemann 1986; Hatt et al. 1990). Examining the impact of this journey on Canadian levels of unemployment, Stephen McBride (1992) identified a marked shift to the right, from Keynesianism to monetarism in matters of monetary policy, labour-market policy, unemployment insurance, and industrial relations. To address the risks this presents for a consensus-based and social democratic Canadian hegemony, the state has sought to "manage consent," a strategy Hatt et al. describe as "governing a country of diverse national and regional interests primarily through the transformation of controversy into technico-bureaucratic problems and the manipulation of complex federal/provincial relations" (1990, 31).

This last point equates to reducing the size of the federal government bureaucracy through a program of downloading previous federal responsibilities to the provinces via such moves as changes to the constitution. For instance, among its prescriptions, the Meech Lake Accord called for a significant decentralization of federal power to the provinces, and while the accord itself failed, this aspect of it has not (McBride 1992).

This is an important component of the neoconservative agenda because of the constitutional principle of the supremacy of Parliament in Canada. This principle in effect prevents the federal state from moving dramatically left or right in response to domestic or foreign economic crises (McBride 1992; Hatt et al. 1990). By offsetting responsibilities to the provinces, however, the latitude required for a neoconservative response to such crises is not only secured, but the agenda itself becomes hidden behind the complexities of federal/provincial relations. As Ratner and McMullan (1985) point out, the neoconservative agenda has a strong localized quality that allows it to operate behind the inevitable regional conflicts and peculiarities that arise from Canadian federal/provincial policy relationships.

The Free Trade Agreement (FTA) Canada signed with the US and then later with Mexico stands as arguably the best national example of this new establishment ideology and as potentially the most significant neoconservative threat to Canadian social democratic hegemony. David Wolfe (1989) argues that while Canada has escaped the worst excesses of Thatcherism and Reaganism, the role of the state in the management of the economy is being replaced by a belief in the primacy of the market, a strategic shift manifested in the details of the FTA. Wolfe's concern is that the agreement presents a backdoor opportunity for the dismantling of Canada's social safety net through claims of unfair subsidies (1989, 120). It presents, in other words, another opportunity to achieve indirectly what the capitalist class has been unable to achieve directly and suggests once more the clandestine, surreptitious nature of Canadian neoconservatism. John Warnock fittingly observes that in the FTA "there was always a hidden agenda – the New Right program of solving the persistent economic crisis ... the reality is that support for free trade comes almost exclusively from big business and its ideological supporters" (1988, 22). With the implementation of the FTA by Brian Mulroney's Progressive Conservative government, Canadians began to experience life driven by a neoconservative economic agenda.

As significant as this event was, it was the emergence of Preston Manning's Reform Party of Canada in 1987 that proved to be the federal watershed moment for the New Right in Canada. Unlike Mulroney's Conservatives, Preston Manning's party embraced a New Right agenda of both economic and social conservatism. The new establishment ideology of this Western-based populist party loudly and proudly articulated a belief in a grassroots, common-sense approach to government and social policy.

Among these common-sense approaches could be found a get tough, law and order approach to crime, support for traditional family values, and a (sometimes thinly) veiled Christian ethos. Economically, the party supported a view recognizing that Canada must take its place in a new global economic order that is "dominated by the three huge trading blocs – the European community, the Asia-Pacific economic community, and the North American free trade area" (Manning 1992, 336). Manning, in his book *The New Canada,* also called for a downsizing of the federal bureaucracy, elimination of grants to special-interest groups, "fiscal responsibility through constitutional reform," distribution of social goods and services through the provinces, and efforts to "develop transition programs to move public-sector workers to more productive employment in the non-governmental sector" (1992, 342, 344).

In attempting to address these economic, social, and administrative issues, the Reform Party chose to focus on Canada's economic problems, believing that, once these were remedied, the social and administrative aspects of its agenda would naturally follow. Brooke Jeffrey points out that, in a "move more reminiscent of Thatcher than of Reagan, those advancing neo-conservative values in Canada emphasized, first and foremost, the *economic* agenda rather than the social and moral aspects" (1999, 50, emphasis in the original).

What this strategy provided for the Reform Party was at least in part a shield for its social conservative ideals. With popular economic motifs such as lower taxes and greater economic prosperity leading the way, the Reform Party could avoid the potential public political controversies that surround social conservative beliefs about such things as traditional families and Christian values. Within party circles, however, these ideals were openly celebrated. Trevor Harrison notes that Canadian pro-family ideologue William Gairdner was a "frequent speaker at Reform party meetings in Ontario. In 1991 he was a featured speaker at the party's Saskatoon convention in 1991. His book [*The Trouble with Canada*] is a fast paced, unrelenting denunciation of such things as bilingualism, multiculturalism, immigration, welfare, feminism, and criminal justice ... Gairdner makes clear in his book that he believes in the natural superiority of traditional Anglo-Saxon culture and fears that heterogeneous cultural, and normative or moral, intrusions are eroding this 'ideal'" (1995, 171).

In 2000, when the Canadian Alliance replaced the Reform Party, only the name and the leader changed; the New Right ideology of Preston Manning's party remained much the same. Under the leadership of Stockwell Day, the Alliance Party's 2000 federal election campaign was accurately characterized by some in the media as similar to "Reagan's 'caring conservatism,'"[4] which hinted not only at the economic and social conservatism of the Alliance's New Right ideology, but also at its inherent populist rhetoric. It was in fact popular enough (at least in the western provinces) to give the party official opposition status on the basis of the sixty-six seats it won in the autumn 2000 election. Of course, a key part of the Alliance's populism was constructed to tap into the strong feelings of alienation in the western provinces, so the regionalized results of the federal election were hardly a surprise, particularly given Alberta's strong conservative political tradition and the fact that Reform/Alliance has its organizational roots there.

Yet in British Columbia, where Reform/Alliance accounted for half of the popular vote, a word of caution is in order. It might appear from the results that British Columbians are becoming more like Albertans in their taste for New Right social and economic policies, but this is likely not the case. As David Laycock points out in a commentary on the election results, "it would be a mistake to read the almost 50 per cent support of BC voters for Alliance party candidates in the 2000 federal election as 50 per cent endorsement among BC voters of the Alliance party's policy agenda" (2001, 16). As Laycock continues, it would be more accurate to assess the results as a reflection of BC's sense of alienation from Ottawa. Or, to use Phil Resnick's (2001) term, these results provide further evidence of his argument that BC voters have a tradition of practising a "politics of resentment." Nonetheless, whether because of their social conservatism or their anti-traditional-politics stance, Reform/Alliance appears to have created a firm federal beachhead for Canada's unique brand of New Right politics.

Provincially, the Conservative government of Mike Harris in Ontario vigorously pursued a neoconservative agenda once it was elected in 1995. The Common Sense Revolution that Harris got under way in the province was characterized by deep budget cuts to the civil service, layoffs, privatization, workfare, and downloading provincial responsibilities to municipal governments.[5] This intention to off-load previously provincial services such as welfare, housing, child care, and policing costs is the logical extension of the neoconservative state decentralization that began at the federal level. It is, in the words of political scientist Andrew Sancton, a functional downloading in which "government simply quits its responsibility for a service and leaves it to other governments."[6] The similarity between the ideology behind the Common Sense Revolution and that of the federal Reform/Alliance party was so striking that Preston Manning came out in open support of Mike Harris's agenda.[7] Further, the rhetoric so resembled that found in the American Republican Party's New Right ideology that "in a direct steal from *Contract with America,* the CSR [manifesto] continued: 'For too long government has grown larger and still failed to meet the needs of the people. We will put people first'" (Jeffrey 1999, 197). Even after Harris's departure, the conservatives continued with his revolution of New Right populism.[8]

But Ontario is only one of the more recent provinces to experience an attempt by neoconservatives to establish a political and economic beach-head at the provincial level. In the early 1990s, Ralph Klein's Conservative government in Alberta undertook equally drastic measures to control the province's downward spiralling economy and was applauded by his rural constituents for his "common sense."[9] Manitoba's Conservative government also followed a similar path in the mid-1990s when it privatized its telephone company, implemented legislation to limit the powers of unions, and took what then Premier Gary Filmon called a "sharp turn to the right."[10] It was reminiscent of Stirling Lyon's neoconservative agenda, implemented as far back as 1981, to deal with Manitoba's chronic struggle for a system of stable economic development. Like all neoconservative projects, this too was characterized by a rolling back of the size of the welfare state (Chorney and Hansen 1985). Yet as Chorney and Hansen point out, this project of massive fiscal restraint, based on faith in free-market ideology, failed to produce the economic and social benefits that were promised.

The Saskatchewan Conservatives under Grant Devine experienced a similar disappointment with their forays into neoconservative ideology in 1982. Pitsula and Rasmussen (1990) document Devine's failed attempt to revitalize the province's economy with his devout belief in the power of the market. They write that "his views parallel those of the entire New Right coalition, whether it be the Chamber of Commerce, REAL Women, the Institute for Saskatchewan Enterprise, or Campaign Life ... Step-by-step the neo-conservative program unfolded: the promotion of Christian right moral values, the experiments with supply-side economics, the touting of free enterprise, the reining in of the Crown corporations, the attacks on the civil service, social programs and trade unions, and the massive push towards privatization" (Pitsula and Rasmussen 1990, 21). Despite Devine's convictions, by 1986 the provincial debt had grown to over $5 billion, ownership and control of large parts of the province's economy had moved to central Canada, and the need for social assistance among Saskatchewan's unemployed and underclass had grown (ibid., 283, 285).

It is British Columbia, however, that has been regarded and extensively analyzed as arguably the purest and most austere example of neoconservatism in Canada (Butcher 1985; Havemann 1986; Marchak 1986; Carroll and Ratner 1989; Shields 1986; Hatt et al. 1990). Bill Bennett's Social Credit government introduced twenty-six pieces of legislation in the summer and autumn of 1983 that, among other things, gutted the rights of unionized public sector employees, reworked the Human Rights Code to narrow the definition of discrimination, eliminated rent controls, eliminated the Human Rights Commission, stripped local school boards of budget authority by centralizing it in the Ministry of Education, and provided the opportunity for doctors to opt out of medicare (Palmer 1987, 22). As Carroll and Ratner point out, in response to BC's fiscal crisis the Socreds had "opted for a cyclical crisis-management strategy, prioritizing the 'balanced budget' over demand management and necessitating coercive interventions vis-à-vis its unionized employees" (1989, 36).

It was not, however, an entirely reactive strategy. As Howlett and Brownsley indicate, the 1983 budget was a culmination of a continued "economic and administrative program pursued by the Social Credit government since it had regained power in late 1975" (1988, 142). Coincidentally, the Fraser Institute, now the country's leading neoconservative think tank, had been formed a year earlier with sponsorship that included the province's forestry and mining sectors (Carroll and Ratner 1989). It was this institute that lent the Socred legislation of 1983 its neoconservative purity.

As the principal architect of the 1983 budget, the Fraser Institute had managed to achieve what American neoconservatives had with the Reagan administration: direct policy influence over a government. In its annual report, the Fraser Institute commented on the 1984 provincial budget, referring to it as "the BC government's experiment with Fraser Institute type economic policies" because of "the four objectives of the BC government's budget: (1) fiscal restraint, (2) downsizing of government, (3) deregulation, and (4) the beginning of a change in the philosophical orientation of government policy" (quoted in Havemann 1986, 19). Havemann goes on to note: "The Fraser Institute's advocacy of self-reliance, church-based charity, voluntarism, and privatization was strikingly paralleled by government policy. The Fraser Institute argued that the welfare state has displaced the family and the churches, which should be central in meeting the needs of the poor" (1986, 20). Yet the British Columbia economy, like those of Saskatchewan and Manitoba, continued to worsen rather than improve. Unemployment increased, as did demands for social assistance, and the provincial debt escalated (Shields 1986).

With the election of Gordon Campbell's Liberal Party in May 2001, British Columbia plunged once again into the chilly waters of neoconservative politics. The provincial Liberals were swept to power on a platform of typical political rhetoric that promised to bring better government and economic times to the province. Having lived with five years of Glen Clark's scandal-plagued and inefficiently run NDP government, few were surprised that voters handed Campbell an overwhelming majority. Having won all but two of the province's seventy-nine legislative seats, the Liberals have been proceeding on a course that seems strikingly similar to the Bill Bennett restraint program of the 1980s. Just as Bennett slashed the civil service and Mike Harris cut taxes in his Common Sense Revolution,

Campbell has cut personal income tax rates, has argued for drastic reductions in the number of people on social assistance, has introduced legislation to reduce the size of the civil service by one-third, and has broken existing collective agreements in order to trim hundreds of millions of dollars from the provincial operating budget. It is an agenda that has come to dominate news headlines not simply because of its draconian neoconservative undertones, but also because the initial effects are akin to those seen in the 1980s: a rising provincial debt and unemployment rate, and an apparent increase in economic instability for the province.

To date, the sum of Canada's experience with neoconservatism continues to be these types of dramatic ideological efforts by provincial and to a lesser extent federal governments to implement draconian economic initiatives to remedy protracted economic crises. Yet such attempts have consistently failed to forge a new conservative, hegemonic project for the provinces or the country. As McBride and Shields put it, "it would seem that Canadian political culture is still inclined towards collective social provision and tolerates reasonable levels of governmental intervention in the economy to moderate the effect of market forces. The current Canadian government may have become 'true believers' in neo-conservative political economy, but in this respect their position is incongruent with the broader political culture" (1993, 115). The altruism and compassion rooted in Canada's social democratic political culture stubbornly refuse to give way to the ascetic neoconservative social philosophy of self-reliance. This was reflected in the Canadian Conference of Catholic Bishops' 1982 condemnation of neoconservative economics and social policy as generating a "moral disorder in the abandoning of the poor, the unemployed and the disenfranchised" (Havemann 1986, 26-27).

It is a position that exposes an apparent socio-political conundrum for social and economic conservatives – that is, how to promote economic and individual self-reliance while maintaining a Christian duty of charity to the underprivileged and socially powerless. In good measure, this problem is the natural tension of conservatism itself, but it is also a product of the allegiance that has developed since the mid-1970s between neoconservative economic ideologues, New Right populists, and politically reinvigorated Christians.

Culture Wars: The American Christian Right

What emerged in Britain, Canada, and the United States in this period as neoconservative and New Right thought was a rather secular phenomenon with a focus on the economic. Little direct attention was paid to socio-moral issues – the feeling was that a properly nurtured free market and a greatly scaled back role for government would take care of whatever social ills had befallen these countries. This simplistic logic is readily seen in the thinking of neoconservative groups like the Fraser Institute: "The market tests of profit and loss ... tend to eliminate from the private sector those who indulge in discriminatory practices" (quoted in Marchak 1985, 8).

It was also politically expedient to lean on what amounts to a hidden pillar of social Darwinism. The Thatcher, Mulroney, and Reagan administrations well understood the populist nature of modern electoral politics and the potential minefield that could result for a conservative government tackling such trigger issues as women's equality, abortion, and gay rights. This left those who considered themselves primarily social or religious conservatives feeling alienated from the mainstream political process. Thus marginalized, Christians began to mobilize behind the organizers of the New Christian Right (NCR).

While the Christian right is active in all three countries, its most mature and successful form can be found in the United States. The NCR has appeared on the political landscape of America within the broader politics of the New Right and has developed over the last twenty years into a well-disciplined, well-organized, and well-financed force. While analysts were surprised by the movement's rapid ascendancy and influence in the 1976 presidential campaign, in fact this mobilization was only a relatively recent instance in a history of activism that spans more than two hundred years (Liebman and Wuthnow 1983; Lienesch 1993). Like others, Michael Lienesch has identified a pattern in the twentieth century that finds Christian activism emerging and then tailing off into prolonged periods of quietude (1997; Smidt and Penning 1997; Wilcox and Rozell 2000). Lienesch points out that the 1920s, 1950s, and 1980s were all decades that exhibited intense activism over predominantly single-issue concerns such as alcohol, the teaching of evolution in public schools, prayer in public schools, and the erosion of the traditional family.

The New Christian Right can be broadly understood as an evangelical Christian movement, a loosely bound and very diverse collective of religious conservatives who have united around specific socio-moral problems. Although commonly held belief tends to identify Christian activists as fervent Southern Baptists or geographically isolated pockets of staunch evangelical Protestants, the NCR is a broad-based national phenomenon (Liebman 1983). Within its fold are numerous religious groups opposing any number of issues that threaten traditional lifestyles. Commenting on a Gallup survey's findings, Lienesch writes that the "millions of religious conservatives were a diverse and divided group," a product of innumerable interpretations of biblical scripture and political preferences (1993, 2). Such theological differences, coupled with the cultural growth of secular and liberal attitudes and the quasi-formal belief in separation of church and state, have all contributed to a general disaffection among Christians for the formal political process.[11]

The separation of church and state is a particularly contentious point for people in the NCR because of the original intention of such a separation. The aim was to limit state interference in religious practice rather than vice versa; it was not done in an effort to diminish the long heritage of religious influence in American politics. As Alex de Tocqueville remarked about American political culture, "religion should ... be considered as the first of their political institutions" (quoted in Hammond 1983, 208), and as Roger Scruton points out, it has been duly noted that "there can be no genuine conservatism which is not founded upon a religious view of the basis of civil obligation" (Lord Hailsham, quoted in Scruton 1984, 170).

For supporters of the NCR, then, political activity independent of a belief in God becomes not only a philosophical and practical impossibility, but counter to American political tradition. This separation of the church from its historical political function also makes religious conservatives, or, as Lienesch describes them, "traditional people struggling to maintain rural religious values in an increasingly urban and secular society," feel disenfranchised. They sense that their political heritage has been left out in the cold.

An important feature of this conservative heritage is the simultaneous stress it places on commitment to the pursuit of individual interests and the elevation of concern for the collective good.[12] This is the source of a cultural tension that generates a social conundrum for the NCR and the American right in general, which Platt and Williams see resolved in a combination of "self-interested individualism with a dogmatic conception of doing good works by providing for, if hesitantly, begrudgingly, and patronizingly, the less fortunate of the community" (1988, 41).

It is arguably this characteristic of the American conservative religious tradition that has proved to be its ideological Achilles heel, presenting for the movement chronic problems of legitimacy and making it vulnerable to caricatures like that presented by comedian George Carlin in his description of the conservative right and its opposition to abortion: "They're all in favor of the unborn ... but once you're born, you're on your own. Pro-life conservatives are obsessed with the fetus from conception 'til nine months. After that, they don't want to hear from you. No neo-natal care, no daycare, no Head Start, no school lunch, no food stamps, no welfare, no nothing" (Carlin 1996). This kind of negative popular imagery, coupled with the secularization of society and politics, created in religious conservatives an acute sense of status frustration and a drive to practise a type of status politics.[13]

In three different books, Sara Diamond (1989, 1995, 1998) has documented the institutionalized form of this frustrated Christian politics. Diamond links American religious conservative activity through to the 1970s with phenomena such as McCarthyism, anti-Communist foreign policy, fundamentalist opposition to employment equity bills and the teaching of evolution in public schools, and support for trickle-down economics. The 1970s ushered in the modern era of the Christian right as religious conservatives found themselves faced with four policies that surely must have constituted their socio-moral apocalypse: Congress's 1972 approval of the Equal Rights Amendment (ERA); the Supreme Court's 1973 *Roe v. Wade* decision, which struck down anti-abortion legislation; the IRS's 1978 attempt to invoke racial quotas in Christian schools; and the ever-progressing gains being made by gay rights movements (Diamond 1995; Wuthnow 1983; Lienesch 1993). Religious conservatives identified these issues as examples of the ever-increasing pervasiveness of the legal and legislative branches of the state in the private institutions of family and religious assemblies.[14] As Diamond describes it:

> The major social issues of the 1970s caused right-wing evangelicals to feel threatened about their ability to promote the supremacy of the traditional nuclear family. Women's equality, abortion, and gay rights were all issues that crossed lines of economic class, and even race ... Also at stake was the drive of evangelical activists to exert their democratic rights to participate in the political process and to assume some measure of political power. These highly charged social issues all involved questions of welfare state spending, law enforcement and business regulation in discrimination cases. (1995, 161)

The personal nature of these social issues fuelled a Christian population with a strong sense of moral urgency that in turn forged novel alliances and activities. For instance, the *Roe v. Wade* decision brought evangelicals into the heretofore Catholic domain of the abortion fight by reconfiguring its previously private moral status into a public political issue (Gottfried and Fleming 1988). Evangelical Christians also experienced a political outing in the 1976 presidential election when they voted in unusually high numbers for Jimmy Carter, a professed evangelical convert (Diamond 1995). As Liebman and Wuthnow (1983) observe, the increasingly blurred line between private morality and public policy, along with the general increase in popular exposure that evangelicals were receiving through the 1970s, gave them a sense of motivation, legitimation, and social connection to engage en masse with the political process.

Despite the overwhelmingly evangelical character of the NCR, however, it is in actuality a movement constructed by Catholic activists involved with the secular New Right movement. In their attempt to build a mass political movement, Catholics like Paul Weyrich (Committee for the Survival of a Free Congress), Richard Viguerie (founder of the *Conservative Digest*), and Howard Phillips (Conservative Caucus) saw the tremendous mobilizing potential of the evangelical community as invaluable to their quest for influence within the Republican Party. With the help of others like Robert Billings (National Christian Action Coalition) and Ed McAteer (Christian Freedom Foundation), these professional activists approached televangelist Jerry Falwell, and the NCR came to organizational life as the Moral Majority in 1979.

It was a movement strategically designed around highly charged moral issues – abortion, gay rights, and women's equality – and the threats they posed to the very foundation of American society: the family. Not defensive or reactionary, "at its inception the New Christian Right, far from being a populist uprising, was an army organized from the top down by those New Right strategists who set much of the early agenda for their politically less sophisticated recruits" (Lienesch 1993, 8). The product was a movement characterized by a high degree of organizational sophistication, frontmen who were popular charismatic preachers, and strategists capable of turning single-issue concerns into general political activism.

Sara Diamond argues that Richard Viguerie identified abortion as an issue capable of unifying divided factions within the evangelical and Catholic communities with the logic of a "hypothetical case of a man, never before politically active, who suddenly becomes disturbed by the image of dead babies. For the first time in his life, he joins a political group and believes naively that change will come when a few citizens get angry. But once he realizes that the outlawing of abortion involves a prolonged struggle, he begins to take an avid interest in electoral politics and in a host of political issues related to his concern about abortion" (1989, 58). It was a strategy that strengthened links between the number of single-issue groups in the country by highlighting the political and moral interconnectedness of concerns over abortion, euthanasia, gay rights, the ERA, foreign policy, and the deficit. Groups like Phyllis Schlafly's Eagle Forum, which was instrumental in the defeat of the Equal Rights Amendment to the constitution, found kindred spirits with the likes of the Conservative Caucus, Christian Roundtable, Christian Voice, and the host of other organizations that arose in the 1980s.[15]

Schlafly's Stop ERA organization, later renamed Eagle Forum, was an exercise in just this kind of socio-moral interconnectedness. Herself a Catholic, Schlafly opposed the ERA on legal and economic grounds, claiming it was a federal power grab that would "destroy the power of state legislatures to make laws on divorce, child custody, inheritance, welfare and labor," as well as threaten the economic security of women by removing their right to child support (Diamond 1995, 169). It would also grant, she argued, "legal sanction to homosexual marriages and make it impossible for the Supreme Court to reverse its 1973 *Roe v. Wade* decision" (ibid., 170). It was an argument that aligned itself naturally with economic neoconservatives, pro-life activists, and opponents of the gay rights movement.

The NCR's drive to restore a traditional moral order by constructing a broad socio-moral program around a single issue found favour with the Republican Party through the 1980s because it presented what the GOP had always lacked, a grassroots constituency (Diamond 1989). By backing Reagan (who claimed an evangelical conversion experience in 1976) in 1980, the NCR did something decidedly political: they compromised on a leader who was "viewed as too liberal and not enough of a leader by some of the clergymen" because "he was all that was left" (Guth 1983, 36). Reagan's two-term presidency did prove a disappointment for the NCR, but their hopes were buoyed by televangelical magnate Pat Robertson's bid for the White House in 1988. Robertson lost the nomination but most of his supporters viewed the 1988 campaign with optimism because of the gains they had made within state and local GOP apparatuses (Diamond 1998).

Political activism at state, local, and school board levels was one of the primary strategies adopted by Robertson's newly formed Christian Coalition. Replacing Falwell's Moral Majority, the coalition was built from the remnants of Robertson's 1988 campaign with the strategic intention of keeping "one figurative foot inside formal Republican Party circles and another planted firmly within evangelical churches ... [and embarking] ... on a 1990s strategy combining issue-based and electoral activism" (Diamond 1995, 290-91). The success of the Christian Coalition within the Republican Party in 1992 was unparalleled in Christian activist politics:

> An estimated 47 percent of the delegates at the 1992 party convention were self-described born-again Christians, and the Christian Right had its way in drafting the party platform ... a constitutional amendment to ban abortion (with no exceptions). Other planks included opposition to any civil rights laws for homosexuals, a call for the government to ban the sale of pornography and for condemnation of public funding for "obscene" art, endorsement of home schooling and school prayer, and opposition to contraception being made available in schools. (ibid., 296)

The growing influence and power of the Christian Coalition reached another peak during the 1996 presidential campaign. During the primaries, potential presidential nominee Steve Forbes had his campaign severely damaged by the coalition in a move described as swift and coordinated: "The Christian Coalition and affiliated groups on the religious right unleashed verbal attacks aimed at destroying Forbes' ... campaign ... The religious groups charged the publishing magnate with being 'soft' on abortion and gay rights and with trying to 'confuse pro-lifers' by fudging on the issues."[16] The coalition was also accused of "hijacking" control of the Republican National Convention with "intimidating" tactics and platforms.[17]

Again, despite losing the White House, the NCR was satisfied with its growing influence and the deeper inroads made at all levels of government policy making. As then Christian Coalition executive director Ralph Reed commented, "instead of focusing on winning the White House ... we're developing a farm team of future officeholders by running people for school boards, city councils and state legislatures ... Now we're seeing those institutions that are closest to people's lives and have the greatest impact on them in the hands of conservative people of faith" (quoted in Diamond 1995, 301).[18]

In a number of publications, Reed outlined the agenda of the Christian Coalition and its religious and pro-family conservative followers.[19] To revitalize an American culture that had supposedly been torn apart by "the sexual revolution, Watergate, Vietnam, the rise of the drug culture, and the explosive growth of the welfare state," he argues that family-centred policies and government initiatives needed to be instituted because "the family is the most efficient and effective Department of Health, Education, and Welfare ever conceived" (Reed 1994b, 3, 8). This broad-based platform aimed at restoring:

> Much of what was good about America ... marriages that work and a far greater proportion of intact two-parent families. Lower taxes, less bureaucracy, leaner government ... Greater empowerment of private citizens to free themselves from dependency on government programs. Abortion rare and largely restricted ... Voluntary, student-initiated school prayer and other public expressions of faith protected as free speech under the First Amendment. Television shows and movies that celebrate the family and elevate the human spirit and do not glorify violence, extramarital sex, vulgar language, and human cruelty ... A tougher criminal-justice system that puts violent offenders behind bars ... Tax policy should reflect two family-friendly policies ... Income dedicated to providing for the basic needs of children ... should be exempt from taxation ... The welfare system subsidizes family breakup ... it fails to address the root cause of government dependency: family breakup and illegitimacy ... We must also provide greater stability for the most important contract in civilized society: the marriage contract. (Reed 1994b, 3, 4, 7, 9, 10)

In his book *Active Faith*, Reed describes this agenda as "bold and ambitious," one based on the "need to affirm the basic social and religious values upon which the nation was built. Ours is largely a defensive movement. We are not revolutionaries but counterrevolutionaries, seeking to resist the left's agenda and to keep them from imposing their values on our homes, churches, and families" (Reed 1996, 203, 195).

The political amalgam of neoconservative economics, Christian morality, charismatic fervour, and sophisticated infrastructure of mobilization that constituted this counterrevolution seemed poised in the mid-1990s to be a powerful and influential political movement. Since the political high-water mark of the 1996 presidential campaign, however, an ebb tide has begun to trouble the NCR. The 1998 elections are viewed by analysts (Green 2000; Wilcox and Rozell 2000) as "a defeat" for the Christian right, and by 2001 both Ralph Reed and Pat Robertson had left the Christian Coalition and less and less was being heard from American Christian right activists. It appeared that the movement had entered one of its cyclic periods of quietude, a time of reorganization and refinements of strategy – as one newspaper headline read, the "religious right is down – but far from out."[20] Given the way it reemerged in 2004, like a political rogue wave seemingly coming from nowhere, it's clear that this was a highly effective time of retreat. It is also clear that this is a powerful, well-organized political movement, one that like-minded Canadians are enviously peering at from over the border.

Christian Politics in Canada: The Canadian Christian Right

Perhaps consistent with Canadian self-definitions, members of the Canadian Christian right (CCR) first describe themselves in terms of difference from Americans. One thing they are not is equivalent to their American counterparts. In his history of Canadian evangelicalism, John Stackhouse points out that while it is a vain effort to find an adequate characterization of Canadian evangelicalism, one can be sure that "this kind of Christianity should not be dismissed as some fringe group or some bizarre American export" (1993, 204). The closest Stackhouse himself comes to defining evangelicalism in Canada is the unexceptional description of its followers as "not all that strange, not all that different from other Canadians" (ibid.). He in fact challenges the view of Canadian evangelicals as being necessarily fundamentalist and conservative and having experienced a conversion.[21]

Historically sectarian until the 1980s, when they began to develop closer transdenominational ties, only in the last few years have evangelicals in Canada begun to assume a more political and populist profile. In a seeming paradox, at a time when Canadian culture is becoming less influenced by Christian values, interest in the evangelical movement is actually growing, particularly in British Columbia[22] – a trend that flies in the face of typical Canadian patterns of religiosity. Reginald Bibby has found a steady decline in Protestant and Catholic membership and church attendance through the latter half of the century. As he describes it, "there's little doubt that organized religion is in very serious shape, its golden years apparently relegated to history" (1993, 115). A 1996 Angus Reid poll also found that only 19 percent of Canadians let religious beliefs influence their political thinking, 18 percent support Christian right politics, and 8 percent consider moral issues a primary electoral issue. These figures stand in sharp opposition to those in the US, where strict belief in biblical doctrine, the importance of conversion, and the priority of promoting family values are much more highly rated.

In British Columbia, the typical religious profile is handily reflected in the observation that "people don't seem to worry very much about churches out here" and Peter Newman's remark that British Columbians are "pioneers, not pilgrims" (quoted in Burkinshaw, 1995, 4). Nonetheless, in *Pilgrims in Lotus Land,* Burkinshaw (1995) argues that while Catholicism never took hold in the transient non-native population of BC, evangelicalism has grown steadily since 1921, opposing the trend Bibby has identified in the rest of Canada.

Like their American brethren, British Columbian evangelicals have through the course of their history "very frequently felt alienated from the religious and social mainstream ... [and] ... did erect, with varying degrees of intensity, defensive walls to hold back the inroads of modernism and secularism" (Burkinshaw 1995, 12, 13). According to popular media accounts, this trend towards isolation is one that appears to be diminishing. The import to the province of organizations like the Promise Keepers, the Christian Coalition, Focus on the Family, and the Toronto Blessing (via the Vineyard congregations) and the continued growth of evangelical denominations all indicate a pattern of increasing attempts to move in from the margins of society.[23] The evangelical population in BC has risen to 290,000 – 8 percent of the provincial population and 3.5 percent higher than the 1921 figures (Burkinshaw 1995). And although religiosity does appear to be on the decline nationally, Dennis Hoover points out that a 1996 poll found that, "18 percent of Canadians feel somewhat or very close to the 'Christian Right,'" versus 34 percent of Americans (1997, 195).

In general, these numbers and small provincial surges have not translated into a cohesive form of political activism like that seen in the US. As their self-definition would indicate, Canadian evangelicals are *not* like their American counterparts. There is none of the organizational sophistication and unity or fervent sense of urgency on the socio-moral issues they see as plaguing modern societies. With the exception of Grant Devine's Conservatives, neoconservative and New Right agendas throughout the country have been secular and economic in focus, not religious or social. Religious activism is present in Canada, but it has tended to be buried deep within party politics or isolated around single socio-moral issues that have yet to be politically interconnected. Opposition to gay rights, abortion, and feminism, support for traditional schools, making governments smaller, and welfare reform are all vibrant issues for Canadian religious conservatives, but it is only the latter two issues that have been of any significant concern to mainstream conservative political parties in Canada. The potential political firestorm that could be sparked by directly confronting abortion or gay rights has tended to keep religious conservative politicians behind the protective curtain of sayings like "You can't legislate morality."

What happened to Stockwell Day when he took over the leadership of the Canadian Alliance attests to these concerns. The woes of the Reform/Alliance Party were blamed in good measure on Day's openly Christian beliefs on such matters as creationism and abortion, issues the Canadian media seized upon to generate rather dramatic headlines that depicted the leader as intolerant.[24] As with their counterparts in the US, Canadian religious conservatives have been increasingly frustrated at being portrayed in such a way and what they perceive as their concomitant lack of political victories.

Loss of their political ground, though, is nothing new. For religious conservatives in Canada, the trouble really began in the 1960s, and things have only been getting worse. The 1969 removal of abortion from the Criminal Code, the slow but steady recognition that homosexual couples should be able to legally marry, and the apparent stranglehold of secular humanism on Canadian culture have all been grist for religious conservatives' political mill. Through the last twenty years, these social trends have been a lightning rod for the gradual strengthening of political resolve among religious conservatives in this country.

Unlike the American state, however, the Canadian party system does not afford pro-family organizations much lobbying power within particular parties. This has forced activism on socio-moral issues down one of three roads: influencing individual sympathetic politicians within parties, formal legal intervention in particular court cases, or civil education campaigns. Each avenue has particular merit and strategic value to an organization and its cause, but none of them offers the entrance into legislative power that is required to effect the kind of social change desired by the Canadian Christian right.

Certainly the odd exception exists – Devine's neoconservative experiment in Saskatchewan was largely centred around the promotion of Christian right moral values. His personal slogan of "God first, family second, and the NDP under my thumb" includes his socio-moral positions on abortion and homosexuality: "I think one of the biggest challenges we face in this country and North America is one of morals ... I would venture to say that 98 percent of the women that you find out peace-marching or against nuclear energy are pro-choice. They haven't got their objectives straight. They are living in the 'I'-centred egotistical society. They don't have God as their focus. Very selfish ... [On homosexuality] I don't want my children thinking that this is a reasonable, normal thing to do" (quoted in Pitsula and Rasmussen 1990, 17).

W.A.C. Bennett's Social Credit Party in BC was also Christian-based but never advanced an agenda as overtly Christian as Devine's.[25] The Socreds did, however, enjoy tremendous support from the evangelical community in BC. Indeed, one of its most flamboyant and popular ministers, "Flying Phil" Gaglardi, was a Pentecostal preacher. Robert Burkinshaw remarks that the Socreds were "at least until the mid-1970s ... composed largely of rural and small-town people from the province's interior and the Fraser Valley, and it functioned as a populist protest movement against the urban elites in Vancouver and Victoria ... While a few Social Credit ministers ... were self-declared evangelicals, as right-of-centre politicians they ideologically supported the concepts of private initiative" (Burkinshaw 1995, 8, 215). The Vander Zalm era of the Socreds in the late 1980s also exhibited strong Christian undertones. His failed 1988 attempt to remove abortion funding from the medicare fee schedule was driven by his strong Catholic convictions on the issue and in many ways characterized the rest of his turbulent time in office.

Frustrated attempts such as Vander Zalm's led many in the CCR to reconsider the utility of continuing to fight within a particular party for these contentious social issues. What took form as a result was a number of new political parties.

Federally, the Christian Heritage Party of Canada (CHP) was formed in 1987 with the view that "the political task we in the CHP have perceived as our God-given duty is to call fellow Canadians back to Bible-obedient lifestyles ... the CHP brought a new perspective ... of principled politics, policies which are rooted in Biblical ethics" (Vanwoudenberg 1989, 20, 22). Founded by Ed Vanwoudenberg, a member of the Canadian (Dutch) Reformed Church, the CHP has a mandate similar to that of the Christian Coalition in the US. Electorally, it has been most successful in rural Ontario. In the 1988 election, for instance, the party garnered over 100,000 votes nationwide, 64,707 of them in Ontario (Harrison 1995). The CHP has run candidates in every federal election since but remains firmly out in the hinterlands of the political margins.

The Reform Party of Canada was also founded in 1987, by Preston Manning, an evangelical whose father directed the radio show *Canada's National Bible Hour* for more than forty years. Manning insists that Reform is not a religious party and actively distances his party from the CHP: "The Reform Party of Canada is not a religious party, nor does it have a hidden religious agenda ... [The pro-life/pro-family agenda] is being pursued by ... a new political party, the Christian Heritage Party. Although I do not deny Christians of the right or the left the right to develop such agendas and to pursue them through political action ... this is not the approach I have taken to politics, nor is the Reform Party of Canada a product of such an approach" (1992, 102, 104). Yet he also contends that "there *is* a relationship between private and public morality, between what one believes and how one responds to public policy issues ... And these relationships should be openly explored ... A different approach to Christian involvement in politics, and the one that I personally favour, might be described as 'working Christianly with the urgent or existing public agenda.' This involves accepting the present political agenda as a legitimate starting point for one's involvement in politics ... and trying to influence it from within by the application of one's most deeply held values" (1992, 103, 104).

The party has been plagued since its inception with not unfounded images of its supporters and members as religious and social intolerants.[26] MP Bob Ringma's infamous "back of the shop" comment about the right of a store owner not to hire gay employees, Manning's well-known evangelical background and anti-abortion stance, activities like MP Herb Grubel's attendance at the libertarian International Society for Individual Liberty 1996 World Conference, MP Lee Morrison's opposition to subsidized daycare, and of course Stockwell Day's well-documented views all paint the Reform/Alliance Party into the Christian right corner, if only at its ecumenical edge.[27]

Provincially, the Ontario and BC Family Coalition parties, founded in 1987 and 1991, respectively, attempted to blend Reform/Alliance's neoconservative economics and populism with the CHP's heavy emphasis on Christian moral fortitude. While neither party formally relies on biblical scripture for policy formation in the manner of the CHP, their constitutions upheld similar doctrine: sanctity of life from the moment of conception to natural death, and recognition of the traditional nuclear family as that of two married people of the opposite sex and the people directly related to them. Like Reform, they adhered to the potential of "doing the Christian thing without mentioning God." As Chapter 1 showed, the unique political feature of these parties, in particular the BC FCP, is their primary focus on the erosion of the traditional family and the social problems this has produced. Unlike those of the American New Right and New Christian Right, their agenda was founded on socio-moral issues for their own sake – they weren't just tagged on to a platform of New Right economism. Nonetheless, these parties still reflect a world view strongly parallel to their American Christian right counterparts.

With such parties, it would appear that the CCR has another important part of its infrastructure in place. To reach the level of sophistication and effectiveness of the American Christian right will require, among other things, formal political access and social movement activism around some clearly defined issues and media access. The Christian Heritage Party, the FCP in Ontario, and to an extent the Reform/Alliance Party of Canada are structurally capable of providing the necessary legislative inroads to make political change. While not as large as the US network, the televangelism of such programs as David Mainse's *100 Huntley Street* and the growth of Christian literature in Canada have the same mass mobilizing potential as the 700 Club and Third Century Publishers.[28] As well, organizations like the Campaign Life Coalition, the National Citizens Coalition, Focus on the Family, and REAL Women continue to perform extensive educational and lobbying functions for the overall movement.

In British Columbia, the CCR's situation is similar. The recently formed Unity Party of British Columbia – the result of the FCP and Reform Party merger – quietly Christian in its ethos but staunchly pro-life and pro-family in its social and economic conservatism, took 3 percent of the 2001 provincial vote and in early 2004 was running at about 7 percent in the polls. Conversions continue to bolster evangelical numbers in the province, and a number of new organizations have formed in recent years to defend and promote traditional social and family orders. The US-based Focus on the Family runs a $6-million-a-year operation from Vancouver's downtown core, Christian Coalition International (Canada) emerged in BC in the mid-1990s, and groups such as the Catholic Civil Rights League have formed in an attempt to instill political vigour into the province's religious conservative community. These are in addition to already existing provincial organizations that are at least sympathetic to a Christian right position: the BC Pro-Life Society, the Citizens' Research Institute of Canada, REAL Women of BC, Vancouver Right to Life, the Euthanasia Prevention Coalition of BC, Westcoast Women for Family Life, and the Campaign Life Coalition BC. While differing in mandate and political involvement, these are the types of organizations from which a more cohesive, interconnected CCR might emerge in the province, and they would be standing on a common platform, one founded on social conservative thought and rooted in the politics of the traditional family.

Family Feud: The Politics of the Family

The importance of the family in the politics of the New Christian Right in the United States and Canada cannot be overstated. From the writings of Edmund Burke through to the brand of Christian right neoconservatism being practised by its adherents today, the family has been identified as the primary socio-political institution that must be supported if a stable social order is to be created and maintained.

For the Christian right, the family has become the main fulcrum for their broad, comprehensive program of social and economic reconstruction. Jerry Falwell has said the family is "the fundamental building block and basic unit of our society, and its continued health is a prerequisite for a healthy and prosperous nation" (quoted in Lienesch 1993, 52). This political vision is entrenched in the policies and dialogue of all Christian right institutions. The Christian Coalition's Contract with the American Family, which, among other provisions, calls for a Mothers' and Home-makers' Rights Act, is, as Ralph Reed states, "not a Christian agenda. It is not a Republican agenda. It is not a special interest agenda. It is a *pro-family* agenda" (Reed 1996, 201-2, emphasis added).[29]

The language of this document reveals it to be in part a resolve to remedy the social pathologies brought on by the erosion of the family in America: "The crime problem can only be solved by strengthening the two-parent, nuclear family," argues Reed (1994b, 87). "No amount of money thrown at education can substitute for strong families and stable homes ... what religious conservatives want is to make the restoration of the two-parent, intact family with children the central and paramount public policy priority of the nation" (ibid., 85, 91). The avenues of dialogue necessary for promoting this pro-family ideology have been expanded through the growth of publications put out by NCR organizations, from *Conservative Digest* and *Journal of Marriage and the Family* to James Dobson's plethora of Focus on the Family publications.

In Canada, the importance of family issues to the politics of religious conservatives is threaded through conversations at the kitchen table through to policy statements of the Reform/Alliance, the CHP, and the FCP. Like Falwell, William Gairdner, a chief ideologue of the Reform/Alliance Party of Canada, sees the family as *the* foundational social unit: "If the first building block of democratic capitalism is the individual and his person-hood, the second is the family, which nurtures and creates this reality. Practically speaking, however, we could reverse this order, and say that the family is first, for it is in the bosom of the family that the crucial values, disciplines, and standards of individual behaviour are formed" (1990, 80).[30] In his latest book, a collection of essays by such New Right ideologues as Michael Walker of the Fraser Institute, Gairdner universalizes the natural family, writing that "this basic unit has been and still is a primordial fact of life in the West, if not for the vast majority of mankind in all of history" (1998, 62). Hidden in the footnote to this passage is what he means by "natural family": "For most of the 1980s and '90s, approximately 76 percent of all Canadian families have been married mother-father-children families. If we include 'common-law' families with children, then about 87 percent of all families still live in the traditional form. (For the sake of my argument, even common-law co-habitation is a form, if far less stable, that models true marriage and thus fits a kind of shadow definition of the natural family)" (ibid., 89).

This sort of belief is reflected demographically in Trevor Harrison's analysis (1995) of polls that indicated that Reform/Alliance is the only federal party that has greater support among married than non-married people and that over 80 percent of Reform members are married. It is also discretely embedded in the party's Statement of Principles, in which the sixth principle states: "We affirm the value and dignity of the individual person and the importance of strengthening and protecting the family unit as essential to the well-being of individuals and society" (Principles and Policies, 1991).

The Christian Heritage Party founds its similar, albeit more biblically doctrinaire and overtly heterosexual, position on the sentiment reflected in Psalm 33:12: "Blessed is the nation whose God is the Lord." The party's constitutional entrenchment of the family is born of the fear that, "knock the family off its God-ordained foundation, and all of society will suffer irreparable harm and damage" (Vanwoudenberg 1989, 78): "We affirm that the family is a God-ordained institution and the fundamental indispensable basis of human society; that it consists of a man and woman lawfully wedded for the purpose of procreation; all in a secure family home. We affirm that heterosexual, monogamous marriage is God-ordained as the foundation of the family, and that any other form of union whatsoever is biblically prohibited" (CHP Policy and Program, 06.4, section 1).

A strong pro-family stance was even to be found in Brian Mulroney's Conservative government. Lorna Erwin (1993) points out that the thirty-two-member Family Caucus would meet with pro-family leaders in an attempt to address what was being perceived among the movement as the dramatic failings of the Conservative majority to deal concretely with family and life issues. Erwin notes that "the Caucus quietly bills itself as a 'defender of Christian values' ... it supports various pro-family positions, including the recriminalization of abortion, the elimination of tax breaks for common-law couples ... It has also been credited with preventing amendments to the *Human Rights Act* that would recognize same-sex marriages" (1993, 416).

The Ontario and British Columbia FCP brought the pro-family concerns of religious conservatives to provincial politics with less stealth than the Family Caucus. In Ontario, the FCP is "a political party based on family values ... the policies of the FCP are based on moral principles expressive of the Judaeo-Christian tradition" and a recognition of "the family as the basic social cell. When family values are strong and promoted by the State, democracy and economic enterprise flourish. When family values falter, society becomes disordered and is in danger of collapse" (Ontario FCP Statement of Principles). Meanwhile, the BC FCP stated its intentions "to enact laws and policies which recognize the right to life of every innocent human being from conception to natural death ... To enact social, educational and economic laws and policies which recognize the family as the basic unit of society" (BC FCP Constitution, purposes 2b and 2c). Family is accepted by its members to mean "TWO OR MORE INDIVIDUALS RELATED BY BLOOD, MARRIAGE OR ADOPTION. The FCP recognizes the definition of *marriage* to mean THE LEGAL UNION OF TWO PEOPLE OF THE OPPOSITE SEX" (BC FCP Constitution, emphasis in the original). This position was carried over to the Unity Party, whose Principles and Policies stated that "the traditional family, individuals related by blood, marriage or adoption is the cornerstone of society. We uphold the definition of marriage as the legal union of two members of the opposite sex" (Unity Party of British Columbia, 2002, Foundational Principles, principle 8).

This emphatic and ubiquitous presence of the family as the key feature of the religious conservative platform suggests an agenda driven by far more than concerns over unemployment and rising deficits. It is important here to understand that the social and economic concerns of the New Right do not necessarily go hand in hand. Far from seamless, there exists at times a sharp scission between these areas. Religious conservatives are as concerned with the present and future threats to the family as they are with the economic state of society.

This last point may make them a convenient and beneficial ally of the secular New Right's promotion of a free-market ideology, but it in no way guarantees the social issues surrounding the former will be addressed or substantively advanced. The social and cultural hegemony in both the United States and Canada has been progressively altered through the hard battles fought and won by women, gays, immigrants, environmentalists, and other traditionally dispossessed citizens and groups. This social metamorphosis has occurred in large part independent of the economic forces that are constantly restructuring labour and financial markets to fit an unfettered global economy. Were a close dependency between conservative economic and cultural imperatives to exist, Canada and the US, as they move more towards strategies of increasingly globalized free-trade accumulation, would be exhibiting socio-cultural patterns and values more reflective of those desired by religious conservatives. Yet quite the opposite seems to be occurring. As the push to economic globalization continues, social patterns reflect an increasing, rather than decreasing, diversity of family structures, marriage patterns, and acceptance towards gay and women's rights.

For religious conservatives, this diversity has brought with it what they regard as an apparent social pestilence in such forms as a growing crime rate among young men who have been stripped of their male authority and their right to a job by the demands of the feminist movement. They also argue that increasing rates of teenage pregnancy, illiteracy, and promiscuity have been brought on by a failing education system that promotes liberal sexual attitudes and lifestyle choices while denying parental involvement in matters of educational policy. Then there is their belief that there has been an increase in social and familial deviancy with the promotion of gay lifestyles. Most serious for them has been a growing disregard for the sanctity of life with the promotion of abortion, euthanasia, and the various reproductive technologies of the day. Religious conservatives believe that redemption and salvation from all this can be sought only through a restoration of the traditional family and its values – in other words, by an appeal to the divinely ordained.

The importance of the family to religious conservative politics and the argument linking such social decay to the erosion of the family is found in the belief that the family is ultimately a transcendent institution because of its universality and naturalness. Divinely ordained, the family is seen as a pre-social body upon which all forms of social order and authority are based. Roger Scruton's (1984) explanation adopts a secular philosophical argument that the family, unlike society at large, is non-contractual, its bonds based not on choice but on natural necessity, giving it an indispensable and transcendent nature. The bonds between parent and child that flow from the family, Scruton continues, are themselves transcendent. The obligation and responsibility a child feels towards its parents are founded not on any notions of socially derived justice, but on a natural sense of honour and respect that is "simply *due* to the parents as a recognition of the filial tie" (Scruton 1984, 32, emphasis in the original). As the child matures, "it is this ability that is transferred by the citizen from hearth and home to place, people and country. The bond of society – as the conservative sees it – is just such a transcendent bond" (ibid., 33). The glue of Scruton's conservative social order, then, is a transcendent authority based on the recognition and acceptance of traditions that command obligations and allegiances not reducible to contractual choice. And when this glue comes unstuck, it is the family that must be attended to and repaired.

Conservatives with strong religious beliefs turn to a second source for proof of the transcendent nature of the family: ecclesiastical doctrine. Very close to the beginning, in the book of Genesis, it is written: "So God created man in his own image, in the image of God created he him; male and female created he them. And God blessed them, and God said unto them, Be fruitful, and multiply, and replenish the earth" (Genesis 1:27-28). John Paul II, in his 1994 *Letter to Families*, uses this passage, among others, to *"discern how the primordial model of the family is to be sought in God himself, in the Trinitarian mystery of his life"* (John Paul II 1994, 13, emphasis in the original). The genealogy of the family cannot only be traced directly back to God, but the family structure of father, mother, and child becomes in some manner a corporeal representation of the holy trinity.

With such an understanding, the sacred and deep commitment religious conservatives exhibit towards the sanctity of the family takes on a dimension greater than simply one of political expediency to achieve economic change. The Holy See's 1983 *Charter of the Rights of the Family* translates the transcendent spirit of the family into a political language: "The family is based on marriage, that intimate union of life in complementarity between a man and a woman ... and is open to the transmission of life ... the family, a natural society, exists prior to the State or any other community, and possesses inherent rights which are inalienable ... the family ... is uniquely suited to teach and transmit cultural, ethical, social, spiritual and religious values, essential for the development and well-being of its own members and of society" (Holy See 1983, 5).

It is in the last part of this passage that a final, and politically the most important, reason can be found for the family's central position in the politics of the Christian right. More than any other social institution, the family is a symbolic repository for a nation's cultural hegemony. As the passage from the Holy See's message suggests, the family is the primary site of transmission for the cultural, economic, spiritual, and moral schemes of a society. It is viewed as the institutional protector and moulder of innocents, a space where the knowledge and wisdom of one generation is passed on to the next. As such, it is a politically vital piece of social terrain that the Christian right is fighting for, not so much for its institutional reality or form, but as *the* site of symbolic ideology for society.

When the monolithic image of the family as a static absolute is replaced by the understanding that the family is a porous construction of intersections and trajectories, this symbolic importance becomes clear. That is, the logic of the Christian right's argument that rising rates of abortion, sexually transmitted diseases, divorce, shoplifting, carjacking, and dropping out of high school are attributable to family dissolution is exposed. As Alan Crawford (1980) has suggested, the movement is symbolic as much as it is political. In an attempt to restore stability to a system in flux, the strategists of the New Christian Right have appropriated the family as a catch basin for all the symbolic examples of a crumbling conservative order. In his discussion of the American NCR and symbolic production, Donald Heinz writes: "The New Christian Right finds in the family a means to recover a lost meaning as well as a lost past. It has become a primary symbol of the worldview, and the story they offer as a countermythology. The family is both a symbol for that mythology, and its primary and necessary socializer" (1983, 142).

The richly emotive images that the symbol of the family and its destruction evoke were not lost on Paul Weyrich as he and others attempted to forge mass support for the New Right agenda in the US. During the 1970s, after Richard Viguerie had identified abortion as the issue capable of mobilizing a previously apolitical mass, Weyrich suggested using the term "pro-family" rather than "pro-life," recognizing the potential of the term to capture a broader spectrum of social issues dear to the hearts of religious conservatives (Diamond 1995). With this, the pro-family movement (PFM) was, if not born, at least developing a morphological identity. The New Right ideologues and strategists had constructed a broad PFM agenda out of previously single-issue concerns and constructed a clear enemy: secular humanism. This became another vital symbolic repository, representing those influences, groups, and people who propagated godlessness, moral relativism, tolerance for pornography, gay lifestyles, the abortion culture, and the destruction of the traditional family.

The pro-family movement was now the New Christian Right with a sharpened focus: to beat back legalized abortion, gay rights, permissive and liberal public education policies, and feminism. Paul Weyrich's Heritage Foundation sought to couch such initiatives in the narratives of "family values" and "conservatism," but in fact he "acknowledged that he does not truly intend to *conserve* anything ... 'We are no longer working to preserve the status quo. We are radicals, working to overturn the present power structure of the country'" (Diamond 1989, 54, emphasis in the original). The urgency and determination reflected in this statement come back to understanding the cultural transmission function of family. Stripped to its core, it is a matter of socializing society's children and "the right to determine how and by whom the minds of children are molded is the most valued prize in the tug of war between the Christian Right and secular society" (ibid., 84).

Three of the earliest PFM initiatives in this tug of war were the walkout staged by the Christian right at Jimmy Carter's 1979 White House Conference on Families, the attempted passage in 1980 of the Pro-Family Act, and the 1981 drafting of the Family Protection Act.

Led by Connaught Marshner, a director of Weyrich's Free Congress Foundation, the walkout by pro-family supporters was in response to the perceived bias against evangelical Christians at the conference and a definition of family that included unmarried and homosexual couples (Diamond 1995).

The Pro-Family Act was brought to the Senate by Ronald Reagan's campaign manager, Paul Laxalt. As Rosemary Ruether points out, the act proposed, among other things, supporting school prayer, banning textbooks, and discouraging "the promotion of shelters for battered wives and abused children, implying that such aid was deleterious to 'the family'" (2000, 169).

In addition to leading the walkout, Marshner was also instrumental in the creation of the Family Protection Act, a traditional-family bill with some thirty-five major provisions that was debated in Congress in 1981 but never passed. Its provisions included restricting abortion and gay rights, tax incentives to encourage mothers to stay home with their children, restrictions on the food stamp program, a return of voluntary prayer to public schools, and a call to end coeducational school sports programs (Diamond 1995).

With such provisions, the Family Protection Act stands as an exemplar of the pro-family strategy in both the United States and Canada: Under the cover of family symbolism, a spectrum of separate socio-moral issues with deep ideological consequences was brought forward in an attempt to rein-vigorate what was being perceived as the passing of a morally virtuous past.[31]

Abortion, Euthanasia, and Reproductive Technology

The highly charged battle over abortion rights has been raging in Canada since the 1969 liberalizing of abortion in the Criminal Code and in the US since 1973, when the Supreme Court legalized a woman's right to an abor-tion on privacy grounds in the *Roe v. Wade* decision. While the issue that breathed life into the pro-family movement still holds sway as the prin-cipal issue for pro-family activists, the growing debates over euthanasia, doctor-assisted suicide, and reproductive technologies are likely to take an equally important place on their agenda.

Traditionally, the abortion fight has been a Catholic one. The supreme value placed on the sanctity of life is so great that even contemplating get-ting an abortion can be considered a mortal sin. As with the protection of the family, a divine defence can be found for protecting the unborn child: "Lo, children are an heritage of the Lord: and the fruit of the womb is his reward. As arrows are in the hand of a mighty man; so are children of the youth" (Psalm 127:3-4). As John Paul II writes in his encyclical *The Gospel of Life*, "the mere possibility of harming, attacking, or actually denying life in these circumstances is completely foreign to the religious and cultural way of thinking of the People of God" (John Paul II 1995, 77).

Divine ordinance aside, it is also interesting to note that the early church did not look favourably upon the institutions of marriage and the family. Marriage was viewed not as natural but as a vocation, and, as such, "marriage was understood to have a peculiar service to the community – namely, it served a symbolic function denoting God's loyalty to his people and as such was the appropriate context for reception of new life ... There-fore, for Christians, having children or getting married is not a 'natural' event but one freighted with the deepest moral and religious significance. Their attitude toward abortion is but an aspect of the conviction that they must be people who are ever ready to welcome children into the world" (Hauerwas 1993, 154-55). With a belief system so deeply rooted in reli-gious conviction, it makes sense that the tenacity and durability of the pro-life movement forms the cornerstone of the pro-family agenda.

Although a sub-movement of pro-family activism, the pro-life move-ment is a well-organized and -operated movement in its own right. In the US, support for the cause rapidly began to expand beyond the Catholic community after the 1973 *Roe v. Wade* decision. This landmark ruling for the pro-choice movement was effectively responsible for the greatest amount of support the pro-life movement had ever known (Luker 1984).[32] The decision also politically coalesced Catholics and evangelicals by trans-forming abortion from a private moral issue into a public political matter.

The pro-life community's opposition to abortion has taken a number of strategic forms, including scholarly refutations in *Human Life Review,* the blockades of abortion clinics by Operation Rescue, the militant tactics of Joe Schiedler's Pro-Life Action League, and the efforts of the National Right to Life Committee.[33] Most troubling for the movement has been the violent tactic of bombing clinics that began in the mid-1980s.[34]

In one way or another, these tactics have been attempts by the movement to mobilize Republican Party support for the pro-life stance. At the 1984 Republican convention, it was affirmed that "the unborn child has a fundamental individual right to life which cannot be infringed upon ... [we therefore] support a human life amendment [which would define human life as beginning with conception]" (Platt and Williams 1988, 44). In 1995, the Republican-dominated house began an attempt to restrict abortion by limiting federal funding and then in 1996 passing a bill that banned the controversial practice of partial-birth abortions.[35] The overall performance of the Republican Party, though, has been viewed as less than stellar by pro-life activists. For instance, as Martin Durham (2000) argues, it was clear that pro-life Republicans had succumbed to party pressure when the issue of abortion was excluded from the party's Contract with America.

Canadian governments have been far more reluctant to tread into the explosive arena of abortion. Since 1969, when abortions became more readily available under the Trudeau government, there have only been a few examples of partisan attempts to develop a legislative platform for a pro-life position: Stockwell Day's well-publicized views on abortion, Preston Manning's foray into the abortion debate, and Bill Vander Zalm's failed attempt to restrict medicare funding for abortions in British Columbia. On the other hand, during the same time period pro-life activism grew steadily. Initially mobilizing under Alliance for Life, Canada's first national pro-life organization, the movement has solidified and diversified itself both nationally and provincially into educational, political, and counselling branches.[36]

Membership patterns in the pro-life movement have been similar to those in the US. Initially Catholic, the movement has enjoyed increasing participation by Protestant evangelicals, yet this has had the effect of splintering the movement into hard and soft factions, with evangelicals tending to be more liberal in their views than Catholics (Herman 1994). Tactically, the Canadians have also followed the US pattern of increasing diversity and violence. The bombing of Henry Morgentaler's Toronto abortion clinic in 1992 and the shooting of Dr. Garson Romalis in Vancouver in 1994 have pushed Canadian pro-life activism to the terrorist end of its movement spectrum.

Since 1989, when the Supreme Court struck down the 1969 abortion law as unconstitutional under the Charter of Rights, Canada has been

without any abortion law. One of the litigants in the case, Dr. Henry Morgentaler, is the pro-life movement's unequivocal archenemy, while Joe
Borowski, who lost a Supreme Court case over fetal rights in part because
of the Morgentaler decision, is their martyr.[37] These clearly identifiable
players give the Canadian pro-life movement a dimension the American
one lacks: adversarial personalities upon which to clearly pin their hopes
and horrors.

In British Columbia, the pro-life movement is trying to revitalize itself
in the wake of a number of setbacks. After a protracted struggle over picketing outside the Everywoman's Health Clinic, the "bubble zone" decision, which prevented picketers from demonstrating within fifty metres of
the clinic, was upheld.[38] The removal of elected health boards at BC hospitals has also limited avenues for pro-life activists. John Hof of Campaign
Life has been quoted as saying this decision was made because the NDP
would "like to see abortion in every hospital."[39] Additionally, in May 2000,
BC became the first province to make the morning-after pill available
without a prescription. Despite its trenchant attitude, established organizational structure, and committed activism, it would seem that the pro-life
community in BC is battling a global flood tide of pro-choice sentiment
among the public that supports these types of decisions.[40]

The core of the abortion debate of course revolves around the status of
personhood and the concomitant rights that accompany that status. For
pro-choice advocates, it is the matter of a woman's right to control her
own body and exercise her reproductive function as she deems fit. Her personhood established, these rights supersede those of the fetus, which at
most enjoys only the status of potentiality.[41] For pro-life supporters, the
right to life *necessarily* extends *equally* to the fetus *because* of this potential,
and the pregnant mother has an inviolable moral obligation to protect
those rights due to her parental status.

This debate over fetal rights has been highlighted by a number of legal
cases in the US and Canada in which the state has attempted to protect
the fetus from the actions of its mother: a Manitoba woman remanded to
a drug rehabilitation centre to protect her fetus, the case of an Ontario
woman who shot her near-term fetus in the head, and identical cases in
the US all raise the issues of fetal rights and the state's right to restrict an
expectant mother's behaviour to protect a fetus. In the Canadian cases,
the courts found it unconstitutional to force a mother into treatment for
drug addiction and charges were dropped against the Ontario mother because under Canadian law the fetus is not considered a person.[42] For the pro-
life movement, such rulings are frustrating defeats, but they serve not only
to fuel their commitment but to redefine their movement away from abortion towards a broader notion of what may be understood as life politics.

This augmentation of their cause has been fuelled by the rapid expansion of reproductive technologies and their implications for fetal rights and family structure. Stories about surrogate grandmothers, test-tube babies for gay couples, rent-a-womb arrangements, destruction of frozen embryos, and book deals based on the survival rate of eight fetuses being carried by a single woman strike horror into the hearts of these activists.[43] Yet it appears that the capacity of reproductive technologies to redefine the traditional familial relationship has not been seriously addressed by pro-life and pro-family activists. At best, there appears to be a vague acknowledgment of the danger this technology represents to their cause, but little strategic attention has been paid to it.[44] It is a curious paradox. While there is currently no abortion law in Canada, and the pro-life movement is desperately seeking a highly restrictive one, they have engaged in little mobilization over attempts to restrict reproductive technologies – this as the federal government, while reticent to act on the abortion issue, seems to be moving steadily towards a position supporting a variety of reproductive and bio-engineering technologies.[45]

Beyond reproductive technologies, the euthanasia and assisted-suicide debate is being viewed as a cause that will reinvigorate the pro-life movement.[46] Abortion, while no less important to the movement, has become a stale issue for mobilization – little significant progress has been made in twenty-five years of activism. However, Canadian cases such as Sue Rodriguez's doctor-assisted suicide and Robert Latimer's euthanizing of his severely handicapped twelve-year-old daughter offer the potential to broaden the support base for a pro-life movement concerned with more than abortion. In the Latimer case, for instance, disability groups opposed the leniency he was shown after killing his daughter. Hugh Scher of the Council of Canadians with Disabilities observed, "We are talking a lot about Robert Latimer and a lot about mercy and compassion or what some perceive that to be, but what's getting lost is the fact that a little girl has been killed."[47]

The euthanasia issue may prove to be just as intractable a fight as abortion has been for the pro-life advocates. In 2000, Holland legalized the practice; France and Belgium are considering similar measures; in 1997, Australia's Northern Territory legalized it, though this was overturned after a year by the federal government; and in the US, Oregon permits doctor-assisted suicide. But for the pro-life and pro-family movements, this is a fight over the sanctity of life and a family's responsibility to it. Anything less than a commitment to protecting life to its natural end is regarded as a violation of that sanctity.

These life politics issues – abortion, euthanasia, and reproductive technology – are at the core of the pro-family movement in the US and

Canada. With the growing support for euthanasia and the rapid growth and advance of reproductive technologies, it would seem these pro-life activists have new battles to wage and the pro-family movement has more perceived threats from which the traditional family must be protected.

Gay Rights

Where abortion is the shame of modern society for the Christian right, homosexuality is the scourge. Banishing it from mainstream society may well be the second-most-important cause on the pro-family movement's agenda. They believe its disappearance would eliminate a prime source of social deviance, violence, pornography, promiscuity, family disintegration, and disease.

The almost comic remark that "God created Adam and Eve, not Adam and Steve" reflects the Christian right's biblical opposition to homosexuality but also disguises what at times is an attitude of violent moral revulsion. Texas evangelist James Robison, well-known for his anti-gay position, has said, "It is perversion of the highest order. It is against God, against God's Word, against society, against nature. It is almost too repulsive to imagine and describe. It is filth" (quoted in Lienesch 1993, 84). Other comments have been similar: one Family Coalition Party member described homosexuality as "sodomy, that's it. Where they put their cock is the dirtiest place in a human being." A supporter of Oregon's attempt to limit gay rights commented, "if someone tells my son it's okay to suck cock, I'll kill the son of a bitch."[48] Martin Durham's work on the Christian right exposes the anti-gay claim that "Nazism should be seen as crucially linked with homosexuality" (2000, 54). For example, he points to an "anti-gay campaigner, Gene Antonio, [who] declared that, far from gays being the victims of the Nazis, 'the Nazi movement – the New World Order of its day – was put on the map by militant homosexuals'" (ibid.). These are inflammatory examples but nonetheless sentiments that point to a strong undercurrent of opinion that informs the Christian right's anti-gay attitude.

Again, the Christian right uses biblical doctrine to defend its opposition to homosexuality. Ralph Reed writes, "the Christian view of homosexual practices derives from a belief in the moral principles of human sexuality found in the Bible. From descriptions in the Book of Genesis of the destruction of Sodom and Gomorrah and the injunctions against sexual misconduct in Leviticus to the apostle Paul's letter to the Romans, in both the Old Testament and the New Testament, the Bible makes it clear that homosexuality is a deviation from normative sexual conduct and God's laws" (1996, 264-65). Moral justification in hand, the Christian right in the US has actively opposed gay rights throughout the country for the past twenty-five years, enjoying a degree of success not found with the abortion cause.

Anita Bryant's Save Our Children campaign was one of the first and most prominent of the Christian right's crusade against homosexuality. In 1977, she successfully managed to overturn a Miami–Dade County ordinance including homosexuals in local anti-discrimination laws (Adam 1995). Bryant explained her opposition to the ordinance by saying, "homosexuals do not suffer discrimination when they keep their perversions in the privacy of their homes ... so long as they do not flaunt their homosexuality and try to establish role models for impressionable young people – our children" (quoted in Lienesch 1993, 85). Barry Adam's (1995) analysis of Bryant's organization identified among its supporters the National Association of Evangelicals, Jerry Falwell, the direct-mail lobby group Christian Cause, and the archbishop of Miami. Bryant toured nationally to promote her opposition to gay rights and also helped organize California's Proposition 6, a bill that would have banned homosexuals from teaching in public schools had it not been defeated (Diamond 1995).

The 1990s brought a continued assault by pro-family forces on gay rights. In Oregon, a 1992 bill that would have restricted gay rights was narrowly defeated, while in Colorado, a group called Colorado for Family Values ran a successful ballot, which was later overturned, preventing local jurisdictions from enacting civil rights ordinances (Ruether 2000).[49] Federally, President Clinton agreed in 1996 to sign a bill restricting same-sex marriages, and the Senate passed bills that would deny the recognition of same-sex marriages under the Defense of Marriage Act and deny gays protection against job discrimination. In Mississippi, a bill was signed banning the recognition of same-sex marriages, and the state of Washington has entertained similar legislation.[50] Rosemary Ruether's analysis of state legislation indicates that in 2000, twenty-one states have laws banning or strictly limiting same-sex sodomy and only an equal number of states have hate-crime laws "that include sexual orientation, while nineteen more have similar laws that do not protect gay people; ten states (including Wyoming) have no hate-crime laws at all" (Ruether 2000, 172). In 2004, gay marriage was banned by voters in eleven states and, with his re-election, it seems likely that George Bush will pursue his goal of a constitutional amendment banning gay marriages.

An emerging part of this issue for the pro-family movement is gay parental rights. In both the US and Canada, gay couples are seeking the right to adopt children – something that is not sitting well with the Christian right. In February 2004, Ken Connor, president of the Family Research Council, was invited to appear on CNN's *America Speaks Out* to debate the American Academy of Pediatrics' statement that legal parental rights should be extended to same-sex couples, which at present is possible in only three states.[51] Some of his remarks encapsulated the anti-gay attitudes of pro-family activists: "The problem with same-sex adoption of course is that it trivializes the important contributions that each gender makes to the development of a child. The data, common sense, and experience show that children do best when they're in families with mothers and fathers who are united in marriage ... what this is really about is normalizing homosexual relationships and trying to equate them with marriage."

Canadian pro-family forces appear to be confronted with a culture more resistant to anti-gay sentiments than that of the US. Although they were not overwhelming majorities, two different news polls showed Canadians support the protection of gays and lesbians under the Human Rights Act (59 percent in favour) and the recognition of gay marriages (49 percent).[52] Some significant policy decisions and legislation also have the potential to advance gay rights in the country. As well, corporations, including the federal government, have begun to extend same-sex benefits to their employees, the British Columbia government has legislated the right of homosexuals to adopt children, the federal government is attempting to pass legislation protecting gays from discrimination, and the Ontario and BC Supreme Courts have struck down Canadian marriage laws that prevented gay couples from legally marrying.[53]

Nonetheless, the pro-family movement in Canada does actively mobilize against gay rights initiatives. In 1986, a campaign in Ontario opposing a "sexual orientation" amendment to the province's Human Rights Code was mounted by REAL Women, the Evangelical Fellowship of Canada, the Ontario Conference of Catholic Bishops, and the National Citizens Coalition (under the banner of the Coalition for Family Values) (Herman 1994). REAL Women has also opposed the proposed protection of homosexuals from discrimination under the federal Human Rights Act. As national vice-president Gwen Landolt argued, changing the act would open the door to homosexual marriages and job quotas.[54] In Ottawa, Catholic bishops have opposed a section of Bill C-41 that would invoke harsher penalties for those convicted of crimes based on race, gender, or sexual orientation.[55]

In British Columbia, there are organizations that take similar stances in opposing gay rights and alternative sexual orientations, including the FCP, Focus on the Family, and the Citizens' Research Institute (CRI). The first two both opposed the legislative changes that allowed gay couples to adopt, while the latter is a pro-family organization that pursues such issues under the guise of parental rights and the pursuit of democratic freedom. The institute's mission statement proclaims that the organization "provides information that will enable Canadians to hold the government accountable and responsible for maintaining an effective democracy," and a featured quote in an institute pamphlet says, "what we need in the development and application of social policy is common sense."

The themes of common sense and democracy are common ones in pro-family discourse, where they are typically used in an effort to normalize their agendas. CRI's common-sense position on sexual orientation becomes clear in a document entitled the Declaration of Family Rights. The institute makes this form available so that parents can sign it and have it placed in their child's formal school records. An information sheet on the declaration states: "*EXERCISE YOUR RIGHTS TO PROTECT YOUR CHILDREN.* Citizens' Research Institute has developed this *DECLARATION OF FAMILY RIGHTS* ... Parents are encouraged to file this Declaration with their school and obtain some assurance that it will be honoured" (emphasis in the original). The declaration states that a parent's child "must not by any teacher or, through the teacher, any other persons or resource materials, or the learning environment, be exposed to and/or involved in any activity or program which: 1. Discusses or portrays the lifestyle of gays, lesbians, bisexual and/or transgendered individuals as one which is normal, acceptable or must be tolerated" (Declaration of Family Rights, 97/03/20).

The ideology behind this opposition to homosexuality can be found in the writings of such people as William Gairdner. On the issue of gay rights, he argues that:

> Canada ... promotes the idea of "families," while providing funds to special-interest groups that promote perverse anti-family sexual "orientations" (Canada has rushed to embrace the entire homosexual agenda, thus weakening the privileges and protections of the natural family) ... Cultures that want to guard against the threat of homosexuality must therefore drive a cultural wedge down hard between maleness and femaleness, for it is no simple coincidence that homosexuality is flourishing in a time of feminism ... they are winning the right to all the privileges of social group membership, but without fulfilling any of the requirements ... young male and female homosexuals demand the legal, tax, and even commercial advantages and privileges of married couples, without submitting to the procreative order of society. (1990, 81, 281, 447)

More than the free-rider problem Gairdner alludes to, for pro-family supporters the threat homosexual couples pose to the traditional family is similar to the one posed by the advent of reproductive technologies: they undermine the cornerstone of the Christian family – procreation. Once this foundation is eroded, it is argued, the family moves onto a slippery slope that sees marriage devalued, the socialization and education of children turned over to public institutions, and Judaeo-Christian morality discarded. For pro-family supporters, avoiding this requires recentring the traditional family through social and economic policy and buttressing it with Christian values. A well-balanced nuclear family, it is believed, with clearly defined roles for its members would help abate not only the general cultural and moral decay of modern society, but homosexuality itself.

Gairdner cites statistics that suggest a child raised in a non-religious home has a 450 percent greater chance of "choosing the homosexual lifestyle" (Gairdner 1992, 366),[56] and American pro-family activists Tim and Beverly LaHaye take the position that "homosexuals are being created all the time, the product of failed families, of weak-willed fathers and overly dominant mothers" (Lienesch 1993, 85).

All of this logic carries with it an underlying belief about gays and lesbians. To quote Didi Herman, "gay sexual behaviour, thus, is not simply anarchic; it is fundamentally pagan – it lacks spiritual, as well as physical, discipline. Ultimately, gay sexuality is satanic in origin" (1997, 82).

The Public Education System

To the Christian right, public schools are the secular institutions of a morally bankrupt liberal society that have usurped the natural function and right of the family to educate children. Bans on school prayer, promotion of sex education curriculums that allegedly promote promiscuity and homosexuality, condom dispensers in school washrooms, youth violence, and an oppressive bureaucratic structure that limits parental input have all mobilized pro-family forces.

This sub-movement of the PFM is far more diverse and amorphous than the pro-life movement. Its concerns include home-schooling, traditional schooling, private schooling, busing, textbook selection, funding, and prayer. This range of issues defies categorizing the movement with a single name, although in the US Paul Weyrich's Heritage Foundation tried to gather them all under the umbrella of the National Congress for Educational Excellence (Crawford 1980). What does link them are two consistent themes: lack of parental control over the education of children and the general moral decay that presides over the current public school system.

In the US, Christian right activist Beverly LaHaye believes that "the public school has turned into a zoo today. Drugs, immorality, pornography, violence, and in some places witchcraft, have replaced what once was a great educational system" (Lienesch 1993, 82). Miriam David points out that, for the Christian right, a partial antidote for this situation is returning to public schools a strong sense of Christian morality that will help "reassert parental influence over children and to ensure instruction in right and proper sex roles in the family as well as the wider society" (1986, 157). This kind of faith even extended as far as the White House when Ronald Reagan stated that, "if our opponents were as vigorous in supporting our voluntary prayer amendment as they are in raising taxes, maybe we could get the Lord back in our schoolrooms and the drugs and violence out" (quoted in Platt and Wiliams 1988, 42).

In particular, efforts to inject moral fibre back into public education have been focused on school textbook selection and sex education curricula.

Since the mid-1970s, the issue of textbook selection has been largely directed by Mel and Norma Gables (Diamond 1989). Removing school library and classroom books that promote secular humanism, occultism, promiscuity, alternative lifestyles, and violence and introducing morally wholesome texts in their place is viewed as a major step to reversing the moral erosion in schools. The Gables, working from their Texas home, have helped numerous parent groups nationwide in having books banned from their local schools, as well as from school libraries in Tennessee, Alabama, and West Virginia (ibid.).

Alice Moore, the protagonist in a West Virginia banning, succinctly placed the issue in its broader agenda: "What we are fighting for is simply who is going to have control over the schools, the parents and the tax-payers and the people who live here, or the educational specialists, the administrators, the people from other places who have been trying to tell us what is best for our children" (quoted in Crawford 1980, 156). For Moore, a school board member at the time, these best interests could be served only if she and her supporters could successfully remove a new set of textbooks "they believed were full of 'obscene, anti-American, and anti-God' themes" (Diamond 1998, 65).

This kind of book banning is also directly tied to the Christian right's opposition to homosexuality and sex education. Their fear is that children will become socialized to what is often referred to as the "homosexual agenda." For instance, James Dobson, founder of Focus on the Family, has actively fought to keep gay teachers from influencing textbook selection in California (Durham 2000), while in British Columbia, the Family Coalition Party supported a local school board that banned books depicting gay families.

Sex education programs are perhaps the most reviled aspect of the liberal education curriculum. For the Christian right, sex is a subject that should be taught in the home and by parents. If it must be taught in the schools at all, Ralph Reed of the Christian Coalition argues that "abstinence-based curricula that encourage young people to resist peer pressure in the area of drugs, alcohol, and sex will greatly reduce the social pathologies that have transformed too many schools into war zones. The prophets of permissiveness have done tremendous harm to our children" (1994b, 257). Or, as Mark Holmes, a Canadian pro-family conservative writes, "Conservatives agree that lessons in sex education should empha-size morality ... that sexual relations should be postponed at least until adulthood, and, for most conservatives, until marriage. Those teachings are easily derived, both from traditional practice and religious belief" (1998, 110). The problem for religious conservatives is that the inclusion of birth control methods, condom machines, and descriptions of gay and lesbian sex have, as US activist Tim LaHaye writes, created a "moral holocaust, a wave of promiscuity, teenage pregnancies, and venereal disease" (quoted in Lienesch 1993, 83).

For pro-family advocates, attempts to regain parental control over the educational system have come primarily through the home-schooling and traditional and private school movements. Traditional and private schools are not religious per se, but they do subscribe to a similar teaching philosophy, and as Susan Rose (1989) points out, the Christian school movement has been one of the most rapidly expanding sectors of private education.

Whether they are religious or not, what the Christian right has with these schools is the opportunity to develop a curriculum for what Miriam David (1986) has called "teaching family matters." Central to this approach is the notion of the teacher-centred classroom and the discipline of children rather than the liberally permissive and self-absorbed focus of the child-centred class. It is believed that this is a necessary shift if children are to be properly trained and taught respect for authority and tradition. As Mark Holmes writes, "authority is an essential, desirable, and visible element in a conservative school" (1998, 110), which in essence seems to be arguing for a "children need to learn their place" philosophy. In addition to this, should the school be a Christian one, there is also an "authoritative, disciplined and God-centred education that emphasizes character development and spiritual training" (Rose 1989, 60). Either way, religious conservatives see this as an essential and long overdue corrective to public education.

For the pro-family movement to gain the power necessary to achieve these goals in the public system, however, requires more than just co-optation to the private sector. Recognizing this, the Christian Coalition's plan for restructuring public education includes a call for aggressive activism at the local school board level and a restructuring of educational funding to a voucher system that would give parents the opportunity to choose where and how to educate their children. It is a plan that emphasizes what Ralph Reed suggests is the creation of a learning environment free of current social pathologies, a back-to-basics curriculum, and greater parental control over school board decisions (1994a, 1994b, 1996).

As the first chapter showed, the Canadian Christian right, through the Family Coalition Party, is strikingly similar to its US counterparts in its views on the current public education system and the remedial measures that need to be taken. As William Gairdner puts it, "the people have allowed the State to take out of their hands the most important task of any nation: the nurturing of the quality of the minds, spirits, and bodies of the young" (1992, 277). In British Columbia, parental reclamation of this task has included a call by the pro-family movement for a voucher system in education funding, a growing pursuit of home-, charter, and traditional schooling, challenges to the sex education program, and keeping a careful watch over literary material in schools.

There is a general agreement among pro-family activists in BC that a voucher system would provide parents with greater choice and control over the education of their children and thus over a lot of these issues. In 1992 the FCP submitted a brief to the provincial government about education funding in which it recommended just this. It is thought that such a system would facilitate the growing variety of school movements in the province and across the country.[57] Gairdner, who sees an inherent superiority in private and denominational schools, contends that putting public education on a voucher system like this would "create competition for educational excellence in all schools. (A parent receives one voucher for each child equal in value to the per-student cost of a year's education, and can 'spend' it at any qualified school he wishes, public or private – if he gets there quickly enough!) This makes the producers of education responsive to the consumers of it, instead of to the government and its ministries" (1990, 244).

The benefits and shortcomings of this funding structure have been debated in the province for the past few years as support for charter and private schools has increased among parents across the country.[58] This trend towards alternative schooling appears not to be restricted to supporters of the pro-family movement, a situation that may provide the movement with an opportunity to increase its popular appeal. The danger for opponents of the Christian right is the potential of having "traditional values" quietly advanced within this larger shell of support.

Challenges to sex education programs and the appropriateness of reading material available to students in schools are also active dimensions of the Canadian pro-family movement in BC. The Surrey School Board ignited a legal battle in the province when in 1997 it banned three primary-grade books because they featured same-sex parents.[59] The ban was overturned in 1998 by the Supreme Court of British Columbia, a decision further upheld by the Supreme Court of Canada in 2003. In part, the courts found that the grounds for the ban contravened the BC School Act because of the religious bias of those supporting the ban. At the centre of the debate was Heather Stilwell, the chair of the Surrey School Board, a long-time pro-life and pro-family activist and the leader of the Family Coalition Party.

Successful or not, to the pro-family movement, the importance of such challenges revolves around regaining social and moral control from what they view as the secular humanists: "Collectivists in the West have long since captured the prime means of media communications, plus the vast majority of schools and universities, which they all but control with 'politically correct' textbooks" (Gairdner 1990, 53). This control, it is argued, has left public schools and school boards without any sense of the need to instill moral values in students.

To Canadian pro-family activists, like their American counterparts, this lack of moral values is nowhere more apparent than in the sex education curricula of public schools. As far back as 1966, claims Gairdner, "sex education in the schools became unrestricted, and it now includes the full range of psycho-social deviations. Special attention is given to the 'restructuring' of student attitudes for eager acceptance of masturbation, oral-genital sex, homosexuality, sodomy, and even animal sex, with abortion-on-demand taught as a basic right" (1992, 249). The fear pro-family activists harbour about such liberal sex education programs is their capacity to redefine social and moral normalcy, thereby displacing traditional family values and leaving children at risk for the many social pathologies secular humanism has supposedly wrought.

To combat this trend, pro-family activists have engaged local school boards and the provincial and federal governments in an attempt to restrict and modify a program that they view as undermining parental control, traditional family authority, and basic Christian morality. For instance, a Health and Welfare Canada video, *What's Wrong with This Picture,* evoked a strong reaction from BC pro-family advocates because of graphic phrases like "Always use a rubber when you screw in the anus or vagina."[60]

This is also part of the broader agenda behind the Citizens' Research Institute's Declaration of Family Rights. An information sheet on the declaration states that it is a "positive instrument for parents to use to defend their values and protect their children ... Big government has demonstrated a tendency to facilitate the self interest groups who see our school children as a captive audience ... Now that ... teachers have admitted they are already discussing the gay and lesbian lifestyle in the classroom, parents are required to take a more effective and constructive step if they are going to protect their children." This is one more example of the normalizing rhetoric used consistently by the pro-family movement in their fight to wrest control of public education from their enemies: the state and secular humanists.

Feminism

The visceral dislike the Christian right has for feminism is neither masked nor difficult to understand, since feminism as an ideology tends to occupy a position diametrically opposed to that of the pro-family movement. Feminism's critique of the traditional family as oppressive and patriarchal, as well as socially and psychologically repressive for women and children, makes it the ideological antichrist to the Christian right. Jerry Falwell considers feminists to be "pro-homosexual and lesbian. In fact, it is shocking how many feminists are lesbians," and Beverly LaHaye views feminism as a "philosophy of death. At its core in modern times there is a stridently anti-life motivation. Radical feminists are self-destructive and are trying to bring about the death of an entire civilization as well" (quoted in Lienesch

1993, 72). Canadian William Gairdner adds that, "every age seems to have its peculiar intellectual cancers ... Like so many, I find myself increasingly surrounded by strident, petty, whining feminist arguments that have by now nibbled their way into every organ of our society ... When studied carefully ... their arguments, taken as a whole, amount to a virulent, cult-ish, man-hating, and family-hating program that threatens the funda-mental health of our society" (1992, 296).

The artifacts that document these attitudes consistently equate femi-nism with sexual orientation and the destruction of society (Durham 2000; Ruether 2000). As the statements above indicate, pro-family activists seem to immediately conclude that to be a feminist is to be a lesbian and hater of families, although this is sometimes qualified as pro-family sup-porters specify that they are referring to "radical" (presumably as opposed to "rational") feminists when they speak in these terms. Gairdner, for one, makes this distinction: "Most women who think of themselves as 'femi-nists' today simply mean that fairness has not always been evenly applied to women in our society, and that it ought to be. (Of course, in some cases they will argue it shouldn't be, because women have advantages they don't want to lose. Paid maternity leave, couches in women's washrooms, re-straints on lifting heavy objects, immunity from military conscription ...)" (1990, 271). Rosemary Ruether sums up this Christian right attitude this way: "The gay-takeover/doomsday scenario promoted by the Christian Right is buttressed by specific rhetoric against lesbians ... lesbians, when they are mentioned, are often identified with feminism. Feminism itself is depicted as a man-hating, child-rejecting perversion of women in rebel-lion against their proper attitude of submission to male authority in fam-ily and in society; its logical consequence is lesbianism" (2000, 174).

At the root of these sentiments is what Berger and Berger (1983) have called "acute value conflicts" between feminists and the pro-family move-ment. More specifically, there exists acutely disparate opinions about the ontology of the family and its function in Western society. The pro-family perspective is one supposedly wrapped in stability, warmth, security, and freedom in following a biblically prescribed natural order. Feminists, how-ever, have challenged that vision with a critical deconstruction of the family that leaves its claims of universality and naturalness on shaky ground. It is not simply the pursuit of such analyses but their cogency that continues to fuel the often virulent hostility the Christian right dis-plays towards the feminist movement. The pro-family movement's inveter-ate position can be understood by examining just what it is feminists have been arguing.

With analytic views like Jacques Donzelot's (1979) conception of the fam-ily as a site of innumerable intersections, feminists have pulled apart the traditional idea of the nuclear family into a complex series of meanings and moral sanctions. In the case of abortion, pro-life activism is interpreted as a social control mechanism aimed at restricting a woman's sexual life. As Rosalind Petchesky argues, "if a woman can control her pregnancies, there is no built-in sanction against her having sex when, how and with whom she pleases – and this, for the 'pro-family'/'pro-life' movement, is the heart of the matter." She continues: "Over and over again in antiabortion and 'pro-family' literature, one is struck with a defiantly traditional middle-class morality regarding sexual behavior and an undisguised antipathy toward all forms of sexuality outside the marital, procreative sphere" (1981, 229-30).

For the Christian right, restricting women's sexual behaviour to the realm of heterosexual marriage and child bearing helps restore the "proper" psychodynamics of the familial relationship and thus the greater social order. In his analysis of the Christian right family, Michael Lienesch (1993) has explored the psychosocial roles of man, woman, and child in the family, concluding that for the pro-family movement, the solution to familial problems is for men to adopt their natural position at the head of the household and for women to submit. It is this structural situation that has led feminists to conclude that the family is an institution that leaves women submissive, oppressed, exploited, and ignored.

These kinds of direct frontal assaults on the traditional family, as well as the political denigration of the Christian and New Right, have further fuelled the antipathy of the pro-family movement towards feminists. Works like Michele Barrett and Mary McIntosh's *The Anti-Social Family* and Pamela Abbott and Claire Wallace's *The Family and the New Right,* for instance, have called for the complete destruction of the nuclear family and questioned the true motivations behind the pro-family movement.

For Barrett and McIntosh, the traditional family is characterized and driven by relations of patriarchal domination and "the principles of selfishness, exclusion, and pursuit of private interest and contravenes those of altruism, community and pursuit of the public good" (1991, 47). Familialism, they argue, is a cloak for the individualist ideology that accompanies capitalist consumption and production patterns, as well as the reproduction of chronic class and gender inequalities. Once it is understood that the family as a private institution is a constructed social process, they argue its essentialist nature can be discarded and it becomes possible to entertain social arrangements that promote a more equitable social collective. In this pursuit, Barrett and McIntosh recommend experimentation with household and personal arrangements, the avoidance of oppressive acts like heterosexual marriage with traditional roles, and a cautionary attitude towards the idea of domestic bliss. Wary of the damage the family as an economic and social institution has done throughout history, Barrett and McIntosh have no wish to see any type of replacement because "as a bastion against a bleak society it has made that society bleak" (ibid., 80).

Abbott and Wallace pursue a more political angle in their analysis of the motivations behind the New Right's attempt to save the traditional family. For them, the entire pro-family agenda is one the New Right has used to politically manipulate popular support for a neoconservative economic plan in the US and Britain. Their exposé of this strategy, mounted by conservative ideologues such as Roger Scruton and Ferdinand Mount in Britain and Charles Murray in the United States, challenges the moral convictions and motives the Christian right put forward as justifications for their agenda. It also casts doubt on a fundamental pro-family argument that sees the secular humanist bias of society as a product of state interference in family life. The Thatcher and Reagan administrations, Abbott and Wallace argue, were strongly pro-family in their policy directions, to the point that internal party groups like the Conservative Family Campaign of the British Conservative Party arose to blatantly promulgate "remoralising the nation's life through the restoration of the traditional patriarchal family and a revival of fundamental Christian values" (1992, 48). The Reagan administration, heavily influenced by neoconservative and New Right advisors, followed a similar path, as did the Republican-dominated Senate of the mid-1990s with its Contract with America – this with the full blessing of the Christian Coalition. In Canada, the Family Caucus of Brian Mulroney's Conservatives had hoped to do the same. In other words, the state has a long history of policy involvement that revolves around trying to maintain the hegemony of the traditional nuclear family.

What this suggests is that the Christian right has erred in blaming what it views as an over-interfering, liberal-minded state. American and Canadian governments have passed increasingly liberal social legislation over the past twenty years, but this is more a reflection of the values and beliefs that the bulk of citizens want their society to practise, rather than vice versa. Certainly the character of Canadian and American cultural hegemony has altered. However, this is likely more a product of successful mobilization on the part of historically disenfranchised citizens and groups and the concomitant belief by the broader society that such injustices needed (and continue to need) cultural and legislative amelioration. It is also readily apparent that there continues to be an active and powerful conservative element within the state – one need only look at the Republican Party in the US and the Reform/Alliance Party in Canada.

This type of argument largely nullifies the Christian right's position on the role of the state and helps expose the pro-family movement to evaluations such as Abbott and Wallace's: "The 'pro-family' movement is concerned with sustaining the patriarchal nuclear family as the norm and it is vigorous in its attack on welfarism, divorce, abortion and sexual deviancy. It is also anti-feminist and racist. The key areas in which it advocates political reform arise from these issues" (1992, 49). Such cogent assessments and arguments evoke infuriated reactions from the Christian right towards a group they often refer to as "femi-nazis," whom they view as attempting to corrupt all that is good and wholesome in society with their toxic blend of gay rights, safe abortion services, universal daycare, and equal opportunity employment.

In railing as they do against feminism, gay rights, and other progressive elements of today's society, the Christian right has become the latest version of an aggressive form of conservatism that emerged with the neoconservatives and New Right of the 1970s. Far from supporting the idea of slow, gradual change, the Christian right set forth on a path that has a broad and dramatic socio-political agenda. Their goal is to save society, and to do this they must save the traditional family, for they believe that as the family goes, so goes society.

To achieve this, pro-family forces argue that a profound change in social and moral attitudes must take place in Canada and the US. That is, there must be a decisive shift away from the allegedly destructive forces of secular humanism towards the safety and truth of social policies and laws informed by biblical scripture. The institution of heterosexual marriage, for instance, must be strengthened by dissuading divorce and homosexual marriages. For a mother to stay at home to raise children should also be recognized as a legitimate career choice, and one that should be actively promoted. Abortion and euthanasia, they continue, must be severely restricted or, ideally, banned, and health care support systems must be structured more towards helping women with crisis pregnancies and people needing palliative care. Further, changes in the economy and size of government must accompany this. Freeing up the capitalist marketplace and getting the government "off the backs of families and on their side," as one FCP member said, must be a priority if the tax burden on families is to be alleviated. Finally, they believe that public education policy should be driven more by parental opinion and less by heavy-handed bureaucracies.

These are the issues of the pro-family movement and, as Chapter 1 showed, the issues of the Family Coalition Party. Its founders and the current supporters of the Unity Party of BC stubbornly cling to a vision of a fading society, and they are determined to resurrect it through a strategy that combines social movement activism with institutionalized political action. It is to the specifics of this plan that the next chapter turns.

3
The Burden of Form:
The Family Coalition Party
as a Movement

As a collective action form, the Family Coalition Party is the historical product of its adherents' frustration and disaffection from not only mainstream political parties and processes but also the ineffectiveness of other movement forms in the pro-life and pro-family industries. In Canada, since the decriminalization of abortion in 1969, the pro-life and more recently the pro-family movements have been confronted with ever-diminishing political opportunities that can be exploited to reaffirm the traditional life and family values its activists hold sacrosanct. They have also been confronted with a social milieu resistant to the messages these movements carry. The cultural beliefs and socio-political policies of Canadian hegemony have shifted continually, albeit slowly, in the past twenty-five years towards the integration of previously marginalized citizens. The activism of women, gays and lesbians, racial and ethnic minorities, and other historically disenfranchised groups has broadened and diversified the popular image of the Canadian cultural landscape to the point where tangible gains have been achieved by these activists.

This progress can be identified in the two spaces critical to achieving social change: the legislative/juridical and the popular consciousness of daily life. As the first two chapters revealed, in British Columbia this progress has included, among other things, the legal right of gays to adopt children, the broad availability of safe, legal abortion services for women, and the emerging acceptance of familial structures other than what is understood as traditional.

For the Canadian Christian right, the witnessing and subsequent opposition to this continuing cultural shift has been an extended period of frustrated attempts to mobilize active support from its seemingly natural constituency of Christian communities. This frustration has also included trying to influence party and legislative policy through federal and provincial state mechanisms and parties. On this latter point, the FCP, like its provincial namesake in Ontario and the Christian Heritage Party federally, was an attempt by pro-family activists to create a political space using a party form to gain access to the polity for the purpose of achieving their movement goals: the legislative and cultural re-establishment of a pro-life and pro-family ideology for Canadian society.[1]

It was this tactic that gave the FCP its party/movement character, and it highlights an intimate yet highly viscous relationship between the form and the function of an organization like the FCP. Its party form is the result of a tactical decision, a movement strategy to deliberately and overtly engage the political system in order to provide the pro-life and pro-family movements with another avenue for activism. In this sense, its form becomes a tool, an organizational crowbar with which to pry open a political access point for entrance into the mechanisms of legislative power. It also implicitly acknowledges the premise that all movements are ultimately political and that movements, at some point in their life cycle, must in some way engage the state to attain their goals.

More specifically, within the pro-family movement industry, the FCP can be understood as a specific and unique social movement organization (SMO) that emerged at a particular historical moment of the current protest cycle, now characterized by a slow but progressive reversal of the movement-countermovement roles previously played by the new social movements (NSMs) and their conservative opponents. The legalization and popular support for the availability of safe abortion services in Canada, for instance, signals a victory for pro-choice forces in the country and now casts them in the role of a countermovement defending these changes against pro-life attempts to limit the availability of abortion services. On the other hand, with this shift in socio-cultural attitudes and politico-legal safeguards, pro-life has become the movement rather than the counter-movement in this battle as its members attempt to promote acceptance of their desire to restrict these services.

Using the analytical concepts made available by social movement theorists in the areas of framing (Snow et al. 1986; Snow and Benford 1988), resource mobilization (McCarthy and Zald 1973, 1977), and political opportunity (McAdam 1982; Tilly 1978; Eisinger 1973; Tarrow 1994), this chapter will establish the FCP as a social movement organization and evaluate the problems it confronts as such. Beyond appreciating the movement function and character of the FCP, this chapter will also argue that conservative movements have to date been underexamined by social movement researchers, which has limited the capacity of social movement theory to fully reflect the temporal dynamic that mediates the interactive relationship between opposing movements and the state during cycles of protest.

Finding a Niche: Resurgence Movements

For understandable reasons, the bulk of social movement research over the past forty years has focused primarily on the collective efforts of disenfranchised groups' efforts to improve their social, political, and economic standing within democratic polities. To this end – and their great credit – social movement theorists have developed an impressive body of work capable of analyzing and understanding various facets of a movement's life cycle: its emergence, the social-psychological requirements of its supporters and mobilizers, its structural requisites and strategies for survival and success, and to a lesser extent movements' outcomes and the end of their life cycle.

Since the early 1960s, when research of this kind tended to depend primarily on social-psychological explanations of collective behaviour (Smelser 1962; Gurr 1970), social movement theory has gone through a period of emphasis on macro- and meso-structural factors such as that found in the work of McCarthy and Zald (1977) on resource mobilization and McAdam's (1982) political process approach, and currently finds itself in a time of theoretical convergence. Movement scholars have recognized the great utility of a multivalent approach to the study of social movements, and consequently there has been an increasing surge of work attempting to bring together micro and macro perspectives, as well as European new social movement theory, with the American-dominated resource mobilization approach (McAdam et al. 1988, 1996; Morris and McClurg Mueller 1992; Buechler 1993; Jenkins 1983; Klandermans and Tarrow 1988; McAdam et al. 2001; Canel 1992).

This theoretical trend is likely in no small part a result of the changing character of the social movements themselves and the socio-political culture in which they do battle. As capitalist accumulation strategies continue to adapt and defy Marx's prognostications, cultural hegemonic programs have concurrently broadened, providing ideological space for previously suppressed systems of belief and furnishing opportunities for groups to challenge the historically dominant Western patriarchal Christian ethos. In the post-industrial age, classic protest movements – typically associated with class struggle and attempts at structural socio-economic transformations in the base of the hegemonic order – have largely been supplanted by the new social movements, with their reformist, anti-institutional, particularistic focus on a variety of single issues that find more prominent articulation in the upper hegemonic domains of culture, lifestyle, ideological belief, and consciousness.

Regardless of such historical form or focus, definitions of what constitutes a social movement tend to reflect consensus about their being a form of collective action by a group of like-minded people who exhibit a degree of organizational formality while operating in a non-institutionalized context to promote or resist issues of social change through campaigns of public awareness and/or the threat of mass mobilization. Descriptions like this abound in the literature (Heberle 1968; Wilkinson 1971; Zurcher and

Snow 1981; Scott 1990; Marx and McAdam 1994; Tarrow 1994; Teske and Tétrault 2000) and, for most movement scholars, provide a satisfactory characterization of what West German sociologists dubbed *Neue soziale Bewegungen,* or new social movements (Dalton 1990, 4), the study of which has largely dominated the field for the past twenty years.

The claimed novelty of these movements has been their characteristic turning away from institutionalized and representative politics, their attention to a diverse range of individual issues, their emphasis on localism and extraparliamentary action, and their predominant concern for culture and lifestyle over the economic (Boggs 1986; Scott 1990; Kelly 2001). The NSMs are largely a form of citizen politics concerned with the expression and validation of identity. With these movements, as Alberto Melucci has observed, "what individuals are claiming collectively is the right to realize their own identity: the possibility of disposing of their personal creativity, their affective life, and their biological and interpersonal existence" (1980, 218).

This means these are struggles not simply about gender and sexuality, but the full spectrum of cultural forces that mould, mitigate, and manage the daily lives and identities of people. Ecological concerns, the peace movement, anti-consumerism, tax revolts, student protests, and opposition to television all share the common feature of trying to reconfigure popular culture in such a way as to free the individual from the workaday corporatist ideology of capitalist social relations. The celebration of personal autonomy, increasing individual control over one's existence, and improving the quality of personal and collective life are the cultural goals of these movements. They are about breaking out of the narrow socio-cultural and political mould of modern society. Crafted from capitalist, patriarchal, and Christian ideals, it is a mould that limits economic and cultural legitimacy to a large paycheque, a traditional family, dominance over the environment, and spiritual salvation. To this end, writes Alain Touraine, *"the positive goal of today's social movements, which oppose both the reign of markets and the domination of communitarian-inspired movements, is the defence of the cultural and social rights of individuals* ... The general principle on which all social movements are now based is the right to cultural equality" (2001, 51, italics in the original).

In rebuking these homogenizing effects of capitalism on social identities, NSMs have taken up an operational locale in civil society, focusing on local issues and forms of mobilization. This emphasis on direct action and participatory styles of engagement reflects an inherent distrust among NSMs for the corporatist practices of the modern state and an intent to take back democratic control of everyday life. The outgrowth of state involvement in the everyday lives of citizens has blurred or, as some argue (Melucci 1980), eliminated the line separating the spheres of public and private, resulting in a creeping strangulation of democratic autonomies and freedoms. Carl Boggs points out that this expansion of the state is inevitable, that the "structural transformation of capitalism – the collapse of market mechanisms giving rise to monopoly control, extensive planning networks, and socialization of production – requires massive state initiative, even where (as in the United States) the myths of free enterprise remain" (1986, 24). Regardless of arguments on autonomy and whether the state operates on behalf of or at the behest of capital, corporatist practices of social control mediation are rebuffed by NSM activists because the goal of such processes remains the maintenance of systemic conditions favourable to fostering extant patterns of accumulation, not the retreat of state mechanisms from private life or the democratization of society in general.

Boggs further argues that the dominant and common theme among all NSMs has been "the commitment to participatory democracy. What galvanized all social forces was a passionately anti-authoritarian ethos, a preoccupation with direct action, community and self-activity that carried into virtually every arena of struggle" (1995, 333). This has necessitated a disavowal of traditional political party systems of representation, or, as Alberto Melucci writes, "essentially they [NSMs] are not oriented toward the conquest of political power or of the state apparatus, but rather toward the control of a field of autonomy or of independence vis-à-vis the system" (1980, 220). The goal of direct action and full political participation cannot be met if the locus of power is transferred from the individual to a representative of conglomerated interests, so NSMs have deliberately stressed the interdependence of the personal and political, and the importance of understanding civil society as a politically engaged space.

For the categories of NSMs that have been generally identified – those concerned with issues of gender, sexuality, race, youth, peace, and ecology (Boggs 1986; Miliband 1989; Johnston et al. 1994) – these attitudes and tactical traits can be accepted as readily applicable. However, the important question at hand is whether an organization like the Family Coalition Party, decidedly conservative and seemingly accepting of traditional protocols of political engagement, can be understood and accepted in similar fashion.

Certainly the FCP is working to resist social change, which squeezes it into the definitional end of a social movement, but it is also focused on promoting social change. Cultural and political gains made by various NSMs have come at the expense of the FCP's belief system and political security. For example, the FCP is not *fighting to prevent* the passage of legislation legalizing abortion or adoption by gays; it is *fighting to promote* support for changing existing laws it views as inherently wrong and unjust. What it is seeking, in other words, is the re-establishment of the ideological and political supremacy of the Western patriarchal Christian ethos that the NSMs have been slowly and successfully eradicating. It may well be that the FCP is attempting a return to the past with this goal, but this is a political and ideological judgment and not the point of concern here. Attempting to change cultural beliefs and influence legislative decisions are goals of any movement, regardless of form or ideology.

As Chapter 1 made clear, the FCP's traditional family value platform is piecemeal compared to the type of complete political package commonly associated with institutionalized parties. There was no real economic policy and little in the way of policy development. Its mandate was driven by a narrow, particular set of issues that constituted a specific politics of identity. Preserving and restoring the traditional family identity within BC's cultural hegemony was the FCP's goal, and its executive considered attempting to acquire parliamentary standing through the electoral process only a method by which to achieve this goal. Apart from Heather Stilwell, none of the executive or the candidates in any election or by-election expressed any interest in a political career or even the opportunity to wield political power beyond that needed to achieve the goals of their movement. Indeed, the entire membership considered the role of the FCP to be more that of a movement focused on increasing awareness and educating the general public about the benefits of traditional family values and the dangers of secular humanist forces in society. Election periods were viewed only as additional opportunities to raise these issues, and the FCP was considered a specialized vehicle within the pro-family movement for that purpose.

It was also regarded, however, as a potentially effective educative body in off-election years. Like the NSMs, the FCP executive operated under the belief that successful social change comes about through the process of people's identifying their values, and that this will primarily be achieved through the institutions and daily life of civil society. Those in the pro-family movement and the FCP believe that only when this shift in values has occurred, only when people have become "cognitively liberated," to use Doug McAdam's (1982) term, will a party like the FCP have the potential to become a viable political force.

Despite its structural form, the FCP as a group harboured a deep disaffection for representative politics. Years of broken promises, doors of political opportunity slammed shut, and backroom party dealings had left the membership with a jaundiced view of the political process. While FCP executives and supporters believe that politicians and their parties should work to represent the wishes of their constituents, they share a strong sentiment that in practice the case is quite the opposite. They believe that the parliamentary system under which Canadian governments operate provides little opportunity for accurate or free representation. The experiences of the Toths and the Stilwells while working in political parties and the examples of pro-life politicians like federal Liberals Tom Wappel and

Roseanne Skoke and BC provincial Liberal John van Dongen, and the way they are consistently silenced by party whips, were regularly used to demonstrate the dangers and ineffectiveness of representative politics. On the other hand, FCP members viewed the Family Coalition as a party capable of providing the opportunity for direct, open, and principled political participation for pro-family supporters.

With its reformist goals, distrust of representative politics, concern for the identity of the traditional family, and belief in direct as well as extra-parliamentary political participation, it would seem the FCP should fall somewhere under the rubric of the new social movements. The danger lies in overstating its fit. The FCP is still the ideological antithesis of what are commonly understood to be NSMs. It embodies a form rejected in principle by most NSMs, it is not pursuing the goal of radically restructuring the democratic process, and it has taken a strategically deliberate turn towards the institutional.

Part of the solution to the puzzle of the new social movement qualities of the FCP is to first recognize the anti-political idealism of the NSMs as rather illusory. The NSMs' "flight from politics," as Boggs (1986) describes it, may be an act of self-distancing from traditional political institutions, but it is equally as much an expansion of what constitutes political terrain. The identity politics of these movements has politicized what were previously non-political spaces by mobilizing around issues of sexuality, gender, and culture, and this has consequently forced mainstream institutions into a politically attentive relationship with them. Yet, as L.A. Kaufmann writes, "the overall effect of this new identity politics was a major shift in political thinking, deemphasizing the role of institutions in perpetuating discrimination and exploitation and highlighting the role of extra-institutional culture ... [and this] tendency to claim political content for changes in lifestyle encourages the view that politics need not necessarily involve engagement with external structures of power" (1990, 71, 77).[2] So deluded, NSM activists risk falling into the trap of denying what they really are – political movements directly engaged with the state.

For all their anti-political idealism, this is precisely what the NSMs are. For all their novelty, NSMs share the same goals and problems as traditional working-class movements. As David Plotke points out, the traditional movement's "aim was not to refuse power, much less destroy it, but to take and reshape it. The problem of identity was in theory already settled ... What remained was the problem of enhancing and guarding identities in practice" (1990, 92). And this is the juncture the NSMs have found themselves at for some time. Identity established, they are now searching for avenues to secure political power and unifying themes that might allow a coming together of disparate interests. They are pursuing what Boggs (1986) has termed a "conversion project."

That the new social movements represent a thematic shift rather than an ontological break from traditional class-based movements has been well argued (Cohen 1983; Plotke 1990; Miliband 1989; Tucker 1991; Calhoun 1993), as has the point that both types of movements are concerned with issues of citizenship, social distribution of power and resources, and the opportunity for political participation. The pursuit of a radical democratic politics by the NSMs (Laclau and Mouffe 1985; Sandilands, 1992), the entrance of the environmental Greens into the political mainstream (Boggs 1986; Kitschelt 1989; Sandilands 1992; Mayer and Ely 1998), and the general pursuit of rights through the legislative and juridical spheres are all deliberately political acts engaging the state.

Indeed, in their examination of the NSMs' principled rejection of the state as a locus of power, Mooers and Sears conclude that "the radical democrats' bold claim to have theoretically transcended the crude Marxist preoccupation with the centrality of state power masks the peace they have made with the state at the level of practical politics. To the extent that much of the baggage of traditional liberalism is smuggled back into radical democratic discourse, its political prescriptions begin to sound like minor variations on an old theme ... This type of politics represents a new form of reformism ... all social movements come up against the state" (1992, 60, 68). Like the FCP, then, the NSMs have not simply taken a decided turn towards the institutional in their pursuit of social change; they may in fact have never really turned away.

For present purposes, the Canadian Greens provide the readiest means to observe a similar engagement with the institutional. In Ontario, the Green Party is introducing a form of radical democracy through its tactical entrance into provincial politics (Sandilands 1989), but it is in BC that politics has made the strangest bedfellows. In the pursuit of electoral reform for the province, the Green Party and the FCP, along with a number of other small parties, joined forces as the Coalition for Electoral Reform in an attempt to press for a system of proportional representation in the province.[3] Dissatisfied with the current form of representation, these parties were pressing for this more directly representative type of electoral system, the likes of which has not been seen since W.A.C. Bennett's Social Credit came to power in British Columbia as a protest party in 1952. Although the environmental and pro-family movements occupy opposite ends of an ideological continuum, this pursuit of electoral reform and participatory democracy vis-à-vis a structural form brings them onto common tactical ground and closes the taxonomic gap between the NSMs and the FCP.

What remains, however, is the ideological orientation of the FCP. It could well be argued that the FCP is in no way similar to a new social movement. In their analysis of modern movements, scholars have tacitly, albeit accurately, accepted NSMs as ideologically and politically left wing –

something the FCP most assuredly cannot claim. In analyzing the use of the term "new social movement," scholars have pointed out that a tendency has arisen to ontologize the characteristics of these collective action forms (Melucci 1989; Johnston et al. 1994). In addition to the traits described above, this argument includes their political orientation. Through years of analytical focus and discussion, popular use of the term now carries with it an implied and accepted understanding that to speak of new social movements is to speak of a leftist political ideology. This is not necessarily an analytical fault, although it needs to be recognized more overtly than the current literature does, but it does little to properly situate a conservative movement like the FCP in this theoretical frame.

Typically, when an organization like the FCP is encountered or analyzed, it is labelled a countermovement and situated somewhere on the perimeter of serious social movement research. As Meyer and Staggenborg (1994) point out, there has been a paucity of theoretical and empirical work available on countermovements, although this situation has improved somewhat in recent years. There is a slowly growing literature that uses social movement theory to analyze conservative or countermovements (Werum and Winders 2000; Anderson and Langford 2001; McCaffrey and Keys 2000; Bendroth 1999).[4]

This historical lack of work on countermovements is an understandable product of movement history over the past four decades, a period that has seen remarkable mobilization by forces on the left and a lesser but growing resistance or counter-mobilization from the right. To use Tarrow's (1994) observation, the social movements that arose in the 1960s in North America constituted a third cycle of protest for the modern age, and these movements have resulted in a number of manifest gains in the Canadian and American polities. Cultural attitudes and acceptance of alternative lifestyles, minority rights, abortion, and the need to protect the environment have grown, and this has been reflected in various legislated bills and applications of law. History, in other words, is not the present. Time has passed and social norms have altered as this cycle of protest has rolled on; the socio-moral and juridico-political status quos in the new millennium are not what they were twenty or even ten years ago. These changes have in many regards reversed the roles of left-wing movements and their adversarial conservative countermovements, making the past practice of automatically labelling conservative and right-wing movements "counter" outdated.

McAdam, McCarthy, and Zald (1988) have pointed out the limited utility of this traditional labelling practice and the importance of timing on the targets of countermovement action, but they did not stress the importance of what could be considered the *historical moment* in situating a collective action form as a movement or countermovement. Like other descriptions of countermovements (Heberle 1968; Benford 1992; Johnson

1999), theirs highlights the fact that any movement will invite opposition (countermovement), that they will interact with one another, and that countermovements attempt to defend the status quo or existing social order. To their credit, and unlike these other descriptions, they did not include the inference of inherent conservatism in a countermovement. Tahi Mottl's formal definition of a countermovement avoids the same potential pitfall: "It is useful to define a countermovement as a conscious, collective, organized attempt to resist or to reverse social change" (1980, 620, emphasis in the original). Clarence Lo (1982) identifies this definition as "opposing not another movement, but rather social change" and suggests instead that a "countermovement may be defined as a movement mobilized against another social movement" (Lo 1982, 118).

Both these definitions have analytic utility for the field, Mottl's because it emphasizes the countermovement's relation to the broader social and historico-temporal context and Lo's because it allows one to sort out the players according to which side you find yourself on. Yet neither of them is adequate to fully reflect the temporal dynamic that comes into play as gains are made by any particular movement during the increasing interplay between opposing movements and the state.[5] What is needed is a point of reference from which the determination of whether a movement is "counter" can be made.

Such criteria can be found in Richard Gale's (1986) work on state-movement interactions, because it provides an opportunity to use the state's actions in response to a movement's success – the passage of favourable laws, the increase of social sanction against the movement, etc. – as a crude indicator of the historical and cultural moment in which opposing movements find themselves. Zald and Useem's (1987) work on movement-countermovement interaction provides the same opportunity, as well as stressing the importance of recognizing that a "mobilization and interaction of M/CM must be nested in a historical context" (Zald and Useem 1987, 254). Nonetheless, their starting supposition, "movements of any visibility and impact create the conditions for the mobilization of countermovements," while true enough, makes the labelling process somewhat akin to deciding who threw the first punch and does not account for actual changes that have occurred in the everyday world.

For instance, the current historical moment in British Columbia is one that has seen the legislative expansion and cultural acceptance of gays increase while popular tolerance for the beliefs of the pro-family movement has diminished. Thirty years ago, the reverse would have been true and the FCP would truly have been a countermovement, attempting to resist change. Today, however, *their* situation has reversed because of the successes of the gay rights movement. In the current moment, the FCP in good measure finds itself in the role of the movement, not the countermovement.

In comparing the mobilization capacities of the pro-life and pro-choice movement, McCarthy alludes to this type of role reversal and the mediating function of the state in this process when he writes: "When pro-choice was the movement, rather than the countermovement, before the 1973 Supreme Court decision, it was not, with the exception of a few areas ... a grass-roots movement" (1987, 64).

Of course, these roles could change again – and in fact, for the pro-family movement, they have not entirely changed now – as the next historical moment is approached and entered. The implication is that the use of the term "countermovement" is moment- and standpoint-specific. It can apply to left- or right-wing movements (Lo 1982), and it can be used by one movement to describe its opponent, but, ultimately, the determining factor in labelling must be the historico-cultural moment in which the opposing movements find themselves. To use the term "countermovement" across historical time and through varying cultural and social norms can only result in a situation that calls forth unwieldy terms such as "counter-countermovement."[6]

While the most popular, countermovement is not the only label that has been used to describe conservative movements like the FCP. Jürgen Habermas (1981) has called them "resistance movements" for their attempts to defend traditional conceptions of the social order, and Klaus Eder (1985) has called them a middle-class form of political protest guided by the "petit bourgeois consciousness" that supports "the orthodoxy of the classical ideal of the family, of deterrence and economic growth" (1985, 877-78). They are viewed, in other words, as "moral crusades." The difficulty with this last term is that it is more an ideological than a theoretical definition, and Eder uses it to deny they are social movements:

> The NSMs manifest a form of middle-class protest which oscillates from moral crusade to political pressure group to social movement ... The moral crusade is the form most favored by the petite bourgeoisie. Petit bourgeois radicalism is of a primarily moral nature. The petite bourgeoisie are predestined by their social situation to be protesting moralists ... The point of reference of this protest is the set of moral principles which have become the basis of modernity. The moral crusades of the NSMs are collective reactions to the cultural modernization which has increasingly widened the gap between morality and the lifeworld. (ibid., 888-89)

Habermas's "resistance movement" comes closer to the mark but is not inclusive enough. The FCP is certainly attempting to resist change, but it can also be seen as attempting to promote change, as do other movements of its type. The question here becomes *why* it is trying to effect social change. It must be more than the fear of losing status privilege or experiencing status frustration, since these motives might only lead to attempts to *prevent* social change. To pursue the promotion of social change, the group must be seeking the acquisition of something it perceives as socially good or beneficial – something not currently reflected in the social and political milieu.

In the case of the FCP, this is the pursuit of a value system it is losing *and in some instances has already lost*. The FCP, in fact the entire pro-family movement, is engaged in a kind of cultural reclamation project as it attempts to forestall any further losses and regain lost ground by trying to generate a surge of support among Eder's petit bourgeois. In this sense, the FCP and the pro-family movement can be understood as a subtype of the new social movements, specifically, a *resurgence movement:* a modern movement attempting to resist social change while simultaneously promoting social change by working towards the re-establishment of lost but previously dominant and popularized cultural beliefs.

Introducing this term into the lexicon of social movement taxonomy creates a theoretical space for an organization like the FCP. By extension, the entire pro-family movement can also now be conceptualized and subsequently analyzed as a modern movement, independent of its ideology but not stripped of its privileged social history. So conceived, a movement like the pro-family one can more accurately be assessed not in an absolutist, ahistorical frame that dichotomizes its position into one of either simple dominance or marginalization, but in one that avoids reification by acknowledging that such clearly marked battle lines do not exist in the dynamic arena of modern social struggle.

Of course, at this time resurgence movements are more likely than not to be conservative in nature, but this may not be the case in the future. Should the gains won by various NSMs be eroded as time goes on, then *they* would become the resurgence movements as they try to prevent further erosion of the ground they have won and to gain back lost ground in what is essentially an endless cycle of social movement conflict.

A Sketch of the Pro-Family Movement in British Columbia

Before assessing the FCP for its efforts in framing, mobilization, and political process, it will be helpful to situate it as a social movement organization within the broader pro-family movement industry. To date, the limited work available on the pro-family movement in Canada (Eichler 1986, 1988; Steuter 1992; Erwin 1993) has used REAL (Realistic, Equal, Active, for Life) Women as the dominant example of the movement. Other organizations in the industry have tended to be mentioned only briefly in the main text or documented in a footnote.[7] To build on this valuable work and better understand the movement's full spectrum, these organizations need to be brought from the footnotes fully into the main text so the functional relationships and operative dynamics of this neophyte Canadian movement can be identified for future exploration. Anderson and Langford's (2001) work on the pro-family movement in Calgary, Alberta, stands as one of the few examples of this kind of analysis and supports findings similar to the situation in British Columbia.

In BC, as in the rest of Canada (Steuter 1992), the pro-life movement currently constitutes the core of the pro-family movement. Of fourteen organizations identified as "pro-family" for this book, six of them are also – and primarily – part of the pro-life movement. This is unsurprising in light of the fact that among the supporters of and activists in the two movements, there is an overwhelmingly dominant view that the relationship between being pro-family and pro-life is natural and inevitable. Interview respondents consistently described life as emerging from family and the function of family as being the source and protector of that life. Consequently, it was argued, those who hold a pro-life position naturally extend that to include support for the pro-family movement.[8]

Also, and of particular note, respondents had consistent difficulty identifying specific organizations they considered "pro-family." While pro-life organizations were immediately and accurately identified,[9] pro-family organizations were described in vague terms like "anyone who supports pro-life," church groups, supporters of home-schooling and traditional schooling, groups seeking tax relief for families, and "anyone but the NDP." One activist said of this trend that "pro-life is an important issue, and it can be even with pro-family, but pro-family requires all kinds of definitions which can be hard to articulate. So defining what is the pro-family movement is more difficult to tackle, but being pro-life is a subset of pro-family." Perhaps surprisingly, this trend held even with those interviews done with directors of provincial pro-life and pro-family groups. The only exceptions to this general pattern were the consistent identification of Focus on the Family Canada as a PFM group and the occasional reference to REAL Women. Nonetheless, when prompted, respondents did agree that the following organizations do work towards the promotion of the pro-family agenda in the province: Focus on the Family Canada, REAL Women, the Christian Coalition of British Columbia, Westcoast Women for Family Life, the Catholic Civil Rights League, the Citizens' Research Institute, the Compassionate Health Care Network, the Euthanasia Prevention Coalition of BC, Respect for Life, the Campaign Life Coalition Canada, the BC Pro-Life Society, local right-to-life associations, Birthright, and Vancouver Right to Life.[10]

Excluding the pro-life organizations, the PFM in British Columbia is a relatively young movement. Focus on the Family, the Citizens' Research Institute (CRI), and REAL Women have existed since the mid-1980s, but the Christian Coalition, the Catholic Civil Rights League, and the Euthanasia

Prevention Coalition emerged only in the mid-1990s. Most of the organizations are affiliated with extra-provincial, national, or international parent organizations. This is the case for Focus, an outgrowth of James Dobson's US-based Focus on the Family; REAL Women; Westcoast Women for Family Life, started by those involved with the Alberta Federation of Women United for Families; the Catholic Civil Rights League, operative since 1985 in Ontario; and all the pro-life organizations. The Christian Coalition, the Compassionate Health Care Network, the Euthanasia Prevention Coalition, and CRI all claim organizational independence. Respect for Life is attached to the Vancouver archdiocese and, through that, other Catholic organizations throughout the country.

As a movement industry composed of these organizations, the PFM is best characterized as one that is underdeveloped. Overall, a strong emphasis is placed on organizational autonomy. A general belief exists that the movement is best served by each organization's maintaining its independent focus and that aggregating into a more functionally interdependent organism would be not only strategically damaging but a practical impossibility. The tendency for PFM activists to be independent and strong-minded and the issue of charitable status are cited as the primary reasons for this impossibility.[11] The connection between these organizations is best thought of as a pattern of loose informational relationships with a small degree of board membership crossover and a high degree of personal association or knowledge between organization directors and activists. At times, the organizations do work together or draw on each other's strengths when dealing with particular issues. For instance, a 1996 appellate case in which the province sought to have the ruling that had gutted its bubble zone legislation overturned saw Respect for Life, BC Pro-Life, Campaign Life Coalition, Feminists for Life, and Physicians for Life all act as legal intervenors on behalf of the original defendant.

A similar pattern prevails between provincial and national organizations. While provincial representatives do attend annual general meetings and other special gatherings of the national organizations, for the most part there is a high degree of organizational autonomy and independence. REAL Women, the Campaign Life Coalition, and the Catholic Civil Rights League, for instance, receive little top-down direction other than the requisite maintenance of the organization's principles. Issues of importance are identified and acted upon with local initiative and with little interference from national boards. Inter- and intra-organizational channels of communication seem strong, although there is an underlying opinion that information exchange at this level could be strengthened. As with the provincial situation, interpersonal knowledge of and connections between activists throughout the country appear to provide a strong element of cohesion for the movement.

Cross-nationally with the United States, no formal organizational associations exist at this time.[12] Directors described relationships as friendly but restricted to the informal exchange of information, general developments within the movement, and the occasional use of guest speakers from the US. An experienced pro-family activist perhaps best described the overall nature of intra-provincial, national, and cross-national relationships between pro-family organizations when he said, "We have informal networking with them, we are on the phone with them, and talking about various issues. We often show up at the same meetings or public forums together and we network with other groups in regards to court intervention, in coalition with three or four of them, or alongside them. We call them together in Ottawa and have a conference on these concerns, send each other briefs, that sort of thing."

In calculating their support base, PFM organizations in the province use either direct membership totals or the size of their mailing list. Focus on the Family and CRI, for instance, claim mailing lists throughout Canada that number 145,000 and 80,000, respectively. An activist knowledgeable about Respect for Life, on the other hand, commented that there is no solicitation of members for that organization but the assumption is made that "everyone who is Roman Catholic and goes to church is the membership." The Campaign Life Coalition of BC has a mailing list of 2,200, but this includes churches and other religious organizations that have their own membership base. The Euthanasia Prevention Coalition of BC organizes exclusively around this concept of member organizations. One EPC activist believes there to be "twenty-nine member organizations who could be said to represent maybe 300,000 in BC."

Membership groups were identified as ranging from various religious groups, the Roman Catholic Church, and several secular groups to pro-life organizations such as Nurses for Life. The pro-life movement as a whole (BC Pro-Life, Vancouver Right to Life, etc.) has a membership of around twenty-five thousand province-wide. As a confidential counselling service, Birthright keeps no records of its clients, which would constitute its membership, but the organization does boast a total of 600 centres throughout North America, with 16 of those in BC. Likewise, a member of REAL Women believes its national membership total stands at fifty thousand and the provincial total runs at roughly three thousand. She pointed out that its membership totals "fluctuate quite a bit – it seems that when issues come up that people are shocked by, then they join, but then they let their memberships lapse after two years. It's not so much lack of support, but people not remembering to renew. If you phone them, they remember." The Christian Coalition's membership stands at only three hundred, but, as this is a new organization, past chairman Clyde Vint says it has only just begun a serious membership drive. Westcoast Women for Family Life's membership total also stands in the hundreds, as does that of the Catholic Civil Rights League (CCRL). One pro-family activist had a feeling that the CCRL's membership records were poorly kept but thought there was a total of about five hundred members across the country. Overall, this is a consistent theme for pro-family organizations. In terms of tracking memberships and generating new support, John Hof, president of Campaign Life Coalition BC, captured the situation when he lamented, "We're a very disorganized group."

For the pro-family movement, the mobilizing resources of money and personnel come virtually exclusively from this pool of constituents. Financial resources are claimed to be entirely by individual or organizational donation, membership dues, and the occasional large anonymous donation.[13] Particularly important to the movement as a whole is that each organization operates without any government funding – a source of both pride and strategy for the PFM.[14] Strategically, it is generally felt that to receive such funding would tether the movement to the state, limiting its freedom of activity. As John Hof of Campaign Life puts it, "we receive no government funding. Some say it would be nice, but I'd say it would be a millstone around our neck. I think when you're independent you don't have anyone telling you what you can or can't say." It is also a generally held belief that their opponents – feminist, pro-choice, and gay rights groups, etc. – would be unable to sustain themselves as movement organizations if it were not for the large amount of state funding they receive. One director commented on years of involvement: "It's cost me – we sacrifice a lot in this movement. It's cost me money. If the other side didn't get their funding from the government, they'd soon go away."

PFM organizations take pride in their financial self-reliance, believing that if the playing field were level, their conservative combination of self-reliance and community focus would prevail over the socialist forces of secular humanism. Most of the organizations operate on per annum budgets running from $3,500 for the Euthanasia Prevention Coalition to Respect for Life's $80,000, which is supplied by the Vancouver archdiocese. The archdiocese also donates collections from one day of the year to the pro-life movement, the proceeds of which are divided between the various provincial organizations. CRI's budget is over $100,000, while Focus on the Family's is about $6 million per annum. Although some donations in kind are made on occasion to these various organizations, this is acknowledged as a minor, sporadic, and therefore unreliable type of support.[15]

These organizations are predominantly headed by directors and board members who work on a voluntary basis, except for some who occasionally receive a small stipend. Only Focus on the Family, the Campaign Life Coalition, and Respect for Life have paid directors and/or staff. Organization workers and personnel are also volunteers and are recruited primarily through word of mouth, which is overwhelmingly felt to be the most effective form of recruitment. There exists a chronic shortage of manpower within the entire movement and a pattern of consistently calling upon the same people when an organization is recruiting help to work on a particular issue. Directors consistently cited a rough figure of 10 percent when identifying the proportion of their constituents who are regularly active in the movement. Volunteer recruitment seems best described as haphazard and most concentrated when an organization is actively engaged in promoting or resisting an issue that has arisen. Only three organizations said they try to recruit help on a regular basis, while four said they did no active recruiting whatsoever, preferring, as one director said, to let "people come to us." Expertise in a specific area of activism is accepted when offered; otherwise, it has been developed by individuals within organizations through years of trial and error. One long-time organizer in the movement summed up the human resource situation of the PFM like this:

> We struggle. There's only so many sources for most of these movements, and we find that all these groups are going to be going to the same well for water all the time and there's a limitation on how many people are willing to participate in this even if they're sympathetic to the movement. I think for those who consider themselves pro-life you're lucky to get 5 percent of them active in any way. You might get 15 percent out to meetings once in a while, 35 to 50 percent of them willing to contribute now and then in some financial way or another, either buying a Christmas cake or whatever, but it's because most groups count on the same general population, whether its FCP, Campaign Life, Pro-Life or Citizens' Research. You do struggle, it's a constant battle.

The combined goals of all these efforts are similar to those of other pro-family movements in Canada and the US: the promotion and re-establishment of an ideology valorizing the traditional patriarchal family and defending an unmitigated respect for human life from conception to natural death. Speaking about Focus on the Family, a pro-family activist said it is "primarily concerned with the whole definition of the family, and we see this eroding by various initiatives, or threatened by various initiatives that have come down the legislative road the last few years." One of the Catholic Civil Rights League's objectives is to "continue to defend the traditional family as the basic unit of society" and "make Canadians aware of what is going on" in response to the fact that "the Canadian delegation to United Nations conferences actively promoted pro-homosexuality and pro-abortion policies and is implementing them with taxpayers' money and without the knowledge or consent of the Canadian public or Parliament."[16] The Christian Coalition, meanwhile, seeks to "affirm the value of protecting the sanctity of all human life, from the point of conception to the point of natural death, [and to] represent the pro-family, pro-community point of view before local, provincial and federal governments."[17]

For BC Pro-Life and its forty-five provincial affiliates, Vancouver Right to Life, Birthright, and the Campaign Life Coalition, the first of the Christian Coalition's objectives is the prime concern.[18] The pro-life movement has been described as a "spiderweb with ten arms on it" and as a "body," with BC Pro-Life the head, Campaign Life the legs, and Birthright the heart. Functionally, they each work towards their goal via different avenues. Birthright provides counselling services for expectant mothers and remains staunchly apolitical, maintaining such a low profile that other pro-life activists commented that they often "don't know what Birthright is up to most of the time." BC Pro-Life and its affiliates and Vancouver Right to Life also maintain an apolitical focus with an emphasis on serving as educative bodies that act as information resources. The Campaign Life Coalition is designated the official non-partisan political body of the pro-life movement and as such acts at different times as a direct political lobby group, legal intervenor, evaluator of political candidates, and distributor of political material on the pro-life issues. Meanwhile, Respect for Life pursues a six-point mandate – education, non-partisan political activity, working with social services, engaging with the broader pro-life movement, working with other churches, and dealing with spiritual activity – as it works towards the pro-life goal in a strategy described as proactive because it is not about "waiting for things to happen but rather getting out and getting members involved in the pro-life movement on a regular basis," as one activist says. The Euthanasia Prevention Coalition works to oppose the promotion and legislation of euthanasia and assisted suicide, as well as to promote palliative care for the dying. In its quest, this fledgling organization is also educational and politically non-partisan.

Commensurate with these concerns, however, is an actively sympathetic standing among these organizations for those who are pursuing the broader pro-family agenda. This includes the Citizens' Research Institute, the Christian Coalition, REAL Women, Focus on the Family, Westcoast Women for Family Life, and the Catholic Civil Rights League, all of which refer to the defence of the traditional family as one of their organizational purposes.[19] Directors of all these organizations cited education as their primary strategic initiative, followed by some type of formal or informal political lobbying.

Consensus exists among pro-family activists that the most important step for this conservative resurgence movement is to disseminate information and educate the public, thereby empowering the average citizen to make informed political and social decisions. Increasing awareness among adherents and bystander publics through educational means and extraparliamentary avenues was identified as the primary function of a social movement and the most critical to generating social change. About this, one director commented that the role of his organization is "making sure people have factual information and giving them a licence to use their voices to allow healthy debate to take place. Canadians have to be informed with factual information to make informed decisions rather than just casting ballots. Bad politicians only occur when good people don't cast ballots. There's more to voting than going to the polls and this is a new realization in our psyche." Another argued that before direct political engagement can occur, a base in civil society must be solidified through increasing people's awareness of pro-family issues, and so, "in terms of a specific agenda, it is to build bridges within the community and also with like-minded organizations and religions. It's sort of a strengthening of the flock and then, when we're secure in our faith and identity, then to get out there and bring the faith out into public affairs."

Politically, all the organizations have adopted a non-partisan stance, believing that working within existing parties at the level of the individual politician and concentrating on changing the attitudes of the general voter will prove to be more effective in the long term than backing a single political party. This is despite a belief that mainstream parties and their politicians consistently exhibit opportunism and careerism, and pursue the adoption of social policy by "sniffing the wind," as one activist put it. But this tendency of mainstream parties to maintain power through practices of political populism leaves pro-family advocates feeling that they are without a representative voice that will sustain an uncompromised position on social issues. Clyde Vint of the Christian Coalition, for instance, believes "there are a lot of good Christians in all parties, but unfortunately the mandate of the party doesn't give them a mandate to speak. If the party as a whole doesn't embrace their ideas, then they have no voice."

In part, this seemingly paradoxical situation may be explained by an underlying belief that in spite of any legislative victories, there is an intrinsic impermanence to the political, so significant and durable social change can only come about with an ideological transformation at the level of the individual. As one activist said, Bob Rae's NDP came to power in Ontario and "got loose in the candy store, brought in labour laws and all sorts of things and in the space of four years it's been dismantled. So that indicates to me it's just not a permanent fix, political alignment is not a panacea."

Nonetheless, as an entire movement, the organizations do believe that formal political representation is imperative to achieving their goals. Years of experience working on the pro-life cause have taught John Hof that "there *has* to be a law. Education in the schools is only a part of it ... one reason they haven't been [politically] activated is because they haven't caught the vision of how effective they can be. Christians need to take their responsibility more seriously at election time. They only need to increase their numbers by 5 percent and we could swing an election. They have to be shown that vision." Articulating the paradoxical relationship that both resurgence movements and new social movements have with the state, another director pointed out, "certainly there has to be [formal political representation] because there is still respect for authority in this country, which is good but not necessarily deserving because government has gotten into areas where it has no business. The only way to get out is through the political process. Because these issues have become political, it's been necessary to use the arena to curb them, so it's necessary to have political representation."

The FCP hoped that it would be the manifest vehicle for this vision of necessary political representation and that it would gain the unilateral support of all those in the pro-family movement. Judging by the election results seen in Chapter 1, this clearly did not happen. While the presence of the FCP on the provincial political landscape was regarded as beneficial, or potentially beneficial, to the movement, its utility remained in its movement rather than its party function. Pro-family supporters did not see the party as politically viable even though unanimity existed within the movement that the FCP did offer a unique opportunity to bring up pro-family issues during election times, in a forum where they would otherwise be ignored. Similarly, most felt that the party was another useful pro-family voice in non-election times, a role not typically associated with political parties. Overall, the party was regarded within the movement as valuable but as having neither more nor less potential institutional influence than any other politically focused pro-family group.

On its potential for effecting change as a political party through the legislative and electoral process, opinions ranged from hope to immediate rejection. The most optimistic saw the FCP as an opportunity lying in wait for the moment of critical awareness or cognitive liberation among pro-family supporters. The thought was that should that moment arrive – the realization that other parties will not attend to pro-family demands – and people look to cast their ballot for a party of pro-family principles, the FCP would be there. One long-time activist said the FCP "represents our political aspirations. We have to have a presence, a state of readiness – we have to have that." Another said they would "love to see them become the political arm of a bunch of groups, but pro-life and pro-family groups would have to realize what you can do from a political view versus a societal view." Still another saw their "primary function is one of having faith – the candidates, the issues, and their time will come."

But beyond these words of support, a more critical view of the party's potential could be found. Directors of other pro-family organizations offered some immediate and pragmatic assessments of the FCP's party potential that highlighted the dangers of having a single-issue image and the importance of presenting itself as a party capable of running the province. Clyde Vint, for instance, said, "The FCP needs to educate its people and the people of BC that they can govern the province," and another director expressed concern that "they might be going the wrong way. I question the effectiveness of their strategy. With a pro-life party, you're really developing an isolationist mentality because you put yourself in a corner."

There were also those in the movement who extended this doubt to full rejection. One activist simply stated that the best the FCP could do was "stop being itself – it's just not the way to go. If I was them, I'd have one last pancake breakfast and then take them swimming." Another critic of the FCP's approach said, "It's an issue of tactics – but they can't appoint themselves as the only pro-life, pro-family party in the province. You can't self-appoint yourself and then expect people to vote for you – it's not a moral issue, it's about political freedom."

What is implied in these observations is that, as an organization within the pro-family movement, the FCP's function as part of the overall movement was tentatively accepted, but the utility of its form for opening further political space for promoting awareness of pro-family issues was never acknowledged nor fully appreciated.

This sketch of the pro-family movement in British Columbia exposes several characteristics of the movement that continue to limit its vision in this regard. These include a tactic of maintaining political non-partisanship, an embedded disaffection with mainstream politics, an emphasis on generating awareness within civil society while maintaining a distance from institutionalized politics, and a focus on specific social issues rather than general political and economic concerns. In other words, the very characteristics of this resurgence movement, like those of NSMs in general, prevent a ready acceptance of mobilizing political power through institutionalized forms. As a pro-family organization with a movement function, however, the FCP had not only to address these hurdles on its way to gaining party legitimacy for the PFM, it also had to attend to matters of framing, mobilizing resources, and creating political opportunities.

Selling the Form: The FCP's Framing Issues

Since David Snow et al. (1986) extended Erving Goffman's (1974) work on frame analysis, framing has emerged as a critical aspect of analyzing and understanding the mobilizing potential of social movements. Work in this area (Snow et al. 1986; Snow and Benford 1988, 1992; Klandermans 1984; Benford 1993) has produced a conceptual lexicon permitting study of a movement's efficacy at constructing the meaning of a social grievance in such a way as to garner support for its cause. Originally conceived as such, framing refers to the "conscious strategic efforts by groups of people to fashion shared understandings of the world and of themselves that legitimate and motivate collective action" (McAdam et al. 1996, 6).

At the core of the framing concept is an appreciation that ideas, meanings, and ideology are not passive or impermeable entities *sui generis*, but dynamic constructions constantly being reconfigured in an effort to maintain an understanding of the social world favourable to the experiences and cognitions of a potentially sympathetic target population. David Snow and Robert Benford, for instance, "do not view social movements merely as carriers of extant ideas and meanings that stand in isomorphic relationship to structural arrangements or unanticipated events. Rather, we see movement organizations and actors as actively engaged in the production and maintenance of meaning for constituents, antagonists and bystanders or observers" (1992, 136). Understood this way, master frames, collective action frames, frame alignment processes, vocabularies of motive, and associated ways of conceptualizing aspects of collective belief systems of protest are, as Bert Klandermans notes, "constructed and reconstructed over and over: in public discourse, during the mobilization of consensus, and in the process of consciousness raising during episodes of collective action" (1992, 99).

Implicit in this conception is that nothing can be taken for granted by movement activists. Meanings and values are never static and are constantly vulnerable to the interpretive character of interpersonal communication. This means that cognitive terrains must be battled over and actively pursued through the construction of collective action frames that generate a reality that makes enough sense to people that they will in some way come to actively participate in the movement. About this, Snow et al. warn, "Frame alignment, once achieved, cannot be taken for granted because it is temporally variable and subject to reassessment and renegotiation" (1986, 476).

Dawn McCaffrey and Jennifer Keys (2000) found this to be the case in their study of the rhetorical strategies used by the New York State National Organization for Women. NYSNOW began altering its collective action frame because of opposition by various pro-life organizations, thus providing evidence supporting Snow's warning. Likewise, applying these concepts to the experiences of the Family Coalition Party shows that such framing analysis is particularly helpful in identifying and understanding any movement organization's mobilizing weaknesses, be it a resurgence party/movement or an NSM.

Taking frame alignment for granted was one of the most significant errors committed by the FCP. As Chapter 1 pointed out, the party executive assumed that the party's existence would be enough to gain the electoral support of the pro-family and pro-life constituency in the province. Party membership and electoral results demonstrated otherwise. Simply laying out the welcome mat and waiting for people to knock on the party's door stunted not only the FCP's political potential, but also its movement potential. In Chapter 1, it became apparent that the party never developed a clear vision of who it was and where it wanted to go. The executive's denial of the party's ideological identity and their failure to lay out a specific course of action left the party unable to properly develop a collective action frame that might have appealed to supporters of the pro-family ideal. Party executives stated a clear understanding of this problem. In essence, they said that only by coming to terms with their party's identity – that is, by resolving the debate over being an overtly Christian, pro-life party – could the party hope to proceed with a framing process that might increase its mobilizing and party/movement potential.

Master Frames and Collective Action Frames

The FCP drew its specific collective action frame from a broader master frame guided by a Judaeo-Christian heritage that valorizes traditional family and social orders and above all else the creation and preservation of human life. As conceived by Snow and Benford, the generic function of master frames is to provide a broad orientation of perspective analogous to "linguistic codes in that they provide a grammar that punctuates and syntactically connects patterns or happenings in the world" (1992, 138). For the FCP and the rest of the pro-family movement, the Western Christian ethos provides these linkages and gives its movement organizations a common source to blame for the problems that beset modern society. This "attribution function," as Snow and Benford call it, provides the "interpretive medium through which collective actors associated with different movements within a cycle assign blame for the problem they are attempting to ameliorate" (ibid., 138-39). In the case of the FCP, the breakdown of the traditional family, which in its members' minds has been wrought by gays, feminists, and the general rise of secular humanism, is largely the cause of the social pathologies they see as so prevalent in modern society.

Given the dominance of Christian beliefs in Western society, it would seem that this ethos should provide the movement with an elaborated master frame that would permit it to incorporate a broad range of interests and groups. However, the FCP – and to a lesser degree the entire movement – with its narrow definition of family and protection/valuation of life, ended up creating, to use Snow and Benford's phrase, a restricted master frame. So limited, the FCP cut itself off from the vast number of moderate evangelicals and Christians who might have provided a broader base of support.

The final feature that Snow and Benford identify as having an impact on a master frame's efficacy is its mobilizing potency. Citing the master frame's restrictive or elaborative status and its resonance, they argue that, "hypothetically, the greater the resonance, the more potent the master frame" (ibid., 140). Evaluating potency is a matter of determining the frame's empirical credibility, experiential commensurability, and narrative fidelity. As a whole, the PFM's empirical credibility – "the apparent evidential basis for a master frame's diagnostic claims" (ibid., 140) – appears high. Interview respondents pointed to the breakdown of the family as the cause of current social crises and believed the messages that organizations like the FCP spread were important to remedying this crisis. Experiential credibility also runs high for the movement and the FCP, particularly around issues like taxation, universal daycare, and the Infants Act. Respondents repeatedly cited these as examples of state interference in their daily lives. Finally, the movement's narrative fidelity – "the way the frame strikes a responsive chord in that it rings true with extant beliefs, myths, folktales and the like" (ibid., 141) – also runs high for the movement and the FCP. Respondents point to their families and communities as examples of the benefits of following a Christian lifestyle and have by and large made folk devils out of feminists, gays, and socialists.

Consequently, the master frame of the PFM can be seen to exhibit a high degree of resonance, giving it a good mobilizing potency, which is diminished only by its restrictive character. This assessment also holds for the FCP. As was mentioned in the first chapter, its executive and candidates were told innumerable times, "I agree with everything you stand for, but I can't vote for you." In other words, the FCP enjoyed a solid level of resonance but ultimately little support because of its party form.

According to Snow and Benford's logic, an SMO's specific collective action frames derive from these larger master frames. They have the purpose of generating mobilization for a particular organization within a movement and are the product of three core framing tasks undertaken by the SMO: diagnostic framing, prognostic framing, and motivational framing (Snow and Benford 1988).

It is at this point that the FCP's difficulties with its collective action frame can be clearly seen, particularly in its potential for mobilization. Its diagnostic frame, which "involves identification of a problem and the attribution of blame or causality" (Snow and Benford 1988, 200), is largely satisfactory. The FCP's diagnostic frame is identical to the attribution assessment of the PFM master frame in that it enjoys a high degree of resonance with other movement organizations – there is agreement on what the problem is and who is to blame. By using the idea of a prognostic frame, however, the disagreements between PFM organizations and the FCP can be identified.

This frame "is not only to suggest solutions to the problems but also to identify strategies, tactics and targets. What is to be done is thereby specified" (ibid., 201). It became clear in Chapter 1 that out of frustration and after all other avenues and forms of collective action were exhausted, the party structure was adopted to pursue social change through the direct path of electoral politics. For the FCP, *what is to be done* was to use this form to educate, agitate, cajole, and lobby the public, the government, and other political parties into adopting pro-family ideology and legislation. At the same time, the party believed pro-family forces should cast ballots in its favour during elections in an attempt to elect an MLA or at least to send up a political flare by collecting a large number of province-wide votes.

The pro-family movement in BC, however, utilizes a prognostic frame that advocates an educational and distinctly non-partisan, multi-party approach. This lack of alignment between the FCP and other organizations seemed to carry down to rank and file pro-family supporters, a situation the FCP definitely believed to exist. Joining the FCP and working for or supporting it in some capacity (not simply voting for it in an election) was often not considered a productive use of scarce manpower resources by activists who believe success will be achieved by maintaining a more broad-based, multivalent approach.

Finally, the FCP's efforts at motivational framing, which aimed to transform consensus into action, can also be evaluated. The principal decision confronting the FCP in this regard was whether or not to invoke an overtly Christian vocabulary in the efforts to mobilize support. Some, like the Stilwells, felt such a move could only benefit the party, while others, like the Toths, believed it would severely restrict the FCP's capacity to attract movement and electoral support. It is a situation characterized by Snow and Benford's observation that, "in some instances these components unwittingly render existing frames impotent or the development of new ones particularly difficult" (ibid., 203). This was the Toths' fear as they and the rest of the executive searched to improve this frame and avoid the dangers of such "framing hazards" (Benford 1993).

In the end, the FCP was between a rock and a hard place in this regard. If they had decided to use a Christian vocabulary, they could very well have ended up even more marginalized. Yet because they downplayed this aspect of their identity, their platform was often seen to be a bit disingenuous by those around them.

Frame Alignment Processes and Framing Battles

To construct an effective collective action frame along the three indices above is to ensure that they exhibit an ideological and structural congruence with the extant beliefs of as wide-ranging a pool of potential adherents as possible. Snow and his colleagues have called this a matter of frame alignment, "the linkage of individual and SMO interpretative orientations, such that some set of individual interests, values and beliefs and SMO activities, goals, and ideology are congruent and complementary" (1986, 464). Of the four processes they identify as critical to frame alignment – bridging, amplification, extension, and transformation – the first three hold some relevance for the FCP.

Frame bridging, "the linkage of two or more ideologically congruent but structurally unconnected frames regarding a particular issue or problem" (ibid., 467), is something the FCP engaged in minimally. This concept can be used to see that the error they committed was to assume that ideological and attributional congruence, *ceteris paribus,* was sufficient to mobilize support for their action form (i.e., having party status). Their bridging efforts, in other words, were largely a passive enterprise except during election periods. There was no concentrated effort to try to convince potential adherents that the FCP's party status held extraparliamentary value for the broader movement. Snow et al. identify the targets of frame bridging as those "aggregates of individuals who share common grievances and attributional orientations, but who lack the organizational base for expressing their discontents and for acting in pursuit of their interests" (ibid., 467). The potential PFM adherent pool did not regard the FCP's form as a legitimate vehicle to perform this latter function.

As party activists like the Toths came to realize, what confronted the FCP in its bridging activities was a twofold challenge. They had to use bridging techniques not only to increase their movement profile by reaching out to potential adherents, but they also had to convince this group that their party form was just as valid and effective, if not more so, for performing movement functions as any other organization's structure. This, of course, as the executive well understood, was contingent on the executive's first coming to a decision on whether their primary function would be that of an educational SMO or a party seeking electoral success.

With frame amplification, the FCP was confronted with a large barrier to developing an appealing pro-family movement collective action frame. Snow et al. identify frame amplification, "the clarification and invigoration of an interpretive frame that bears on a particular issue, problem or set of events," as important because "support for and participation in movement activities is frequently contingent on the clarification and reinvigoration of an interpretive frame" (ibid., 468). The FCP was predominantly associated with the pro-life cause. Media, the general public, and other political parties all identified the FCP as the right-to-life party. The value and belief components of this amplification process over-identified the party with the pro-life movement, which concomitantly diminished its broader pro-family agenda. To shift the FCP's collective action frame into closer alignment with the pro-family adherents, the party executive became aware that they needed to not only amplify the frame's broader pro-family character, but also actively engage in a process of what could be called *frame deamplification* whereby its pro-life character held less frame dominance. While this strategy was discussed by the executive, it remained a highly contentious issue for the party. Some members felt this was a strategically necessary step, while others, including the Toths, felt this would dilute the ideological purity of the party.

These acts of amplification and deamplification can be assisted by a frame extension effort, in which "an SMO may have to extend the boundaries of its primary framework so as to encompass interests or points of view that are incidental to its primary objective" (ibid., 472). It may well be that the FCP's primary goal was the legislated protection of life from conception to natural death, but as the Toths and others in the party pointed out, this proved to be insufficient in mobilizing support. They suspected that by actively extending its frame and amplifying its pro-family concerns, the party could broaden its base of potential adherents and improve its overall frame alignment with the PFM.

For instance, several pro-family activists and FCP members pointed to euthanasia as the next pro-life issue likely to concern the general public. They believe that, unlike the abortion issue, which they suspect the general public has tired of, euthanasia has the potential to directly touch people's life experiences in an ever-increasing way, given the aging baby boomer population. They argue that this issue thus has the capacity to reinvigorate support for the movement as a whole. And in terms of frame extension strategies, euthanasia is only one example. Like the Christian right in the US, the FCP clearly had a range of issues to which it could extend its frame: child care, family taxation laws, parental control over education, traditional schools and home-schooling, euthanasia and palliative care, electoral reform, homesteading opportunities for young couples, etc.

While all of these are pro-family concerns, none is inherently linked to a staunch pro-life position like the FCP's and any one of them had the potential to increase the FCP's adherent pool. All of this framing work was something the FCP began to realize it needed to develop aggressively, rather than simply assuming, as it typically did, that individuals will make these connections and efforts themselves. The importance of this task is underscored by Philip Converse's still astute observation that, "for the truly involved citizen, the development of political sophistication means the absorption of contextual information that makes clear to him the connections of the policy area of his initial interest with policy differences in other areas; and that these broader configurations of policy positions are describable quite economically in the basic abstraction of ideology. Most members of the mass public, however, fail to proceed so far" (1964, 246).

Of course, all of these framing efforts are focused on internal considerations and presumed to be socially free-standing, unaffected by external contingencies. Obviously this is not the case. Every social movement interacts within the broader social context of its oppositional movement, the state, and the media, as well as any other supporting or opposing groups or individuals, and this creates an environment where "framing contests" occur (McAdam et al. 1996; Zald 1996). McAdam and his colleagues point out that these contests emerge during later framing stages because if, at the outset, the "political establishment is apt to be either unaware or amused and unconcerned by initial framing efforts, their reaction is expected to change if and when the movement is able to establish itself as a serious force for social change" (1996, 17).

This is the situation the FCP perceived itself to be in. Executives and members hold the opinion that the FCP was so small and ineffective that potential opponents were dismissive of the organization and that this attitude was behind the lack of active resistance to the party's activities. Nonetheless, had they grown – or should the Unity Party yet grow – into a more potent political force, such framing contests would have been inevitable.

These are not so much contests, however, as they are *framing battles*. Social movement theorists have pointed out that during movement-countermovement interactions, each side attacks the other in attempts to simultaneously generate solidarity among movement supporters while discrediting the other side. These rhetorical attempts at what has been called polarization and vilification can be found in arenas as diverse as the abortion debate and the environmental movement (Woliver 1998; Gerlach 1999; McCaffrey and Keys 2000). Additionally, movements engage in what McCaffrey and Keys call frame debunking and frame saving, which capture a movement's efforts to discredit an opponent's frame (debunking) and repair a frame (saving) damaged by that opponent's own debunking efforts.

Keep in mind that these are tactical maneouvres by adversaries, not friendly rivals – the goal is conclusive domination of one opponent over another, rather than just efforts of casual one-upmanship. Such framing battles require developing the skills to manage a dynamic interactive process in which an organization's (in this case the FCP's) *offensive frame* – essentially its collective action frame – is *counterframed* by its opponents in an attempt to generally discredit its message and dissuade potential adherents and bystander publics from mobilizing on behalf of the FCP. (At the same time, these efforts will also constitute attempts to gain active support by this oppositional movement for its own cause.) This counterframing in turn necessitates a *defensive framing* by the FCP in which it attempts to deflect and resist the labels its opponents hope to affix to its public image. These efforts of offensive, defensive, and counterframing are not simply reactive or antagonistic. In equal measure, they are also proactive in their attempts to avoid the damaging effects of an opponent's framing attacks and in their efforts to generate solidarity and new support for their movement.

This is the framing battle that has been under way for years between the pro-life and pro-choice movements. Both groups counterframe the other as an "anti" group, refusing to acknowledge any merit in the other's position in an effort to diminish the potency of their respective offensive frames. Both groups also attempt to resist this label by presenting a defensive frame that broadens the issue from simply fetal status and rights to matters that include individual rights within a democratic polity and socio-moral concerns for the common good of such a society. These acts help diffuse the impact of the counterframe by exposing the connections of the primary framing concern to other less amplified issues that are nonetheless salient and can positively contribute to the public image of the movement.

The pro-family movement in BC appears to be only at the cusp of this kind of framing battle. Still in a predominantly emergent state, the movement has yet to encounter much publicized resistance other than some scattered grumblings about its stands on various issues. For instance, the conflict that arose over the Surrey School Board's banning of several primary-grade books that depict gay family structures (see Chapter 2) did exhibit these framing battle characteristics.[20] Likewise, the Citizens' Research Institute has been labelled anti-gay in the local media and was denounced as such in 1997 by then NDP minister of education Paul Ramsey.[21] It seems a defensive frame has yet to be developed by CRI, other than what may be an attempt to normalize the institute's views. A *Vancouver Sun* article reported that, "the group would help any gay student who was facing discrimination in school."[22]

The impact of such framing battles is not limited to a specific organization. In this instance, the counterframing of CRI as anti-gay, coupled with Heather Stilwell's vote, as a trustee, to ban the books, could easily have had a negative impact on the Family Coalition Party. The web of interpersonal connections, cross-board directorships, and communications networks that provides a movement with much of its infrastructural cohesiveness and micromobilization potential can also act as the conduit through which counterframing efforts against one organization can spread to have an impact on the entire movement. This in turn can have a significantly negative impact on a movement organization's ability to generate the resources it needs to pursue its goals.

Mobilizing Resources and Looking for Political Opportunities

Already hamstrung by its small size, political party form, and restricted master frame, the FCP executive knew they faced a tremendous challenge when it came to securing the resources the party needed. With respect to mobilization, the most formidable challenge they faced was to demonstrate to the party's potential adherents and its supposed natural constituency that its political form could provide a unique and effective movement function for the pro-family cause. Repeatedly, Mrs. Toth tried to highlight that the FCP's form allowed it political access not granted other pro-family organizations. The most prominent example of this, of course, comes during election times, when candidates are able to speak at all-candidates meetings, but less obvious opportunities also present themselves. The FCP's presence at early meetings of the Enterprise League of British Columbia, which aimed to unify right-wing parties in the province, provided an opportunity to lobby for the adoption of the party's core principles. The result of such access was seen in the first chapter. Without the presence of the FCP at these and similar meetings, it is unlikely that Unity would have formally adopted the pro-life and pro-family principles that now characterize this fledging party. For the Toths and others in the FCP, this success was the direct result of their decision to adopt a party form for their movement organization.

In a broader context, the importance to any social movement organization of meeting this challenge to mobilizing resources lies with the link that exists between the legitimacy of an organization's structure and goals and its mobilizing or recruitment opportunities (Snow et al. 1980; Klandermans and Tarrow 1988; McAdam et al. 1996). In other words, a social movement organization relies heavily on its goals in order to foster a healthy interactive relationship with its broader movement environment. This in turn is vital to its resource mobilization activities. What hampered the FCP in this regard was its failure to clearly identify for the broader movement just what its goals were. Unable to do this, the FCP doomed its resource mobilization potential within the movement as a whole.

There is also Zald and Ash's (1966) observation that the viability of a movement increases as different organizations with different functions and strategic initiatives arise. In general, there appears to be no lack of what have been called micromobilization contexts, mesomobilization actors, or recruitment networks (McAdam 1988; Klandermans and Tarrow 1988; Gerhards and Rucht 1992; McAdam et al. 1996) within the pro-family movement in British Columbia. This argument suggests that the PFM has a diverse number of organizations, connections, and activists, but the FCP failed to convince the movement – or the movement itself failed to realize – that a political party form was an equally vital part of this growing viability. Had the FCP created this realization through its framing activities, thereby winning converts to the view that its party form was legitimately congruent with social movement functions, its mobilizing efforts might have been more richly rewarded. That is, its situation supports

Charles Tilly's (1975) observation that the mobilizing potential of a movement organization is limited by its structural features.

It has been noted that efforts to mobilize are in effect attempts at generating solidarity and commitment to the means and goals of the organization (Zurcher and Snow 1981; Jenkins 1983; Borgatta and Borgatta 1992). If this is true, the FCP cadre's commitment to the organization's structure and strategy should have been absolute. Zurcher and Snow point out that, "to be committed in this sense is not only to follow a line of action consistent with the expectations of the movement, but it is to follow a line that rigidly circumscribes or cuts off other possible lines of action ... within most movements there is usually a corps of participants who are devoted to advancing the cause on purely 'moral' grounds. Simply put, they think it is right. They see it as the 'one way'" (1981, 458, 460).

The Toths, the Stilwells, and other long-time executives and supporters of the party constituted this moral core. Theirs was a commitment of resolute dedication that drove their donation of time, money, energy, and other valuable personal resources to the organization's goals. Time, money, and family commitments were all cited among this group as the primary costs of their deep involvement with the FCP and the pro-family movement in general. As Heather Stilwell put it, "when I'm an old woman, I want to be able to say I did what I could. Truthfully, it's not very practical with the family, but the job needs to be done and I can do some of those things."

Yet this kind of dedicated commitment did not extend beyond this core group. While it was enough to have kept the organization alive, the first chapter exposed the executive's awareness that the FCP consistently needed to improve its recruitment efforts, not only for the organization to grow, but also to rejuvenate the spirits of these core constituents. Like others, Heather Stilwell pointed out that "there's not much recruitment. We really need to get into a whole different level of activity – people to do phoning, get out and bang on doors, that sort of thing. It requires a concerted effort and we don't have that level of work available."

That is, the party knew it needed people to *do things* for it: take out a membership, donate some money, make some phone calls to promote its objectives, bring its name up in casual conversations, organize a bake or rummage sale and the like. If we apply Jo Freeman's (1979) division of resources into tangible and intangible, all of these activities require people, the primary intangible resource available to a movement, for the generation of tangible resources such as money, space, office equipment and so forth.

According to Freeman, there are two types of intangible resources people can contribute, specialized and unspecialized, and the FCP was keenly aware it needed both. By specialized resources, Freeman is referring to those skills that activists bring to the movement and help it in specific areas, which may include media relations, fundraising, gaining access to politicians, and intermovement networking. Of particular note in this category is status. The FCP cadre's activist and political past gave the group a wealth of experience in collective action in most of these areas, but as Chapter 1 showed, they knew they desperately needed expertise in the area of governmental policy development because of their party form. The thin policies they developed on health, labour, economics, and other areas were unsatisfactory for mobilizing pro-family political support under the FCP banner, and there was quite simply no one within the party with the necessary skills to guide and develop this area. The executive further identified their own limitations with regard to expertise in media relations, advertising, and membership recruitment. Several of them commented that there was a definite need for the executive to consult with experts on how to effectively pursue these activities.

The importance of status to a movement's mobilizing potential could be emphasized in no better manner than with Bill Vander Zalm's involvement with the FCP. During his time with the party, it enjoyed not only its greatest period of membership growth but also public profile and media coverage. Nonetheless, although Vander Zalm's involvement may overshadow Mrs. Toth's status within the pro-family movement, it must not lead to underestimating it. The immense respect and admiration the pro-family community has for the FCP's founder in fact provided a greater source of mobilization potential than did Mr. Vander Zalm's role. Pro-family activists and FCP members constantly cited Mrs. Toth as a source of inspiration for their continued involvement with the broader movement and/or as their reason for joining the FCP. Such contributions suggest that, as a valuable specialized resource, status can take on different forms and functions. Mrs. Toth gave the organization its principled foundation, everyday work ethic, and long-term vision, all of which helped the FCP project the image of a serious organization that would not squander any resources that potential constituents might have wished to provide.

Mr. Vander Zalm, on the other hand, gave the organization a charismatic and populist presence, as well as linking its political roots with the history of the Social Credit Party in BC. Validating Max Weber's (1946) work stressing the importance of charisma to organizational fortunes, Vander Zalm's involvement demonstrated the mobilizing power that charismatic leadership can bring to a movement. A legitimate authority figure in pro-family work because of his extensive political background, in 1993 Vander Zalm was able to mobilize more support for the FCP in a few weeks than the party had been able to secure over the previous two years. However, this support, or consensus mobilization, did not translate into any significant action. Two of the areas in which the Vander Zalm rallies were held, and the bulk of the 250 memberships taken out, continued to be largely dormant even after 1993. The support attributable to Mrs. Toth, on the other hand, generated a consistent level of action on behalf of the party. These different effects point to a need to distinguish between the different mobilizing functions that status types perform for an organization.

Moving to the source of unspecialized intangible resources, Freeman considers these to be time and commitment, because "any participant could contribute them if so inclined" (1979, 173). These are the resources that the FCP identified as desperately required and for which it needed to develop a strategy for acquiring. Generating *commitment* through the elaboration of its collective action frame was dealt with, but *time* was a different matter. As Oliver and Marwell point out, time is the most precious of resource commodities, "the ultimate resource for collective action. The entire collective action sector is labor-intensive ... the basic production activities always involve people doing things" (1992, 257). The problem for potential constituents, however, is finding the time to work on behalf of the movement. Limited time due to family responsibilities was overwhelmingly the most frequently cited reason for respondents' reluctance to become involved, or more involved, with the FCP.

To help ease this inevitable tension for potential constituents, and to more effectively engage in what Oliver and Marwell call mobilizing technologies, the FCP became aware that it needed to develop active networks of communication and some kind of formal action schedule. The former were already in play with the pro-family movement micromobilization contexts and the FCP's list of some ten thousand people who wished to see a referendum held on abortion funding in the province. This list, with its names, addresses, and phone numbers, is what John McCarthy has called a "thin structure," a list that has "been gathered initially for other purposes" (1987, 59).

But to effectively utilize these microstructures, the party cadre knew it must develop the latter: a specific schedule of activities, jobs, and duties that needed to be done on behalf of the party during a specified period, including but not exclusive to election times, along with the demands of each task. They recognized in their own way that "a lot of technological knowledge about mobilizing volunteer time is about organizing and dividing labor and structuring events and jobs so that people can be invited to participate in well-defined and limited ways" (Oliver and Marwell 1992, 266). Darren Lowe, past president and executive member, stressed the importance of having such an understanding. Commenting on how to get people involved, he said, "I think it helps to have specific jobs for people to do. You give people small, manageable projects to work on. If you have someone who wants to be an activist and there is nothing to do, they will drift off into something else." And this is the type of specialized knowledge that years of activism should have allowed the cadre to gain. What is involved, for instance, in phoning to solicit new memberships or renew old ones, or the time necessary to organize an information campaign on a particular pro-family issue, are vital ingredients this group should already have gathered from past experience. This is what they were trying to pass on through strategies like Darren Lowe's.

The actual mobilizing technologies utilized by the FCP were typically unremarkable and fell within the types described by Oliver and Marwell: annual general meetings, auctions, calls for donations through newsletters, requests for assistance on special projects, small social gatherings to generate funds, and similar activities. Most donations of time or money outside such activities tended to be small in nature, most of the people who turned up or helped out at FCP events tended to be the same ones, and most of these events are similar to those held by other movements. It is a situation summed up by Oliver and Marwell this way: "Volunteer activists try to think up new attractive events or execute the ritualized ones well. They mobilize through the people they know: the same people go to the same events, and they exchange the currency of mutual obligation – I went to your event, so you come to mine ... This is not the stuff of transcendent social change ... This is the world as it looks most of the time" (ibid., 270).

In this regard, the FCP was no different from any other pro-family movement organization or any other organization in the entire social movement sector. The difficulties of mobilizing resources are ubiquitous, the work mundane. To complicate matters, the FCP compounded this challenge by choosing an organizational form it hoped would provide the entire pro-family movement with a legitimate political access point that had been unavailable since Bill Vander Zalm's days with the Social Credit Party.

Creating a Political Opportunity
The deliberate adoption of an institutional form for the FCP was an attempt by its founders to establish a political beachhead that they hoped would provide the pro-family movement with an alternative form of political opportunity to those already available. It was a tactical decision that implied these other forms of political access had proven inadequate, at least in the eyes of the FCP members, for effecting the social change they were pursuing.

The unresponsiveness of the government and other provincial political parties to the pro-family concerns of the FCP, as the first chapter made clear, was the very reason for the party's existence. Although British Columbia's parliamentary system has various mechanisms in place that movement organizations can use to access the policy-making process – opportunites for legal intervention and presentations at standing committees and policy review boards, for instance – supporters of the FCP found these avenues to be largely dead ends. Working from within other political parties also proved to be frustrating and fruitless. The structural dynamics of the current party system in British Columbia (and Canada) makes it virtually impossible for a cause to be promoted and supported within that party without the support of the party leader and executive board. For instance, as Chapter 1 revealed, this became obvious to the Toths, the Stilwells, and others when changes took place in the Social Credit Party. It is a situation that has been described elsewhere, one in which formal policy access has not translated into substantive policy gains for the movement in question (Jenkins 1983; Rochon and Mazmanian 1993).

This situation was further accentuated when the NDP government replaced elected members of hospital boards with government-appointed ones.[23] In pursuing this action, then Minister of Health Joy MacPhail was quoted as saying: "In the communities where certain special-interest groups have made it their goal to impose an anti-choice point of view, those communities' activists were not put forward to be appointed to the board. Basically, everybody on the board was required to support our government's view that all legitimate health-care services, including therapeutic abortion, be provided."[24] Until this time, elected hospital boards had been a prime site of political opportunity for the pro-life movement in BC, but with this change, one more leverage point that the movement could use was eliminated. With available routes of opportunity like this one being closed off and others consistently failing to be effective, the FCP drew a simple conclusion: British Columbia lacked effective structures of political opportunity that could be exploited to promote its cause.

Since Peter Eisinger (1973) operationalized the term "structure of political opportunities" to emphasize the impact of political climates and structures on the development and mobilization of movements, the bulk of this type of macrostructural analysis has focused on systemic facilitation. McAdam, McCarthy, and Zald's definition reflects this analytical trend when they write: "By structure of political opportunities we refer to the receptivity or vulnerability of the political system to organized protest by a given challenging group" (1988, 699). The important work that has taken this path includes that by Eisinger (1973), Gamson (1975), Jenkins and Perrow (1977), and Piven and Cloward (1977). Their commonality lies in the emphasis they place on the importance of recognizing the influence political and state variables can have on the emergence and potential success of a movement.

What is problematic about this approach, however, is that it hides the dialectical relationship that exists between a movement and the state, risking a view of the movement as a strictly passive actor in this process. Consequently, the possibility that a movement might be able to create its own political opportunity also tends to remain hidden. Nonetheless, this work does make the critical point that social movements are eminently political and, as Sidney Tarrow points out, "what has been learned about the importance of political opportunities and the links between the social movement sector and politics suggests that both individuals and organizational choices are conditioned by the political process" (1988, 435).

Political process theorists (Tilly 1978; McAdam 1982; Kitschelt 1986; Tarrow 1983) have built on this tradition and expanded it to include a sensitivity to the historical moment and the structural opposition that movements generally face. McAdam's description of political opportunity structures broadens to accommodate these recognitions: "By 'structure of political opportunities' we mean the distribution of member support and opposition to the political aims of a given challenging group. Characteristically, challengers are excluded from any real participation in institutionalized politics because of strong opposition on the part of most polity members. This unfavourable structure of political opportunities is hardly immutable, however ... Challenging groups can count on facing very different levels of support and opposition over time" (1988, 128).

Certainly this reflects the experiences of those involved with the FCP. Under Bill Vander Zalm, political opportunity existed within the Social Credit Party for pro-family activists to at least have some institutionalized representation for their concerns, but with the elimination of the Christianity clause and the announcement by then Premier Rita Johnston that the party was pro-choice, this political access point disappeared.

It is a scenario similar to McAdam's description of the impact the Nixon presidency had on the political opportunities the gay rights movement had enjoyed to that point in the US. He writes that the movement was "preceded by a highly significant electoral realignment that can only be seen as disadvantageous to gays ... If anything, then, it would appear as if the movement arose in a context of *contracting* political opportunities" (McAdam 1996, 32). Yet these political opportunities seem to have expanded once again. Werum and Winders' study of gay rights activism in the US from 1974 to 1999 indicates that "gay rights proponents increasingly succeed when using central governmental channels (legislature, courts) which remain contested" (2001, 386).

At the other end of the ideological spectrum, the experiences of the New Christian Right in the US are similar. Green et al. (2001) note that, despite variations in success, this movement has been most active where the political opportunities were most readily accessible. However, nothing is permanent when it comes to state-controlled political opportunities. As Vernon Bates (2000) argues, for instance, efforts by the Oregon Citizens Alliance, a New Christian Right lobbying organization, were seriously hampered because of a diminishment in the political opportunity structures available to it.

This permeability of the state in terms of political opportunities for collective action by movements has been described as a cycle of thawing and contraction (Tarrow 1983) and the opening and closing of political space (Gamson and Meyer 1996), but as Gamson and Meyer point out, these historical patterns are more dependent on the volatile, as opposed to stable, aspects of political opportunity. These volatile elements, "shifting with events, policies, and political actors ... are at the heart of explanations of mobilization and demobilization that emphasize the interaction between movement strategy and the opening and closing of those oft cited windows of opportunity" (1996, 277). Again, the diminishing opportunities of those who founded the FCP are well captured. Micro events such as these were responsible for closing this window of opportunity, but it is at the macro level – the stable elements of political opportunity, as Gamson and Meyer call them – that the reason for the FCP's form can be found.

Cross-national observations and studies have highlighted the important role a nation's political structure plays in the development of movement activists' attitudes and strategies, as well as an organization's political opportunities (Nelkin and Pollak 1981; Kitschelt 1986; Klandermans and Tarrow 1988; Kriesi 1996; McAdam et al. 1996). In his study of the antinuclear movement in four countries, Herbert Kitschelt concluded that "the mobilization strategies and impacts of social movements can, to a significant degree, be explained by the general characteristics of domestic political opportunity structures" (1986, 84).

Christopher Soper's (1994) comparative study of the pro-life movement in Britain and the US amply demonstrates this point. He notes that while "the market for conservative morality" was virtually identical in the two countries, the New Christian Right in America has enjoyed far greater success at influencing policy than evangelicals in Britain because of differing state systems. The British organizations, he notes,

> were frustrated in their efforts less by their lack of size than by the absence of support from key political elites and the paucity of opportunities for meaningful activism which their political system afforded them. The British state dominate the policymaking process on abortion, which meant that pro-life groups could not succeed against state resistance and without state support. With its concentration of power in the hands of the Prime Minister and Cabinet, Britain's parliamentary regime placed few obstacles to abortion reform if the Conservative Party leadership had political or ideological reasons to support them. (1994, 130)

Canada's and British Columbia's parliamentary systems, born of the British Empire as they are, present the same obstacles to the pro-family movement as those experienced by the pro-life movement in Britain.

Conversely, "America's weak state allowed them [the NCR] direct access to the policymaking process at local, state and national levels. It became apparent in the aftermath of the Roe decision that the national state did not have the capacity to impose policy coherence on abortion, a sign of state weakness which provided pro-life groups the opportunity to organize their efforts against a number of state officials and institutions" (ibid.). Because of the permeable nature of the American state and the good political opportunities it provides, the American pro-family movement has been able to mobilize within the Republican Party with sometimes striking effectiveness. The structure of the American political system is such that pro-family forces are able to develop mobilizing strategies that use various lobby groups and political action committees and target the GOP as their sole point of political access and influence.

Meanwhile, the pro-family movement in Canada continues to face a political structure that concentrates state and party power to such a degree that any available political opportunities turn into mirages of political access. Yet the predominant strategy continues to be a multi-party, non-partisan approach to gaining political access and influence. In response to this chronic situation, the founders of the FCP decided to create their own space of political opportunity by taking on the institutionalized form of a political party.

The challenge faced by the FCP once it made this decision was to convince others in the movement that its party form was a legitimate vehicle for pursuing these demands. This was an effort characteristic of what Rochon and Mazmanian suggest when they write that "the task of any social movement may be that it takes an unlikely idea, makes it seem feasible, and then puts it into practice" (1993, 87). This implies that the FCP, and indeed the entire movement, had to acknowledge three specific things.

First, the pro-family community needed to recognize the benefits that an institutional party form had for creating political opportunity. As David Meyer put it regarding the peace movement, "opportunities are not opportunities unless perceived as such" (2000, 46). Second, there is a tendency among movement activists to overestimate the degree of political opportunity available to them (Gamson and Meyer 1996). This is very true of the PFM as a whole. For instance, despite pointing to and supporting pro-life and pro-family politicians in various parties, the movement appears to have placed too much faith in the power of these politicians to achieve any of the real change it is seeking from within these existing parties. Third, the FCP itself needed to determine its primary function and goal – social movement or electoral party.

With various levels of awareness, those involved with the FCP seemed to have an understanding of all these points. That is, they knew they had to convince those in the broader movement, and some in the party itself, that form need not dictate function.

That the FCP failed in this regard is not entirely of its own doing. The pro-family movement as a whole seems not to have understood that, as Sidney Tarrow notes, "protesting groups can increase their opportunities by expanding the repertoire of collective action into new forms" (1996, 58). Had the broader movement recognized this, and had the FCP been more effective in its framing efforts, the possibility for viewing an organization like the Family Coalition Party as a viable and legitimate addition to the pro-family movement industry as a whole may well have emerged. In turn, this would have improved the mobilizing potential and survivability of a party/movement like the FCP.

This failure of the PFM is linked to the typical assumption regarding what forms parties and movements should take in their efforts, but if form and function are separated, then the FCP can be understood to be a social movement organization working towards social movement goals. It must also be remembered that this was a resurgence movement *reluctantly* cum political party – one of its principal aims was to have its beliefs adopted by another political party so it could disband the FCP as a political entity. As Alan Scott argues, this idea of disappearance as movement success is a valid one: "'Success' takes the form of integrating previously excluded issues and groups into the 'normal' political process ... Success is thus quite compatible with, and indeed overlaps, the disappearance of the movement as a movement" (1990, 10). When the FCP merged to form the Unity Party of BC, its success did indeed lay in its disappearance.

What remains to be seen, however, is whether or not this is in fact a victory for the FCP. Certainly some of the FCP's goals were achieved: it was able to merge into a larger political party with its core pro-family and pro-life principles intact; with this platform, the Unity Party did receive over 3 percent of the popular vote in BC's 2001 provincial election, more than triple what the old FCP was able to generate in any of its campaigns; and there is a strong FCP contingent among the Unity Party membership and on its executive board.

Despite these early signs of success, the Unity Party is still very much a fledgling and marginal political party in the province, and as the first chapter argued, at this point there is little reason to believe it will move beyond this status. Should this be the case, the movement efforts of the FCP activists will indeed have failed. For the FCP, the goal of a merger was to become part of a larger party that has real access to the political process. If Unity remains on the political fringe, it will be no more helpful to the pro-family movement in the province than the FCP, and in some ways it will be significantly less helpful. The Unity Party, after all, is not a party/movement the way the FCP was. It is clear that the primary goal of Unity is to win political office and be a mainstream political party. Advancing or even representing the goals of the pro-life and pro-family movement in the province seem to be regarded as almost counterproductive to the party's electoral goals.

As the next chapter will show, this is a situation that worries a number of FCP supporters. Because Unity supports the idea of public referendums on social policy and downplays the pro-life principles of the party, FCP members fear that it will devolve into nothing more than, as one member put it, "a typical power-hungry party without principles." If this happens, the FCP as a party/movement will have disappeared along with its goals.

Nonetheless, as a conservative resurgence movement working towards this merger, the FCP faced the same organizational problems that any movement faces in terms of developing an effective collective action frame, mobilizing resources, and finding political opportunities to exploit as it pursues its goals. Additionally, in taking the bold step to create its own political opportunity through adopting an institutionalized party form, the FCP compounded the challenges and obstacles it faced. Over the years, it became apparent to the executive that it needed to manage not only the difficulties associated with functioning as a social movement, but the challenges of convincing pro-family activists that its form offered a legitimate opportunity of political access for the entire movement. In part, this involved persuading pro-family activists that the movement's interests would be better served by abandoning their strategy of non-partisanship and adopting a deliberately partisan stance through the FCP.

To win this argument, the FCP executive came to realize that they must attend to the popular expectations that accompanied its form. Despite its function as a movement, the FCP was a formal provincial political party in British Columbia. When it was registered as such in June 1991, the FCP became a potential representative body for those who would cast a vote in its favour, and, for the voter, governmental representation includes far more than support for pro-life and pro-family issues. Like the many minor parties that have preceded it, the FCP was faced with some formidable obstacles if it was to be accepted as a legitimate political entity within the institutionalized realm of provincial politics. The next chapter will turn to understanding the FCP as a minor political party in British Columbia and the challenges it was confronted with in terms of the confines of the Canadian political system and the expectations of Canadian political culture.

4
The Function of Form:
Family Coalition as a Political Party

When the founders of the Family Coalition Party chose to construct a political party in their attempt to create a political access point for the pro-family movement in British Columbia, they also brought upon themselves the popular and systemic expectations that accompany such an institutional form. Most important is the reasonable assumption that registered political parties set as one of their primary goals the attainment of legislative office for the purpose of representing the broad spectrum of political wishes held by those who voted for the party during an election. Systemically, political parties, unlike social movement organizations, are required to abide by a rigorous set of mandates and formal procedures, usually set out in some type of Elections Act.

For a small party with a narrow-issue focus like the FCP, the cultural and structural challenges these expectations present can be formidable. With limited resources and political expertise at their disposal, in addition to a sometimes questionable commitment to the ultimate goal of actually attaining political power, small political parties in Canada generally find it difficult to gain not only electoral support from their supposed natural constituencies, but political legitimacy for their cause in general.

Despite these obstacles, the Family Coalition Party became part of the long political bloodline of minor political parties in Canada. At both the federal and provincial levels, Canadian political culture has been characterized by the presence of minor political parties. Federally this has existed from the time of the Progressives in 1921 and continues most recently with the emergence in the 1980s and 1990s of the Bloc Québécois and the Reform/Alliance Party. Provincially, William Aberhart's Social Credit League of the 1930s in Alberta represents one of the most successful efforts by a minor party to succeed politically, while the Toth's Family Coalition Party in BC represents one of the most recent efforts. The focus of this chapter is to explore the challenges and benefits created by a party/movement such as the FCP in joining the ranks of the Co-operative Commonwealth Federation (CCF), the Social Credit Party, the Green Party, and others.

Political scientists have argued that the consistent presence of these minor parties signals a chronic deficit in the representative capacity of parliamentary democracies like Canada's. This is generally regarded as a crisis of representation, a situation that leaves average Canadians few opportunities to exercise their political will or even have their interests properly articulated by major parties. This crisis, scholars argue (Covell 1991; Phillips 1996; Tanguay and Gagnon 1996), has led not only to a rise in minor parties, but also to other forms of extraparliamentary representation, including new social movements. This dynamic is at work both federally and provincially. Major parties are being seen as increasingly dysfunctional and unable to satisfactorily aggregate and represent an ever-increasing number of interests. Consequently, there is growing support for abandoning the Westminster model in favour of some type of proportional representation system that would loosen the current stranglehold of elite parties on Canada's political process.[1]

The Political Representation of Issues:
Is the Party at Westminster Over?

The term "democracy" often evokes the ideal vision of full citizen participation in the political process. Images of the Greek polis alive with debate over the daily concerns of ancient city-states come to mind as we ponder the democratic process. Yet in modern liberal democracies like Canada's, sheer geographic mass and population size prevent the practical implementation of any such kind of direct democracy. David Elkins points out that there is an "impossibility, on practical grounds, of direct democracy in countries ... Hence, one has to delegate authority to representatives who can, for a period of time, speak on behalf of those too numerous to attend the place where decisions are made" (1991, 16). It is this delegation of political authority that provides the cornerstone of what is commonly understood in Canada as representative democracy. And as Elkins continues, this issue of political representation is fraught with argumentative questions surrounding who should qualify as a representative, on the basis of what authority this role is bestowed, and what types of issues should be represented.

Given that a primary aim of liberal democracies like the ones in Canada and Britain is maintaining social stability and order, there is an inherent conservatism to the political systems of both countries. To grasp the historical depths of this still pervasive character, it is once again useful to return to the work of Edmund Burke.

Sitting as a member of Parliament in the House of Commons for close to thirty years, Burke had the opportunity not only to comment on the issue of political representation but to act on those beliefs.[2] Supportive of political and social orders based on traditional hierarchies, Burke considered classical democracy an anathema and opposed any notions of political representation based on direct citizen participation (Kornberg et al. 1982). According to Francis Canavan, political authority was for Burke correctly understood as a delegated authority "set in the framework of the Christian doctrine of creation," for despite the social contract basis of government, "God, as the Creator of human nature, is also the ultimate author of the state" (1987, 117). Burke believed the proper recipients for this mantle of divinely ordained authority were those demonstrating a strong capacity for exercising solid reasoning and judgments that would benefit the whole of society. Michael Freeman (1980) argues that Burke had in mind here citizens of high social status, education levels, and occupations that promoted the development of leadership qualities, such as landowners, merchants, professors, and clergy.

What emerges with these points in Burke's prescription for the exercise of good government is a belief that political inequality is a natural and desirable feature for democratic societies and that there exists a natural and traditional ruling class. Burke's advocacy for this type of elitist democracy has at its root a deep commitment to the belief that only the virtuous and wise members of the aristocracy have a true understanding of the function of government and its relation to those it represents. In an oft-quoted passage from a speech in 1774, Burke commented that the function of Parliament "is not a congress of ambassadors from different and hostile interests; which interests each must maintain, as an agent and advocate, against other agents and advocates; but parliament is deliberative assembly of one nation [sic], with one interest, that of the whole; where, not local purposes, not local prejudices ought to guide, but the general good, resulting from the general reason of the whole" (quoted in Eulau 1978, 113).

This vision demanded, Burke believed, that reason triumph over will in matters of political decision making, and that representatives, although acting on behalf of their constituencies, must nonetheless be free to act on their own judgments, regardless of constituency opinion. "This right and duty of the Member of Parliament," Michael Freeman observes, "to follow his independent judgement against the wishes or instructions of his constituents is one of Burke's most famous doctrines ... it is often cited today, typically with approval, when similar problems of the relation between M.P. and his constituents arise" (1980, 124).

To pursue these duties effectively and to protect "honest men" from the potentially corrupting effects of extraparliamentary influences, Burke became a reticent supporter of the political party.[3] Burke thought of a political party as "a body of men united, for promoting by their joint endeavours the national interest, upon some particular principle in which they are all agreed" (quoted in Macpherson 1980, 23). Burke believed that in this manner parties could successfully represent the populace and work towards the common good of society, so long as their members had the individual freedom to exercise their good judgment. Yet despite his recognition of parties as necessary and potentially beneficial to the political process, Burke was not a strong defender of them, seeing in them the potential danger of usurping this political freedom. Grant Amyot (1996), for instance, argues that Burke's position on this has no room for the strong party disciplines exhibited by today's modern parties.

It should also be noted that Burke opposed the democratic reform movement of the eighteenth century, which sought to bring a greater degree of representation to the majority of Britons, who were underrepresented in the House of Commons. As Michael Freeman argues, Burke considered "reform ... not merely unnecessary, it was fraught with great peril ... the system worked and most of the people were satisfied with it" (1980, 127). Such opposition was likely a product of Burke's concern with the potentially destabilizing effects on the social order in increasing the opportunities for direct democratic participation by the masses, as well as his trenchant belief in the merits of maintaining a hierarchical political and social order.

After more than two hundred years, many of these issues still characterize the political process. Certainly Burke's concern with political parties stifling the individual freedom of politicians has persisted. As Chapter 1 pointed out, members of the Family Coalition Party routinely expressed frustration at the consistent party suppression of individual pro-life politicians. Governments and major parties have also been reluctant to support any initiatives seeking to increase the participation of the average citizen.

In Canada, though, perhaps the most significant testimony to the durability of Burke's political philosophy on representation is the socioeconomic makeup of the House of Commons in Ottawa. Despite attempts to make the House more reflective of the nation's social character and the ideal vision that a "representative should be a member of the group represented, should share personal and social characteristics with those represented" (Elkins 1991, 18), a study by Guppy et al. (1987) concluded that, historically, members of Parliament, and overwhelmingly those in cabinet, have backgrounds of high social status and education and occupational status.

Mainstream Parties Today: No More "Loose Fish"

In Canada, as in other Western liberal democracies, political parties have developed into sophisticated, disciplined organizations that claim the virtually exclusive right to represent a nation's citizens politically. While Burke might have favoured the predominantly upper-middle-class character of Canada's House of Commons, the limitations that today's strict party discipline places on members' freedom to vote according to their individual judgment would surely exemplify the inherent dangers he saw in the adoption of a strong party system. Under the Westminster first-past-the-post electoral system, modern political parties in Canada reflect just such a disciplined rigour. In its defence, advocates argue that only through a strong party system can the diverse range of issues that characterize heterogeneous societies like Canada's be effectively aggregated and represented. Opponents deny this, claiming that modern party dynamics concentrate power in the hands of leaders and other party elite, thereby denying the opportunity for viable representation of issues beyond those deemed important by a party's executive.

Canada's parliamentary parties did not take on the current disciplined form until late in the nineteenth century. Before that, party processes and election dynamics reflected a more Burkean tradition based on the freedom of the individual politician. Elected candidates often aligned themselves not based on party loyalty but on the basis of which party or "leadership clique" promised to win material benefits for the candidate's constituency (McMenemy 1976b).

This problem of "loose fish," as Sir John A. Macdonald called them, was a product of the fact that the precursors of Canadian political parties were loosely knit coalitions of local leaders representing the local concerns of the dominant class (Covell 1991; Lyon 1992). Originally held together by various acts of overt patronage, the class-based character and regional power bases of these early coalitions still exist within the major parties today. For example, the Liberals and Conservatives continue to find their support among the economic elite of central Canada, while Reform/Alliance finds its support all but entirely in western Canada. In fact, the history of the development of Canadian political parties is in many respects a reflection of Antonio Gramsci's observation that, "if it is true that parties are only the nomenclature for classes, it is also true that parties are not simply a mechanical and passive expression of those classes, but react energetically upon them in order to develop, solidify, and universalise them ... Classes produce parties, and parties form the personnel of State and government, the leaders of civil and political society" (1971, 227).

Regardless of such class bias or regional origins, modern parties must still fulfill two primary functions within the Canadian polity: the aggregation of diverse interests and the institutionalized representation of those interests. These responsibilities, beyond any others, are widely understood and accepted to be the primary functions of any legitimate political party (Covell 1991; Chandler and Siaroff 1991; Lyon 1996; King 1969). Modern parties are also generally held to the Burkean expectation that their representation will reflect a responsibility to the needs of the entire provincial or national community, not simply factional interests (Lyon 1992). This expectation is of course compounded should the party form the government, since then, as John McMenemy points out, "the parliamentary system requires the governing party to act in the name of the crown and be responsible to the legislature rather than to act in the name of ... a party convention" (1976c, 102, 103).

Beyond representation and aggregating interests, Anthony King (1969) identified five other general functions performed by mainstream political parties in liberal democracies. As they perform these functions, King makes the important observation that "parties and party systems play a large part in creating and maintaining the political culture and political structures which characterize political systems as a whole and in the context of which particular situations develop" (1969, 118). With this in mind, it is worth briefly reviewing what King described as these "alleged functions of party" and their potential impact on a polity (ibid., 120).

Structuring the vote is the first function King identifies, which he equates with opinion structuring and what Vaughan Lyon means when he notes that parties "exist to persuade people to accept their definition of what is good for the community" (1996, 534). Should a party prove successful in this task, it would expect to be rewarded at the ballot box.

Next King discusses the *integration and mobilization function* of parties. These are the acts of political socialization by which people come to develop psychological and social attachments to parties. In this regard, John McMenemy observes that "parties acquire potent institutional memories and socialize new generations of members and supporters to the myth of the group" (1976b, 10). If parties are performing these functions effectively, partisan activity on their behalf should remain constant or increase as the myth is embraced.

Leadership recruitment is a function King sees parties as deeply implicated in, given that leaders are elected through parties, though he also questions the importance of their role in *actually* recruiting them by suggesting that extraparty influences often play a dominant role in the selection process.

The *organization of government* and *policy formation* are two other functions King believes parties have been overly implicated with. Although parties that have formed the government are in a position to alter some aspects of the parliamentary system, this is really the responsibility of the government acting on behalf of the Crown, rather than the party acting on behalf of its supporters. In terms of policy formation and influence, King also argues that parties tend to take policy stances, but this does not necessarily mean that the party itself developed the policies it is seen to support. The idea here is that parties sometimes adopt policies due more to external social or political pressures than internal development and desire.

Canadian political parties, federal and provincial, claim to perform all of these functions in their quest to gain access to the halls of legislative power. Yet it must be remembered that the execution of these functions is not free of structural constraints. Just as King observed that parties assist in the creation and maintenance of the political system in which they exist, so too does the system influence the character and actions of the party (Chandler and Siaroff 1991). In fact, it may well be argued that this dialectical relationship between parties and the electoral system has a greater and more immediate impact on the nature and fortunes of a party than on the structure of the political system itself. Rejean Pelletier (1996), for instance, argues that the concentration of power in the hands of a party's leader and its executive elite is a direct result of Canada's adopting Britain's Westminster parliamentary system, which sought to transfer power from the monarch directly into the hands of the prime minister rather than to the legislature. Also, the shift in 1878 from an open to a secret ballot vote for general elections (McMenemy 1976b), combined with a simple first-past-the-post electoral system, had the eventual effect of casting a tight party net around those "loose fish." These changes effectively made the party, rather than the individual candidate, the central figure in the election process.

In summarizing Canada's Westminster-style parliamentary system, Chandler and Siaroff (1991) identify the following seven structural features: general elections central to the determination of government; a majoritarian, first-past-the-post electoral system; a predominantly although not exclusively two-party system in which these two parties alternate in power; government by a one-party cabinet; a powerful prime minister; a weak legislature; and a formal opposition that has little input in governmental policy formation and implementation.

In making this assessment, Chandler and Siaroff make three observations that are critical to the issue of effective political representation in Canada. First, they note that while this system provides a "strong institutional basis for party government ... parties themselves are not organizationally strong, and *lack deeper penetration into civil society*" (1991, 209-10; emphasis added). Second, the "system dynamics and party discipline" the Westminster model demands "ensures that individual deputies are constrained in their behaviour and have little policy influence" (ibid., 202). In other words, individual legislative members are forced to toe the party line rather than act on behalf of the wishes of their constituencies. Finally, they remark that "the Westminster version of party government does not require a perfect two-party system" (ibid., 200). The important implication here is that while Canada's political history has been dominated by the exchange of power between the Liberals and the Conservatives, there is room for the existence of other parties without jeopardizing the stability or functioning of the entire system.

Excluding their last point, Chandler and Siaroff's analysis, like King's and Burke's before them, suggests not only that political parties may not be the best of representative vehicles for democratic societies, but that the Westminster system itself may make things even worse. These are all parts of the debate that has been growing for some years over the representative efficacy of parties and the political system in Canada. Post-material Canadian society, with its emphasis on identity and issue politics, is a long way from the politics based on principle that characterized the parties of Burke's day. Increasing numbers of groups have been seeking alternative forms and forums to represent and articulate their interests as mainstream political parties remain unable or unwilling to perform these functions for such groups. This has led to what is now commonly referred to by political scientists as the decline of parties (Meisel 1985) in Canada and other liberal democratic societies.

A Crisis of Representation: The Decline and Transformation of Mainstream Parties

The popular tendency to view politics, parties, and politicians with cynicism and distrust is so extensive in Canada that this perception has become a truism. The electorates' disaffection from mainstream political parties and politics is deep and pervasive, penetrating federal and provincial levels, as it has in other democracies such as Britain and Germany (Braunthal 1996; Amyot 1996).

Opinions held by members of the Family Coalition Party reflected this trend. Asked to give a definition of the function of political parties, a vast majority offered a two-part answer. In terms of an ideal type, they defined parties as political organizations with a mandate to govern the nation or province in the best interests of all its citizens while its members simultaneously represent their constituents in a conscientious and accurate fashion. They added, however, that in reality parties and politicians are power-hungry and opportunistic, willing to say anything, during an election, to win office, after which they either ignore the wishes of their constituents or are forced to toe the party line.

The crisis of legitimacy reflected here is born largely out of the inability or unwillingness of parties to effectively aggregate and then represent the ever-increasing diversity of interests in post-industrial societies. As Ronald Inglehart (1977) has pointed out, modern democratic societies are increasingly characterized by populations embracing post-material values – those beyond the basic material necessities of sustenance (economic growth and stability) and safety (social order and national security). The politics of identity and involvement that form the base of many new social movements revolve around the set of post-material values that emphasize quality-of-life issues (environment, peace, gender and sexual equality, and leisure) and the importance of direct participation in the political process. This last point has proven particularly troubling for political parties, as their structural constraints and historical patterns of interest intermediation have prevented them from accommodating this demand for direct citizen involvement. In turn, this has exposed aspects of their nature as undemocratic and unrepresentative.

Much of the blame for this crisis that mainstream parties are perpetually confronting can be placed at the feet of party-dominating elites and their long-standing tradition of practising brokerage politics. From the early party days of loosely knit local coalitions to current corporate party structures, Canada's economic elite have remained solidly in control of the party system, structuring its operational dynamics to favourably reflect their interests and continued dominance (Lyon 1996). Elites, Lyon (1983) argues, have consistently overemphasized the importance of parties in the democratic process. "Parties," he writes elsewhere, "are easily made 'inevitable' in a democracy by simply defining 'democracy' as a political system characterized by competing parties" (1996, 532). The Canadian electorate's accepted view of their inevitability permits parties to occupy the privileged position in the political process, providing elites with a legitimated institution for the continued representation of their selective interests.

In his analysis of the Reform Party of Canada, David Laycock points out that in the 1920s, parties were objects of "prairie populist criticism because they were held to be complicit in the overrepresentation of elite interests in the formulation of public policy" and that today this sentiment is a predominant one throughout not only Canada but North America (1994, 219-20). This view can also be found in British Columbia's pro-life and pro-family movement's general disdain for mainstream parties. One pro-life member, for instance, commented: "Our problem in Canada is that the Liberal and the Tory parties are both owned by a few wealthy families in Canada. As far as believing that there's anything along the line of democracy in this country, I don't believe it anymore." While this may be a perception that elite interests might want to alter, according to Lyon (1996) it is certainly not a reality they wish to surrender or modify. The failure of the major federal political parties to substantially implement any of the 1991 Lortie Commission's recommendations on electoral reform (Tanguay and Gagnon 1996) suggests that Lyon's argument may in fact not be overstated.

Further inhibiting effective broad-based representation by parties have been the deeply historical practices of brokerage politics and what S.J.R. Noel (1976) calls "clientalism" in Canadian politics. Canadian political scientists have characterized the dominant form of political representation in the country as a brokerage style of politics in which mediation and patronage are used to elicit factional interest support for deals made behind closed doors. These deals form the basis upon which more general policy packages are developed and then presented to voters as widely favourable to them in the hope that these packages will win voter approval during an election (Elkins 1991; Covell 1991). This practice of "clientalism" is one in which a party, as patron, bestows material benefits such as patronage appointments, or preferential access to certain economic or political opportunities, on a potential source of support – the client – to secure that support in terms of "voting, campaigning, [or] organizing for the patron or the patron's candidate" (Noel 1976, 197). These are the underpinnings of what might be thought of as a kind of party corporatism, a degree removed from the corporatist practices of the state but nonetheless reflecting a similar approach to the mediation of social conflict and interest aggregation as parties attempt to win the right to wield state power.

For mainstream parties, the realized danger of brokerage politics via clientalism has been the loss of representative legitimacy among the Canadian population. The failure of parties to include the growing number of alternative interest groups in their decision-making processes means that more and more voters are feeling politically shunned – and they aren't wrong. These groups do not hail from the elite cohort that dominates party infrastructures, so in the first place they tend not to be even invited behind the closed door. Maureen Covell, for instance, argues that "the overall conservatism of the system can also be seen in political recruitment which underrepresents new groups and those who do not enjoy the advantage of social prestige" (1991, 69).

In addition to being excluded from the domains of decision-making power, the interests or concerns of issue-oriented groups, should they actually receive any recognition from party elites, tend to disappear in the facile platforms of parties that "try to attract as broad a spectrum of voters as possible by avoiding a distinct and therefore limiting ideological or policy image" (ibid., 85). In this regard, a party elected to form the government has executed its brokerage tactics par excellence: it has successfully convinced the electorate that its policy packages are in their best interests without having to commit itself to any overt ideological position or expose its entrenched, class-biased, and corporatist executed agenda.

Beyond the system-maintenance intentions of elite interests and the issue-deadening practice of brokerage politics, political scientists have identified a number of other factors contributing to the decline of mainstream parties in Canada in the face of their crisis of representation (Meisel 1985; Tanguay and Gagnon 1996; Covell 1991; Lawson 1988). While Meisel's is the best known of these analyses, the others have made similar identifications, which can be placed in four general categories.

First, major federal parties have failed to adequately accommodate the diverse range of regional and cultural interests in Canada. The results of the 2000 federal election make this point with crystalline clarity: while the Liberals maintained their majority, winning 173 seats, the bulk of their support came from Ontario and Quebec; the opposition Reform/Alliance's

66 seats came exclusively from western Canada; and the Bloc Québécois' 37 seats were, not surprisingly, restricted to Quebec.

Second, the inability or unwillingness of parties to accommodate the post-material values and concerns of an increasingly well-educated and materially secure public has given rise to a search for alternative forms of representation. Unwilling to accept politics as usual, supporters of new social movements and other post-material-value projects are seeking to redefine the very meaning and practice of political representation. What is emerging is a new form of politics that reflects not simply a disenchantment with traditional party representation, but a legitimating embrace of other political institutions and practices. In this case, Maureen Covell sees that "one characteristic of the new politics [is] a willingness to use political tactics that do not involve links with parties. These include demonstrations, direct mobilization of groups, helped by modern techniques of communication, including the fax revolution, media campaigns, and access to the courts as well as direct links with the bureaucracy" (1991, 80).

Covell's mention of communications technology leads into the third general factor contributing to the decline of parties – the roles of media and technology. Opinion polling, direct-mail canvassing, televoting, and the growth of the Internet have all diminished the importance of a party organization to winning an election (Tanguay and Gagnon 1996). These technologies have made traditional methods of political canvassing largely superfluous and generated a party dependent on the services of professional pollsters and media consultants rather than political strategists.

Of all the media and communications technologies available, however, it is television that has had the greatest impact on the role of parties in the political process. As John Meisel points out, "until the advent of radio and particularly of television, politicians were the most effective means through which the public learned about political events ... television has, to a great extent, changed all that ... Public views and public opinion on almost everything is being shaped by television programming and television advertising. Politics and politicians are filtered by a medium in which the primary concern is often not enlightenment, knowledge or consciousness-raising, but maximal audiences and profits" (1991, 184).

One of the most significant impacts of this reality has been the further concentration of a party's political power and fortunes into the hands and image of its leader. The problem for parties and their representative function in this regard is that it heightens the perception among a disaffected electorate that, as past Family Coalition Party president Darren Lowe remarked, "under our Canadian system our leadership has quite a bit of power, more so than in the States." Mark Toth reflected the frustration among the party membership and the pro-family community about this situation in his comment that, "in this country I think there is something wrong with the political system, because members of the majority who vote on issues are considered outcasts if their view is different from the prime minister's. Take [Roseanne] Skoke and [Tom] Wappel, for example."[4] Pro-life politician Roseanne Skoke in fact lost her 1997 renomination bid in the Nova Scotia riding of Pictou–Antigonish–Guysborough. In the paper, it was reported that, "blocked by a 'hardcore' party establishment from seeking another term in Parliament, controversial family-rights champion Roseanne Skoke says she will campaign to lead the Nova Scotia Liberals: ... 'As long as our people are there, they're going to continue to be oppressed.'"[5]

The fourth and final factor concerns the features of Canada's socio-economic and political structures. Corporatism continues to be a dominant characteristic of Canadian politics. Commensurate with this reality is a diminishing role for political parties as "the large organized economic groups such as business, labour, agriculture, and consumers have increasingly been compelled to press their demands through the direct lobbying of the administrative apparatus of the state" (Tanguay and Gagnon 1996, 4). There is also the mundane reality observed by Anthony King, that the actions or policies of parties may "as often as not, be the product largely of force of circumstances" (1969, 137). The demands of economic crises, international policy trends, and domestic social policies all place tremendous pressure on parties to develop platforms that reflect their capacity to manage a country's or a province's economic affairs should they form the government. This kind of situation has existed for the Liberals in Canada since they came to power in 1993. Despite promises to restore Canada's social programs, which had suffered under the Mulroney Conservatives, the Liberals found themselves pressured by the dynamics of the international market to make deficit and debt reduction the top priority, thereby stalling any significant attempt to restore the social safety net.[6]

In varying degrees of concert, all of these factors have contributed to dislodging political parties from their privileged position in the political psyches of the Canadian electorate. Yet there continues to be a debate as to whether their manifest impact on parties is enough to claim that parties will soon be or have already become inert and atavistic political institutions. Vaughan Lyon (1996) argues for just such a fate, believing that democracy in Canada would be well served should government by parties, what he calls "partycracy," come to an end. Then again, among political scientists there is also the acknowledgment that while the influence of parties is declining and public cynicism towards them is rising, this is not an inevitable situation (Paltiel 1996; Tanguay and Gagnon 1996; Amyot 1996; Covell 1991). Paltiel, for instance, takes the position that, given the consistent levels of voter turnout, competition for party nominations, and delegates at party conventions, there is little empirical support for the view that "Canadian parliamentary parties are either moribund or in decline" (1996, 414).

If parties are not edging towards the political scrapyard, however, they are still faced with the very tangible reality that their privileged position of representation is being challenged. In a follow-up article to "Decline of Party in Canada," Meisel points to ten dysfunctions that parties create for themselves, thereby self-limiting their potential.[7] Of these, two – limiting political discourse and ignoring important issues – are of particular importance to the emergence of alternative organizations of representation.

For those individuals who have sought political expression from within parties, like those who founded the Family Coalition Party, these are precisely the limitations that frustrated their efforts in other parties. The removal of the Christianity clause from the Social Credit constitution and Rita Johnston's proclamation of the party as pro-choice (see Chapter 1) were both examples of a mainstream party deliberately ignoring and silencing part of its membership. This kind of marginalization typically revolves around quality-of-life issues (abortion, the environment, etc.) that demand a party take a firm ideological stance on the issue. This occurs because, as one Family Coalition Member observed, "big parties don't take on serious issues." The resulting tension, created by the desire of citizens for more direct political participation over social issues and the reticence of parties to make such an accommodation, has led not only to rising voter cynicism and distrust of mainstream parties, but a deliberate attempt to sidestep them via the establishment of minor parties and other political vehicles of representation.

It seems clear that for a variety of self-inflicted and externally imposed reasons, the crisis of representation faced by political parties in Canada has fostered this disaffected and cynical voter culture in Canada. Among the members of the Family Coalition Party, it was a thriving trend. The vast majority of FCP members, for instance, had never belonged to any other political party before the FCP because of their disenchantment with the disingenuous, opportunistic nature of parties and politicians. One member's comment sums up their view this way: "I'm suspicious of all parties. Ninety of ninety-five politicians are not concerned to serve the people, they're concerned with their own interests. But the FCP is sincere, they do want to serve and are motivated by what's right and wrong – by principles."[8] Another member said:

Historically, if you look at the democratic process, it's supposed to be representation for the people, in pure form, a voice for the people. But over time this voice has been influenced by outside interests with money which has been created by or given to the parties. It's unfortunate, because Canada is supposed to be democratic, but I don't think I'm being represented at the provincial or federal level – and I'm not alone, I don't think. Something's gone wrong or I've turned cynical along the way, but I just don't feel represented because oftentimes the party that's in doesn't share my beliefs. Second, in the past I've been lied to – if I've voted for a particular person or leader, I've been let down. Often my requests for answers or action have been completely ignored by my representative in government, and they've never been ridiculous questions, just ones I want honest answers to.

For such disaffected citizens, there would appear to be only two options: first, to seek out alternative forms of representation, such as those offered by the new social movements, interest groups, or political pressure groups in the hopes that they can better articulate the issues of concern for that individual. Second, cynicism and disenchantment may cause people to opt out of the political process entirely. With the increase in the activity of social movement organizations and decreasing or at best stable voter turnouts for elections in general, it would appear both options are being exercised as Canadians grow increasingly tired and frustrated with parties' continued practice of politics as usual.[9] Yet, at the same time, the creation of new political parties appears to be a continuing and viable option in the attempt by politically concerned citizens to find alternative vehicles for the expression and representation of their political ideals. The 1991 Royal Commission on Electoral Reform and Party Financing – the Lortie Commission – noted:

In many ways we seem to be in an era of anti-politics, although the rapid emergence of new parties points to the need to exercise caution in drawing conclusions. Canadians appear to distrust their political leaders, the political process and political institutions. Parties themselves may be contributing to the malaise of voters ... Whatever the cause, there is little doubt that Canadian political parties are held in low public esteem, and that their standing has declined steadily over the past decade ... [Nonetheless] many smaller parties have developed partisan constituencies of loyal and committed supporters ... Further, electoral support for these parties indicates that, despite the increased activism of interest groups, Canadians are hesitant to abandon the institution of party. (Canada, RCERPF 1991, vol. 1, 223, 228)

Although there is little doubt that the major parties are in serious crisis, the raft of minor and protest parties that have dotted the federal and provincial landscapes of Canada throughout the twentieth century indicate a continued overall faith in the Canadian political system and its parties despite their myriad dysfunctions. Perhaps the important distinction to make here on the crisis faced by parties is just that: it is the mainstream or major parties, historically the Liberals and the Conservatives but now also Reform/Alliance, that are in a crisis of representation, not the small parties that emerge from social movements or on the basis of strongly held social beliefs. These minor parties, like the FCP and the Greens, with their grassroots support, issue-based and principled platforms, and calls for electoral reform, may well be what keeps the party at Westminster going.

Keeping the Issues Alive: Minor Parties in Canadian Politics

The existence of minor political parties of protest at the federal and provincial levels has constituted one of the most unique and enduring features of Canadian political culture. Since the Progressives entered the federal election of 1921, minor political parties have distinguished Canada's Westminster parliamentary model from other first-past-the-post systems by creating a uniquely Canadian, hybrid political system characterized by two-party dominance with the continuous presence of minor parties (Bickerton 1996). When the Toths and others chose the Family Coalition Party as their alternative means of political representation, they became part of the historical stream of Canadian political consciousness that has manifested itself in party form and been committed to the belief and pursuit of full democratic participation in Canada throughout the twentieth century. Like the Progressives, the Co-operative Commonwealth Federation (CCF, later the NDP), the Christian Heritage Party, and Social Credit in Alberta, the FCP was made up of a membership of aggrieved citizens with strong feelings of political disenfranchisement resulting from the failure of major parties to represent their interests.

Despite the considerable obstacles and challenges that confront these parties in the face of such resistance, they press on, motivated by such past successes as those of the Socreds in BC and Alberta and the CCF/NDP at both the federal and provincial levels. In fact, notes Maureen Covell, with the rise of the Bloc Québécois and the Reform/Alliance Party of Canada, "it is possible that we are entering another period of party effervescence. The Reform Party and the Bloc Québécois have been formed to run candidates in the next federal election, and parties such as the Christian Heritage Party have entered politics at both the provincial and federal levels, and in a small number of cases have gained enough votes to affect the result, usually by causing the defeat of the candidate closest to them in ideological terms" (1991, 102). Since this was written in 1991, the Bloc (1993), Reform/Alliance (1997, 2000), and the new Conservative Party (2004) have all formed the official federal opposition to the Liberals, and in 1994 the 275 votes the Family Coalition Party received in the Matsqui provincial by-election were enough to send Socred matriarch Grace McCarthy down to defeat, losing as she did by only 67 votes (see Chapter

1). Such victories, large or small and regardless of political stripe, have created a deep well of political folklore and tradition from which neophyte minor parties draw their strength.

In categorizing these small parties, scholars have used a range of terms, calling them minor parties, mass parties, protest parties, third parties, flash parties, and movement parties (Duverger 1959; Pinard 1975; McMenemy 1976a; Gagnon and Tanguay 1996; Carty 1996). The source of the distinctions between the terms can be found in the criteria that are used to define the origins, size, and trajectories of such parties. For example, Maurice Pinard's notion of a "third party" is based on the size of the popular vote received by the party and the subsequent threat it poses to the dominant party in the system. In this case, Pinard (1971, 1973) argues that a party must receive 15 percent of the popular vote to qualify as a legitimate third party. Duverger (1959) and McMenemy (1976a), on the other hand, define mass and movement parties, respectively, by their origins.

Duverger's differentiation between mass and cadre parties is one of the most commonly used to differentiate between traditional mainstream parties and smaller parties like the CCF/NDP or the FCP. Cadre parties, such as the federal Liberals or Conservatives, are professional electoral machines with extensive financial and technical expertise that has been developed for the express purpose of conducting successful election campaigns. Mass parties, on the other hand, have a grassroots base, arise from civil society, and rely exclusively on their membership for support. "The members," writes Duverger, "are therefore the very substance of the party, the stuff of its activity" (1959, 63). But he stresses that it is not membership size that separates cadre from mass parties, it is structure. Mass parties, for instance, engage in acts of political education to gain support from which the party derives its financial resources, so "the party is essentially based upon the subscriptions paid by its members ... In this way the party gathers the funds required for its work of political education and for its day-to-day activity; in the same way it is enabled to finance electioneering: the financial and the political are here at one ... The mass party technique in effect replaces the capitalist financing of electioneering by democratic financing" (ibid., 63).

As became evident in the first chapter, this description of gathering financial support is a good fit for the Family Coalition Party, with its membership dues and annual party banquet constituting virtually all of the party's revenue sources. Yet the FCP did not have a sufficiently extensive membership base to be considered a mass party in the same way that the CCF/NDP or Social Credit might be.

Beyond cadre and mass parties, Duverger indicates that one "concept, 'minor party,' deserves special consideration" for its ability to capture the activities of parties that exist and operate at the edges of parliamentary legitimacy (1959, 290). Personality parties and permanent minority parties are the two variants of minor parties that Duverger identifies. In a parallel discussion on minor third parties in Canada, John McMenemy (1976a) classifies them into fragment, movement, and mixed fragment-movement parties, creating a distinction similar to Duverger's.

The critical distinction between both formulations of these party sub-types lies in their point of origin. Personality or fragment parties are the product of party fractures within a sitting parliamentary party. Of personality parties, Duverger writes that they "are purely parliamentary groups having no real party organization in the country, no true social substructure. They are made up of deputies who chafe under the discipline imposed by major parties" (1959, 290). In Canada, Henri Bourassa's Nationalists and H.H. Stevens' Reconstruction Party, both of which enjoyed a modicum of electoral success during the first half of the century, were just such parties.

Movement or permanent minor parties, meanwhile, have their genesis in issues that have generated social unrest in civil society; they are, in other words, extraparliamentary in their origins. Originating as they do in civil society, these parties tend to enjoy a solid, albeit usually small, base of support. This base of support tends to be a political minority, something Duverger says is "a 'spiritual family' quite well marked off, very much in a minority, relatively stable and not reducible to the major tendencies which divide the country" (1959, 292). McMenemy summarizes the political mobilization and intentions of these movement or permanent minor parties this way: "Movement parties arise in times of social crises to articulate grievances. Their leaders and adherents may not seek political office wholeheartedly at first. Instead, the aims of the movement party may be limited to obtaining only sufficient representation to impress the governing parliamentary party. If the party is primarily interested in radical social reform, political power is seen as a long-term goal and less important than educating the public" (1976b, 14). While not quite accurate for parties like the FCP or the Greens, this is traditionally the conceptual space they have been placed in.

In Canada's historical experience, three main catalysts of social crisis that have spawned movement parties can be identified. The first is economic. Norman Penner (1996) argues that it was during the Depression years of 1929 to 1939 that parties like the Social Credit League and the Co-operative Commonwealth Federation emerged, in part as a protest to the protracted economic crises of the period. He further contends that the chronically sluggish economy of the 1990s gave a similar boost to the Reform/Alliance and the Bloc Québécois as the Progressive Conservatives collapsed under the weight of a Mulroney administration unable to halt the economy's downward spiral.

The second catalyst is regional exploitation and alienation. Much of the strength of parties like the Social Credit League, Reform/Alliance, the Union Nationale, and the Bloc Québécois comes from a deeply rooted belief that the demands of western Canada and Quebec are not satisfactorily articulated or represented by the major parties (Thorburn 1991a).

Finally, what can be termed the *crisis of post-material values* has provided the impetus for several parties that have emerged in the 1980s and 1990s.[10] The Feminist Party of Canada, the Green Party (federal and provincial), the Christian Heritage Party, and the Family Coalition parties in Ontario and British Columbia were all developed on platforms of strong principles on quality-of-life or post-material issues. Social and political equality, ecological destruction, the diminishing influence of Christian values in Canadian society, and the erosion of the traditional family – all of these issues, despite obvious political and ideological antagonisms, have been identified by supporters as critical to the future social well-being of the country and as being denied effective representation in mainstream parties.

These minor parties of protest have taken form as a way of giving a formal political voice to these issues and simultaneously protesting the constrictions of practising politics as usual in mainstream parties. One Family Coalition Party member reflected a dominant membership belief about the lack of representation for pro-family issues in mainstream parties when she said, "I think it's been proven you can't change anything in an old party," and as two pro-family activists commented about the FCP, "I think it formed as a kind of protest party," and "the FCP is made up of people disaffected from the parties they worked in before."

In their critique of the dominant theories about how these parties form, Tanguay and Gagnon (1996) identify the lack of cadre party representation and cultural, systemic, and structural factors. They also correctly conclude that no single perspective has satisfactory explanatory power and that in actuality, "any hope for a general model of minor-party development that would permit the researcher to predict with confidence the times and places in which minor parties will emerge is likely to be disappointed" (1996, 127). Nonetheless, several requisite general conditions can be gleaned from the theoretical and empirical work that has been done on the emergence of minor parties.

Beyond a lack of cadre party representation, the next most important factor in minor-party development is the presence of a political system conducive to their presence. Although the rules of the Westminster parliamentary game make it difficult for a party to form and survive, they are not so prohibitive as to make it impossible. The institutional characteristics of Canada's political system, with its strict party discipline and reliance on constituency-focused elections, simultaneously makes working from within an existing cadre party unattractive while offering the possibility of alternative party representation. John McMenemy argues, for instance, that, "under the Westminster parliamentary system employed in this country, the focus of electoral activity is the constituency election. The election of only a handful of Members of Parliament gives minor parties a certain legitimacy and credibility" (1976a, 29). Although the challenge of actually getting elected poses some monumental challenges for minor parties, they are at least able to gain access to the election forum, unlike, say, the American political system, where restrictions to ballot access for minor parties are formidable.

Second, certain structural socio-economic and socio-political factors consistently appear in explanations concerning the rise of minor parties. Three types of social and economic crises – economic, regional exploitation and alienation, and post-material values – have already been pointed out, but the importance of one- or two-party dominance and group homogeneity must also be mentioned. In looking at the rise of the Social Credit Party in Quebec during the early 1960s, Maurice Pinard (1971) argued that a political situation where one party is dominant and no effective opposition is felt to exist will give rise to a third party during times of socio-economic crises. Although Pinard (1973) subsequently reformulated his original argument to make one-party dominance one of several intertwined factors leading to the rise of minor parties, the point remains that the persistent "presence of a single dominant party leaves all groups opposing it without viable channels of political representation ... [and even] a strong two-party system ... could as well be nonrepresentative for groups who feel their central ideology and long-term grievances cannot be accommodated through any of the existing parties" (1973, 442).

C.B. Macpherson's conclusions on the emergence and political success of the Social Credit Party in Alberta, on the other hand, rested on two different characteristics particular to the province: "One was their relatively homogenous class composition, the other was their quasi-colonial status" (1953, 21). Albertans' sense of regional exploitation with the province's "subordination to the outside economy ... [specifically] the interests of eastern capital" and the heavy predominance of a petit bourgeois, small-propertied class, argued Macpherson, were the principal structural features upon which the United Farmers of Alberta and then the Social Credit Party were able to politically dominate the province from 1921 to 1967 (1953, 6). Paul Taggart's (2000) study on political populism adds further support when he stresses that the religious imagery and overtones in William Aberhart's rhetoric did much to galvanize Social Credit supporters. Like Duverger's metaphor of a "spiritual family," Macpherson's and Taggart's analyses rest on an unstated acknowledgment that the group cohesion that is so vital to a minor party of protest is based in large part on socio-economic and socio-political similarities between members.

Finally, a variety of trends in popular and political culture aid the development of minor parties. Most obvious at this historical moment are the cynical and disaffected attitudes of the electorate in Canada. The result is that any politician claiming moral high ground or speaking of working from new or principled positions tends to quickly be labelled insincere, because, as Warren Magnusson notes, "our culture makes such claims deeply suspect, and demands of the politically active constant proof of public-spiritedness and self-sacrifice. Respectability is more easily conceded to those who deny political ambitions" (1990, 526).

Such political disenchantment is both the product and producer of such a cultural norm, which works to the disadvantage of cadre parties but fosters the credibility of the activists in minor parties, who are working from a position of principle. If Covell (1991) is correct and the two principal options available in the midst of this crisis of parties are system decay or the formation of new parties, then it is likely these cultural traits would defer to the latter, not the former. Given Canada's long history of minor-party formation and relative lack of social and political upheaval over its political system, this would appear to be the case.

Minor Parties of Protest: Features and Functions

When the conjunctural moment arrives with all the requisite conditions and elements for the development of a minor party of protest, what emerges is a movement party with a set of characteristics and functions common to its political brethren. Once it has entered the political arena, the party's potential is wholly contingent on the mandate set by its members and its capacity to meet the opposition and challenges that a hostile political environment presents. Cadre parties, the media, the general voter, and even their natural constituents can ostracize, ignore, or oppose a new party. All this, combined with a first-past-the-post electoral system and demanding Elections Act requirements, create a formidable environment for minor parties of protest like the Family Coalition and the Greens. In such a climate, simple organizational survival is cause for celebration.

A primary feature of minor parties of protest is, as it is for any political party, that they engage in election campaigns and pursue political office by running candidates during general and by-elections. They also predominantly reflect a typical administrative infrastructure complete with executive boards, constituency associations, and officials formally elected to such positions as the party's leader. While not as sophisticated or fully developed as professionalized cadre parties, minor-party organizations like the Family Coalition do utilize this administrative form in pursuing their goals.

Beyond this structural similarity, however, minor parties possess unique qualities that markedly differentiate them from cadre parties. For one thing, their intention to give a grievance an organizational form through which supporters can represent it means that most minor parties have a narrow- or single-issue focus. The term "single-issue" may in fact be misleading, given that most minor parties in fact have a platform based on *issue clusters*, which can be understood as a small number of interrelated issues clustered around one dominant or higher-profile issue. The Family Coalition Party is typical of this in that it was most commonly identified as a pro-life party, but it did give equal if not greater focus to pro-family issues such as education and child care. The Green Party also reflects this trend. Its popular image in British Columbia is as a party concerned primarily with forestry and fishery practices, but its broader – and more international – agenda includes other popular environmental struggles including anti-nuclear issues, disarmament, and toxic waste disposal.

Related to their relatively narrow focus is another feature of minor parties: their emphasis on principled, value-oriented platforms. Unlike cadre parties, which maintain a flexible and populist approach to ideological positions, parties like the CCF/NDP, the Greens, and the FCP operate according to a strict adherence to their foundational policies. The Reform Party of BC's reliance on popular referendum to decide the party's position on social issues, for example, was the sole issue that prevented the Unity merger from occurring years earlier. One activist within the FCP commented on Reform: "It's a total waste of time. If a party gets in because they stand for certain principles, then they should be able to act on them. But if they say, 'Vote for us and then we'll have a referendum to decide the issue,' you don't stand for anything." Carried forward into the constitution of the Unity Party, this issue of referendum-based politics has FCP members concerned about their principles being sacrificed through acts of political opportunism. For this reason, several FCP members refused to join the new party.

Clearly, then, this is a situation that both helps and hinders these minor parties. Unwavering commitment to their principal grievances ensures the solid loyalty of their "spiritual family," providing them with a grassroots legitimacy and a source of support from civil society. However, this base of support is often small, and the uncompromising position taken by these parties denies them the flexibility larger parties have to adapt policy and organizational directions in their pursuit of broad-based support.

This inflexibility is generally born of the social movement foundations these parties frequently have. As in the case of the FCP, this fact is not simply the source of a minor party's commitment to its principles, it is the very reason for its formation – a party like the FCP exists because of its principles, not in spite of them. Asked, for instance, whether they felt another pro-life party would emerge in British Columbia, FCP members were virtually unanimous in believing one would, if Unity failed to uphold the pro-life and pro-family principles upon which it was founded.

Beyond the uncompromising stance on foundational principles, the feature next most cherished by supporters of minor parties is their internally democratic nature. Whereas the leadership and executive of cadre parties tend towards oligopolistic practices in adopting party policy and strategy, in minor parties, "legislative leadership is not only formally accountable to the extra-legislative organization, but appears to share power with the extra-legislative leadership of the party. The rank-and-file members of these parties value democratic internal procedures and correct policy more highly than electoral success" (McMenemy 1976c, 104). The CCF/NDP, the Greens in Ontario, and the FCP in British Columbia all emphasize the importance of the direct involvement of their members in the decision-making processes of the executive (Young 1992; Sandilands 1992). Past FCP president John O'Flynn saw this as one of the most attractive features of the party for him: "I like how it goes through the democratic process as a way to develop policy. It was the only way, I felt, to do it at the political level. At least, it seemed to be the most attractive way for me, even though there are other ways."

This belief in direct democratic participation also extends into a commitment by minor parties to reform the political system in which they exist. The United Farmers of Alberta and the Social Credit Party in Alberta were, observed C.B. Macpherson, "based on a novel theory of democratic government, and each was carried into effect by a popular movement broader than a political party" (1953, 3). Similarly, the Greens, the Progressives, and the CCF, with their goals of implementing a program that promotes a more direct and participatory democracy, all hoped to reform the Canadian political system to allow for more effective articulation, representation, and accountability in government (Sandilands 1992; Covell 1991). In BC, the Family Coalition Party joined the British Columbia Coalition for Electoral Reform (BCCFER) in support of that organization's goal of altering the current provincial electoral system from its first-past-the-post style to some type of proportional representation.[11] A majority of FCP members supported this initiative, believing it would help democratize BC's political system and create the potential for a more representative legislature.

The last and one of the most vital features of movement parties is their educational aspect. In the case of Social Credit in Alberta, Paul Taggart writes that "it also had, in the early part of the period, a strong educational strategy ... the cultivation of study groups by Aberhart had the effect of building up the basis for his political movement" (2000, 70, 71). This role of movement parties as political educators is recognized as one of the most important distinctions between movement and cadre parties (Covell 1991; Lyon 1992). In fact, it could be argued that this is the defining feature of a minor party of protest. In this way, the identity of a movement party becomes an inseparable melange of its institutional form, educational purpose, electoral hopes, and resource accumulation strategies, but standing out most prominently is a belief in social change through political education.

In Chapter 1, it became clear that the goals of the FCP reflected a greater interest in social change through political education than in acquiring legislative power. From the outset, the Toths' concern was to have family-friendly legislation enacted, to educate the general public as to the merits of the traditional family and the threat secular humanism poses for its future, and to convince larger, cadre parties to adopt their two founding principles. In pursuing these goals, Mrs. Toth remarked "there's more than one way to skin a cat," her hope being that these goals could be reached and the FCP dissolved as a formal political institution.

To this end, the potential of the party form for organizations like the FCP, the Greens, and the Feminist Party rests less exclusively with their intentions and hopes of electoral success than with their capacity to function as political agitators and educators from within the institutionalized setting of party politics. Expanding the terrain of political activism from civil society to include the political sphere permits these aggrieved groups to continue their movement functions from within a realm that has been steadily appropriated by cadre parties and their elite supporters for their own purposes. One of the principal functions of movement parties, then, is to repoliticize and redemocratize the political process. Where the new social movements expanded the notion of legitimate political terrain to include all aspects of civil society, from institutions such as the family to the individual and corporeal body, now the Greens and conservative resurgence movement groups like the FCP are returning to the political sphere with the intent of relegitimating it as a site for political debate and social change. In large part, this is achieved by mobilizing citizens into active political participants in the party, the potential result being a reinvigorated political system.

Beyond acting as political educators and sources of democratic revitalization for the parliamentary system, movement parties are also sentinels of political discontent. Their presence is a political flare, a warning sign signalling the inadequacy of engaging in politics as usual and the public's dissatisfaction with all the practices that accompany that condition. "Almost by definition," Covell argues, "the rise of new parties is a sign that the established parties of a system are not accommodating important shades of political opinion in that system" (1991, 91). At the same time, movement parties also signal a deeper malady – disaffection from the entire status quo political system and process (Gagnon and Tanguay 1996). For the political activists who work within the Greens or the FCP, these discontents revolve around the systemic inability or cadre party unwillingness to tackle social issues. Mark Toth, for example, commented that, "I don't think a political party is doing its job unless it deals with social problems." The FCP was an institutional expression of this discontent, a sign of cadre party dysfunction and the democratic shortcomings of British Columbia's political system.

Through their work, movement parties also perform an accountability function. With a candidate's mere presence at an all-candidates meeting during an election, a movement party can force mainstream parties to confront issues they would otherwise avoid. During the 1996 British Columbia provincial election, for example, Family Coalition Party candidates were able on several occasions to bring their pro-family and pro-life concerns into the debate, forcing cadre party candidates to state their position or to at least expose an evasive attitude towards such issues.[12] Likewise, outside of election periods, movement parties are often able to participate in forums not available to other organizational types. To return to the first chapter here, the FCP made a number of presentations to standing committees on issues such as financing public schools and child protection, and of course it was involved with the Enterprise League of British Columbia. Both sets of involvement were possible only because of its standing as a provincial political party. As Kathleen Toth sees it, without the presence of the FCP at these latter meetings, the Unity Party would have formed, but without the formal inclusion of pro-life and pro-family principles. Their form, in other words, provides opportunities not only for movement parties to demand accountability, but simultaneously lets them articulate their grievances in the hopes of at least slowly working towards policy concessions if not winning them outright.

In this vein, one of the most overt functions of movement parties is to create a formal political domain for the issue clusters that form the basis of their platform. John O'Flynn of the FCP commented that the party "gives public visibility to your stance," an agreed-upon belief of the membership, which felt that without the party, pro-family issues would have received no political articulation whatsoever. Echoing this belief, FCP leader Heather Stilwell remarked, "if we are not there, and not given the time, the issues will not be talked about by the other political parties. They are uncomfortable with them. The other parties do have pro-life people within them but they are silent, and so you can't impact upon society if the issues can't be discussed."

The Greens, the FCP, and other issue-oriented parties all popularize agendas that are downplayed or simply ignored by mainstream parties. This means that citizens who live their lives based on any number or type of inviolable principles can find themselves in the politically untenable situation of having to cast a vote for a party that does not profess a similar degree of commitment to those principles. Whatever the issue, these voters first look to cast their ballots on the basis of social principle. FCP members admitted to frequently spoiling ballots or not voting and express utter disdain for practices such as voting purely on the basis of potential economic gains or voting negatively to ensure a particular party does not form the government. For committed pro-family or pro-life ideologues, the FCP provided them with an opportunity to vote purely on the basis of conscience. As Mrs. Toth said, "I suppose we are an electoral vehicle for people who hold those socially moral values, social conservatives and moral conservatives – it gives people a place to put their vote." One FCP member who ran in 1987 as a pro-life candidate recalled "a number of people who said to me, 'If it wasn't for you, I wouldn't be able to vote.'"

A final function of minor parties of protest is that they create political opportunities for the broader social movements to which they are related or sympathetic. The form and institutional presence of these parties provides a political access point through which movements have the potential to influence the policy process or other, larger parties. Although in the case of the FCP this potential wasn't recognized or embraced by the pro-family movement as a whole (see Chapter 3), movement parties can and do create unique opportunities for intrusion into the political process that can be exploited by other social movement organizations in their work. The most obvious example is during an election, when parties have privileged access to public forums, the media, all-candidates meetings, and general campaigning, all of which can be used as sites for education, agitation, and demands for representation. By using elections in this fashion, movement parties can help transform them into forums of rigorous political action that addresses their grievances – grievances that have been politically legitimized by the institutionalized form that represents them and thus cannot be easily dismissed as the spurious rhetoric of election debates.

To fully capture the essence of minor parties of protest or movement parties is to understand that all of their functions and features are not mutually exclusive, nor do the parties exhibit them to the same degree. At particular stages of a movement party's development, it will manifest some traits and execute some functions more conspicuously than others, while still others may remain entirely latent. For the most part, these characteristics and functions can be readily identified in fledgling organizations like the FCP, the now defunct Feminist Party of Canada, and the Communist Party of BC as they either struggled through their parties' infancy or remained fastidiously true to their principles. Other movement-originating parties, like the CCF/NDP, the Progressives, and the United Farmers of Alberta, evolved to various points of maturation that resulted in the shifting, masking, or abandoning of their original movement traits. Yet they remain movement parties: formal articulations of particular grievances that provided opportunities for the casting of votes based on social principle and political dissatisfaction.

In this sense, movement parties embody an inherent paradox. Their existence is symptomatic of system and cadre party dysfunction, and as such they can be contemplated as a destabilizing force threatening the operational integrity of the parliamentary system. But while their presence agitates traditional parties and makes those supporting the political status quo nervous, ironically, these parties are the true sources of system validation. Rather than posing a threat to democratic politics in Canada, as those who practise politics as usual might argue, small parties do quite the opposite. They help increase citizen involvement and interest in politics, confirm the viability and potential of Canada's parliamentary system, and breathe democratic life back into the political process with each mobilizing effort they undertake. Mark Toth summed it up this way when he commented on the importance of movement parties: "They are a good thing because they tend to bring the large parties into line. It is good for democracy to have small parties that are trying to increase justice and the fight against the injustice of bad laws."

The Challenge of Being Small: Beating the System and the Problem of the Vote

Not surprisingly, any new party will find itself confronted by a number of formidable obstacles on its road to not only success but even mere survival. These barriers all combine to create a political climate that is structurally and culturally reticent to bestow political legitimacy on new parties. It is a situation that adds another twist to the complexities of Canadian politics – the socio-political elements that nurture the democratic possibilities of new parties are the same as those that work to prevent their manifest realization and efficacy.

The challenges that these elements present for new parties can be generally grouped into four categories: systemic, structural, cultural, and organizational. Systemic obstacles include Canada's Westminster, first-past-the-post electoral model and the Elections Act regulations that set out the rules of the election game, while the political cleavages and socio-political characteristics of the province or the country are the source of structural obstacles for new parties. Popular beliefs about the role of parties, the concept of the vote, typical voting patterns, and decision-making processes on casting a ballot make up the cultural obstacles faced by a new party. Organizational challenges refer to a party's own inadequacies, which can include lack of political expertise, operational resources, policy development, and lack of leadership.

The individual effect each of these factors has on new parties share a common result: the prevention of vote acquisition by new parties in an election. Regardless of its origin, its issues, or its other functions, the potential and political legitimacy of any political party in a parliamentary system like Canada's ultimately rests upon its ability to attract votes. In the popular consciousness of Canadians, the relationship is a simple one – the more votes a party receives, the greater its potential for wielding political power. In this regard, all the challenges that confront new parties can be compressed into a single conceptual difficulty, what may be thought of as the *problem of the vote.*

Systems of representative democracy rely on the concept of citizens each casting a single ballot to express their choice. The inherently reductionist nature of this practice is captured by Lyon's description of voting: "All the citizen's formal/authoritative input to government must be compressed into a single pencilled x after a candidate's name on a ballot every four years. With this x the person is, at various times, urged to pass judgement on the performance of the incumbent government, choose the best local representative, express an opinion on various issues before the public, and so on ... Small wonder that for most citizens voting is a symbolic act rather than a serious attempt to influence policy" (1992, 135).

Two particularly important points concerning the vote are embedded in this passage. First, the vote is an act of socio-political reductionism where the citizen has to cast an opinion on a broad range of social, political, economic, and moral issues in an exclusively singular fashion. It is a circumstance that forces compromise upon voters as the only option – there is little room for the expression of absolutes at the ballot box. Similarly, the process demands that voters blend socio-moral and socio-economic issues together – issues they may view as mutually exclusive – in their decision-making process. The result is that voters must choose between ensuring the continued material security of their families by voting for a party acknowledged to be competent in managing the economic affairs of the country or promoting their post-material concerns through a vote for a sympathetic new party that has yet to prove its managerial competence.

Since most new parties arise on the basis of some issue cluster that has been underrepresented by cadre parties, their implicit request is for voters at the ballot box to attenuate concerns for their personal socio-economic security and draw electoral attention to that unrepresented issue. New parties' electoral results suggest this is not a request that is readily granted by voters. Results for the Greens, with 2.7 percent of the 1990 popular provincial vote in Ontario (Sandilands 1992), and the FCP, with 1 percent of the popular vote in the 1996 BC provincial election, for instance, indicate that people are largely unwilling to vote purely on the basis of social issues. In discussing the electoral fortunes and potential of the FCP, one pro-family activist summed up this tension by saying, "We wouldn't necessarily vote for a conservative party that only had social issues at its heart because if the economy doesn't work and the nation is not secure and all those other good things, then there is no platform on which the family can flourish anyway."

Another important point in Lyon's passage is the implied cultural importance placed upon voting and the limited systemic opportunities for the average citizen to engage in the political process. These have combined to compress the legitimate exercising of political power into this episodic and singular act. This restrictive situation gives citizens only one opportunity every three to five years via a single avenue by which they are able to participate in the political process. In this way, the act of voting becomes a momentary and truncated demonstration of political will into which voters must distill all their political opinions. The representative aspect of the individual vote is thereby reduced and diluted to such an extent that it becomes unencumbered by the complexities of the very thing it is supposed to represent: the broad spectrum of desires and concerns that most political citizens hold.

Confronted with such a circumstance, and if the act of voting is the one occasion that people have for input into the type of representation they want, the reductive nature of the vote itself demands that the voter exercise this limited power to seek effective socio-economic representation before addressing socio-moral concerns. Frustrated by the inevitable reality created by the nature of the vote in parliamentary systems, one long-time pro-life activist and FCP member remarked that people "are torn between the ideal and the pragmatic. In a pure sense they want to support the party, but they want their vote to count, even if it means holding their nose."

The problem of the vote for new parties, then, can be found in the limited capacity of the vote for political expression and representation. Lyon points out that "general elections are not single-issue referendums" (1992, 135), which is true, but there is more to it than that if voting is actually a meaningful form of political expression. Systems of representative democracy operate on the principles of simplification and reductionism, which force voters to exercise their single act of political power in support of maintaining the material and economic security that has created the conditions under which activism for socio-moral issues (i.e., social movements) has been able to flourish. Until a new party can demonstrate an ability to ensure the former, it is not likely to receive many votes on the basis of the latter. As Maureen Hynes of the Feminist Party of Canada observed, "the significance of operating on any electoral level is clear – numbers are needed" (1980, 8), and in the simple world of majoritarian politics, with greater numbers comes greater political power and the likelihood of greater popular support.

To achieve this potential, a top priority for new parties is to develop into and present themselves as a legitimate political alternative capable of managing the governmental affairs of the province or the country. This is no small task. As Paul Taggart concludes about William Aberhart's Socreds in Alberta, "Social Credit was an extremely successful social movement. In government its record was more problematic. It certainly failed consistently or systematically to put the ideas of social credit into practice as government ... as an anti-party its appeal was strong, but this limited the degree to which it could sustain itself once Aberhart took control in Alberta" (2000, 71, 72). In a similar vein, Clyde Vint, past president of the Christian Coalition of British Columbia, observed that "the FCP needs to educate their people and the people of BC that they can govern the province," and Heather Stilwell remarked that one of the biggest disadvantages the party faced was that "people don't take you seriously. We will have to get ourselves organized enough as a real political party so that people outside of the social movement will consider us as capable to govern."

Meeting the organizational challenges of a neophyte party like the FCP is a matter of developing this type of political respectability. In Chapters 1 and 3, it emerged that the FCP was burdened in this regard by a lack of financial resources, political expertise, comprehensive policy development, and vibrant candidates with political ambition. With Bill Vander Zalm's period of involvement with the FCP, the first chapter also highlighted the importance to a new party of charismatic, politically recognizable figures. Similarly, the success of Social Credit in Alberta "was built on the foundation of a movement fundamentally dependent on the charismatic and personalized leadership of Aberhart" (Taggart 2000, 70). Many of the FCP membership pointed to this critical variable of charisma for the potential of the party. One founding member of the party believed that overcoming many of the obstacles faced by a small party like the FCP required "a really charismatic leader, some sort that can really overcome these barriers and really seduce the media and really get up there and sway people when they spoke. I guess that would probably be the big break that we would need." Again, this was part of the hope that accompanied Bill Vander Zalm's involvement with the party.

As Gagnon and Tanguay (1996) further suggest, attractive, articulate candidates are also vital to developing a small party's political legitimacy. Of the fourteen candidates the FCP ran during the 1996 provincial election in BC, it was West Vancouver–Capilano candidate Jim Kelly who was consistently pointed to by Lower Mainland members as the ideal type of candidate the party should be putting forward. Personable, handsome, and articulate, he was the only candidate besides Heather Stilwell to receive mainstream television and newspaper attention.[13] Other FCP candidates who ran in the election received less favourable evaluations from local members. Of one candidate, members said, "He was a funny little guy, he was a sacrificial lamb – he was just tongue-tied." Other candidates were also regarded as detrimental to the image of the party as legitimate and serious because of the overtly controversial tactics and an apparent lack of thorough understanding of party principles they demonstrated during the election. The potential harm such candidates could do to the party image was recognized by members in their common belief that candidates needed to be selected with care.

The importance of running a full slate of seventy-nine candidates, one in each provincial riding, was also identified by members as important to the image of the party as a capable alternative, but far and away the most important image members felt the party needed to project was that of youth. Again, Jim Kelly was pointed to by those who knew the candidate as offering the ideal profile. One thing the party membership became acutely aware of was the danger of projecting an image, as one member put it, "as a bunch of little old ladies in running shoes who couldn't have a baby even if they wanted to." Another member said, "The last thing we need is men and women my age running for families under this label, because people will say, 'Oh well, that was in the old days.' You need young men and women acting out their beliefs and saying, 'Yes, this is the way to go.'"

This suggests a belief that selecting quality candidates, developing or acquiring political expertise, and attempting to attract a charismatic, committed leader might enable new and small parties like the FCP to move towards dealing with many of the organizational challenges that can otherwise limit the development of their image as a credible political alternative.

As for the systemic obstacles faced by small parties, the benefit of organizational expertise in the area of party administration might help mitigate the restrictive effects of Elections Act regulations, but meeting the challenges posed by a first-past-the-post electoral system will likely require modifications to the system itself. Institutional resistance to small parties is well acknowledged as a significant limiting factor to their development and potential influence (Lyon 1992, 1996; Chandler and Siaroff 1991; Covell 1991; Paltiel 1996). In British Columbia, institutional yokes for small parties are believed to be provided by the Election Act. One FCP member noted that "the trouble with our electoral system is that it isn't built for more than two parties ... the Election Act is designed for two parties." Mrs. Toth reflected the sentiments of several FCP members when she said, "the act is terrible. It discourages any small party from forming. We decided if you follow the rules they can't kick you out, but if you once slip up, well, then they say you are gone. I think they want a lot more control, they want to know who is funding you and it works for us as well as for anybody else. Small parties like us might say, 'Don't bother, it isn't worth the hassle.'"

While there was agreement among the executive and general membership that the Election Act is problematic, surprisingly, most FCP members did not feel that its design is a deliberate attempt to eliminate small parties, but rather that this effect is an inadvertent result of attempting to make cadre parties more accountable. Similarly, Paltiel (1996) argues that at the federal level attempts to increase accountability of major parties through Elections Act regulations have further professionalized the party process and that "there is little evidence that minor parties or independent candidates have benefitted from the controls" (1996, 418).

Such professionalization works to the distinct disadvantage of small parties, which have neither the expertise nor the resources to hire consultants to manage the intricacies of election acts. The membership gave Mrs. Toth full credit for the FCP's survival in her tenacious attention to what the act demands. As she says, "I am particularly careful about filing everything on time, and doing everything the way it is supposed to be, so they can never use that as an excuse for getting rid of the party." The act was such a contentious matter that the party identified its ability to adhere to its demanding regulations as one of its few successes. In one newsletter, it was reported that:

> There is no doubt in the minds of most non-socialist party organizers that this Act was meant to rid British Columbia once and for all of small political parties like ours who split the vote and make polling predictions inaccurate and useless ... How the NDP would love to get rid of the Greens who take votes away from them ... You will be happy to know that every one of our fourteen candidates, all eighteen constituencies and the Party met the requirements and survived to fight another day! We've learned to avoid the traps they set and we've deciphered their deliberately-confusing accounting system.[14]

After two provincial parties were deregistered and forty-one candidates faced a ban for failing to submit the appropriate documentation following the 1996 provincial election, calls arose for changes to the Election Act.[15] To this end, meetings sponsored by the Liberal Party began and were attended by representatives of provincial parties to develop a package of Election Act reforms aimed at making compliance easier.[16] Echoing a sentiment of the FCP executive, BC Green Party leader Stuart Parker was quoted in the *Vancouver Sun* as saying: "A lot of our energy is going into coping with the act. The act has already taken out two parties so we're taking this very seriously ... We need some changes in the act so that small parties can get on with their activities."[17] One of the promises made by the BC Liberals prior to their victory in the 2001 provincial election was electoral reform. This began to materialize with the formation of the Citizens' Assembly on Electoral Reform in late 2002, but whether this will produce any significant alterations to the electoral system remains to be seen.

Where a small party's tactics for managing and combatting such restrictive election acts are predominantly a matter of *organizational survival,* minor-party support for alterations to Canada's and British Columbia's first-past-the-post electoral system is more about increasing *organizational potency.* The history of small parties in Canadian politics is also a history of attempts to increase the democratic potential of the Westminster system and provide minor parties with increased opportunities to become viable representative bodies. As Lyon wryly notes, "writing about parliamentary reform is an academic growth industry" (1983, 123), one that has documented reform initiatives from the United Farmers of Alberta and the CCF in the early 1900s to the current efforts of the Greens and the FCP in British Columbia (Whitehorn 1991).

This minor-party support for reform is a product of the systemic realities that Canada's "plurality system most often overrepresents, sometimes significantly, the party with the most votes," and it disadvantages parties with diffuse geographic support (Seidle 1996, 283). These factors have the effect of heavily favouring strong cadre parties and systemically marginalizing small parties like the Greens and the FCP. The 2001 provincial election in BC demonstrated this amply: the Liberals took 58 percent of the popular vote but 97 percent (77 of 79) of the legislative seats in Victoria. Apart from two seats won by the NDP, all the other parties were shut out. In this kind of situation, one long-involved FCP member remarked that, to get credibility, "we have to change the system – we do have enough votes to get people in, but with this system we have to change people's attitudes [about voting]. Under this system, I don't see the party growing very much." About the current system in general, another member remarked that, "right now you could have it so that more than 50 percent of the people don't have a voice in government. I don't think that's very good democracy, certainly not in an ancient Greek way."

For the FCP and other minor parties, the preferred alternative to a first-past-the-post system is some form of proportional representation system akin to Germany's Hare quota, or Neimeyer method, or the single transferable vote system used in British Columbia during the 1952 and 1953 provincial elections.[18] Expressing support for this kind of reform, Gerhard Herwig, a long-time FCP executive and a candidate in the 1996 provincial election, commented that, "in Germany, with mixed member proportional representation, there is a chance for smaller parties if they get 5 percent of the total votes cast in an election. The Green Party jumped that hurdle many years ago and since has been a growing force in government. I am convinced that under that kind of system the FCP would elect members to the legislature. Giving voice to different points of view would make for better government." Another active party member remarked that proportional representation would help because "tons of people say I'd vote FCP if they could win," but under the current system, this is a faint hope.

Even Bill Vander Zalm, the former Socred leader, supports the idea of adopting a more representative electoral system: "Hopefully one day in this country, when we move to a more democratic approach, including perhaps such things as proportional representation, we will see more views represented on our legislature – including anything from the Communists through to FCP through to Green through to labour, business or whatever. I think it is the healthiest type of system. Ours is very unhealthy. If we had proportional representation, then every view could be reasonably represented within the voice of government or within the legislature and the [FCP] results would be very, very different."[19]

After the 1996 provincial election in British Columbia and the 1997 federal election, general debate favouring electoral reform increased in the popular media and the activities of the Coalition for Electoral Reform (CFER) accelerated.[20] CFER – now called Fair Vote Canada and Fair Vote BC – operates federally and formed provincially in British Columbia in April 1997 with the principal objective of promoting a more democratic and representative electoral system and pressuring the government to accommodate such demands.[21]

Whether these attempts to provide small parties with an opportunity to overcome this systemic hurdle will prove effective remains speculative both federally and provincially. Part of the problem here, as Duverger notes, is that while such changes do provide a greater advantage to those parties currently in the most disadvantaged position, "nevertheless this effect of proportional representation is very limited; on the whole P.R. maintains almost intact the structure of parties existing at the time of its appearance" (1959, 252). And as Lyon points out, elites "will support only those institutional changes which will leave the party/parliamentary system fundamentally intact" (1983, 118). This was Bill Vander Zalm's concern when he talked about the Recall and Initiative Act he initiated as premier: "[In] my last year of government I fought very hard for the introduction of the referendum and initiative and my reasoning for a good part was I could foresee no change coming within the system as long as the politicians, particularly those governing, had the final say. They would always tend to protect the status quo because they were the status quo, and had I been able to introduce referenda and initiative in the form that I saw fit, we definitely would be looking already today at changing the way we are being governed." Despite Vander Zalm's optimistic view, the conclusion still seems clear: even with the adoption of some variation of proportional representation, small parties like the FCP would still be faced with an enormous systemic hurdle to overcome.

There are also structural hurdles that small parties must not only face but have virtually no power to control. Traditional political and socioeconomic cleavages play a significant role in a party's fortunes, and unless new parties align themselves with these cleavages, their potential remains extremely limited. In this regard, Jane Jenson (1976) argues that, federally, Canadian political parties have traditionally run on cleavage lines based on language, religion, and region. The most prominent of these in the past has been the cleavage between Catholics and non-Catholics, with Catholics strongly favouring support for the Liberal Party (Jenson 1976). However, it has been argued that religion is no longer a relevant cleavage in Canadian politics (Irvine 1991; Johnston 1991)· "The religious disputes that have divided the major parties, over schooling or property, are ancient and are usually regarded as settled. The religious questions that presently divide Canadians, over abortion for instance, cut across parties" (Johnston 1991, 93).

In relating this trend to British Columbia, Bill Vander Zalm reflected that, "short term, particularly, and perhaps long term as well, a party whose strength and future growth is dependent on Christian principles has troubles. This is no longer a predominantly Christian province – it is agnostic, they have over 30 percent of the population, the non-religious, and we have an ever-increasing influence of people that are either Sikh, Hindu, and Buddhist – so if your whole thrust is based upon being Christian, you're rowing against some heavy water. It's going to be an uphill battle." For a party like the FCP, the absence of a marked political cleavage based on Christianity, Catholicism, or traditional values, combined with a general decline in the importance of religion in politics, leaves it without a natural structural cleavage to exploit for electoral support.

Additionally, the sharp bipolar cleavage between left and right that has characterized British Columbia politics since the turn of the century (Dyck 1991; Blake 1996) further hinders the party. As Cairns and Wong (1991) note, this cleavage consistently gives the NDP a good one-third of the provincial vote and puts pressure on conservative parties and voters to coalesce – people do this by voting for the largest conservative party and parties do it by trying to amalgamate. As mentioned in Chapter 1, the latter became manifest most recently in the efforts of the Enterprise League of British Columbia, which sought to create a single, united conservative and free-enterprise party from existing ones.[22] The result of these talks, of course, was the creation of the Unity Party, but it is misleading to assume that the existence of Unity led to a united political right in BC. It may have presented itself that way, but in fact only the FCP formally deregistered as a party. The Reform, Conservative, Social Credit, and British Columbia parties all remain registered, and many of their members did not join Unity. The fractured state of the right in the province remains and is one of the reasons some FCP members regard Unity as primarily a bigger and better FCP rather than the second coming of Social Credit.

As far as conservative voters go, there is little doubt in the minds of the

FCP executive that the presence of this left/right cleavage prevented potential supporters from casting a vote for the FCP because of an acute concern about the importance of defeating the NDP and returning a right-wing party to power. Certainly this anti-NDP sentiment was a strong force behind the Liberals' overwhelming majority victory in 2001. Bill Vander Zalm sees this practice of negative voting as a systemically created feature of contemporary politics, since, "realistically, within the system as we know it today, people tend to vote more against something than for something." That religious conservatives were engaged in this kind of negative voting was something Mrs. Toth subscribed to: "People were so scared the NDP would win. I don't know what the logic is behind it. It's a sort of silly way of voting strategically, because if you have principles and you believe in them, then if you can't vote for them, you might as well not vote at all."

Overall, there is little a small party can do to increase or diminish the importance of structural cleavages within its polity, but the presence or absence of particular cleavages can dramatically hinder the potential growth of a new party. For the FCP, this left/right cleavage was a pronounced obstacle, and not one that appears surmountable for any staunchly social conservative party, at least in the near future – the halcyon days of the Socreds in Alberta and BC are long past, relegated to a political memory that can do no more than draw a fond smile across the faces of religious conservatives.

Finally, a number of cultural trends, beliefs, and practices must also be overcome if new parties are to realize their potential. The predominant tactic in this effort is engaging in a concerted commitment to politically educate the electorate about the importance of active political participation, the importance of seeing small parties as viable bodies of political representation, and the importance of opposing the unrepresentative, dysfunctional aspects of cadre parties. In particular, there exist four areas in which cultural attitudes act as a barrier to the growth of new parties.

Arguably the most important among these is the limited level of political participation among Canadian citizens. As Kornberg et al. argue, Canadians "tend to be deferential to the 'betters' and are content to be spectators rather than players in the 'political game'" (1982, 56). This tendency towards deference is likely a product of the inherent conservatism in Canada's political system and tailings of a Burkean attitude that, as William Mishler notes, "stems from elitists' observations that few citizens possess these qualities and their fears that increased participation would, as a consequence, jeopardize the quality of democratic life" (1979, 109). In this vein, there was a general opinion among the FCP membership that, as one member put it, "Canadians are a little more apathetic than others – more laid back, they don't want confrontation, they're very much 'live and let live.'" Many in the pro-family movement seem to concur. One activist described the attitude towards politics in Canada this way: "Here in Canada, the complacency issue – Canadians are a very deferential bunch and believe that, normally, authority should be deferred to rather than challenged." Such attitudes of course favour the larger, more established parties and limit the potential of small parties to generate sympathetic political activism.

Long-standing party loyalties erect another obstacle new parties face in their attempt to build a credible membership base. Party loyalties and the political cleavages that sustain them are largely a product of political socialization within the family (Kornberg et al. 1982; Johnston 1991). As one pro-family activist put it while contemplating the FCP's lack of electoral support, "You know – if you're born a Liberal, you die a Liberal." This intractable trend quickly became apparent to the Toths in the formative days of the FCP. In their efforts to recruit members, they discovered that while religious conservative members of the Social Credit Party supported the Toths' efforts, they refused to leave the Socreds and join the newly formed FCP. Even after the merger in late 2000, stalwart Socreds kept the party registered, and in the 2001 election, Socred Grant Mitton finished a comfortable second in Peace River South based on this kind of party devotion. Again, cadre parties enjoy the benefit of this situation – to whatever extent Canadians do participate in the political process, they tend to do so through the party their parents supported.

A third cultural obstacle facing new or small parties is the popular attitude towards parties in general. British Columbia's political culture, for example, reflects moralistic trends, a belief that individuals can make a political difference, suspicion of traditional political elites, and support for populism (Blake 1996). At first glance, this might appear to be a climate conducive to a minor party like the FCP, but it must be remembered that new or small parties are still political parties and as such still subject to the cynical, distrustful assessments of a disenchanted electorate. Having roots in a social movement, or arising to give principled representation to a social grievance, does not provide immunity from the criticisms of a disenchanted electorate for an organization with party form.

Last, cultural attitudes towards the vote prevent small parties from gaining political legitimacy at the ballot box. Part of this problem of the vote for parties like the FCP is that it is popularly conceived as an instrument not only for political representation but political victory. Casting a vote for a cadre party that can viably compete for the right to become the government is popularly thought of as a potentially "winning" vote and therefore a preferred option for the voter. In the case of a party like the Family Coalition, this results in votes being cast for the most viable party with the closest ideological orientation to the FCP. Some FCP members, for instance, reported that they fully supported the party's ideals, and intended to continue their membership, but would – and in fact did – vote for the Reform Party of BC in the 1996 election because it was a party that had a better chance of winning.

In a political culture that stresses victory and socio-economic representation as the critical features of the vote, small parties trying to gain a political foothold for their cause through the electoral process suffer a serious disadvantage. A vote for a small party in a culture where such opinions dominate can only be viewed as wasted, and the FCP executive identified this *wasted-vote syndrome* as the single most debilitating factor in their electoral efforts. Not surprisingly, FCP members unanimously share Bill Vander Zalm's position that, "I personally don't feel there is such a thing as a wasted vote. There is a message in the results." Mrs. Toth feels "our votes are as individual as our name. If you can't cast your vote with integrity, then you have lost your access to the democratic process." Bill Stilwell of the FCP summed up the wasted-vote issue this way: "The vote, the way I see it is, 'Who did you vote for in the last election [1996], Liberal?' Well then you wasted your vote, you didn't get elected, the NDP got elected. So you still wasted your vote, you may as well have voted for us. You voted for them because they might get elected – because they had a better chance of getting elected. In other words, you took the lesser of two evils. I can address it from a practical point in that unless you vote for the winning candidate, you waste your vote."

For small parties to increase their electoral potential, they must confront the cultural challenge posed by the wasted-vote syndrome and the other aspects of the problem of the vote. If the vote continues to be conceptualized in terms of purely competitive and economic variables, then it seems unlikely that small parties will enjoy much success.

Unlike the structural obstacles facing small parties, however, these cultural challenges could possibly be addressed through political education. As William Mishler (1979) points out, Canadians are not born with political predispositions. Political attitudes and beliefs that govern a citizen's political actions are the products of political socialization and education. Mishler even argues that, "far from being an inevitable consequence of man's inherent apathy, the oligarchic structure of political activity in Canada appears to be learned – the result of a combination of individual experiences and historical events" (1979, 108). Similarly, Munroe Eagles (1996) argues that citizens need opportunities to participate directly in the decision-making processes in a variety of non-political settings if they are to increase their participation levels in the formal political process.

Implied here is a recognition that people's belief in their ability to exert a political influence is something that can be learned and developed through alternative forms of political involvement. For small parties like the Greens, the FCP, and others, these are important points. If they are able to develop and engage in effective programs of political education that focus on changing common cultural beliefs about and practices around the political process, they may be able to increase their own potential. Likewise, they may be able to expose some of the myths that protect current electoral practices and shroud the unrepresentative nature of mainstream parties.

The organizational, systemic, structural, and cultural obstacles that new and small parties confront all act as barriers to electoral success. They are formidable challenges, in some cases uncontrollable by parties, and the probability that parties like the FCP will overcome them and enjoy electoral success seems remote, given the history of minor parties in Canada. While the NDP has become a major party in Canadian politics, for instance, Hugh Thorburn (1991b) points out that the party is the product of a merger between the CCF and the Canadian labour movement as the CCF sought to escape the obstacles presented to it by a narrow base of support and limited resources. Further, the Green Party, existent federally since 1983, has yet to gain any parliamentary standing in Ottawa. In British Columbia, through the 1990s, only Gordon Wilson's Progressive Democratic Alliance had any electoral success among the minor parties in the province, and that success was due solely to Wilson's populist standing in the province and his previous work in the late 1980s to rejuvenate the provincial Liberal Party.[23]

With the electoral potential of minor parties appearing so bleak, their value must lie elsewhere, and it is here: the true importance of minor parties does not rest in their chances of victory during an election, but rather in their mere presence on the ballot at election time. From the crisis of representation to the problem of the vote, it is clear that symptoms of an ailing Canadian political system are everywhere. However, it is the continued presence of minor parties in the system that offers hope for democratic representation and participation in Canada. The presence of the FCP and the Greens validates and strengthens Canada's parliamentary system. Party goals of raising awareness about social grievances, educating the general public about Canadian democracy's need for citizen involvement, manifestly increasing direct participation in the political process, and injecting principled representation into politics – all of these minor-party actions increase the democratic character of Canada, and it is in this ability that the true value of minor parties resides.

For parties like the Family Coalition, this is a conclusion that offers limited hope for electoral success in the near future. Worse, what compounds this prognosis for these parties are the additional challenges they heaped on themselves by choosing to use a party form to pursue movement functions. The next chapter examines these problems and the various tensions they produce.

5
The Tensions of Form: Family Coalition as a Party/Movement

Although the Family Coalition Party of BC can be understood as both a social movement and a political party, there is a critical caveat. While it is analytically useful to separate and distinguish the function and form of the FCP this way, it also produces an artificial distinction between them. No different from a child born of two parents, the FCP and similar organizations embody characteristics of both social movement and political party but ultimately stand as unique entities, their true nature fully understandable only as that of a party/movement. Blending party form and movement function is largely an act of political movement fusion that creates an organization with the form/function of a party/movement. It is an identity that carries with it some unique challenges, and the purpose of this chapter is to identify some of the tensions that emerge from the creation of a political organization like the Family Coalition Party.

Like the Co-operative Commonwealth Federation, the Greens, and the Feminist parties before it, the FCP discovered that a byproduct of fusing party form and movement function is a number of tensions that go beyond the difficulties already faced by social movement organizations (SMOs) and minor political parties. These tensions of fusion retard the development of party/movements in two main ways. First, their hybrid identity *creates* for party/movements a number of unique problems that simple movement organizations or political parties do not experience. Second, their party/movement duality exacerbates or *compounds* difficulties that are common to both SMOs and minor political parties.

SMOs and minor parties, for instance, both face similar obstacles to mobilizing resources with the limited financial and human means at their disposal. Party/movements like the FCP have compounded this dilemma with their strategic decision to commingle form and function. In some respects, they have confronted themselves with the worst retardants of both organizational types – not accepted by movement activists or potential voters as either a legitimate movement or political party, the party/movement doubly constrains the efficacy of its resource mobilization capacity by using a party form to create political opportunities for its movement functions. Conscience constituents of the pro-family movement become reticent to support what they view as an unviable SMO because of the FCP's party status, and potential electoral supporters withhold their involvement and vote because of the organization's narrow-issue focus and lack of governmental viability. Beyond such compounded challenges, party/movements must also manage various organizational, institutional, and cultural challenges unique to their character. All of these exist in concert and construct additional walls that groups like the FCP must hurdle if they are to effect the changes they are seeking.

Ways of Relating Parties and Movements

Before considering the specific tensions of fusion to which party/movements must attend, it is worth commenting on the distinction in nomenclature between a movement party and a party/movement, as well as the approaches that have been used in analyzing and describing the relationship between social movements and political parties. That parties and movements experience an intimate connection has been broadly recognized by political scientists and movement scholars alike, from Susan Phillips's (1996) and John Green et al.'s (2001) discussions on the systemic relationship between movements and parties to Herbert Kitschelt's (1989) study on the rise of left-libertarian parties in Europe. As will become apparent in the upcoming discussion, this book resonates more with Kitschelt's study, but Phillips's work provides a useful way to appreciate how party and movement relations are commonly approached.

The importance of the distinction between a movement party and a party/movement can be seen in the history of the CCF/NDP. It is common to refer to the CCF/NDP as a movement party, which implies that it grew out of an extraparliamentary social movement organization and then simply functioned as a typical institutionalized political party. However, at the CCF's 1932 organizational conference in Calgary and its founding convention in Regina the following year, the party was intending to function as much as a movement as a political party. Walter Young makes this point clear in his analysis of the CCF: "The CCF began in the West because it was there that the roots of protest had grown strong in the soil of discontent, that the isolation of the frontier, the malevolence of nature and eastern business were most keenly felt, driving the people to build their own organic society, expressing values foreign to industrial capitalism ... *Its approach was that of a movement,* predicated on the assumption that there is universal agreement on the cause and cure of sin and that if such agreement is lacking it is the result of ignorance which education will remedy" (1992, 219, 221, emphasis added). Young goes on to write that, "as the argument is pursued it is increasingly difficult to disentangle one from the other because, of course, the CCF was a *party-movement"* (1992, 234, emphasis in the original).

The point is that from its inception, the CCF was a party/movement, an organization with a party form and institutionalized standing but a social movement agenda. It was not until after the NDP merged with the Canadian Labour Congress around 1960 to "escape the trap of inadequate campaign funds and too narrow a base" (Thorburn 1991b) that it began to drift away "from its original *movement* functions towards a more electorally focused party" (Penner 1996, italics added).[1] That is, the organization fell victim to professionalization and organizational drift, abandoning its party/movement status for that of a more typical mainstream party. As Chapter 1 made clear, the FCP's experience is the same: it spent its political life as a party/movement, with its supporters using its party structure to pursue a social movement agenda of consciousness raising. With the emergence of the Unity Party, however, the FCP's party/movement status was replaced by Unity's status as a party with a typically singular focus on electoral victory.

Traditional, Derivational, Complementary, and Fusionist Perspectives

Typical treatments of the relationship between political parties and social movements reflect an organizational separation similar to the linguistic separation found in the term "movement party." For sound analytical reasons, the dynamics between parties and movements are predominantly examined by both political scientists and movement scholars as a product of the complementarities and differences between these two separate organizational forms. Depending on the organizational focus (i.e., a social movement) of the research in question, the alternative organization (i.e., a political party) is treated as an oppositional body that exerts a varying degree of force on the fortunes and strategies of the principal organization under study.

The work of John Green and his colleagues (2001) on the relationship between the Christian right movement and the Republican Party in the US is one such example. They argue that movements relate to major parties in three general ways: contention, confrontation, and consolidation. When a movement engages with a party, it must confront forces such as the party's receptivity to its issues, as well as other movements competing for the party's attention. Their conclusion reflects the fragile and dialectical relationship between the two when they write: "In a political process outcomes are not strictly determined by inputs. Movement contention can hurt a major party, but it can also bolster it, under the right circumstances" (2001, 424).

This kind of analysis has provided important insights and advances to the understanding of the exogenous relations between movements and parties, but it is an inadequate approach to understanding organizations like the FCP and the CCF as party/movements. Susan Phillips (1996) has also roughly taxonomized three predominant ways in which analysts tend to approach relational studies on movements and parties by identifying what can be conceptualized as traditional, derivational, and complementary perspectives on this problem.[2] However, a fourth perspective, such as that found in the work of Young (1992) on the CCF and Kitschelt (1989, 1990) on left-libertarian parties in Europe, is vital to properly understanding the full impact of fusing party form with movement function. By adopting what can be called a *fusionist* view, the hidden tensions peculiar to these party/movements can be brought out.

The first and arguably most dominant of these perspectives is the traditional, or competitive: "The traditional view," writes Phillips, "is that interest groups and social movements are in competition with parties, the consequence of which is usually seen to be destructive to the organizational base and representative capacities of parties" (1996, 440). The growth of social movement organizations, in particular the new social movements (NSMs), from the 1960s onwards, has been identified by political scientists, as well as the Lortie Commission, as contributing to the crisis of legitimation being experienced by political parties (see Chapter 4). Whether the NSMs are the cause or effect of the voting public's waning faith in the representational efficacy of parties is debatable, but the Lortie Commission clearly sees them as the cause:

> The rapid rise of organized interest group politics during the 1970s and 1980s ... further undermined the credibility of political parties as primary vehicles for articulating and promoting political ideas and interests ... As a result, many citizens, especially large numbers of well-educated activists, have eschewed partisan politics, and thus political parties, as mechanisms of dimensions of this phenomenon are critical ... many of these activists express, explicitly or implicitly, strong anti-party attitudes. The legitimacy of political parties as primary political organizations is questioned in ways reminiscent of earlier populist movements such as the Progressives. (Canada, RCERPF 1991, vol. 1, 222-23)

Implicit in this view is that representation and articulation of post-material issues is being usurped by movements adopting strategies for support that are at least in part exploiting the public's disenchantment with political parties. As Phillips suggests, then, this orientation results in a clear sense that parties and movements are antagonistic and ultimately destructive to one another.

This antagonistic attitude of movements towards parties has been commented on by other political scientists and broadened to include various minor parties of protest that were born out of social movements (Covell 1991; Duverger 1959; Pinard 1973). Of particular interest in this regard is Pinard's comment about "radical movements": "[They] believe that none of the existing parties can be counted on. In such situations, what is abandoned in favour of a new party is not a weak traditional opposition party, but all existing parties. Indeed, the latter are not only abandoned, they are positively rejected as unsuitable channels for the expression of a rather precise set of concerns ... As examples of radical movements, one could mention the following parties during their 'real' phase: the Farmers and Labour movements and the Progressives of the 1920s and the CCF/NDP" (1973, 442).

The importance of Pinard's argument is the identification not only of an antagonistic and competitive climate between parties and movements, but also of the strategic adoption of party form to perform movement functions during this "real phase" (i.e., party/movement phase) of organizations like the CCF/NDP. The point is that none of these four perspectives are mutually exclusive – they are separable and identifiable only by the degree of weight awarded them in a given analysis.

Research focusing on social movements also reflects this competitive view of parties and movements. In criticizing the decision of the Canadian environmental movement to form a political party, Helga Hoffman and David Orton write: "We believe that building a green movement in Canada was seriously undermined by the formation of the federal green party and also the formation of green provincial parties in BC and Ontario" (1989, 21). In their opinion, such a tactical decision undermines the democratizing potential of a social movement like the Greens by reconfirming current institutional arrangements as the only legitimate repositories of political power in Canada. For the most part, then, whether the primary subject of study is a party or a movement, this perspective appears to have room only for a combative relationship between the two forms.

In considering the second way of viewing the party-movement relationship, Phillips writes of the derivational perspective that it "recognizes there is often a direct connection between social movements and parties because it is not uncommon for a movement to develop the apparatus to contest elections" (1996, 441). The Family Coalition Party, the Christian Heritage Party, the Feminist Party of Canada, and the Green Party – both in Canada and West Germany – are all parties born out of broader social movements. Like the Progressives, the CCF/NDP, and the Social Credit League of Alberta, these parties were formed to give formal institutional and political voice to the social grievances that had catalyzed their respective movements.

When asked about the relationship between political parties and social movements, all of the FCP members interviewed for this book remarked that a relationship did exist. Executive member Gerhard Herwig commented that, "at the root of every party is a movement trying to bring change in a certain direction. Parties probably spring from movements because there isn't an expression in the existing political structure that brought results [for the issue of concern]." A majority of FCP members shared Mr. Herwig's opinion and directly connected parties and movements by commenting that many parties arise from social movements.[3]

That parties like the FCP, the CCF/NDP, and the Greens derive their support and owe their existence to founding social movements is commonly noted by political scientists and movement scholars alike (Boggs 1986; Offe 1998; Zirakzadeh 1997; Braunthal 1996; Phillips 1996; Penner 1996; Thorburn 1991b; Kornberg et al. 1982; Heberle 1968). Boggs, for one, writes of the German Greens that "the uniqueness of the West German Greens – and a vital source of their political strength – lies in their organic relationship to emergent popular struggles" (1986, 178). Of left-libertarian efforts to "develop new vehicles of political mobilization" in Europe, Herbert Kitschelt writes that "social movements represent a first step in this direction ... Founding new parties ... constitutes a second step" (1990, 184), while Young (1992) makes a parallel observation about the evolution of the CCF in Canada.

Even Hoffman and Orton, despite their opposition to the formation of the Green Party in Canada in 1983, do not dismiss this aspect of the movement-party relationship. They include, for instance, a temporal caveat in their criticism by commenting that "it is a *movement* that has to be built at this time, not a federal political party" (1989, 21, emphasis in the original). Implicit although unacknowledged in their argument is that *at some point* a political party may be useful or even essential to the success of the Greens. Their criticism thus appears to be concerned more with the historical moment at which the party was formed than with its ultimate formation. Before the embrace of an institutional form that may undermine the Green project is contemplated, the work of the movement must first, they argue, "focus on practical environmental work and develop green consciousness ... To put forth ... some concrete green programs and policies around which the public can be mobilized" (1989, 23). Their message is that a radical democratic agenda of ecology-centred politics must first be solidified by the work of the movement within civil society before a party form can be contemplated. Without these foundations, any party arising from a movement runs a tremendous risk of ideological compromise and of self-co-opting its strategic initiatives. Once such groundwork is laid, however, the possibility of utilizing a party form to achieve the movement's goals may become more viable.

Phillips brings the relationship of parties and movements even closer with her third view of the dynamic between them. By regarding the two as complementary, she argues that both organizational forms, rather than being regarded as solely engaged in the adversarial tactics of competition, can be seen as working collaboratively to reinvigorate Canadian democracy. As Phillips describes them, the new politics of the NSMs, with their intent to make politically normative the concerns of a post-material society, have transformed political engagement and representation in three important ways. By emphasizing a "politics of difference" that promotes "inclusiveness, democratization, and cultural relativity rather than homogeneity or sameness," the NSMs have forced a reappraisal and expansion of what is constituted as the political (1996, 455). They have also stretched the realm of what is accepted as legitimate political space by pointing out the simultaneously localizing and globalizing effects of governmental decisions, an effort that also increases and redefines what might be considered a site of political engagement. Finally, argues Phillips, all these trajectories have demanded an alteration in the "style of representation of politics" (ibid.). That is, "the politics of difference necessarily entails a shift of emphasis from what is being represented ... to how it is being represented and who is making the claim" (ibid.).

In this respect, the activities of NSMs have in some sense forcibly constructed the need for a perspective of complementarity. By altering the political landscape in such a dramatic and non-traditional way, social movements have made it increasingly difficult for parties to engage in politics as usual. This means that parties may no longer be able to satisfactorily articulate and represent the interests of an ever-diversifying political culture like Canada's, and so may have to accede a legitimate political role to social movements.

In similar fashion, this complementarity has been identified, albeit in a more synergistic way, in work by Galipeau (1989) and also by Rohrschneider (1993). Galipeau points out that in their attempts to maintain the privileged standing and accommodate the demands required by a "politics of difference," parties have "stretched their brokerage capacities to include women's issues, peace issues, the demand for gay rights, a clean environment, and a host of other special and general interests. Instead of being initiators of policy debates, parties must now react to an increasing number of politicized social cleavages" (1989, 418). For the Family Coalition Party founders, this impact of movements on parties was at no point felt more sharply than when British Columbia Premier Rita Johnston declared Social Credit a pro-choice party (see Chapter 1). It was a clear example to them that, within a party, principles can be quickly compromised by the dynamics of political opportunism. In this case, Social Credit was stretching its brokerage capacity to make itself more attractive to the very groups that the FCP opposed – pro-choice, gay rights, etc.

In another example of this complementarity, Robert Rohrschneider argues that "the evolution of NSMs may fundamentally alter the internal processes of political parties" because movement activists have a preference for non-hierarchical decision-making structures within parties (1993, 168). He points out that these preferences "find their most visible expression in the organizations of green or other New Left parties" and that "there is evidence that movement proponents are increasingly represented within established Old Left parties, which in turn may alter their internal dynamic" (ibid.). Murray Cooke (2000), in examining the German Greens and the Brazilian Workers' Party, also found an internal decision-making process that reflects a social movement organization rather than the typical mainstream party. While there appears to be little evidence of this kind of open, non-stratified organization in Canadian mainstream parties, the Green and Feminist parties and the FCP have all emphasized the importance of an organizational infrastructure that promotes a fully democratic decision-making process (Sandilands 1992; Hynes 1980).

When Rohrschneider remarked that parties like the Greens operated according to a set of non-hierarchical decision-making principles preferred by its activist supporters, he was articulating an example of a manifest characteristic produced by fusing party form with movement function. Young's (1992) analysis of the CCF and Herbert Kitschelt's (1989) study of left-libertarian parties in Europe both use a fusionist perspective to identify the tensions produced by melding form with function. When the relationship between movements and parties is interpreted through such a perspective, a number of unique traits and characteristic tensions shared by party/movements like the FCP and the Greens emerge.

If the four views presented are understood as a relational continuum, then this fusionist perspective stands as the polar opposite to the competitive view. From a position of antagonisms, the movement-party relationship has been drawn ever closer together, through the derivational and complementary perspectives to a point of apparent paradox. The fusionist view offers the closest possible relationship between a party and a movement, but in fact the fusing of party form with movement function to create a party/movement produces an organizational unity: movement and party are no longer related, they are one. This fusing leaves no buffer between the structural and cultural demands of the two organizational types that might otherwise be used to mitigate antagonist tensions that arise between the differing requirements of each. In other words, once the decision has been made to use a party form to pursue movement goals, there's no place left to hide.

For example, Kitschelt (1989) argues that left-libertarian parties are confronted with resolving the tension created by a party's demand to pursue a *logic of party competition* versus a movement's preference for a *logic of constituency representation*. Kitschelt maintains that these parties pursue a strategy congruent with the latter, but that this is not an easy task. Here, Joachim Hirsch, writing about the German Greens, concludes: "Party and social movement? As the recent history of the Federal Republic has shown, these phenomena follow rather different conditional constellations and logics, and they embody forms of politics that are in the end irreconcilable" (1998, 189). Claus Offe goes on to say: "The Greens are currently in a developmental dilemma. They can afford neither to remain as they are nor to become like a normal party without completely breaking with their identity" (1998, 166). Kitschelt's two logics, in other words, put party/movements between the rock of politics as usual and the hard place of maintaining their movement idealism. It means that these organizations cannot simply retreat to the idealism of their movement principles or focus on electoral opportunism. Instead, they are forced to deal with the organizational, institutional, and cultural tensions that accompany the strategic decision to become a party/movement.

Organizational Tensions: Compounded and Created Effects

One activist summed up the Family Coalition Party's difficulties as a party/movement succinctly: "It is damn hard to be a prophet and a king at the same time because of the complexity of our times – they may be no more complex than the past in some ways, but you cannot be Peter and Caesar at the same time."

Beyond the problems that beset all movements and minor parties, party/movements like the FCP have created for themselves a number of tensions unique to their identity as they attempt to meet the requirements that accompany status as a political party while maintaining the focus on and commitment to their movement ideals. Finding a sustainable balance between a movement's role as educator and political agitator and the formal and cultural expectations put on a political party is a tricky balancing act – one that most party/movements have had little success in achieving. The slow abandonment of movement idealism by the German Greens, the Ontario Greens, and the CCF/NDP (Cooke 2000; Hirsch 1998; Braunthal 1996; Offe 1990; Sandilands 1992; Young 1992) is largely a product of their failure to achieve and then sustain this balance, demanding as it does the successful navigation of these tensions of fusion.

Compounded Effects

One set of these tensions is the compounded problems party/movement activists have to confront. These are issues that exist for all movements and minor parties but are exacerbated for party/movements. The FCP, for instance, had to attend not only to the movement issues of resource mobilization and framing, but also to the party issues of developing broad party policy, campaign expertise, and an image of governmental viability. By themselves, each of these issues was a formidable task for the FCP, but efforts by party/movements must be redoubled if they are to overcome them and evolve into viable socio-political actors.

On mobilizing resources for their cause, John McCarthy notes that "the choices that activists make about how to more or less formally pursue change have consequences for their ability to raise material resources and mobilize dissident efforts, as well as for society-wide legitimacy – all of which can directly affect the chances that their common efforts will succeed" (1996, 141).

Financially, the Family Coalition Party subsisted on the meagre funds raised through its membership dues, annual lunches and dinner banquets, and the odd donation or small fundraising effort (see Chapters 1 and 3). Most interviewees reported that while they helped the party at times by donating small amounts of money, they also financially supported other pro-life or pro-family organizations. The implication is that the FCP had to compete with other, more established organizations for donations from conscience constituents. All social movement organizations are confronted with such competition, but, in addition, the FCP had to convince potential donors that its organizational form was, or had the potential to be, as efficacious for the pro-family cause as more traditionally structured SMOs.

Of course, attracting supporters as a political party presented the FCP with the same problem but for the opposite reason. As a party/movement, the FCP reflected the narrow-issue focus of the concerns of the pro-family movement, and this was a situation that made generating political support difficult. Unable to portray itself as an organization with the potential to govern the province, the FCP found it virtually impossible to receive financial support from those religious conservatives that do support political parties. In this way, each half of the party/movement duality dilutes the financial mobilization potential of the other, a dilemma that traces its way through all of the organizational challenges that were faced by the FCP.

Now, much of a party/movement's financial prospects has to do with its ability to generate, sustain, and expand its membership base. In 1993, when Bill Vander Zalm spoke on behalf of the FCP, the party enjoyed its healthiest period of membership growth and financial stability. One of the most oft-cited laments of the FCP executive was that their restrictive financial situation was due in large part to their small membership base. The compounded challenge of broadening and strengthening this base for the FCP was the product of a logic analogous to its financial resources predicament: the various rationales that individuals apply in their decision to join or become involved with a party or movement may be at odds with each other when it comes to a party/movement like the FCP. People join parties and movements for different reasons, and the rationales for taking out membership in the former may dissuade potential members from joining the FCP because of its movement functions, and vice versa. Herein lies the importance of what Carl Boggs calls "maintaining popular mobilization" (Boggs 1986, 204), and the difficulty in achieving this for party/movements has been identified by a number of scholars of the Greens in Germany and Canada, as well as various left-libertarian parties in Europe (Boggs 1986; Phillips 1996; Kitschelt 1990). People may be willing to join a party or a movement, but the hybrid nature of the party/ movement may act as a kind of pyscho-cultural barrier that prevents people from supporting an organization like the FCP because they cannot clearly identify its goals, objectives, or the potential benefits of its form.

Additionally, as Susan Phillips argues, it is often erroneously "assumed that one of the strengths of movement parties is their close interconnection with social-movement organizations" (1996, 450). As an example, Erin Steuter points out that in Canada, "the pro-family network is located in the fundamentalist and Catholic churches, which provide some important advantages including: a large potential support base of sympathetic, like-minded people, as well as financial support, office space, equipment and free advertising in religious publications" (1992, 297).

Steuter's subject, REAL Women, may indeed benefit from some important linkages, but as comments made by the FCP executive in the first chapter made abundantly clear, the FCP enjoyed no such advantage. The strength of the pro-life and pro-family movements in British Columbia did not translate into support for the FCP. Asked, for instance, if the failure of the party would matter to these movements, Mrs. Toth replied, "Not a hoot. They can't seem to take that next step. You see six thousand people lining the street, it doesn't follow they will vote pro-life. This is what surprised me. We thought these people were looking for a place to vote, but they weren't." This observation was further evidence for the FCP executive that they had failed to construct the linkages and interdependencies with the broader movement that would be required if the organization was to develop into a viable political force.

The importance of these linkages and relationships can be found with the Greens. In their early days, the German "Green Party declared its intention to act as an electoral and (where successful) a parliamentary amplifier and extended arm of social movements" (Offe 1998, 169). In part, this potential lay in their capacity to construct a system of organic links with the ecology movement (Boggs 1986). As is well known, this strategy met with decent success for the German Greens, but as Kate Sandilands (1992) points out, the failings of the Ontario Greens have been in part due to their inability to construct just these kinds of relationships. In developing these linkages, argues Herbert Kitschelt, time is a critical variable, because, with its passage, party/movements drift further from their natural source of constituent support through a process he terms "organizational dealignment"

(1990, 180). It is difficult to conclude whether or not this was a significant factor in the FCP's marginal status within the pro-family movement, but without question the party had a greater political and membership presence in its first five years than in its last four.

Two other factors also contribute to the compounded problems of membership recruitment faced by party/movements. First, the organization had a relatively narrow-issue movement focus rather than a platform based on a sense of regional alienation. This means that unlike the Progressives of the 1920s, Alberta's Social Credit League, the CCF, Reform/Alliance, the Bloc Québécois, or W.A.C. Bennett's Social Credit Party in British Columbia, the FCP did not have a strong regional base from which to draw membership support. Resurgence movements or NSMs, being issue-driven, do not have concentrated geographies of support to draw upon, so support for them appears far weaker and more scattered than for a group like the old CCF.

Second, by adopting a party form, party/movements have inadvertently limited their opportunities for recruiting members. Unlike social movement organizations that can viably recruit members year-round, and particularly at times when their issues are enjoying a period of high public salience, party/movements have largely restricted their membership drives to the twenty-eight days leading up to an election. This is a restriction produced in part by an attitude in the public consciousness that sets aside the potential for party involvement until election times roll around. In the days leading up to the 1996 provincial election, the FCP was receiving a steadily increasing number of new and renewed memberships, but outside of election periods, its membership drives consistently stalled and produced little in the way of dramatic increases.

Party/movements also face a debilitating mobilization tension within their ranks. Young, writing about the CCF, points out that, "because it was a movement the CCF attracted only those who were dedicated, and who gave freely of their time and money and stayed with the party through defeat after defeat" (1992, 224). And about the reasons people give for joining political parties, Kornberg et al. conclude that "an examination of the reasons officials give for joining party organizations and the conditions under which they enter suggest that as a group they are not really committed politicians consumed with ideological fervour. Some join of their own accord. Others join to accommodate a friend or acquaintance already in a party. People who join parties as a convenience to others rarely develop intense political ambitions. However, they also do not expect to work very hard" (1982, 149).

These two passages reflect the membership tension of party/movements like the FCP. If individuals join because of the party form, they may be unprepared or unwilling to put forth the effort needed for the organization to perform its movement function. In this case, the difficulties faced by any SMO in soliciting membership help are compounded, and it may be that only those dedicated to the movement aspect of the party/movement can be counted on for active participation. Within the FCP, the dedicated, committed activists were to be found exclusively on the executive board, and even then can be narrowed to the handful of people identified in Chapter 1 as those doing most of the work for the party. The Toths' frustration – that they had difficulty finding people to be active on behalf of the party – was a product of the fact that much of their membership was constituted on a show of loyalty towards Mrs. Toth rather than any firm commitment to work towards the party/movement's goals.

Finally, there is the issue of maintaining member support and commitment to the party/movement in the face of tremendous odds against survival and even greater odds against success. McAdam et al. point out that "nothing sustains the commitment of activists, nor draws others to a political movement, quite like victories" (1988, 726). Yet party/movements like the Canadian Greens and the FCP have few tangible victories to draw upon in their attempts to foster intra-member support. Unable to point to electoral success or influential movement activity, party/movements have a doubly hard time finding rallying points of motivation for their membership. The FCP relied most heavily on a survivalist mentality. Without the anticipated support of the pro-family movement or any significant electoral breakthroughs, a party/movement uses its very existence as its primary manifest success. Yet without some eventual tangible victories – the emergence of the Unity Party notwithstanding, should it become a political force – the FCP was going be confronted with a growing problem of membership disaffection and the risk of organizational erosion.

For instance, Boggs indicates that, within the German Greens, "pessimism and even apathy began to overcome many Green activists after mid-1985, in the aftermath of electoral defeats in the Saarland and in North Rheinland–Westphalis ... Moreover, the period of fascination with the Green upsurge between 1980 and 1983 seemed to have crested. An increasing number of members and supporters could be heard complaining that being a Green was no longer exciting" (1986, 217). Klotzsch and her colleagues (1998) draw a similar conclusion in their analysis of the effects an organizational drift towards professionalism has had on the party. With the decline and concomitant lack of success in the party's extraparliamentary movement activities, interest and membership in the party began to wane, leaving it very susceptible to the forces of political professionalization.

In the case of the CCF in Canada, Young highlights the similar risks that constant defeat presents for a party/movement's democratic integrity when he remarks that "a succession of failures encourages independence and irresponsibility among the militants in a party" (1992, 225). While the FCP was never in danger of having its executives behave in this way, without question its lack of substantive successes limited not only its membership potential but also its future. At the time of the merger with Reform BC, the FCP had been hanging around the province's political and pro-family margins for nine years. Its membership base had settled between eight hundred and nine hundred, and it was showing no signs of organizational growth. In such a state, the party's future rested firmly on the ability and willingness of the Toths to keep it alive.

Kitschelt's (1990) four-point evaluation of the membership difficulties faced by left-libertarian parties in Europe is also worth mentioning here. First, "few sympathizers actually join and contribute to the parties" (1990, 191), a situation consistently reflected in the financial and membership status of the FCP. Second, "many who join become disaffected with the party quickly," and third, "the importance militants attribute to purposive commitments inevitably leads to a certain sense of disappointment with the parties' accomplishments. Purposively motivated activists want to change the world" (ibid.). In this vein, Bill Stilwell of the FCP remarked that, "unfortunately, human nature being what it is, people are so desperate for success that they look for a party to succeed right away." And as Mrs. Toth commented, "some people discover the party, and if they never heard of it before, they become very enthusiastic and we hook them right away. You can't know who is going to stay and who is going to go. It was difficult to make people make it a priority. Some people are not on a political wavelength at all, they can't see the importance of doing this – they get discouraged to the point of not continuing."

Kitschelt's last point, that activist commitment can undercut the "social incentives (atmosphere, friendship, social events)" (1990, 191) for less enthusiastic members, did not appear to apply in the case of the FCP. In fact, it appears that these "secondary incentives," as he calls them, actually buttressed and fuelled the continued commitment of FCP activists and vice versa – this was one thing that actually helped them keep going. Nonetheless, it is clear that the FCP compounded the resource mobilization challenges it faced by fusing form with function and thereby steepened the grade of its road to socio-political success.

Mobilizing popular and active support may be the most important of the compounded challenges the FCP set for itself, but related to the party/movement's potential in this area are the issues of developing effective collective action frames, political policies, and governmental expertise. With its party/movement typology, the FCP could not address any of these matters without paying attention to the impact its duality had on them.

Framing efforts, in other words, cannot simply focus on movement function but must also convince potential adherents of the utility to be found in adopting a party form. In Chapter 3, it was argued that the FCP executive came to realize it had been deficient in developing an effective and comprehensive collective action frame. Specifically, this is about experiential commensurability and the prognostic function of a collective action frame (Snow and Benford 1988, 1992; Snow et al. 1986). Does the first of these, inquire Snow and Benford, "suggest answers and solutions to troublesome events and situations which harmonize with the ways in which these conditions have been or are currently experienced? Or is the framing too abstract and distant from the everyday experiences of potential participants?" (1988, 208). Simultaneously, the prognostic function must adequately and acceptably suggest "both a general line of action for ameliorating the problem and the assignment of responsibility for carrying out that action" (1992, 137).

By introducing the notion of using a party form to achieve movement ends, the FCP created a frame that promoted a political strategy too divergent for the pro-family movement to accept. In dealing with this reality, the FCP slowly came to the realization that it needed to construct its collective action frame in such a way that it would not only exhibit ideological congruence with the broader movement, but also convince movement supporters of the legitimacy of its new tactical repertoire. Of course, this latter effort would not have been required if the FCP had emerged with a traditional social movement organizational form.

In terms of political expertise and policy development, the FCP executive were fully cognizant early on that they had to generate a comprehensive base in these areas if they were to present themselves as a legitimate political option for the vote-casting electorate. Like for all minor parties, this was a major challenge for the FCP, but it was magnified by the fact that the expertise of its personnel lay in movement activism, not party politics. Chapter 4 presented the argument that even committed pro-family supporters cannot be expected to vote on the basis of a limited-focus issue cluster such as the one offered by the FCP. Material concerns for economic security and social stability still dominate the vote process, so a party/movement must develop a base of political expertise beyond its post-material concerns if it is to even attract the votes of its natural constituents. In Chapter 1, John O'Flynn of the FCP remarked that most activists have little taste for policy development beyond their movement interests and that the thin policies of the FCP reflected this deficiency. Likewise, R. Kenneth Carty wrote of the Christian Heritage Party that, "despite its preoccupation with public policy, there appears to be less policy study in the CHP than in other parties. Perhaps that is because the party is clear on where it stands, and is more concerned with propagating its views by holding public meetings and publishing newsletters than with debating the fine points of its policies" (1991, 236).

This observation suggests the tension created between the demands of party politics and the movement goals of a party/movement. Political education comes at the expense of policy formation because movement functions take precedence. At the same time, party/movement activists frequently lack expertise in governmental issues. The result is that a party/movement becomes unable to generate electoral support beyond those willing to vote on the basis of a single issue cluster and so may well be doomed to electoral failure.

All minor parties face this problem of evolving into serious political contenders, but, again, party/movements magnify these difficulties. Unlike fragment parties, whose founding leaders and supporting members are already skilled in the art of conventional politics, or parties with regional strongholds – like Reform/Alliance, which can gain legitimacy from its concentrated base of support – party/movements have no strategic advantage they can use as leverage to speed their maturation process. Limited by the commitment to their movement's principles and role as political educator, party/movements like the FCP have no alternative than to focus the development of their political legitimacy on small, incremental goals. Most FCP executives recognized this, accepted it, and shared one member's view that "one of the things is, we're not very experienced. Yeah, being a small party means you have to think small – looking for how you can meet five new members in a year or something – that's quite a leap for us, and then of course your goals and methods to find five members are different from finding five hundred." On gaining political legitimacy, the same member continued: "You don't want to be seen, and we probably are, as 'abortion protester plays politics.' I think unless we can be as visible as the Greens with their issues, then we're not there. The Greens are presented as the authority on their issues and can't be challenged on those issues, and until we're perceived like that we can't say we're successful. I don't know when we will wake up and say we've arrived, but you need to present yourself like that."

Created Effects
Beyond managing compounded problems, party/movements must additionally resolve a number of unique and significant tensions that result from this political fusion. Movement researchers and political scientists both identify these tensions as presenting the most serious threat to the survival of a party/movement in its purest form (Kitschelt 1989, 1990; Young 1992; Offe 1990, 1998; Hirsch 1998; Sandilands 1992; Braunthal 1996; Lyon 1983, 1992). Oligarchization, professionalization, institutionalization, cooptation, or absorption – for a party/movement, these are all terms reflecting the tension between maintaining the integrity of movement principles and engaging in broad-based political compromise. Resisting these powerful

forces demands that activists maintain the will to resist electoral fortune and give primacy to the movement agenda of their organization. These are dangers that must be confronted if the organization is to achieve its goals of helping to effect change by acting as a political opportunity structure for its associated movement.

These tensions can be attributed to two general and powerful forces that act upon organizations like the FCP. The first has been conceptualized by Hans Kriesi (1996) as "internal structuration" and refers to the processes of oligarchization, professionalization, and institutionalization. Kriesi argues that "the process of internal structuration is virtually inevitable, if the SMO is to have success in the long run" (1996, 155) and points, as others have, to the case of the German Greens (Offe 1998; Hirsch 1998; Zirakzadeh 1997).

Claus Offe (1990) refers to the second force as the "logic of institutional politics," which can be understood to include the problem of co-optation or absorption, as well as the tensions between the demands of movement function and electoral success. Offe writes of this force, "so effective seems to be the logic of institutional politics, and so pervasive its impact upon individual actors who learn and practice the rules of the institutional game, that this rapid evolutionary self-transformation does not need to be explained" (1990, 246). Self-explanation aside, an effort should be made to understand the effect these forces can have on party/movements.

As noted earlier, a characteristic of party/movements is to embrace an internal decision-making structure based on non-hierarchical and democratic principles. The German and Ontario Greens, the old Feminist Party of Canada, the CCF, and the Family Coalition Party all exhibit this type of internal structure (Boggs 1986; Hynes 1980; Sandilands 1992; Young 1992; Lyon 1992; Braunthal 1996; Cooke 2000). In this regard, one FCP member said, "We go by the democratic process," and another stated, "It's more grassroots because there is no hierarchy or structure, so it doesn't give the appearance of being a political party, so in that respect it encourages involvement. If there were political aspirations to unify them, yeah, it would be a detriment."

The impact of the dynamics of internal structuration on other party/movements suggests that this observation is well founded, but while the FCP never reached a developmental stage where the drift towards institutionalization and oligarchization was an imminent danger, the same cannot be said for the Unity Party. From the outset, and particularly during the 2001 provincial election, there were grumblings from FCP members about the autocratic and undemocratic methods being used in the Unity Party.

In evaluating this situation, we must keep two things in mind. First, it was never intended to produce a party/movement – the goal was to create a viable pro-life neoconservative party capable of challenging the NDP and Liberal parties for governmental power. Second, it must be remembered that a primary goal of the Family Coalition was to merge or be absorbed by a larger mainstream party. By seeking this end, FCP executives implicitly acknowledged the limited political potential of party/movements and the need for a more conventional internal decision-making process. That Unity is more typically hierarchical in its power structure, then, is not analytically surprising, and its emergence in relation to the FCP confirms once more the risks and perhaps ultimate necessity of this organizational drift to party institutionalization – a result consistent with the history of other party/movements.

In their early days of party/movement activism, the CCF in Canada and the Green Party in Germany were both heralded as novel and principled organizations that could be expected to resist the lure of parliamentary power. Young writes: "The fact the CCF was a movement meant that its participations in the party battle did not contaminate its goals so much that its influence in politics was lost. Its operation within the political system and its gradual acceptance of the rules of the game did bring about a dilution of its ideology in the programmatic sense, but did not significantly alter the party's goals" (1992, 229). And even after several years of existence, Carl Boggs believed the "Greens remain a party sui generis, and there are factors operating in their case that might resist the Michelsian pattern ... The Green program – in the attention it lavishes on participatory democracy, qualitative change, and cultural radicalism – is designed to subvert the pressures toward assimilation" (1986, 214).

With the passage of time, the prognoses for these party/movements have proven overly optimistic. The CCF merger with the Canadian Labour Congress, with the intention of broadening the party's base of popular support (Thorburn 1991b), heralded the emergence of the New Democratic Party (NDP), an organization far more focused on electoral success and pursuing a logic of institutional politics than its organizational predecessor. Unlike the CCF, the NDP has been accused by the more organically pure left in Canada of electoralism and bureaucratization (Howlett 1989) and of being a "capitalist reform party" (Hoffman and Orton 1989, 23). Vaughan Lyon also points out that it may not be possible to turn back the ideological clock on the CCF/NDP: "Making the party 'radical' again might not sit well with leaders who are now serious contenders for power nationally as well as provincially" (1992, 130).

In Germany, the Greens have suffered a similar evaluative fate. Offe observes that, "in its short parliamentary history, the Green party has not only ... abandoned most of its partly naïve experiments in mingling the forms of movement politics and parliamentary politics, but it has also adopted much of the conventional tactical repertoire of (oppositional) parliamentary politics and party competition" (1990, 244). The logic of institutional politics has exerted such a pull on the Greens, in fact, that in May 1993 they merged with Alliance 90, an ideologically centrist and politically pragmatic party, to form what is now known as the Alliance 90/The Greens coalition (Braunthal 1996).[4]

Fear of such institutionalization and of becoming another validating example of Robert Michels's "iron law of oligarchy" (see Rohrschneider 1993) leads to the creation of a serious factional tension within most party/ movements. Opinions about the wisdom of using a party form to achieve movement goals fall into one of two sharply divided camps. Those committed to the ideological purity of the movement's message and educative function oppose the adoption of a party form, fearing that it will corrupt the integrity of the movement via the logic and processes of institutional politics. More pragmatically minded activists, such as the Toths and most of the Family Coalition Party executive, believe the party form can act as an effective political opportunity structure for the movement and that the lure of political power can be resisted if the goals of the movement are kept paramount.

For the German Greens, this divide came in the form of the battle between the fundamentalists, or Fundis, and the realists, or Realos (Boggs 1986; Braunthal 1996; Roth and Murphy 1998), while within the Feminist Party of Canada, "there was some division over the question of participating in elections, but the idea was finally accepted ... It was felt involvement would take the Party one step beyond previous feminist pressure groups" (Hynes 1980, 8). For the Canadian Greens, this tension is present at both the federal and provincial levels. Hoffman and Orton, in their opposition to the formation of a Green Party, wrote: "We believe that building a green movement in Canada was seriously undermined by the formation of the federal green party and also the formation of green provincial parties in BC and Ontario ... For all the talk of consensus decision making, there seems to be a reliance on Robert's Rules of Order and bureaucratic legalisms" (1989, 21). In her study of the Ontario Greens, Kate Sandilands observed the same tactical fissure: "Greens were divided about the election process: some felt that more emphasis should have been placed on the [1990] campaign ... that electoral politics provide an essential educative platform for Green issues. Others felt that Green efforts would have been better spent in organizing community forums around local issues ... that electoral politics divert Greens from the more transformative process of building grassroots activities and alliances" (1992, 157). Young identified a similar tension within the old CCF: "The militants opposed the development of the CCF as a political party ... Success, they feared, would transform the CCF from a vehicle of protest into a disciplined party in which there would be little room to rebel" (1992, 224). The ideological dilution that accompanied the pursuit of conventional politics by the CCF/NDP even aroused these sentiments in the NDP. In the late 1960s and early 1970s, the internal left-wing faction of the NDP known as the Waffle group became openly critical of the conventional political direction the party had taken since formalizing ties with organized labour and sought to redirect the party back towards its original party/movement agenda (McMenemy 1976a; Kornberg et al. 1982).

The danger of this factional tension for party/movements lies in its capacity to drain the time and energy of the organization's activists. Precious resources that could otherwise be spent attending to the mandate of the party/movement are spent trying to put out the fires created by the friction of the two opposing sides and unifying the activist body. The effect of this infighting on a party/movement can be devastating. Braunthal notes that the German Greens' loss of all their Bundestag seats in the 1990 German general election was in no small part due to this factional tension and the disputes it gave rise to.

Yet this battle is not purely symbolic or a matter of egoistic pigheadedness on the parts of the respective strategists within the party/movement. There is ample evidence that the fears of movement fundamentalists are well founded – pursuing movement goals through a party form makes the mandate and structure of the organization highly susceptible to the logic of institutional politics. At the same time, pragmatic-minded activists are correct in their assumption that the internal structure of party/movements is not conducive to growth or the exercise of political influence in the institutional arena. The internally democratic structure of the CCF and the Ontario Greens has in fact been identified as limiting their capacities to achieve their goals as party/movements (Young 1992; Sandilands 1992). Young notes of the CCF that, "although there is much evidence to demonstrate the relevance to the CCF of Robert Michels' Iron Law of Oligarchy, it is also true that the activities of the leaders were limited by citizen participation – enough at least to make participation in the party battle more awkward than if their control was absolute" (1992, 225).

This tension ultimately forces party/movements into making a decision critical to their futures. Herbert Kitschelt (1989) articulates this decision as the choice between pursuing the "logic of constituency representation" or that of the "logic of party competition." The former he conceptualizes as being driven by a commitment on the part of activists to the ideologies and policies of the movement aspect of the party/movement, while the latter refers to the "exigencies of vote-getting" and the institutional and strategic initiatives this logic demands (1990, 180).

For a party/movement, it is a decision that pointedly exposes the tension between maintaining movement principles or adopting the practices of brokerage politics. The difficulty this decision presents is that to shift one way is to engage in a concomitant retreat from the other. That is, to pursue a strategy of brokerage politics is to dilute the ideological purity of movement principles; conversely, to steadfastly maintain a position of principle diminishes the party's potential for exerting institutional policy influence. Kitschelt captures the contradictory nature of this tension by observing that, "on the one hand, they must preserve the fluid, open organizational form and obstructionist quality that challenge the highly institutionalized corporatist welfare state and maintain the loyalty of their core constituencies. On the other hand, they must become effective political players in terms of both electoral appeal and impact on public policy" (1989, 40).

The decision to pursue one avenue over the other is not one generally made on absolute terms or even with conscious deliberation. By their nature, party/movements are seeking to strike the perfect balance between the two options, so the shifts witnessed in a particular organization would tend to be partial and perhaps even temporary as they search for their elusive centre. But organizations like the Family Coalition Party have betrayed a bias for the institutional merely by deciding to engage in an act of political fusion. This suggests that the lure of political power – not for its own sake, but for the goals of the broader movement – may naturally cause a party/movement to slowly and incrementally drift more towards an institutionalized form of party competition than away from it. Further, as Young points out, "the internal pressures of the party-movement they have espoused help them resist any return; for another, a return to the status quo would constitute an admission of error" (1992, 230). Supporters of the party/movement form are unlikely to shift back to a strict social movement organizational form – not only would it be an admission of error, but, more important, they have been down that road and it led them nowhere. With these forces and biases acting upon their tactical resolve, adopting a pure logic of constituency representation seems unlikely.

Beyond these psycho-emotive and motivational forces, there are also tangible reasons for pursuing, to some degree, a logic of party competition. Offe (1990) highlights three such reasons in trying to understand the reality that, in Germany, "Green members of parliament have quickly and effectively adopted all the essential elements of the parliamentary discourse, and simultaneously abandoned much of the discourse of anti-institutional movement politics" (1990, 245).

First, Offe argues, there is the pragmatic issue of "facilitating the survival of the political causes and activities of the movement by making use of the protection and recognition of established political institutions" (ibid.). Second, he notes the absence in democratic polities of alternative forms of representational organizations. Despite their progress, social movements still predominantly occupy a space on the periphery of the institutional, and parties still dominate the political landscape as the only true agents of political representation. Finally, he cites solid historical precedence for such actions: "There are compelling reasons to embark on this (only available) road in good political conscience" (ibid.). That is, there is a long and honourable history of groups' pursuing a logic of institutional politics in an attempt to have their social grievances addressed. In the case of the Family Coalition Party, this lineage has included the Progressives, the CCF, and the Social Credit League.

With one of its aims being to merge with a mainstream party, there was within the FCP an almost innate understanding of all these arguments. Throughout its nine years as a party/movement, support for pursuing the logic of institutional politics was simmering beneath the surface, but not at the expense of the party's core principles. Any discussions of mergers, absorption, or organizational drift were always quickly qualified with that proviso. The ultimate strength of the party lay in its members' unwavering commitment to its principles. Asked if they felt the FCP was vulnerable to losing its movement soul, respondents felt this was extremely unlikely because of the individuals involved with the party, but did recognize that such a risk did exist. One pro-family activist said this about the potential of the FCP's losing its soul:

> On the whole, I'd say not, because I don't see them as moving into the mainstream in the usual way. For example, it's not a move for more power in BC. If there were a party with power connected to the movement and the members of the movement joined it, say the Conservative Party, it seems to me that inevitably there would be compromises there because of joining a major party and perhaps having a chance at power. There might be some tradeoffs. But in the case of a party like the FCP, I can't see such a party attracting people who are willing to make the sorts of tradeoffs which any hypothetical group wanting power in BC would be willing to make. I can't imagine at the moment that happening, so I don't think there's a real risk there with the FCP.

On this issue, one member said, "I would not advocate changing the priorities of the party to achieve electoral success. Our priorities are right." Several long-time members did not support the Unity merger precisely because of the threat it posed to these priorities. Even before the merger talks began, there were those who expressed concern over the dangers of organizational drift and the inherent conflict between movement and party goals. On the latter, one activist remarked that "the movement can't translate into a party without losing a great deal along the way." Another pro-family activist said he felt the FCP does not risk losing its soul, but a party or movement has other ways of selling its soul – when it goes big time and establishes its own bureaucracy, its job becomes to maintain itself; its main job, it seems, is to do the things it needs to provide the money it needs to maintain the infrastructure. Greenpeace is the perfect example of that kind of thing, where it was the most effective, I think, when it was in its small day – sort of volunteers and idealism working towards a certain end. Now it's a big structure, it's a bureaucracy and people are looking at it that way. It doesn't have the credibility, so that's what takes the soul out of the movement. It goes through that stage of movement and developing into a political party and it suddenly realizes it must deal with other issues that it really has not much interest in and that dilutes and waters down the prime issue.

Certainly the history of the Family Coalition Party suggests that it was able to resist this kind of bureaucratization. But it also suggests that in many ways its executive deliberately pursued a logic of institutional politics.

This appears to have been an initially successful strategy. The FCP was a key party in the Unity merger, and it did manage to have its core principles included in the Unity constitution. With its principles intact, the FCP's soul lives on in Unity. Nonetheless, this may be a tenuous situation, and in the end the FCP may still fall victim to a final danger that confronts party/movements: the risk of absorption by another political party and the evaporation of its movement principles.

Movement scholars have pointed to this risk in analyzing other social movement organizations (McAdam 1982; Rochon and Mazmanian 1993). Sandilands sees it happening with the ecology message of the Green Party in Ontario: "Ecology, as common sense, has been increasingly absorbed by dominant discursive formations and transformed into a narrow and limited environmentalism" (1992, 171). For party/movements, the tension created by their duality forces this risk more into the institutional realm of party politics rather than into the domain of the social movement industry. It is perhaps more fitting, then, to speak not of the co-optation of party/movements – although, in another instance of compounding their challenges, party/movements must also guard against this – but rather the absorption of their agendas and/or body politic by larger cadre parties. Political scientists (Lawson 1988; Covell 1991) point to the risks party/movements face in this regard if they begin to achieve the goals of their movement agenda. Covell argues, for instance, "if their educational efforts succeed and their policies begin to attract large-scale electoral support, they are notoriously vulnerable to having those policies stolen in piecemeal fashion by the major parties of the system" (1991, 85-86).

This was precisely the situation the CCF found itself in in 1933 (Penner 1996; Young 1992). As its popularity surged, Liberal opposition leader

Mackenzie King recognized the threat the CCF posed to the cadre parties, prompting him to stand up in the House of Commons and claim that the "Liberal party in power could enact everything in Woodsworth's [the CCF leader's] speech *without* reverting to socialism" (Penner 1996, 91). As Young makes clear, in this case, "it was the movement that triumphed as Mackenzie King read the signs and moved leftward ... What the establishment feared was not the CCF party so much as the CCF movement" (1992, 223, 229).

The issue of absorption is critical to defining the goals and the concept of success as it pertains to a party/movement. The story goes, for instance, that Ed Broadbent, past leader of the NDP, was once asked if he regretted never becoming prime minister so he could enact the policies of the NDP. He replied in the negative, noting that a close look at many of the policies implemented at the federal level of government were originally NDP initiatives. In the case of the Green Party and Sandilands's (1992) analysis, it can be argued that while their efforts have not translated into policy with the ideological purity they seek, their presence as a party/movement has at least contributed to a shift towards greater ecological commitment and consciousness on the part of the major parties.

As for the Family Coalition, it is evident that in many ways its goal was absorption and that it has initially succeeded in this regard. Yet its efforts have not evinced a social conservative shift on governmental policy. Unity as a party remains on the political fringe in the province and the FCP's core principles under Unity are now as susceptible to the forces of political expediency as they were under the old Social Credit Party. Unless the Unity Party becomes a political force in the province, is able and willing to fight for the pro-family and life principles of the FCP, and is successful in doing so, the Family Coalition will become one more party/movement that succumbed to the logic of institutional politics.

Institutional and Cultural Tensions: Hidden Limitations

While it is true that the bulk of particular tensions that face a party/movement exist within its organizational domain, there are also some latent institutional and cultural obstacles that must be overcome. Institutionally, party/movements come to discover that parliamentary systems like Canada's possess a number of characteristic traits that are not sympathetic to their presence. In addition, the administrative demands required to maintain an institutional presence are a particular drain on a party/movement's resources, energy, and motivation. Finally, a party/movement finds itself in a difficult position in its relation with the media.

The media are vital to both parties and movements to develop their potential, so effectively managing this institution becomes vital for the success of any party or movement. Yet a party/movement finds itself in the position of deciding what strategies – those of a party, of a movement, or a combination of both – can best be deployed to attract the attention any political organization requires.

Culturally, party/movements discover they must deal with a *cultural lag*. Supporters of party/movements like the FCP and the Greens view the party form as a legitimate part of a social movement's tactical repertoire. They also view the act of voting as a viable form of social movement action and the electoral arena as a site for the expression of quality-of-life concerns rather than for simply maintaining materialist security. However, potential adherents of the party/movement, both from within the particular social movement community and from the general population, have yet to accept these visions. These discoveries provide a rude awakening for party/movements and add to the lengthy list of obstacles that already confront them.

Institutional Tensions

These tensions, faced by all minor parties but particularly salient for party/movements, manifest a political system resistant to change and not designed for the type of representation the Family Coalition Party was seeking. Quite simply, Canada's and British Columbia's electoral system has not been structured to accommodate organizations that seek to represent constituents on the basis of issues. Rather, it is a system founded on geographic constituency representation, and, therefore, party/movements find it difficult to promote their agenda via an institutional presence because post-material issues cannot be articulated in regional terms.

The problem that emerges for party/movements becomes obvious. Without some degree of spatial concentration of its issue cluster, a party/movement has little hope of wielding the kind of political influence it is seeking. In a system that stresses a geographic perspective, however few votes a party/movement might receive in an election, their results will appear more impressive if they are concentrated in one area rather than scattered across the entire province or country. The Progressives, the CCF/NDP, the Social Credit League, and Reform/Alliance all had the advantage of regional protest that translated into concentrated geographic support. This in turn gave them the necessary base of popular support in institutionalized form from which they could then launch more issue-driven concerns. For the Greens and the FCP, this means that unless their supporters move into specifically designated ridings, they have little hope of demonstrating their political viability.

There is also the problem for party/movements of the overall resilience of the extant political system and institutions in Canada. Offe's (1990) earlier remark, that at present there exists no viable alternative system of political representation in democratic societies, is in part the product of a system stubbornly resistant to change. In the preceding chapter, it was argued that a critical catalyst for the emergence of minor parties in Canada was the crisis of representation being experienced by the country's cadre parties. Yet despite the protracted nature of this crisis, there are at best only discussions taking place about reforming the system and the Lortie Commission's report has gone largely unnoticed. Further, cadre parties themselves show no real signs of any declining legitimacy. For instance, despite the federal Progressive Conservative Party's devastating defeat in the 1993 federal election, in which it won only two seats, the party began to show signs of renewed life after it won twenty seats in the 1997 federal election and in 2004 became the official opposition when the party merged with the merger of Reform/Alliance under the old Conservative banner. Finally, it needs to be recalled that the Lortie Commission went so far as to blame the new social movements for the current crisis of parties. Not surprisingly, as one analyst noted, the NSMs and other interest groups were "cool in their response" to the report (Phillips 1996). As an organic outgrowth of social movements, party/movements like the Family Coalition Party are, by extension, subject to these same forces of institutional resistance and antagonism that have plagued attempts by social movements to construct an alternative system of representation.

These tensions of resistance are in no minor way due directly to this paradoxical relation between party/movements and the political system. In effect, the Greens in Europe and Canada, the Progressives, the CCF, and in a less dramatic way the FCP are attempting to alter the current system by using the institutional mechanisms of the system itself (Sandilands 1992; Braunthal 1996). In Germany, "what inspired the Greens," observes Boggs, "to construct an alternative party in the first place was deep hostility to the corporatist state, to which the party system was viewed as a mere appendage" (1986, 180). Likewise, in Canada, the Ontario Greens have made the intention "to point the way toward alternative forms of political life in the public sphere" (Sandilands 1992, 163) a major part of their political project.

Such motivations create an inevitable tension for party/movements as they attempt to reinvigorate representation by immersing themselves in the institutional realm in order to change it by using the very protocols of conduct that maintain this system. It is a situation that escalates the institutional tension between party/movements and a system reticent to change.

The Media Problematic

Beyond the political system itself, party/movements must also address the challenges presented by another institution pivotal to their fortunes, the media.[5] The need to attract media coverage and formulate a productive relationship with the media is so great, in fact, that general strategies of both parties and movements are heavily shaped by the potential for developing such a relationship (Taras 1996; McAdam et al. 1988; Carroll and

Ratner, 1999). In the case of British Columbia, McLintock and Kristianson state that "the success and failure of the contenders for political office depend in large part on their ability to court positive news coverage, while a variety of interest groups attempt to create a climate within which their particular issues are high on the public and political agenda" (1996, 123).

In this vein, Carroll and Ratner (1999) argue that movements like Green-peace, End Legislated Poverty, and The Centre (formerly the Gay and Lesbian Centre) in British Columbia have all developed media strategies contingent on their desired level of interaction with the mainstream media. For example, they remark that, within Greenpeace, "the commit-ment to a media-oriented political strategy was deeply inscribed in the group's initial formation" and that this strategy has been so masterful that one interviewed activist suggests that, "Greenpeace has positioned itself in a way that *the media will now come to Greenpeace for information or opinion without us going to them because we've established credibility* (Ken)" (Carroll and Ratner 1999, 11, emphasis in the original). Alternatively, the Gay and Lesbian Centre in Vancouver, "anticipating little support from the domi-nant heterosexist media ... reduces dependency on mainstream accounts through sponsorship of independent alternative newspapers" (ibid., 25). As Carroll and Ratner's research suggests, a movement's level of interac-tion with the mainstream media may vary, but deliberate strategies for engagement do exist, and even if the mainstream is shunned, alternative media sources are sought out.

Political parties, meanwhile, have traditionally embraced the main-stream media in their efforts to gain electoral office. In British Columbia, this has historically been a relationship coloured by overt political parti-sanship. McLintock and Kristianson point out that early BC newspapers adopted partisan stands and that "one of BC's most colourful early politi-cians, Amor de Cosmos, founded the British Colonist newspaper in 1860, in part to provide a vehicle with which to oppose what he saw as efforts by Governor Sir James Douglas 'to concentrate power in his own hand'" (1996, 123).[6] Today, although overt partisanship may have disappeared or is at least being hidden, this intimate relationship between parties and the media has not abated. The importance of favourable media coverage has such a high priority that parties "routinely devote approximately half of their campaign expenditures to TV advertising" (Taras 1996, 433) and construct their campaigns in an effort to maximize the probability of favourable news coverage (McLintock and Kristianson 1996).

These party efforts necessarily come at the expense of articulating and defending specific policy positions, because, as Brian Tanguay points out, "[in] contemporary Canadian politics, all three major parties obscure their principles and programs in an attempt to cobble together a winning elec-toral coalition of heterogeneous social groups ... At a time when the major parties are marketing themselves and their programs in the same way that the big breweries flog their homogenized and insipid products, it is highly unlikely that any party will run the risk of crafting intelligent policy responses to issues that are now clamouring for attention" (1992, 484-85). Even the NDP, in an attempt to abide by what Claude Galipeau (1989) has termed the "law of the inclusive middle," has been observed to be increasingly opportunistic and vulgar in its pursuit of media attention (Tanguay 1992). In the end, the discussion and representation of social issues are readily sacrificed to capture an attractive sound bite for the party on the evening news or a good photo-op for the morning paper.

This situation poses a significant problem for party/movements and movements alike because the media are so important to them. Following Gamson and Wolfsfeld's (1993) work, it can be seen that these organizations need the media for the purposes of mobilization (activating constituency support), validation (granting political legitimacy through coverage), and scope enlargement (the drawing in to the cause of potentially sympathetic third parties). If these things can be achieved even in part, Gamson and Wolfsfeld's scheme seems to suggest that the potential for a movement to grow should increase. The problem, of course, is how to achieve this without appearing as politically opportunistic as cadre parties have become.

For the Family Coalition and other party/movements, this is a particularly challenging task. Not surprisingly, within the FCP there was unanimous recognition that the media are vitally important to the growth of the organization. Asked about the importance of the media, Bill Vander Zalm replied that it was "all-important, the media is the most powerful force in society, far more powerful than the government even. Today, the media is the most powerful influence."

Yet despite the acceptance of this position, the FCP executive seemed at a loss as to how to gain standing for the party among the media. The impression they felt the media had of the FCP was captured by Mrs. Toth's remark that "they don't think the FCP is a legitimate party, they never could get the name right. They mixed us up with the CHP [Christian Heritage Party], sometimes I think it was on purpose. They think we are fringe and outside the mainstream. They are certainly not supportive of what we stand for, they are quite openly hostile." And Mr. Vander Zalm commented, "I think they [the media] may see it as a group that may be better ignored than given too much attention and probably often view them as a radical bunch of oddballs."

Efforts to shed this perception and to develop standing with the media were largely limited to election periods and attempts by individual candidates to develop a rapport with local media personnel. During the 1996 provincial election, this strategy was reported by candidates as having been moderately successful. One FCP member said, for example, "I was surprised how well the local media covered us. I felt nervous at the time, and I felt when he covered me he was kind of confrontational, but in the end he gave me a pretty good writeup. I was impressed with how well the local press did this." Other candidates reported similar experiences and levels of satisfaction, although some, like Mark Toth, felt they were entirely ignored. Frustrated at having the *Vancouver Sun* leave his candidacy off the list of those running in the riding of Vancouver–Kensington, Mr. Toth reported that, "I took my sign with the taped article and took it to the office on Granville Street and I handed it to the receptionist."

Overall, the 1996 provincial election provided the FCP with a level of media exposure paralleled only by the attention it received during Vander Zalm's involvement with the party. In terms of the mainstream media, the FCP received coverage from BCTV on two separate occasions, as well as a large article by Douglas Todd, the religion reporter for the *Vancouver Sun*.[7] It was a result that pleased both Mr. and Mrs. Toth, respectively:

> The *Vancouver Sun* put out a rather beautiful photo of the Stilwells and I think that helped them greatly. If they had done that for Kathleen and I, it might have helped our cause. I think it helped the party in general as well.

> During the election campaign, they are in constant contact to find out what you are doing. BCTV was very good this time about putting us on – covering the fundraiser in North Van and that. They did come out and I was pleased they did that. They did a lot of good for the party, we had calls saying, "I saw Heather and please send me stuff." So it is very important. If we could afford to buy TV time, that would be super.

By and large, though, most candidates and executives, while appreciative of the mainstream coverage and recognizing its importance, felt that the FCP had the most success with small local newspapers and radio talk shows.

To improve their chances of gaining standing with the mainstream media, there was agreement that the FCP had to do more between elections to foster a constructive relationship with the media. One FCP member commented that "you have to let them know about your presence constantly so that when an election comes up, they know you're there. Also, you need to develop credibility, be articulate, intelligent and have something to say. To do this you have to constantly pursue it – letters to the editor, talk to reporters on issues, get to know them." Mr. Toth concurred: "I believe we have to try harder, I think we should meet regularly with the media – other organizations do that." Yet part of the objective in gaining standing is to win sympathy and acts of preferential framing from the media, a difficult proposition if the media bias perceived by the FCP membership was valid.

The FCP executive, as well as pro-life and pro-family activists, tend to believe the media harbours an ideological bias against their cause. One pro-family activist stated quite simply, "The media hate us." Bill Vander Zalm, meanwhile, sees the bias as

> an understandable one, I think. You know, regardless of where a person sits, you have to believe in what you do, you might be wrong but you believe in it. The bulk of the media, not only in this country but generally speaking – the people that work in the media for the most part came out of the generation that would encompass the sixties, the late fifties, a generation of conflict. Many or the majority of my media friends, which are mostly a little bit younger than me – I say the majority but that may be overstated – many of those media friends actually became involved in the media because that was their vehicle to protest society as they knew it then. So they are liberal people. There is nothing necessarily wrong with that, but certainly they play hell with where it is you are at when you are taking a more conservative stance. The media generally is very liberal.

This view of a liberal-minded media is shared by the FCP membership and creates an interesting ideological juxtaposition with those involved with the gay rights movement. Diametrically opposite from the activists of the Gay and Lesbian Centre in Vancouver – an organization that believes in the bias of "heterosexual normativity that infuses the world of mainstream media" – whom Carroll and Ratner (1999) interviewed for their study, the pro-family community supports a thesis that the media is sympathetic to the gay rights movement while remaining openly antagonistic to the pro-family message. This circumstance lends credibility to Gamson and Wolfsfeld's argument that, "movement activists tend to view mainstream media not as autonomous and neutral actors but as agents and handmaidens of dominant groups whom they are challenging" (1993, 119). Regardless of where one is positioned on an ideological spectrum, it is not uncommon to regard the media as an ideological antagonist.[8]

To escape the perception of being persecuted or ignored because of an ideological slant on the part of the media, what political organizations may need to realize is that the media are driven in large part by the marketplace. Some in the pro-family movement already recognize this. For instance, Gerhard Herwig of the FCP commented that "the media don't give us a break. We've released lots of press releases and they were ignored. But you have to understand the media. We think they have to be fair and report, but they don't. What drives the media is sales and advertising. To sell, they have to make judgments about what goes in, same with radio and talk shows." And one activist remarked that other pro-family organizations have "by and large pitted the media as the enemy, but the organizations have to understand their role. The media is the vehicle and we're the role player. Not seeing that is the deficiency in other groups. You have to do the physical work [to foster a relationship], you have to provide the tools. The media is a business and money is the bottom line. Know it. Deal with it. That's the fact, it will rule." But escaping the trap of perceived bias is only part of the solution for a party/movement like the FCP as it looks to gain standing and sympathy from the media. The party executive realized, for instance, that they needed to also develop a tactical repertoire capable of avoiding the tension that accompanies being a party/movement.

To promote their agenda successfully and use the media effectively, social movements develop media strategies that will maximize the chances of attracting attention. Movements often adopt tactics ranging from quiet demonstrations and picketing to noisy acts of civil disobedience in a deliberate attempt to draw media attention by providing them with the entertainment value of high spectacle – waving banners and having people arrested makes good copy. Greenpeace may be the acknowledged master of such tactics, but the pro-life movement, with, among other things, its annual life-chain demonstration, provides ample proof of a willingness to use similar strategies. These tactics all provide movements with the opportunity to profile the principles of their various causes and are considered legitimate means of political expression. One FCP member, when asked about the acceptability of demonstrations, replied that he supported them because, after all, "the poor man's media is the street."

For a party/movement, however, the situation is dramatically different. Pro-family activists and FCP members were virtually unanimous in their opposition to the FCP's sponsoring or engaging in demonstrations or other tactics used by social movements to promote their cause. While they found it acceptable for individuals to participate in such social movement actions, to do so as a representative of the party was deemed inappropriate and potentially damaging to the credibility of the FCP as a legitimate political organization. The implication is that, in spite of its movement function and focus, the party form of the FCP ultimately dictates the acceptability of its media strategies. Its form effectively eliminates the tactical repertoires available to social movements because with its party status comes the expectation that the membership will abide by a protocol commensurate with official provincial party standing. This means that a party/movement must, like other parties, concentrate on developing a professionalized approach to mainstream media relations and attract personnel capable of drawing media attention if it is to gain standing. In the case of the FCP, the importance of this was most evident between 1993 and 1994, when Bill Vander Zalm was involved with the party (see Chapter 1).

This situation suggests that a party/movement is forced into deciding whether to pursue what can be regarded as a *strategy of media populism* in which principles are abandoned for the popularized attention the mainstream media give political parties, or what may be thought of as a *strategy of media circumvention* in which alternative sources of media exposure are sought and the mainstream media are, if not avoided, at least not actively sought out. The former is the typical strategy of parties, with their emphasis on leadership style and personality rather than policy substance. The latter can be found in a media strategy like that adopted by the Vancouver Gay and Lesbian Centre as it is described by Carroll and Ratner (1999).

Party/movements like the FCP are caught between the two because of their hybrid nature. They can ill afford to ignore the benefits to be derived from pursuing a strategy of media populism, but to do so risks compromising the public appearance of being firmly committed to the principles of their movement. Yet the pursuit of media circumvention, while perhaps allowing them to maintain a position of undiluted principle, carries with it the risk of not being regarded as a serious or legitimate political force in the electoral arena.

The FCP never really decided upon a strategy of media populism or media circumvention. For the most part, they were simply "taking what they could get," as one member put it. To this end, they entertained any number of tactics to try to gain media exposure. To recall from the first chapter, for example, during the 1996 provincial election, candidates Mark Toth and Brian Zacharias both attempted to gain media attention by being deliberately controversial; both were ignored by the media. Of his sign that read, in part, "Your Taxes Pay for Killing Unborn Babies," Mr. Toth said, "Not one single media took a picture of that sign. The media didn't pay attention, but I thought if they did that would help my cause, it would give me more publicity, and they didn't simply because it was pro-life." In Campbell River, however, John Krell's campaign received a lot of media coverage, albeit negative, in the local papers after he condemned homosexuality during a high school all-candidates debate. Party executives were thrilled with the attention it drew to the party in spite of its negativity. It was a situation of some coverage being better than none, but overall the FCP executive evaluated their attempts at forging a media strategy as inadequate and constantly in need of vigorous development.

Even efforts at utilizing alternative media sources were also evaluated by the FCP as wanting. The executive had little success in promoting the FCP through various Catholic, pro-life, and pro-family media channels because of a commitment on the part of these publications to remain politically non-partisan. Unlike REAL Women, which Steuter argues has the advantage of "free advertising in religious publications" (1992, 297), the FCP was granted no such advantage. Members also commented that ideologically sympathetic publications like *BC Report* are not as supportive of the FCP's goals as they would expect. One member remarked that the media in general is "ignoring us more than anything, we're a nothing, we don't rate mention, definitely not accolades. Even *BC Report*, which I support, I love it, don't give us the time of day."

On the other hand, new media technologies, in particular the Internet, were viewed as viable alternatives for listening to the FCP's voice. One member believes that the Internet may be the answer to the media problematic faced by small political organizations: "It's hard to connect with people when you can't give them a message. I believe myself that the election we just had will be the last where TV and cable will be so important. It will switch to being in front of a computer and direct communication because you can reach people with computers a lot more cost-effectively than through commercial broadcast media. By the next election, there could be Internet in every living room, so you could go direct and don't have to worry about what the media gives you, so maybe it will happen." Another pro-family activist shares a similar vision: "Political parties are trying to do politics the old way, but the game of politics has changed because the tools have changed. We can talk to each other – the Internet, fax machines, cellphones and that. Politicians haven't computed that yet and they should."

Certainly the Family Coalition Party's website provided the party with the greatest amount of exposure it had ever enjoyed. From the 1996 provincial election until the Unity merger in November 2000, the FCP website showed a consistent growth in its level of sophistication and the number of visitors to the site. Even though this trend did not translate into a growing membership base or broader public awareness of the party, it does seem that the advent of new media technologies and the capacity of party/movements to exploit them will be critical to their success.

Cultural Tensions
One more tension of fusion for party/movements is the cultural lag that exists between the vision of its activists and the appreciation of the institutionalized political arena by potential supporters. In Canada, the prevailing cultural attitude is that elections and institutionalized politics are events and sites for settling the materialist concerns of society, not the quality-of-life issues of a post-materialist ethos. These latter concerns are still predominantly regarded as being properly fought over and articulated on the terrain of civil society and in its extraparliamentary spaces. Founders of party/movements, however, have been inspired by a view of the electoral arena as eminently and legitimately suitable for engaging in struggles over the issues that affect the quality of modern life. Party/movement activists, by the very presence of their organizations, deny that institutional politics should be the exclusive domain of corporatist economic agendas and materialist issues.

Such a perspective also allows party/movement activists to reconceptu-alize the purpose and role of a political party. Chapter 3 argued that the founders of the Family Coalition viewed the organization as creating a political opportunity structure for the broader pro-family movement. Party/movement activists regard the party form as a tool for prying open an avenue for the movement to potentially influence governmental and political party policies, but the dominant cultural attitude towards voting and institutionalized politics seems to have prevented the rest of the pro-family movement from seeing this. Party/movement activists, that is, appear to have moved beyond this parochial view of parties and voting. Those involved with the Progressives in the 1920s, the CCF, the Greens, the Feminist Party, the Christian Heritage Party, and the Family Coalition Party all understood that the institutional arena must be expanded, rein-vigorated, and repoliticized so that it can accommodate struggles around the issues of social and moral concern that motivated their decision to cre-ate a party/movement.

This vision of a socio-politically expanded electoral arena necessarily includes viewing the act of voting as more than just ensuring continued material security. This is an understandably dominant attitude, given Canadians' severely limited opportunity for formal political expression (see Chapter 4), but it does little for party/movements. The impact of this situation on them can be seen by the meagre number of votes they garner at the polls. Certainly the election results of the FCP and the Greens indi-cate that their "electoral fate," as Covell describes the Greens' general re-sults, "does not support the idea that there is a large share of the electorate willing to change its vote on the basis of this issue [the environment] alone" (1991, 83). The Feminist Party (Phillips 1996) and the FCP also found this to be the case.

The root of this challenge lies in how the act of voting is perceived by potential supporters. Unlike those not willing to vote for the Greens or the FCP, party/movement supporters seem to identify voting not just as a defence against the erosion of material security, but as a direct form of political and social movement action. FCP leader Heather Stilwell, in de-scribing the dynamics of social movement action, commented that "social movements are when a whole bunch of people in many organizations and outside organizations start to question the status quo, are being heard by the status quo, and take action to achieve that end. [What kind of action?] Well, *the action can be voting,* supporting organizations that they can see are working to effect the change, forming these organizations, working within them, volunteering time" (emphasis added).

These different appreciations of the nature of voting may help explain Covell's observation that "support for new-politics issues in the abstract may be on the increase, but this support has not yet been translated into votes for a successful challenger party based on a new-politics agenda" (1991, 83). They at least help make sense of the response to the FCP's efforts that the Toths have heard continually since 1991: "I like everything you stand for, but I can't vote for you."

By envisioning the electoral arena as a legitimate site for popular struggles over socio-moral issues, party/movement activists are pushing forward this reconceptualized role for political parties and voting. The presence of the FCP, the Greens, and others in the institutionalized domain of party politics is evidence that committed activists are willing to challenge the cultural norms of the political status quo. Their efforts to democratize the political process and make it more representative of a post-materialist value system are also proof that such norms are not the unalterable constructs of political elites but gelatinous formulations that can be modified and reconstructed through acts of political will and movement commitment. Yet their vision of opening up the political sphere and stripping corporatist economic agendas of their political privilege appears to be inhibited by this cultural lag between their activist strategies and potential sympathetic adherents' continued belief that the electoral arena should remain a site primarily for the expression and defence of materialist concerns.

The myriad obstacles that are created and become manifest when political form and movement function are fused to create a party/movement beg questions about the strategic efficacy and organizational stability of an organization like the Family Coalition Party. In an institutionalized political culture driven by concerns for material prosperity, the formation of a party/movement on the basis of quality-of-life issues is a tactical manoeuvre that may well lack practicality. Susan Phillips, in examining the Green Party in Canada, writes that "the limited success of the Greens in Canadian elections indicate that this strategy may not be worth the effort, especially in electoral campaigns focused on the economy and debt reduction" (1996, 453). Likewise, Kitschelt remarks about left-libertarian party efforts in Europe that "a logic of constituency representation and organizational dealignment may not be the most promising of strategies to be successful in electoral competition" (1990, 181). And both Offe (1998) and Hirsch (1998) express similar sentiments about the German Greens.

In Canada, the political track record of party/movements without strong regional bases of support has certainly been dismal, both electorally and in terms of influencing policy. The Canadian Greens have yet to elect a provincial or federal member, the Feminist Party was a short-lived phenomenon, and the FCP failed to exert any serious influence over government policies on the family. Given these contingencies, Kitschelt and Phillips appear to be correct in their assessments of the wisdom of forming a party/movement.

Yet it must be remembered that electoral success is only a secondary goal of most party/movements. Chapters 1 and 3 made it clear that the primary goal of the Family Coalition Party was to effect policy change, either within the government or within another political party with which it would then consider merging. This latter strategy came to fruition late in the autumn of 2000, and for those FCP members who supported the Unity merger, it offers the hope of success, however remote. Should the Unity Party of British Columbia evolve into a pro-life and pro-family political force in the province, the experiences of the FCP will suggest that there is in fact some wisdom in the decision to form a party/movement.

Regardless of this potential outcome, though, one thing these experiences have clearly shown is that pure party/movements like the FCP have limited lifespans. Structurally, party/movements are inherently unstable organizations because of the tensions that the act of political fusion presents for them. Likewise, the forces of internal structuration and the logic of party competition combine to drive party/movements like the German Greens and the Canadian CCF/NDP away from their movement roots and towards the seductive powers of political professionalization. In the end, it may well be the fate of party/movements that they are temporary manifestations in the transition from movement to party. It may be that they cannot be more than intermediary structures with exceptionally volatile and unstable cores whose political half-life is determined only by the commitment and integrity of their activists. Such a reality sets a temporal limit on not only their structural existence but their strategic efficacy, because if it is inevitable that they drift towards party institutionalization, the time that an organization like the FCP has to effect the change it seeks is therefore quite limited.

This is why a strategy of *assimilation* (absorption by or merging with another political party) may not be an objectionable goal for a party/movement. By attending to the objective of influencing the policies of another party to the point of considering a merger, a party/movement alters its requisite organizational demands and cultural expectations. Primarily, party/movements would be able to at least partially avoid the tension between Kitschelt's logic of party competition and the logic of constituency representation. By engaging in a strategy of assimilation, an organization like the FCP might attract members more easily by advancing to potential adherents the benefits of joining the party, not for the purpose of voting for it, but to demonstrate a show of strength for its issue cluster. This in turn would demonstrate a source of potential electoral support for a party willing to adopt as policy the issues of the party/movement. Such a strategy might also partially eliminate the need for a party/movement to develop its internal base of political expertise and the other demands to which a minor party must attend (see Chapter 4).

Of course, a strategy of assimilation still presents a party/movement with the problem of convincing a populist-oriented party to adopt a set of inviolable principles. This would require the party targeted for assimilation to adopt firm policy positions, a practice which is counterproductive to the pursuit of power in modern politics and thus one not likely to be readily endorsed by this party's elite. Historically, this has certainly been the case for the FCP. The initial efforts of the FCP executive to merge with the Reform Party of BC and then to have the Enterprise League of BC formally adopt their founding principles were thwarted by the executive in both organizations (see Chapter 1).

Furthermore, even if a strategy of assimilation is successful, there is no guarantee that the issues of concern for a party/movement will not be removed from the targeted party's policies in the future. It is important to remember that it was just such an act within the Social Credit Party – the removal of the Christianity clause and the adoption of a pro-choice position on abortion – that prompted the Toths to form the Family Coalition Party to begin with. It is also this risk that has caused many FCP members to view the Unity merger with a skeptical if not disdainful eye. Within the Unity Party, there are factions that will likely seek to remove the overtly pro-life if not the pro-family principles in the party's preamble and constitution. During the May 2001 provincial election, there were Unity candidates who were not pro-life, and at the party's first annual general meeting, there were rumblings of dissatisfaction about the FCP's principles. If these rumblings grow and the pro-life/pro-family principles are removed, the FCP may well find itself back at the kitchen table, where it began.

In the end, then, it may well be that the created and emergent tensions experienced by a party/movement make its goals unattainable. But perhaps attaining its goals is not where its true value lies. Rather, it sits hidden in the very existence of party/movements and the processes used by their activists in their struggle to achieve their aims. There is little ideological agreement between the Family Coalition Party and the Green Party, but both share an unwavering commitment to their principles and to their respective struggles to have them realized in popular culture and formal law, and their efforts – through education, raising awareness, encouraging political participation, and fighting to make the political system in British Columbia more democratic – more than their victories or defeats, are what make party/movements an invaluable and integral part of the democratic process.

Conclusion

The experience of Western societies suggests that where
power is both worth having and hard to get, men and women
will combine to form political parties.

– Anthony King (1969)

Cause by cause they fight,
One by one they lose

– Melissa Etheridge, "Testify"

An underlying motif of this book is that ideology offers no buffer to the
obstacles faced by small political organizations. Those who have lived in the
industrialized West and witnessed the struggles of progressive movements
over the past forty years might be tempted to assume that a group like the
Family Coalition Party would have an easier go of it as it works to promote
its highly conservative economic and social causes. Certainly support for
the free market and traditional values seems to be everywhere – in Canada,
one need only look at the continued election of neoconservative governments like Gordon Campbell's Liberals in British Columbia for proof.

Yet it isn't as simple as all that. While support for the economic freedoms that capitalism provides is as strong as ever, the same cannot be said
for the ideals of social conservatism, and herein lies the rub. Those on the
hard right of the conservative spectrum have discovered that a strategy of
dovetailing social conservative beliefs with economic ones does not lead
to unilateral support, even among their supposed natural constituents.

Analytically, this is a situation that makes for some strange bedfellows.
While the foregoing chapters demonstrated the FCP has a high degree of
ideological resonance with Christian right and pro-family supporters in the
United States and Canada, they also showed the FCP to have an equally
high *organizational* resonance with groups like the Green Party, who represent virtually everything the FCP fought against. Consequently, the FCP
can be evaluated as a political organization in the same way that progressive parties, movements, and party/movements have been for the past
quarter-century.

In this case, as a party/movement, the FCP, like the Greens or the CCF,
had to fight to maintain a balance between keeping a principled movement position and meeting the requisite demands of party politics. In this
struggle, party activists were confronted with a series of problems unique

to the organization's dual identity, as well as those problems that exist for any social movement or minor political party. The experiences of the CCF and the Green Party suggest that this is a daunting if not impossible task, as both parties have fallen prey to the powerful forces of political institutionalization. When the Family Coalition merged with Reform BC to become the Unity Party of British Columbia, it too turned down this road.

Because party/movements are fraught with the risk of such transience, the wisdom of forming them might well be questioned were it not for the initial motivations of those involved. For the FCP, this motivation came in the form of its founders becoming so frustrated and disaffected by mainstream social movements and political parties that they took matters into their own hands. Witnessing the inability of pro-family movements to influence government policy and finding themselves shut out of the Social Credit Party, they sought to create their own vehicle for social change. To this end, the FCP was formed to act as a formal political conduit for the pro-family movement in BC, as well as a vehicle for engaging in education, particularly during election times.

In this respect, the FCP shares a number of characteristics with other party/movements such as the Greens, the old CCF, and the now defunct Feminist Party of Canada. Foremost, there is a primary concern for raising awareness about their issue cluster of concerns, then there is a recognition of the need for formal access to the realm of institutionalized politics, and finally there is a concern for winning elected office.

It is this last point that is perhaps the most distinctive feature of a party/movement. It could well be argued that the first two features are shared by all minor parties, even though the political education function of most mainstream parties may be more of a hazy apparition. But party/movements are unique in their partially abstentionist approach to electoral politics. Those involved with the FCP believed that the role of a political party is far more than just that of a vote-generating machine, that it must first be an organization of principle and be used to create awareness of the issues it represents. As they saw it, a party gives formal political access and voice to their entire movement, as well as lending it a certain political legitimacy, all of which they hoped would facilitate the educational efforts of the cause. As one member remarked about the FCP's existence, "if it's a political party, there must be something to it."

Two other traits that characterize party/movements are their agendas of systemic democratic reform and their related internal commitment to operate via a fully democratic, non hierarchical decision making process. The latter has been observed in most party/movements, including the FCP and the Greens. The former is most apparent with the Greens, who have been the most vociferous in their intentions to implement a systemic program of radicalized democracy (Boggs 1986; Sandilands 1992), although the CCF, the Progressives, and left-libertarian parties in Europe all had as part of their package for socio-political change a mandate to increase direct citizen participation. This has included intentions to infuse their respective parliamentary systems with a greater sense of representative responsibility, usually through calls for the adoption of some type of proportional representation system. In the case of the Family Coalition Party, while there was this kind of support for electoral reforms, it was not committed to a program of radical democratization in the way the Greens are. Here it departed from its organizational cousins on the left and reflected its conservative roots by advocating gradual electoral change rather than radical reform.

It is these characteristics, and their strategic combination, that find the goal of electoral success subsumed under a program that seeks to educate, represent, and reform – and this is what makes a party/movement like the FCP distinguishable from any other political party or social movement organization. The decision by the founders of the FCP to use a party form to directly address the concerns of the pro-family movement was a decisive tactical maneouvre aimed at creating a political opportunity structure through which they hoped to have an impact on the policies of other political organizations around them. To proceed down such a path, however, required that they attach their movement function of consciousness raising to a party form that carried with it a set of organizational, institutional, and cultural hurdles that most movement activists are ill-equipped to manage and uninterested in pursuing.

Organizationally, party/movements must address both created and compounded difficulties. The difficulties created by the fusing of form and function pose the most serious threat to the internal stability and organizational future of a group like the FCP, and it is with these tensions that the impact of internal structuration and the logic of institutional politics on party/movements can be clearly seen. What party/movements strive to achieve is a balance between the requisite demands of their party form and the continued commitment to the purity of their movement principles. The force of internal structuration, however, increasingly pushes an organization like the FCP towards professionalization and the risks of co-optation or absorption. Simultaneously, the logic of institutional politics pressures the executive of a party/movement to choose between remaining true to their ideological commitments or abandoning them in favour of political populism. It appears to be the fate of most party/movements, and it certainly has been in the case of the German Greens and the CCF/NDP in Canada, that they succumb to the power of these two forces and to varying degrees jettison the ideological commitment of their movement for the chance to gain political power by pursuing a strategy of party populism.

From the beginning, there were signs that the FCP was not immune to these forces. Simply by virtue of choosing a strategy that involved using a party form, the founders betrayed a bias for the institutional, and there were always those within the membership who did not oppose more flexibility around the party's positions on its pro-life and pro-family principles. One member, for instance, said, "They could soften their stand on abortion, I think, and still get the hard-line support and also get others to support them," while another said the party's "absolute stand on abortion frightens me." In becoming the Unity Party, the Family Coalition was not only forced to soften its pro-life rhetoric but began what may be for party/movements the inescapable slide to institutionalization.

This inevitability is directly linked to the compounded difficulties that arise for a party/movement around membership recruitment, financial stability, and activist motivation. For example, minor political parties and social movement organizations both tend to experience chronic problems with mobilizing resources, and a party/movement like the FCP compounds these difficulties with their organizational duality. Members and/or financial supporters of movements and parties become involved with the expectation that these organizations will fulfill the mandates typically associated with their form. That is, supporters of political parties anticipate that their party of choice has the potential for governance, while movement supporters expect a protocol of activism and constant public education. Most people do not join a political party with the intention of actively working for it, but this was the very thing the movement aspect of the FCP desperately required. The long-term result was that one small core of activists continued to perform the bulk of the work for the party, and by the time of the Unity merger, even they were feeling the effects of the past nine years. Just after the merger, one long-serving executive member said about the FCP, "I kind of think we'd run our course, heavens to goodness. We were just tired."

The FCP was also confronted with challenges of an institutional and cultural nature. The overall resistance of the current parliamentary model to systemic reform, coupled with the geographic base of the electoral system's mode of representation, has created a significant institutional barrier for party/movements. The post-materialist nature of party/movement grievances requires an electoral system capable of representation based on issues rather than spatial proximity. Unless an issue is geographically concentrated, it is virtually impossible for a party/movement to gain the electoral clout required for its organization and for its issue cluster to be perceived as politically legitimate. In this regard, party/movements like the FCP and the Greens differ dramatically from the likes of the old CCF and the Bloc Québécois in that they have no regional stronghold of support that they can use to give political voice to their social grievances. In part, this is the motivation behind Canadian minor parties like the FCP supporting calls for the adoption of a proportional representation system.

As an institution unto itself, the media also pose a vexing challenge for party/movements. The media are of such paramount importance to the fortunes of political parties and movements alike that political organizations must develop highly effective strategies for attracting and utilizing them to their advantage. For parties, this translates into popularizing their message for mass consumption and articulating it through a charismatic leader in a manner that remains flexibly noncommittal on issues of policy. For movements, this necessity demands a specific media strategy that either deliberately avoids or deliberately targets the media by presenting them with irresistible images of confrontation and spectacle. Party/movements, however, are trapped between the two and must choose between a strategy of media populism or a strategy of media circumvention.

The Family Coalition Party membership did not support the notion of the party's engaging in movement strategies for gaining media attention because it felt party status carries with it an expectation of proper institutional conduct. On the other hand, had the party pursued a strategy of media populism and presented itself as an organization willing to dilute its ideological fervour to win media attention as a populist party, it risked alienating its supporters. The result is another tension of fusion that retards the potential of a party/movement.

The current popular beliefs of Canadian political culture contribute yet another barrier to the efforts of party/movements. The strategic vision of party/movement activists is one founded on a belief that the electoral arena is a site of contestation for social and not simply economic grievances. In turn, this has led activists within the Family Coalition Party to regard political parties as a specialized type of social movement organization and the act of voting as a deliberate and legitimate social movement action.

What the FCP and other party/movements discovered, though, is that there is a cultural lag within their constituencies that inhibits potential adherents from adopting this vision. Political parties, elections, and voting are embraced by the average pro-family supporter (and the average citizen) as vehicles and opportunities to ensure continued material security – they simply do not vote with a primary concern for quality-of-life issues. In other words, these political institutions and acts have yet to be identified by movement supporters as equally valid opportunities to engage in struggles informed by a post-material ethos. This cultural lag of political vision has limited the ability of party/movements like the FCP to mobilize support among their natural movement constituencies. Consequently, it has restricted their capacity to present themselves as a serious political force, not only to potential supporters, but to the very parties and government bureaucracies they are seeking to influence.

Regardless of these obstacles, minor parties, movements, and party/ movements do not go away. They are a permanent feature of Canada's political landscape, betraying by their presence a systemic ill. These beacons of discontent most commonly take the form of social movements, about which Alberto Melucci wrote: "These groups become the indicators, the symptoms of the structural problems of the system. Through their visible action they publicize existing conflicts, even though their mobilization is limited to a specific time and place" (1980, 55).

Since the 1960s, the new social movements have been playing this role. And what has been particularly unique about NSMs has been their abstentionist attitude towards institutional politics and their concomitant claiming of arenas in civil society as legitimate terrain for political action and expression. This deliberate refusal to acquiesce to the practices of the political status quo, combined with the opening up of previously apolitical spheres for political engagement, has produced a groundswell of popular support for the feminist movement, the peace movement, and other NSMs. Through their presence and work, NSMs have been able to provide minority voices with a means of articulating grievances without the risk of censure by hegemonic elites. Over thirty years of vigorous movement activism, substantial gains in the realms of popular consciousness, formal law, and political policy have subsequently transpired. In British Columbia, this has meant, among other things, increased recognition for gay marriages, the right of gays to adopt children, the ready availability of abortion services in hospitals and private clinics, and a public education system that is committed to educating students about homosexuality and presenting the gay family as a legitimate family form.

Naturally, the NSMs have faced opposition from their detractors, most often religious and/or conservative-minded ideologues and activists who regard the gains won by NSMs as a threat to the dominant hegemonic order and to the status of their own historically privileged ideology. The most prominent of these oppositional groups have been the pro-life and pro-family movements. Predominantly religious conservatives who have set out not simply to oppose the agendas of various NSMs but to actively work towards the popularized and legal acceptance of a Christian and conservative-based lifestyle, members of the pro-family movement widely believe that the secular humanist ideology that undergirds the NSMs has spread throughout civil and political society and is threatening to dismantle the structures that have provided social order and material security for generations of Canadians.

Scholars have typically regarded these movements as ancillary to the efforts of the NSMs and categorized them as countermovements – movements that arise in opposition to the initial efforts of other movements and resist them with varying degrees of success. While this conceptualization may have been empirically valid in the 1960s and even through the 1980s, since the 1990s it has become inadequate for three main reasons.

First, during any historical moment, the observer's standpoint largely determines which is the movement and which is the counter. Pro-life supporters have always considered pro-choice advocates as the counter-movement and vice versa, so it is important to remember that the analytic distinction is largely an artificial one.

Second, various NSMs can claim cultural and policy victories over the last twenty-five years. Abortion laws are the most evident example of this: with the decriminalization of abortion in Canada in 1969 and the 1973 *Roe v. Wade* decision in the US, coupled with the general cultural acceptance of a woman's right to access to safe abortions, the pro-choice and pro-life movements have reversed their categorical roles. The pro-life movement no longer works as a countermovement trying to prevent or resist the efforts of the pro-choice movement, but rather is working towards reversing pro-choice victories with their movement efforts to have more restrictive abortion laws enacted. It is now the pro-choice movement that is in the defensive position of being a countermovement.

Finally and most importantly, the pro-family and pro-life movements are, like the NSMs, extraparliamentary and concerned primarily with quality-of-life issues. This is what brings them into the orbit of NSM analysis, even though their ideology, combined with the popular use of the term, does make it implausible to call them a new social movement.

Instead, the pro-family and pro-life movements are best thought of as conservative *resurgence movements* that are attempting to resist social change while simultaneously promoting social change by working towards the re-establishment of lost but previously dominant and popular cultural beliefs. Appreciated as such, it becomes possible to evaluate pro-family movement organizations using the concepts that have been applied by movement scholars in their analytical attempts to understand contemporary movements.

To examine the Family Coalition Party this way, it was necessary to separate the party form from movement function, but once this was done, the FCP could be seen as a social movement organization that faces the same difficulties with resource mobilization, framing, and political opportunity that all contemporary movements confront. There was, however, a novelty to its tactical approach as an SMO. Most analysts point to how important available political opportunities are to SMOs' goals. In the case of the Family Coalition Party, none appeared satisfactory, so it created its own.

As a conservative resurgence movement that created its own political opportunity, the FCP represented a challenge to contemporary social movement research because its presence exposed what Steven Buechler (1993) has called the discipline's "theoretical silences" on substantive theoretical and empirical analysis of such movement organizations. In part, this book has attempted to remedy this with its conclusion that all party/ movements and social movement organizations, irrespective of ideological orientation, face the same myriad difficulties in their efforts to gain support and socio-political legitimacy for their cause.

Yet it cannot be forgotten that the Family Coalition Party, while organizationally similar to, say, the Greens in the problems it faces, has a singularly different set of ideological foundations. The pro-family movements in Canada and the US have their roots in the deep traditions of conservative political thought and Christian orthodoxy. After untangling the ideological, religious, and political strands that give the pro-family movements in the two countries their socio-political vision, three conclusions can be drawn.

First, throughout the various mutations that conservative thought has undergone in Britain, the United States, and Canada, it has exhibited a remarkable resiliency. At its core, conservatism continues to reflect a belief in God, a minimalist state, free-market economics, individual responsibility, and the importance of the traditional family as the cornerstone of a civilized society. Second, although these tenets are equivalent in both traditions, Canadian and American brands of conservatism do differ because of Canada's tradition of socialism and America's mainly liberal political legacy. Third, conservative traditions in Canada and the US have always overtly emphasized the intimate relation between the stability of the traditional family and the general health of the nation.

The pro-family movement is at its most mature and powerful in the US. The Christian Coalition and other pro-family organizations have exerted tremendous influence on the American polity through their effective lobbying efforts within the Republican Party. A relatively permeable American state, with its diffuse system of political power, provides numerous political opportunities for PFM activists to gain access to the policy process necessary for promoting their agenda. Also, the lack of a socialist tradition in the United States has permitted pro-family organizers to frame their agenda with support for neoconservative economic policies. What has resulted is a cohesive New Right program of pro-family values, neoconservative economics, and minimalist government that has a broad base of support rooted in the evangelical Christian community. Through the coordinated use of lobby groups, public awareness campaigns, political action committees, and televangelism, the pro-family movement in the United States has been highly effective at combatting the advances of new social movement organizations and, after re-electing one of their own as president in 2004, appears poised to exert even more influence in the future.

By contrast, the Canadian pro-family movement, certainly in British Columbia, is still in a stage of mobilizational infancy, even though many of its organizations have been in existence for years. For the most part, pro-life and pro-family organizations engage in their activism independent of one another. There is no sense of overall organizational or strategic unity among these movement organizations, nor does it appear that any such effort is forthcoming. Asked about the possibility and potential benefit of coalescing under some kind of umbrella organization, pro-life and pro-family activists, as well as FCP members, offered mixed responses. A few believe the possibility exists. Others acknowledge potential benefits to such an arrangement but think it unlikely because the separate organizations appear to relish their autonomy. Still another group felt it would be detrimental to the overall movement as well as an impossibility, again because of the strongly independent nature of the people running the organizations. Another particularly evident obstacle limiting the potential of the PFM in British Columbia to unite is the staunchly apolitical and non-partisan position of most of the organizations. There continues to be a belief within the movement that change must come from civil society and that this can only be achieved by a strategy of maintaining the appearance of political neutrality. Summed up, the pro-family movement in BC is best thought of as existing in a state of organizational disunity and political indirection.

Adding to the movement's challenges is Canada's socio-political culture, which is resistant to an economic system based purely on the principles of the free market. The infusion of socialist doctrine in Canadian socio-economic traditions makes it more difficult for the PFM in Canada to include a program of neoconservative economics in its agenda, even among its own ranks. As Lorna Erwin's (1993) research points out, the pro-family organization REAL Women found its support waning after it began to incorporate support for neoconservative economic policies in its pro-family message.

The same phenomenon could be found in the Family Coalition Party. While the party was made up of economic conservatives, they were opposed to the draconian implications associated with a complete dismantling of BC's social safety net. In discussing the party's position on public funding for abortions, for instance, Heather Stilwell acknowledged that "we are hard on abortion funding, and I don't know if that would be right wing, and we are not going to allow the public purse to pay for abortion. But then that doesn't mean we are miserable and hard-nosed, that we are going to be sending pregnant girls off on a leaky raft. The government can also be used for helping them through the difficulty."

In the hypothetical case that the FCP – or now Unity – were to form the provincial government, this remark hints at a funding redistribution and change in social policy direction more than an ipso facto abandonment of the Canadian tradition of maintaining a social safety net. Of course, strong deconstructive measures have been attempted, federally under Brian Mulroney's Conservatives and provincially with the conservatives in

Ontario, Saskatchewan, and Alberta, but most notably in BC during the early 1980s, where, among other drastic measures, "in the social services area, the Bennett government eliminated the Family Support Worker Program, the Provincial Inservice Resource Team, and Mental Retardation Coordinator positions as part of a major downsizing of the staff in the then Ministry of Human Resources" (Prince 1996, 255). In 2004, these kinds of harsh, ideology-driven measures are once again being visited upon British Columbians by Gordon Campbell's Liberals.

Historically, these kinds of efforts have been sporadic and scattered and have met with swift and vehement opposition. While nothing is guaranteed, Canada's social democratic tradition does seem to provide a partial buffer that has to date prevented the long-term implementation of neoconservatism's harsh socio-economic realities. It has at least prevented the pro-family movement in British Columbia from incorporating the most austere aspects of neoconservative economic doctrine into its agenda.

But it has not quelled the strong social conservative beliefs of pro-family advocates like the Toths. The hard-fought advances for gay rights, abortion, and women's rights won by the new social movements and social democratic parties have only served to fuel their resolve. With social attitudes changing and political opportunities drying up, the Toths saw no other option than to create an organization they hoped would advance the pro-family agenda. For nine years, though, despite the best efforts of its supporters, it remained, as one member put it, "a voice in the wilderness." It was a realistic way to put it – the party would have had great difficulty electing a member based on a platform with a narrow issue cluster of traditional family values in a popular culture that reflects growing support for familial diversity and a political culture that emphasizes materialist over quality-of-life concerns during election periods. Even members, true to the party/movement character of their organization, saw electoral success as a long-term and highly challenging goal. Heather Stilwell estimated it would have been at least ten years before the party won a legislative seat, while another member remarked, "I think it's faced by a difficult role. It could be eight years to get a candidate elected."

Due to these prospects, the merger with the Reform Party to become Unity was the FCP's only legitimate hope of moving forward or even continuing. While Kathleen Toth was adamant about the merger, saying, "if it doesn't work, we'll just carry on," the sentiment of several members was probably more realistic. They felt that once the Toths were no longer active in the party, it would collapse.

With the Unity Party, some life has been breathed into the ideals of the Family Coalition, but the challenges remain largely the same. To become a pro-life party with political force, Unity must win over supporters of the broader movement – a movement that is itself in a relative state of dis-unity. One FCP member commented about the PFM: "Right now they're not together, of course, and a lot of these people are lone riders, as it were, saying, 'Let's ride in and shoot up the town.' So I don't know if they want to be involved in that kind of action [coalition formation]."

If those in Unity can persuade these fragmented pro-family supporters to politically support the party, social conservatives may have a Social Credit Party for the new millennium. Certainly there is enough motivation among these religious conservatives to keep them going. The successes of the pro-family movement in the United States and the high degree of reso-nance between the agendas of the American PFM and the Unity Party con-tributes to the old FCP membership's belief that it is pursuing a course of action that will eventually result in victory.

Then there are the new battlefronts they see on the horizon, around issues they believe will have the power to mobilize people far beyond that of abortion. Past FCP president John O'Flynn, for one, thinks the future of pro-life politics "depends on where euthanasia goes. We'll sit back and see what's happening in this country. This is where the movement will go. The abortion issue is stale, there's not much happening. Genetic engineer-ing, reproductive technologies – these will add to the debate, some of the adoption issues will add to the movement, but I think it's going to be con-tingent on euthanasia."

Others think that what pro-family supporters see as they live their every-day lives is enough to keep them going: "It's done to them, not by them-selves – every time they see the abortion-on-demand issue in the paper or on TV, condoms in schools, see the issue of drugs in schools, sex education in schools – they see it and say this is wrong, we could sit down as the FCP and do something. This impetus drives them further and further on."

In the end, though, it will probably be the deeply historical and reli-gious roots of their conservative and Christian beliefs that keep them bat-tling in the eye of the political storm over family values. For many Family Coalition members, the Unity Party's position in this storm seems to fit a description of the FCP that Norm Herriott, a long-committed member of the executive, offered before the merger: "I think we're poised. If this movement gets off the ground and migrates north, it'll happen. That's the only real hope we have of becoming a party of significant size – if we're poised, ready to become the party for families."

Predicting the future of any political organization is fraught with con-tingencies, but, for the present, British Columbia's newest pro-life/pro-family party does seem destined to remain poised on the political margins. All that seems safe to conclude is that supporters of the ideals that gave birth to the Family Coalition Party will fight on, and with equal commit-ment, so too will those who have struggled to advance the rights of gays, women, and other historically disenfranchised groups. From all this, then, it seems only two things have become abundantly clear. Mobilizing political support for matters of social and moral conscience of any type is a tricky business. And the hotly contested debates that make up the politics of the family will continue well into the future.

Appendix:
Note on Methodology

The research for this study was conducted between 1996 and 2004 using a combination of non-participant field observation, an interview sample survey, and a historical sociological approach. The combination of these strategies made it possible to generate a source of data that provided a rich knowledge base about the Family Coalition Party and thus the opportunity for gaining a detailed understanding of the FCP and its associated movement. Archival material, media searches, party and public meetings, and formal and informal interviews with party personnel were all used in this effort. Interviews were also conducted with directors and activists of pro-life and pro-family organizations to gain insight into their organizations, their opinions about the pro-family movement, and their knowledge and thoughts on the FCP.

The field work specifically included attending five FCP annual general meetings, the Unity Party founding convention, its first leadership convention, and its first AGM. During the 1996 and 2001 provincial elections, a dozen all-candidates meetings were attended and four all-candidates debates on local cable stations were reviewed (this was limited by geography and simultaneous meetings, but most significantly by FCP candidates not being invited to participate).

In total, 102 interviews were conducted over the research period. This included roughly 7 percent of the FCP membership and 17 directors and activists in pro-family and pro-life organizations in the province, as well as executive members of the Unity Party. The FCP members interviewed included all but one of the people who ran as candidates in any general or by-election for the party, executive members, party founders, and general members. Interviewed general members were selected to correlate geographically the ridings of the candidates who ran in elections. Candidates were used in this sense as markers to establish the combined criteria of party activity and provincial distribution of FCP membership. An attempt was made to have this part of the sample include recent and long-term members, as well as reflect gender and age differences. As a result of this strategy, interviews were conducted province-wide, particularly in the Lower Mainland, the Fraser Valley, Hope, the Nelson–Creston region, and southern, northern, and mid–Vancouver Island.

When interviews were conducted, they were done at a time and place that was convenient for the interviewee. For the most part, this involved going to interviewees' homes, but interviews were also conducted in coffee shops, parks, schoolyards, places of employment, shopping malls, and in one instance a camper van parked on a small town's main street. The interviews combined open and closed questions and, although standardized, were executed in a semi-structured way that gave primary respect to the interview situation and the respondent's knowledge of the subject under question. Paramount attention was also given to ensuring the interview situation was as comfortable and free of friction as possible for the respondent. Whether or not this was achieved is difficult to assess, other than to recall that coffee cups were refilled and respondents' answers were thoughtful and at times spirited. Respondents also showed sincerity and a willingness to divulge a level of detail that has contributed to the flavour of the interviewer's research findings.

Quotes from these interviews, as well as the pro-family material that appears in the book, were selected to capture the political and cultural attitudes of the FCP membership and its associated movement in as much ethnographic detail as possible. The selective attribution of names to the quotes was guided by three factors. First, most of the names that do appear are individuals who were either central figures in the FCP's life as a party/movement or involved with the broader movement. Their roles with the FCP and the movement were important, and by being willing and kind enough to let their names be used, they have contributed to the richness of the book's detail. Second, some of the interviewees preferred to remain anonymous, and naturally this request was respected. Finally, it was felt that there was no need to attribute names to quotes that were used only to illustrate a general position, argument, or opinion. This was all done to provide the reader with the opportunity to understand the movement from its own voices and to draw his or her own conclusions about it while still being able to examine the characteristics and struggles common to all party/movements.

Notes

Introduction

1 John Ibitson, "Day's Plan Found in Secret Paper," *Globe and Mail*, 7 November 2000, A1; Peter O'Neil, "Day Defends Creation Beliefs, Attacks 'Lies' on His Ethnic Views," *Vancouver Sun*, 16 November 2000, A1.

2 Julian Bettrame, "Christian Right's Newest Convert Is Robert Dole," *Vancouver Sun*, 16 June 1996, A21; Rupert Cornwall, "Ultra-Conservative Mood Dominates Perot Meeting," *Vancouver Sun*, 14 August 1995, A7.

3 Julian Bettrame, "Christian Right's Newest Convert Is Robert Dole," *Vancouver Sun*, 16 June 1996, A21.

4 Paul Wells, "Groups Voice Opposition to Republican Convention," *Vancouver Sun*, 14 August 1996, A10.

Chapter 1: The Family Coalition Party of British Columbia

1 Until 1990, the first stated principle and objective of the Social Credit Party was to "foster and encourage the universally recognized principles of Christianity in human relationships" (Social Credit Constitution and Bylaws, 1988, section 2a). After his acclamation as leader in 1986, Vander Zalm, in an interview with the *Vancouver Province*, admitted that, "I am pro-life and I am alarmed that the percentage of abortions to live births is so much higher in BC than in other parts of Canada." As well, Vander Zalm supported the return of prayers in public schools while he was minister of education. See Malcolm Turnbull, "Vander Zalm Outlines Priorities," *Vancouver Province*, 1 August 1986, 4.

2 The Toths had originally met Vander Zalm in 1970 through their involvement with Birthright, a counselling service for expectant mothers. They have maintained contact over the years, and upon returning to BC after a ten-year absence, Mr. Toth contacted Vander Zalm to offer their support and help should he decide to run for the Socred leadership.

3 British Columbia, Legislative Assembly, *Debates (Hansard)*, 29 February 1988, 3163-65.

4 For instance, the Toths suggested that Vander Zalm was given the wrong information by members of his inner cabinet regarding the power a premier has to make such proclamations. They also said Vander Zalm viewed his not being a lawyer, which would have eliminated such a dependency, as the largest handicap he faced during his time in government.

5 Bill Vander Zalm, "'What Really Killed Social Credit,'" *BC Report*, 25 April 1994, 10-11. For analyses of Bill Vander Zalm's troubled premiership and time with the Social Credit Party, see, for instance, Persky 1989; and Leslie 1991.

6 Part of Mrs. Toth's motivation for running for this nomination was to counter Susan Brice's platform, which was based on opposition to the premier and the abortion battles that had been going on in the riding. See Barbara McLintock, "Brice Re-entering Fray for Johnston's Team," *Vancouver Province*, 24 July 1991; Malcolm Curtis, "Brice Switches Back to Politics in Seeking Socred Nomination," *Victoria Times-Colonist*, 24 July 1991; Tom Henry, "Church and Province," *Monday Magazine*, 30 May 1991.

7 One report said that Toth "accused the Socred establishment of trying to torpedo her efforts and threatened that neither she, nor her supporters, would back them in an election." See Tom Henry, "Church and Province," *Monday Magazine*, 30 May 1991.

8 Mrs. Toth said these ministers included Claude Richmond, Brian Smith, and Elwood Veitch.

9 Tim Gallagher, "The Socreds Dodge the 'Christian' Clause," *BC Report*, 18 June 1990, 7.

10 The amendment for section 2(a) said, "The principles of the Society recognize the supremacy of God and the rule of law." This is followed by a new subsection, 3(a): "3. The objectives of the Society are: (a) to foster and encourage the development of those social, moral and ethical principles which have historically guided the people of the Province in the pursuit of their individual goals regardless of gender, ethnic origin or religious affiliation." British Columbia Social Credit Party, Constitutional Review Committee 1990 Report.

11 A *BC Report* article even reported that "some suspect the entire fracas may have been part of a continuing assault by Mrs. McCarthy and others on the Vander Zalm leadership." See Tim Gallagher, "The Socreds Dodge the 'Christian' Clause," *BC Report*, 18 June 1990, 7.

12 Mrs. Toth recalls that during an exchange in the 1994 by-election in Matsqui, Mrs. McCarthy accused her of telling lies because of this description of the vote. Toth says she reminded McCarthy that she had in fact been standing at the microphone waiting to speak when the votes were held and so saw firsthand how the event unfolded. Overall, however, Mrs. McCarthy did support the change. She was quoted as saying, "We are, after all, a political organization, not a religious organization." See Les Leyne, "Socred Constitution Drops Christianity," *Victoria Times-Colonist*, 5 June 1990.

13 Bill Vander Zalm, "'What Really Killed Social Credit,'" *BC Report*, 25 April 1994, 10-11.

14 Tom McFeely, "At the Crossroads," *BC Report*, 15 April 1991, 6.

15 Mark B. Toth, "Convicted out of Court," *Victoria Times-Colonist*, 16 April 1991. For the rally, the Toths set up a phone tree to recruit support and brought seven busloads of people over from the mainland in an attempt to dissuade Vander Zalm from resigning.

16 Tom Henry, "Church and Province," *Monday Magazine*, 30 May 1991; Canadian Press, "Right-Wing Christians Welcomed by Socred," *Victoria Times-Colonist*, 10 January 1992.

17 Tim Gallagher, "The Socreds Dodge the 'Christian' Clause," *BC Report*, 18 June 1990, 7.

18 Mike Crawley, "Shut-Out Social Credit Party Will Consider Name Change," *Vancouver Sun*, 18 July 1996, B8.

19 Terry O'Neill, "Mixed Messages and a Moribund Convention," *BC Report*, 21 November 1994, 9.

20 Mike Crawley, "Shut-Out Social Credit Party Will Consider Name Change," *Vancouver Sun*, 18 July 1996, B8.

21 Mike Crawley, "Right-Wing Leaders Urged to Forget Egos and Form New Party," *Vancouver Sun*, 30 May 1996, B5; Jim Beatty and Justine Hunter, "Liberals, Reform Discuss Union," *Vancouver Sun*, 24 February 1997, A1, A9.

22 The Ontario constitution reflected several pieces of legislation that did not apply to British Columbia. For instance, Ontario has a different voting age, and regulation of Sunday shopping had been an issue there.

23 This was a health care resolution passed at the 1993 annual general meeting. The opposition to appointed regional health boards arose because such a situation closes off an avenue for pro-life activists to restrict abortions in hospitals. Locally elected hospital boards provided an opportunity for pro-life activists to elect pro-life supporters to the board and wield some political power. The 1997 battle in Langley was typical. When the government put Langley Memorial Hospital under the control of the South Fraser Regional Health Board, opponents feared the amalgamation would result in the hospital's being forced to perform abortions, which it did not at the time. In point of fact, then NDP Minister of Health Joy McPhail came out with the statement that, "In the communities where certain special-interest groups have made it their goal to impose an anti-choice point of view, those communities' activists were not put forward to be appointed to the board ... Basically, everybody on the board was required to support our government's view that all legitimate health care services, including therapeutic abortion, be provided" (*BCTV*

Late News, 11 March 1997). See Justine Hunter, "Anti-Abortion Activists Barred from Health Boards," *Vancouver Sun,* 13 March 1997, A1, A9.

24 FCP board of directors' policy meeting, 3 August 1991; FCP labour policy resolution, 1992.

25 Family Coalition Party of BC, "Family," Newsletter no. 6 (January 1996). One vigorous pro-life activist purchased a private house that sits within the fifty-metre limit of the bubble zone ruling to allow signs opposing abortion to sit on the lawn. Because the property is a private residence, the bubble zone legislation does not cover it. Known as Gianna House, it operates as a counselling service for expectant mothers.

26 Legislature staff, "1 Million Cold Cash Found for Women's Centres," *Victoria Times-Colonist,* 7 March 1992; Karen Gram, "Women's Groups Pleased with Money for 28 Centres," *Vancouver Sun,* 7 March 1992.

27 It was reported in the *Victoria Times-Colonist* that, "Family Coalition Party of BC leader Kathleen Toth urged the crowd to muster support for a plebiscite on abortion funding." The crowd referred to was the close to one thousand pro-life activists who had gathered on the steps of the legislature in Victoria to oppose this funding. See Katherine Dedyna, "Anti-Abortion Throng Howls for Health Minister to Resign," *Victoria Times-Colonist,* 27 March 1992, A16.

28 Although the party was unsuccessful with this bid, it did present over six thousand signatures along with its brief opposing the regulations and time constraints of the referendum process to the standing committee on the new act. See Family Coalition Party of British Columbia, "Initiative, Referendum and Recall: A Brief to the Standing Committee," 4 November 1992. The FCP had an official position on the initiative and referendum process that supported the process but opposed the mechanism of the enabling legislation in Bill 36. The party considered it "unworkable" because of the time constraints and percentage of signatures required. As it stands, within a ninety-day period, 10 percent of eligible voters in each of the province's seventy-five ridings must sign the petition requesting a referendum.

29 All-candidates meeting at West Vancouver Secondary School, West Vancouver–Capilano riding, 24 May 1996.

30 Ironically, the sign was designed to be deliberately confrontational in the hope of attracting some media attention, but Mr. Toth said the sign – in fact his entire campaign – was completely ignored by the media.

31 Family Coalition Party of BC, "A Brief to the Human Rights Review from the Family Coalition Party of BC," 2 June 1994. Along with all of the party's other briefs, this also appeared on its website.

32 Ibid., 3.

33 Bill 33 protects classes of people – based on race, colour, ancestry, place of origin, religion, marital status, family status, physical or mental disability, sex, age, or *sexual orientation* – from discrimination, hatred, or contempt. Bill 32 changed the Human Rights Act to the Human Rights Code and established a Human Rights Commission.

34 A worry existed that under Bill 33, FCP candidates could be found guilty of spreading hate by openly stating their opposition to homosexuality. However, it was found that section 37 of the bill exempts specific political beliefs.

35 Family Coalition Party of BC, Leader's Report, 1994-95, 1.

36 Family Coalition Party of BC, "Family," Newsletter no. 4 (February 1995), 2; Justine Hunter, "New Law Allows Gays to Adopt," *Vancouver Sun,* 21 June 1996.

37 Mr. Zacharias admits he has been "accused of being racist, anti-Semitic, white supremacist [sic]" but points out, "Those labels are tossed around to destroy my credibility and you have to look where the accusations are coming from." He also said the sign shocked some people and, "Some gave me the finger, some gave me the thumbs up."

38 Dan MacLennan, "Krell Promotes Discrimination," *Courier-Islander,* 22 May 1996, 1.

39 Ibid.

40 Editors, "Unacceptable," *Courier-Islander,* 22 May 1996.

41 Becky Lockhart, "Morality Offered," *Comox Valley Record,* 24 May 1996, A8.

42 Family Coalition Party of BC, "Education Funding Review: A Submission by the Family Coalition Party of British Columbia to the BC Government's Position Paper: Financing

Public Schools: Issues and Options," October 1992. This paper is based largely on the opinions of the Brookings Institute, a neoconservative think tank in Washington, DC, that published a study on education, *Politics, Markets and America's Schools* (Washington, DC: Brookings Institute, 1990). In the study, authors John Chubb and Terry Moe advocated a return of control to local levels through a voucher system.

43 Surrey–Cloverdale all-candidates meeting, 23 May 1996.

44 West Vancouver–Capilano all-candidates meeting, 24 May 1996.

45 Mr. Toth sat on the board for independent schools during this period. Unsuccessful with W.A.C. Bennett's government, they nonetheless persevered and won the battle when the Socreds were returned to power in 1975. Bill Bennett's government agreed to fund one-third of an independent school's cost, a funding level that has since risen to 50 percent.

46 Mrs. Stilwell was also the current president of the school, which receives its funding from the Ministry of Education but has a specific mandate that calls for "teacher-centred" classrooms, committed parental involvement with the school and curriculum, and school uniforms. It is a secular school that follows the provincial curriculum guidelines but teaches the subjects discreetly and emphasizes a back-to-basics approach to learning and respect for traditional orders of authority. The school currently has roughly 250 students and a waiting list in "the hundreds," according to Mrs. Stilwell. There is also a movement to fund a traditional high school in Surrey. General support for traditional schools seems to be growing. In Richmond, for instance, there is strong support for opening a traditional school, though the proposal was recently turned down. See Harold Munro, "Traditional School's Leader Says Other Classes Just as Good," *Vancouver Sun,* 21 January 1997, B1, B2; Susan Balcom, "Back-to-Basics High School Sought in Surrey," *Vancouver Sun,* 12 January 1996, A1, A4; Susan Balcom, "Richmond Board Rejects Bid for Traditional School," *Vancouver Sun,* 7 March 1996, B6; Brenda Bow, "Private Schools Gain in Popularity as Experts Predict Numbers Will Rise," *Vancouver Sun,* 27 August 1996, B1.

47 Mrs. Stilwell first sat on the Surrey School Board from 1990 to 1993. Then in the 1997 election, she garnered roughly 17,000 votes, only 200 behind the top vote earner. In 1999 she was re-elected, receiving more votes than any other trustee elected. The board was dominated by conservatives, with the Surrey Electors Team holding five positions, the NDP one, and the White Rock representative the other.

48 Province of British Columbia, Ministry of Education, *Career and Personal Planning: Draft Learning Outcomes,* Appendix A: Learning Outcomes, Personal Development, "Family Life Education," 170.

49 Province of British Columbia, Ministry of Education, *Career and Personal Planning: Draft Learning Outcomes,* Appendix A: Learning Outcomes, Personal Development, "Collecting Information," 161.

50 Ibid.

51 This aspect of a student's privacy is actually a product of changes to the Infants Act that the FCP also opposes.

52 Province of British Columbia, Ministry of Education, *Career and Personal Planning: Draft Learning Outcomes,* Appendix A: Learning Outcomes, "Healthy Living," 167.

53 Family Coalition Party of BC, West Vancouver–Capilano, "May '96 Newsletter."

54 Family Coalition Party of BC, "A Brief to the Human Rights Review from the Family Coalition Party of BC," 2 June 1994, 3.

55 Jerry Collins, "Social Engineering Dropouts," *BC Report*, 30 December 1996, 34. A *Vancouver Sun* article also reported on the findings of the privacy commission's review of the program after it received numerous complaints about the "Collecting Information" component of CAPP. See the editorial "How Secret Are Those Tell-All School Assignments?" *Vancouver Sun,* 8 March 1997, A13.

56 In 1995, a resolution was submitted at the party's annual general meeting stating that "the Family Coalition Party of BC would remove provincial government funding for English as a Second Language programs in BC schools." See Family Coalition Party of BC, Policy Resolutions Submitted in 1994.

57 Ibid.

58 Kim Bolan, "Teachers' Resolution Aims at Fighting Homophobia," *Vancouver Sun,* 14 March 1997, B3. In a vote on 17 March 1997, BCTF members overwhelmingly supported passage of the resolution (*UTV News,* 17 March 1997). See also Kim Bolan, "Teachers Move to Tackle Homophobia in Province's Schools," *Vancouver Sun,* 18 March 1997, B1.

59 Kim Bolan, "Demonstrators Face Off over Homosexuality Issue," *Vancouver Sun,* 17 March 1997, A1, A6; "Readers Strongly Divided over BCTF's Anti-Homophobia Stand," *Vancouver Sun,* 31 March 1997, A11. An informal televote poll by UTV asked viewers "Should respect for homosexuals be taught in our schools?" and 75 percent of those who responded said no (*UTV News,* 17 March 1997). A *Vancouver Sun* editorial has also come out in opposition to passage of the resolution. See "Sex Education: Shaping Students' Attitudes to Sexuality Is the Job of Parents, Not Teachers," *Vancouver Sun,* 31 March 1997, A18.

60 New party president Darren Lowe wrote a letter to the local Coquitlam community newspaper opposing Resolution 102. Subsequently the party received over a dozen phone calls from parents about the resolution and the party in general, asking the party for support in their opposition to the resolution. The party responded by submitting a letter of opposition to the Coquitlam School Board.

61 Family Coalition Party of BC Constitution and Policies, 1994, "Finance Policies."

62 Constitution and Policies of the Family Coalition Party of BC, 1994, "The Family."

63 Constitution of the Family Coalition Party of BC, 1994, section 2c.

64 Constitution and Policies of the Family Coalition Party of BC, 1994, "The Family."

65 Ibid. Family Coalition Party of BC, "Resolutions Passed at 1996 Convention," Minutes: 1996 Annual General Meeting, 19 October 1996, 2.

66 Family Coalition Party of BC, "A Brief from the Family Coalition Party of BC to the BC Child Care Regulation Review," April 1993, 1, 3.

67 Constitution and Policies of the Family Coalition Party of BC, Health Care. Subsection 16(2) of the Infants Act states that, "Subject to subsection (3), an infant may consent to health care whether or not that health care would, in the absence of consent, constitute a trespass to the infant's person, and where an infant provides that consent, the consent is effective and *it is not necessary to obtain a consent to the health care from the infant's parent or guardian*" (emphasis added). British Columbia Infants Act, Part 2: Medical Treatment, 25 November 1993. In a newsletter, the FCP remarked that this amendment was part of the "socialist philosophy" that "works to undermine the bonds of love within families by legislating away the rights children have to the wisdom, the protection and the love of their parents until they are grown." See Family Coalition Party of BC, "Family," Newsletter no. 2 (Spring/Summer 1993), 1.

68 Family Coalition Party of BC, "Child Protection Legislation Review: A Presentation to the Committee by the Family Coalition Party of British Columbia," 31 March 1992.

69 Constitution and Policies of the Family Coalition Party of BC, Social Services.

70 Rebecca Hudson, "Big Mamma vs. the Family," *BC Report,* 14 October 1996, 8. Among the pro-family groups opposing the formation of this ministry were Focus on the Family and the Citizens' Research Institute.

71 Constitution and Policies of the Family Coalition Party of BC, Finance.

72 Constitution and Policies of the Family Coalition Party of BC, Electoral Reform.

73 Of the respondents, 79 percent indicated their ethnic heritage was a Western European nation – 47 percent reported it to be either English, Scottish, or Irish, while 32 percent reported another country of ethnic origin, in particular Germany, France, or Holland – 18.5 percent indicated their heritage was Canadian, and only two were of Asian descent. All of the respondents reported being Christian, with 72 percent of total respondents indicating they were practising Catholics. The rest of the sample was spread evenly among Protestants, evangelical Christians, Mormons, and non-denominational Christians.

74 These include the ridings of Abbotsford, Chilliwack, Fort Langley–Aldergrove, Matsqui, and Mission–Kent.

75 Originally the party offered one-year memberships for $10 per individual and $15 for families. In 1992, they were switched to four-year memberships for $15 and $20, respectively. It was also a party practice to carry expired memberships over for a year to allow leeway for those who had forgotten to renew.

76 Family Coalition Party of BC, Minutes: First Annual General Meeting, 14 November 1992, 1.
77 Family Coalition Party of BC, Leader's Report, 1991-1992, 14 November 1992.
78 This included coverage in a number of different provincial publications: "Bill Vander Zalm Returns to His Roots," *Kelowna Daily Courier,* 12 May 1993; Canadian Press, "Values Eroding – Vander Zalm," *Victoria Times-Colonist,* 13 May 1993; Steve Vanagas, "A New Family for Conservatives: Vander Zalm Inspires High Hopes for the Fledgling FCP," *BC Report,* December 1993; Paul Chapman, "Vander Zalm Joins a Party," *Vancover Province,* 28 November 1993; Kenneth Whyte, "The Family Coalition Knows We Have to Develop Our Moral Priorities," *Globe and Mail,* 4 December 1993, D2; Steve Vanagas, "Seeking Friends of the Family," *BC Report,* 24 May 1993, 8.
79 "Toth: Zalm Brings Values to Reform," *Abbotsford News,* 17 May 1995.
80 Steve Vanagas, "A New Family for Conservatives: Vander Zalm Inspires High Hopes for the Fledgling FCP," *BC Report,* December 1993; Paul Chapman, "Vander Zalm Joins a Party," *Vancouver Province,* 28 November 1993; Kenneth Whyte, "The Family Coalition Knows We Have to Develop Our Moral Priorities," *Globe and Mail,* 4 December 1993, D2; Jim Hume, "Political Carousel Easing into High Gear," *Victoria Times-Colonist,* 7 December 1993.
81 Canadian Press, "Vander Zalm, McCarthy May Battle Again," *Lethbridge Herald,* n.d.; Canadian Press, "Family Party Urges Vander Zalm to Fight McCarthy in By-election," *Victoria Times-Colonist,* 28 November 1993.
82 Canadian Press, "McCarthy: By-election Losses Would Be Disaster for Leaders," *Victoria Times-Colonist,* 3 December 1993, B11.
83 The Mandate to Meet policy reads: "The Executive of the Family Coalition Party is mandated to meet with other free enterprise parties with the view to deciding a strategy or perhaps forming a coalition to defeat the NDP. The two FCP Constitutional clauses on the protection of innocent human life and the preservation of the traditional family must be publicly agreed to by all representatives of any new coalition."
84 Dan MacLennan, "Krell Promotes Discrimination," *Courier-Islander,* 22 May 1996, 1.
85 Ian Mulgrew, "What Makes BC Reform's Hanni Run?" *Vancouver Sun,* 9 December 1997, A17.
86 Ian Mulgrew, "BC Reform Leader Vows to Restore Respect for Party," *Vancouver Sun,* 8 December 1997, A4.
87 Family Coalition Party of BC, "Family," Newsletter no. 10 (Spring 1998).
88 Vaughn Palmer, "Party Leaders of the Right Gather in a Surrey Summit," <www.vancouversun.com/newsite/opinion>, 11 April 2000; Terry O'Neill, "The Third Way or the Highway," *Report,* 5 June 2000, 13.
89 The five parties were the Family Coalition Party of British Columbia, the Reform Party of British Columbia, the Social Credit Party of British Columbia, the British Columbia Party, and the British Columbia Conservative Party.
90 Chris Delaney, letter to Kathleen Toth, 10 April 2000.
91 *BCTV News,* 24 February 2001; "Five BC Conservative Parties Unite to Form Pro-Life Front," *BC Catholic,* 4 December 2000.
92 Vaughn Palmer, "BC Reform Discusses Merger with Evangelical Zeal," <www.vancouversun.com/newsite/opinion> (12 June 2000).

Chapter 2: The Pro-Family Movement
1 Seymour Martin Lipset (1988) argues that the label "neoconservative" was attached to this group by Michael Harrington to discredit and distance it from the democratic socialists and attempt to have it viewed as the left wing of the right rather than the right wing of the left. It has proven to be an excellent sociological example of the power of labelling.
2 Their anti-Communism did not bring the neoconservatives to jettison social democrat beliefs entirely. But as Lipset indicates, tension arose within the Republican Party between the neoconservatives and the classic laissez-faire conservatives – a tension that likely began to tug at the neoconservative commitment to the welfare state.
3 The Adolph Coors Company is but one of the most prominent corporate contributors to

and supporters of the New Right. Val Burris (1987) outlines the diverse corporate support that the New Right enjoys. Supporters include Dr. Pepper, Kraft, and 7-Eleven, with the oil industry being by far the largest contributor. See also Jenkins and Shumate (1985).

4 "Day's Campaign Has Earmarks of Reagan's 'Caring Conservatism,'" *Vancouver Sun*, 24 October 2000, A5.

5 "Welfare-Cuts Horror Story Probed," "Ontario Plans to Axe 10,000 Jobs," *Vancouver Sun*, 10 April 1996, A5; "Ontario Set to Make People Work for Their Welfare Money," *Vancouver Sun*, 6 April 1996, A5; "Ontario Unsheathes Sharp Knife to Cut Spending by 5.5 Billion," *Vancouver Sun*, 11 April 1996, A4; "Cuts to the Bone Feared in Ontario Services," *Vancouver Sun*, 16 January 1997, A3; "Ontario Unloads Housing, Welfare Costs," *Vancouver Sun*, 15 January 1997, A6.

6 "The Ontario Revolution: Now It's the Turn of Local Government," *Vancouver Sun*, 25 January 1997, A23.

7 "Manning, Harris Form Reform-Tory Alliance," *Vancouver Sun*, 30 August 1995, A4, notes that Manning sees, "An alliance with Harris is natural since a number of the themes that he is pressing are ones that Reform has plowed the ground on in Ontario and other places." See also "Ambitious Conservative Helped Craft Ontario's Common Sense Revolution," *Vancouver Sun*, 28 April 2000.

8 "Resignation Stuns Tory Insiders," *National Post*, 17 October 2001, A9. Several undeclared leadership candidates were described at the time as neoconservative and "hard-line" neoconservatives.

9 "To Rural Albertans, Klein Represents 'Common Sense,'" *Vancouver Sun*, 26 September 1996, B8.

10 "Manitoba Tories to Veer Right," *Vancouver Sun*, 16 September 1996, A5.

11 See Carter (1993), which demonstrates how legal and judicial actions have structurally and culturally dissuaded people from engaging in religion-based political activity.

12 See, for example, Robert Bellah's "Civil Religion in America," in *Daedalus*, 1967.

13 The collection of essays edited by Daniel Bell (1963), *The Radical Right*, thoroughly explores the theme of personal frustration and the extremist political activism it can generate. See also Simpson (1983).

14 Kent Tedin's study of support for the ERA issue concluded, for instance, that conservative evangelical denominations were overwhelmingly opposed to the ERA. See Tedin (1978).

15 These included grassroots organizations for mobilization like the American Coalition for Traditional Values, Concerned Women for America, and the American Freedom Council, as well as various political action committees (PAC): the National Conservative PAC, Life Amendment PAC, Moral Majority PAC. See Guth (1983); Latus (1992); and Moen (1992).

16 "Religious Right Rips into Campaign of Republican Dark Horse," *Vancouver Sun*, 12 February 1996, A1, A7.

17 "Christians 'On Mission,'" *Victoria Times-Colonist*, 13 August 1996, A2.

18 For instance, in the 1996 Washington State gubernatorial race, "Christian radical" Ellen Craswell won the Republican nomination on a platform that included such views as "Homosexuals can become heterosexuals if they work hard enough at it" and "The righteous should go into government." See "'Christian Radical' Candidate Splits Washington State GOP," *Vancouver Sun*, 24 October 1996, A14.

19 These include *Politically Incorrect: The Emerging Faith Factor in American Politics* (1994a), "What Do Religious Conservatives Really Want?" (1994b), and *Active Faith* (1996).

20 "Religious Right Is Down – But Far from Out," *Vancouver Sun*, 14 March 1998, A1, A10.

21 "Onward Evangelicals," *Vancouver Sun*, 15 July 1995, D15.

22 "Search for Values Brings Boomers Back to Church," *Vancouver Sun*, 27 July 1996, C3; "Lower Mainland Evangelical Churches Lead Membership Race," *Vancouver Sun*, 24 August 1995, B1; "Christians Search for a Renewed Faith," *Vancouver Sun*, 7 October 1995, A4.

23 "Lower Mainland Evangelical Churches Lead Membership Race," *Vancouver Sun*, 24 August 1995, B1; "Christians Search for a Renewed Faith," *Vancouver Sun*, 7 October 1995, A4; "Search for Values Brings Boomers Back to Church," *Vancouver Sun*, 27 July 1996, C3; "11,000 'Take Charge of Family' Christian Men Plan Rally at Coliseum," *Vancouver Sun*, 15 November 1996, B1, B4.

24 "Day Defends Creation Beliefs, Attacks 'Lies' on His Ethnic Views," *Vancouver Sun,* 16 November 2000, A1; "Day's Plan Found in Secret Paper," "Abortion Issue Ignited by Alliance Document, Cleric's Blast at PM," *Globe and Mail,* 7 November 2000, A1.

25 From its inception, the Social Credit's constitution contained a Christianity clause as the first of its principles and objectives: "2(a) To foster and encourage the universally recognized principles of Christianity in human relationships."

26 "Topics Show Reform Not a Party for Middle-of-the-Road," *Vancouver Sun,* 6 June 1996, A3; "Manning Bids to Curb Radicals, but Abortion, Gays Still an Issue," *Vancouver Sun,* 8 June 1996, A1; "Manning Wants Vote to Ban Abortion," *Vancouver Sun,* 31 October 1996, A1.

27 "Day Care a Perk that Subsidizes the Rich, Reform MP Says," *Vancouver Sun,* 23 November 1996, A3; "Reform MP Can't Understand Fuss about Him Attending Conference," *Vancouver Sun,* 21 August 1996, B1, B4; "Reformer Sticks to Back-of-Shop Remark," *Vancouver Sun,* 1 May 1996, A1, A8; "Manning's Morals," *Vancouver Sun,* 2 November 1996, A18.

28 See Haiven (1984).

29 Modelled after the Republican Party's Contract with America, the Christian Coalition's Contract with the American Family was unveiled in May 1995. It includes ten clauses to promote the pro-family agenda, including a ban on partial-birth abortions, promotion of religious liberty, and a return of local control over education. In *Active Faith,* Reed has said this is a document of long-term vision and activism, a "measured and gradual passage of key provisions that built momentum over a period of years" (1996, 202).

30 If there are two books that can be held up as examples of the fundamental doctrine of the pro-family and CCR movement in Canada, they are William Gairdner's *The Trouble with Canada: A Citizen Speaks Out* (1990) and *The War against the Family: A Parent Speaks Out* (1992). Virtually biblical in their immensity, they outline the religious conservative arguments and fears about the decay of the traditional Anglo-Saxon family in Canada at the hands of liberal social policies on gay and women's rights, abortion, immigration, and sex education in schools. A pop culture driven by a secular humanist ethic and a state overly intruding into the realm of private life are Gairdner's focus of attack in works that make no attempt to hide their ideological bent in chapter titles that include "The Feminist Mistake: Women against the Family," "The Great Welfare Rip-Off: Soaking Everyone, to Pay Everyone," and "The Silent Destruction of English Canada: Multiculturalism, Bilingualism, and Immigration."

31 This strategy can consistently be found in the themes of pro-family advocates in the US, Britain, and Canada. In the US, presidential policy advisors like George Gilder, Charles Murray, and Martin Anderson have all pursued this trajectory. In Britain, Roger Scruton and Ferdinand Mount, both advisors to Margaret Thatcher, have done the same. Canadian William Gairdner is continuing this trend with his work. While not always an overt strategy, their defence of the traditional nuclear family, patriarchal social order, and bourgeois morality is also an opposition to the growth of secular humanism and liberal social policies. See, for instance, George Gilder, *Men and Marriage* (Gretna: Pelican Publishing, 1988), Charles Murray, *In Pursuit of Happiness and Good Government* (New York: Simon and Shuster, 1988), Ferdinand Mount, *The Subversive Family* (London: Unwin, 1982), Roger Scruton, *Sexual Desire* (New York: Free Press, 1986), and William Gairdner, *The War against the Family: A Parent Speaks Out* (Toronto: Stoddart, 1992).

32 Luker (1984) provides a good sociological analysis of the abortion debate in the US.

33 In addition, there are pro-life political action committees like National Pro-Life (NPLPAC) and Life Amendment (LAPAC). The direct political action of these groups has been credited with, among other things, the 1976 passing of the Hyde Amendment prohibiting government funding of abortions except when the mother's life is at risk and the election of several pro-life New Right senators (Durham 2000; Diamond 1995, 1998; Luker 1984).

34 Diamond (1989) estimates that between 1982 and 1985, thirty women's health clinics were firebombed. On 16 January 1997, two bombs exploded at an Atlanta abortion clinic, five days before the twenty-fifth anniversary of the *Roe v. Wade* decision (*CBS Evening News,* 16 January 1997; "Six Hurt as Bombs Rock Abortion Clinic in US," *Vancouver Sun,* 17 January 1997, A22). Other violent attacks have included John Salvi's murder of two people at abortion clinics in 1994, for which he was sentenced to life imprisonment

("Killer of Two at US Abortion Clinics Guilty of Murder," *Vancouver Sun,* 30 November 1995, A13).

35 "Republicans Eye Abortion," *Vancouver Sun,* 20 June 1995, A12; "US Pro-Choice Supporters Alarmed after Congress Bans Type of Late-Term Abortion," *Vancouver Sun,* 23 March 1996, A8. President Clinton vetoed this bill in April 1996.

36 For example, the Campaign Life Coalition is the politically active arm of the movement, while Birthright is strictly an apolitical counselling service for expectant mothers. Provincial organizations such as BC Pro-Life and Vancouver Right to Life are educational in focus. To protect the latter's charitable-tax status, each supports the other in spirit but not action.

37 Borowski died of cancer in September of 1996. See "Abortion Foe Borowski Dies," *Vancouver Sun,* 24 September 1996, A3. His struggle against abortion spanned more than twenty years and included founding several pro-life groups, hunger strikes, and most prominently his legal battles over fetal rights.

38 The case revolved around the actions of pro-life protester Maurice Lewis. After Lewis violated the bubble zone and was convicted, an appellate decision ruled the zone unconstitutional. A subsequent appeal filed by the government of BC overturned the first appeal's ruling with the argument that a woman's right to privacy overrode an individual's right to free speech. See "Bubble Zone Law Gutted by Court," *Vancouver Sun,* 24 January 1996, A1; "Government to Appeal Bubble Zone Ruling," *Vancouver Sun,* 25 January 1996, B1; "Court Ruling on Bubble Zones 'A Victory,'" *Vancouver Sun,* 10 October 1996, B2.

39 "Abortion Foes Angry over Health Board Plan," *Vancouver Sun,* 2 December 1996, B1, B2.

40 See, for example, "Angering Pope, Poland Relaxes Abortion Law," *New York Times,* 25 October 1996, A6; "US Decides RU-486 Abortion Pill 'Approvable,'" *Vancouver Sun,* 19 September 1996, A12; "'94 Abortion Numbers Set Record," *Vancouver Sun,* 26 September 1996, A4.

41 For a philosophical argument on the rights of the fetus and the issue of potentiality as it applies to the fetus as a victim, see Winkler (1984).

42 "Charge against Mother to Test Canadian Laws," *Vancouver Sun,* 27 November 1996, A9; "Fetus Rights Issue Left to Lawmakers," *Vancouver Sun,* 24 December 1996, A3; "In Utero Shooting Case Advances, Raising Issue of Whether Fetuses Possess Human Status under Law," *Vancouver Sun,* 26 July 1996, A8; "Attempt to Protect Fetus from Addict Questioned," *Vancouver Sun,* 3 August 1996, A4; "Abuse Care Ordered to Save Fetus," *Globe and Mail,* 7 August 1996, A1; "Court Rules against Forced Treatment for Glue-Sniffing Mother," *Vancouver Sun,* 13 September 1996, A1, A2. In the US, a Wisconsin mother was remanded to a drug treatment centre to protect her fetus, in Florida a mother was charged with murder for shooting her fetus, and in South Carolina a mother was charged with child abuse for using cocaine during her pregnancy (*NBC Nightly News,* 6 February 1997).

43 "First UK Surrogate Granny," *Vancouver Sun,* 9 December 1996, A8; "Kirk Fights Test-Tube Baby for Lesbian," *Weekly Telegraph,* 14 October 1996, 7; "Rent-a-Womb Deals to Face Ban," *Vancouver Sun,* 14 June 1996, A3; "Abandoned UK Embryos to Be Killed," *Vancouver Sun,* 1 August 1996, A8; "Woman Carrying Eight Babies Signs Deal Based on How Many Survive," *Vancouver Sun,* 12 August 1996, A1, A2.

44 For instance, neither Ralph Reed nor William Gairdner, in four books between them, list "reproductive technology" in their indexes.

45 "Marleau Calls for Restraint in Reproductive Technology," *Vancouver Sun,* 28 July 1995, A5; "Liberals Will Allow Some Embryo Study," *National Post,* 8 December 2001, A8; "Fertility Research Opens the Door to Male-Male Procreation," *Vancouver Sun,* 29 December 2000, A1, A4.

46 For background on the euthanasia debate in Canada, see Gentles (1995). For a history of euthanasia in the US, see, for instance, Humphrey and Wickett (1986).

47 Latimer killed his twelve-year-old daughter, who was suffering from severe cerebral palsy, by carbon monoxide poisoning. Sue Rodriguez took her fight for the right to a doctor-assisted suicide to the Supreme Court of Canada. Despite losing, with the assistance of NDP MP Svend Robinson, she enlisted the aid of an anonymous physician to help her commit suicide before Lou Gehrig's disease left her unable to do so. See "Farmer Hopes for Acquittal in Daughter's Mercy Killing," *Vancouver Sun,* 25 November 1996, A7; "Mom Wants Parliament to Decide Right to Die," *Vancouver Sun,* 14 November 1996, A1.

48 Documentary on the reactions to Bill 9 in Oregon, KCTS TV, Seattle, 11 November 1995.
49 The US Supreme Court overturned the Colorado legislation by a vote of 6–3, stating such legislation denied Colorado homosexuals constitutional protection enjoyed by those in other states. See "Colorado Anti-Gay Legislation Struck Down," *Vancouver Sun*, 21 May 1996, A8.
50 "Clinton Agrees to Same-Sex Curbs," *Vancouver Sun*, 23 May 1996, A13; "Same-Sex Marriages Barred," *Vancouver Sun*, 24 August 1996, A9; "Homosexuals in US Dealt Double Setback," *Vancouver Sun*, 11 September 1996, A8; KIRO TV news, Seattle, 12 February 1997.
51 California, Connecticut, and Vermont are the only states that permit second-parent adoptions. The episode of *America Speaks Out* was aired on CNN on 4 February 2002. See also "Let Homosexuals Adopt Children, Pediatricians Say," *National Post*, 5 February 2002, A13.
52 "Gay Marriages Gain Acceptance," *Vancouver Sun*, 7 June 1996; "Poll Shows Support for Gay, Lesbian Rights," *Vancouver Sun*, 27 April 1996, A1; "Top Court Recognizes Gay Couples," *Vancouver Sun*, 21 May 1999, A1; "Same-Sex Spouses to Get New Rights," *Vancouver Sun*, 9 July 1999, B7.
53 "Same-Sex Benefits Approved," *Vancouver Sun*, 27 October 1995, A10; "Homosexual Benefits Won," *Vancouver Sun*, 1 August 1995, A3; "Ottawa to Pay Some Benefits to Same-Sex Mates," *Vancouver Sun*, 16 July 1996, A1; "New Law Allows Gays to Adopt," *Vancouver Sun*, 21 June 1995, A1; "Gay Rights Bill Expected to Be Introduced by Spring," *Vancouver Sun*, 25 November 1995, A3; "Same-Sex Couples Win Parental Rights," *Vancouver Sun*, 29 August 2001, A1, A2; "First Gay Marriage Legal, for Now," *National Post*, 15 January 2001, A1.
54 "Some Catholics Want to Halt 'Pro-Gay Bill,'" *Vancouver Sun*, 15 June 1996, A6.
55 "Women's Group Argues against Gay Rights Bill," *Vancouver Sun*, 20 April 1996, A6.
56 The statistics Gairdner cites are from a study conducted by the Institute for the Scientific Investigation of Sexuality, a Christian right organization run by Dr. Paul Cameron. Adopting various anti-gay positions, Cameron has linked gays to mass murder and child molestation, and he is a proponent of quarantining gays to stop the spread of AIDS (Diamond 1989).
57 Gairdner (1992), for instance, has claimed the home-schooling movement has grown to twenty thousand throughout Canada. In BC, interest in traditional schools continues to grow. Richmond parents lobbied unsuccessfully for a traditional school, while in Surrey the traditional school has parents lining up a week in advance of registration. See "Traditional School's Leader Says Other Classes Just as Good," *Vancouver Sun*, 21 January 1997, B1, B2.
58 "Private Schools Gain in Popularity as Experts Predict Numbers Will Rise," *Vancouver Sun*, 27 August 1997, B1; "Charter School Conference Draws Fire and Praise," *Vancouver Sun*, 6 November 1995, B1; "71 Percent Favour Charter Schools: Poll," *National Post*, 8 September 2001, A1; "Back to Basics High School Sought in Surrey," *Vancouver Sun*, 12 January 1996, A1, A14.
59 The books were *Asha's Mums, Belinda's Bouquet*, and *One Dad, Two Dads, Brown Dads, Blue Dads*. They were chosen by James Chamberlain, a gay educator who teaches kindergarten and Grade 1. See "Surrey Book Ban Overturned Due to Role of Religious Views," *Vancouver Sun*, 17 December 1998, A1, A2; "Banned Books Aimed at 'Inculcating Values,'" *Vancouver Sun*, 11 July 1998, A3; "Religious Group Raising Funds in Surrey Fight over Gay Issue," *Vancouver Sun*, 22 March 1998, B4; "Surrey School Board Loses Same-Sex Book Fight," *Vancouver Sun*, 21 December 2002, A5.
60 "Homosexual Teachings in Sex Course Upsetting to Some Parents," *Vancouver Sun*, 28 June 1995, A3; "What's Wrong with Sodomy and Needles," *BC Report*, 24 August 1992, 22.

Chapter 3: The Burden of Form
1 To simplify matters, the FCP will from here out be referred to primarily in its relation to the pro family movement. As Chapter 2 showed, although pro-life is a movement in its own right, it is also considered a subset of the broader pro-family movement. In this light, the FCP can be seen to serve both movements simultaneously.
2 Kaufmann also makes the cogent point that "The most striking aspect of this broad transformation of identity politics into an introspective, fragmented antipolitics of lifestyle is the extent to which the values it promotes – individual solutions to social problems,

attention to lifestyle, choice – mirror the ideology of the marketplace" (1990, 78). This turning away from politics simultaneously reinforces the relations of consumption promoted by post-industrial capitalism – a move that does little to articulate strategies for radicalizing the cultural relations that mediate the individual's daily life and extant social structures and expectations. Indeed, Boggs (1986) points out that one glaring characteristic of the new social movements is the lack of an alternative economic strategy for society. Like the FCP, the NSMs emphasize social and cultural rather than economic reforms.

3 For instance, Mrs. Toth noted that Stuart Parker, past leader of the Green Party of BC, provided copies of virtually all of the Greens' information and material on electoral reform to the FCP.

4 While there is no shortage of general work on the radical or Christian right, few analyses appear to have used social movement theory directly. Sara Diamond's 1995 work, *Roads to Dominion*, acknowledges the political process model as guiding her examination of the Christian right in the US, and Liebman and Wuthnow's *The New Christian Right* (1983) loosely uses social movement theory for their similar analyses, but beyond these, much remains to be done in this field. One exception, among others, is Burstein (1991). Canadian work includes Steuter (1992); Erwin (1993); Anderson and Langford (2001).

5 For work focusing on the interactions between opposing movements, as well as opposing movements and the state, see, for instance, Gale (1986); and Zald and Useem (1987).

6 This is the situation that arises with Zald and Useem's work on the interaction between movements as they describe a movement's passage through periods of mobilization, demobilization, and remobilization. See Zald and Useem (1987).

7 For instance, Erin Steuter writes, "The largest and best-known of the women's pro-family groups in Canada is R.E.A.L. Women" (1992, 297) and identifies only the Christian Heritage Party, the Ontario FCP, pro-life groups, and the Alberta Federation of Women United for Families as other PFM organizations. In a footnote, Lorna Erwin (1993) identifies five specific PFM groups – including the Coalition for Family Values, Renaissance Canada, and Positive Parents – and, in general, pro-life organizations and "religiously based groups."

8 Although being a pro-life supporter was seen as inevitably leading to similar sympathies for the pro-family position, occasionally the observation was made that the reverse pattern was not as dependable. A small minority of respondents said a pro-family advocate could not automatically be relied upon to support an absolutist position opposing abortion although it was likely that such people were "generally" pro-life.

9 These pro-life groups were Campaign Life Canada, BC Pro-Life, Birthright, and Vancouver Right to Life.

10 This is of course not presented as an exhaustive list of pro-family organizations in the province, and certainly not for across the country. These organizations were identified as the most prominent groups currently active in the province and were chosen for that reason. For instance, although home-schooling and traditional school supporters were identified as "pro-family" and are active in the promotion of alternative education forms in BC, they have no formal or even informal organizational structure.

11 Most of these organizations have charitable status, which allows them to be tax-exempt but prevents them from engaging in direct political work. The Campaign Life Coalition, CRI, the Christian Coalition, REAL Women, and the Catholic Civil Rights League have deliberately not applied for this status because it is felt that such standing would hamper their activities. All of the organizations are non-profit.

12 The one exception to this is Focus on the Family. A pro-family activist thought Focus Canada is like a corporate entity, similar in purpose but autonomous from its American base: "Dr. Dobson sits on the board, as do the other American vice-presidents, but they are outnumbered by nine or more Canadians. So it is an autonomous board, but obviously we exist for the vision of what Dr. Dobson is doing and what he represents."

13 Even Focus on the Family Canada claims its financial resources are derived from donations, despite having an annual budget of $6 million.

14 REAL Women has accepted grants from the federal government in the past but emphasizes that the $6,000 it received to hold a conference in 1996 is far less than what other special-interest groups like the National Action Committee on Women receive.

15 It was reported that such items as office space, fax machines, computers, computer soft-ware, office supplies, etc. have been donated in the past but for the most part such goods are purchased or leased using money from annual budgets.

16 Catholic Civil Rights League promotional brochure.

17 Christian Coalition of British Columbia promotional brochure.

18 For more on the pro-life movement in Canada, see Cuneo (1989); and Brodie et al. (1992).

19 For instance, their brochures say: "To affirm the value of protecting the sanctity of all human life, from the point of conception to the point of natural death ... To promote the protection of the vulnerable in our society, recognize traditional family values" (Christian Coalition); "The CCRL will continue to defend the traditional family as the basic unit of society" (Catholic Civil Rights League); "To promote, secure and defend legislation which upholds the Judeo-Christian values of marriage and family life" (REAL Women); "We acknowledge the need to foster healthy family units, since only through strong families will we have strong communities" (Citizens' Research Institute).

20 Trinity Western University's lawsuit against the British Columbia College of Teachers showed similar signs of a framing battle. In response to a handout from the defence attorney that stated the CCRL believes "a Catholic teacher has a right, indeed a duty, to tell homosexuals that homosexual behaviour is depraved and disordered," a spokesman for the Catholic Civil Rights League was quoted as claiming the defendant's description of Catholic teachers "is trying to make Catholics and Christians look like wild-eyed papists. They're painting us to be fascists." See Sandra Thomas, "Leader Denies Catholics 'Fascists,'" *Vancouver Sun,* 10 May 1997, A20.

21 Robert Pickering, who voted in favour of the ban, sat on the board of CRI at the time. See Kim Bolan, "Surrey School Chair Linked to Anti-Gay Group," *Vancouver Sun,* 6 May 1997, A1, A8; Kim Bolan, "Ramsey Decries 'Intolerance' on Surrey Board," *Vancouver Sun,* 7 May 1997, A1, A6; Kim Bolan, "Surrey's Lawyer Seeks to Keep 'Gay' Quote out of Book Battle," *Vancouver Sun,* 30 June, 1998, A1, A2. One letter to the editor of the *Vancouver Sun* about its description of CRI as "anti-gay" asked, "Does the *Sun* really think Surrey school board chair Robert Pickering's association with Citizens' Research Institute, a pro-family group, should be described as a link to an anti-gay group?" (Letter to the Editor, "Defining the Boundaries of Religious Freedom," *Vancouver Sun,* 12 May 1997, A12).

22 Kim Bolan, "Ramsey Decries 'Intolerance' on Surrey Board," *Vancouver Sun,* 7 May 1997, A1, A6; Kim Bolan, "Surrey School Chair Linked to Anti-Gay Group," *Vancouver Sun,* 6 May 1997, A1, A8.

23 Justine Hunter, "Anti-Abortion Activist Barred from Health Boards," *Vancouver Sun,* 13 March 1997, A1, A9; Dianne Rinehart, "Abortion Foes Allege Bias by Health Minister," *Vancouver Sun,* 4 April 1997; Dianne Rinehart and Justine Hunter, "Protesters Fear Hospital Merger Will Open Door to Abortions," *Vancouver Sun,* 2 April 1997, A1, A14.

24 Justine Hunter, "Anti-Abortion Activist Barred from Health Boards," *Vancouver Sun,* 13 March 1997, A1, A9.

Chapter 4: The Function of Form

1 Federal groups like Canadians for Direct Democracy (CDD) and the Coalition for Electoral Reform (CFER) – now Fair Vote Canada – are lobbying for the adoption of some type of proportional representation system. In British Columbia, the British Columbia Coalition for Electoral Reform, now Fair Vote BC, has done similar work and the Citizens' Assembly on Electoral Reform is formally investigating this issue.

2 Believing that MPs should act according to their best judgment and not necessarily the wishes of their constituents, Burke lost his seat in the House of Commons in 1780 for refusing to defer to the demands of his Bristol constituency (see Macpherson 1980, 12).

3 According to C.B. Macpherson, Burke became a supporter of the party form after witnessing an "attempt by the Court cabal to reduce Parliament to impotence" (1980, 23). Concerned over the vulnerability of individual politicians to exploits by extraparliamentary bodies trying to undermine the proper function of the government, Burke supported the idea of a party system to provide some form of institutional protection for politicians.

4 Roseanne Skoke and Tom Wappel were pro-life federal Liberal MPs whom the FCP believed

were consistently silenced by the party whip when they attempted to bring up pro-life issues.

5   "Skoke to Seek Liberal Leadership in Nova Scotia," *Vancouver Sun,* 24 March 1997, A3.

6   Eric Beauchesne, "Cost of Deep Cuts to Transfer Payments Tallied," *Vancouver Sun,* 9 July 1997, A3.

7   These ten dysfunctions are as follows: limiting political discourse; institutionalizing confrontation; undermining the legitimacy of the political system; attenuating the public philosophy; confusing the government mandate; encouraging wasteful government expenditures; ignoring some important issues; misrepresenting political forces; weakening the central government; and neglecting the policy role. See Meisel (1991).

8   In a bit of an ironic twist, the NDP's Svend Robinson was often cited by FCP members as an example of what a truly principled and representative politician should be.

9   In the 2004 federal election, voter turnout was around 60 percent. In 2000 voter turnout was roughly 61 percent. In 1997, voter turnout was 66.7 percent, in 1993 it was 69.9 percent, and in 1984 and 1988 it was 75 percent. The British Columbia turnout of 68 percent for the 1997 federal election was just above the national average. See Lindsay Kines, "Campaign Blamed as Voters Stay Away," *Vancouver Sun,* 4 June 1997, A4.

10 The use of the term "post-material" here may be seen a problematic, given that it is being used to describe not only new social movements but also conservative organizations like the Christian Heritage Party and the Family Coalition Party, groups that still have firm roots in materialist conceptions of social hierarchy and respect for traditional authority patterns and free-market economics. The use of the term in this case, however, should not be interpreted as an attempt to equate these two types of movements and their different value systems. Rather, it is to simply point out that the FCP activists enjoy a level of material security that permits them to turn their attention and efforts to effecting change that they believe will improve the quality of their lives and those of society at large. As Ronald Inglehart writes, "The values of Western publics have been shifting from an overwhelming emphasis on material well-being and physical security toward greater emphasis on the quality of life ... Today, an unprecedentedly large portion of Western populations have been raised under conditions of exceptional economic security. Economic and physical security continue to be valued positively, but their relative priority is lower than in the past" (1977, 3). In his scheme, Inglehart includes under post-materialist concerns things such as "more say in government," "more say on job, community," and a "less impersonal society" (1977, 42), all of which can be found in the ideas of the Family Coalition Party.

11 The Social Credit Party, the Reform Party, the Progressive Democratic Alliance, the Green Party, the BC Conservative Party, the Communist Party, and the Natural Law Party were the other initial members of BCCFER.

12 For example, during both the Matsqui (21 May 1996) and West Vancouver–Capilano (24 May 1996) all-candidates meetings, the issues of abortion funding and child care were brought up by either the candidates themselves or through questions in the open-mike sessions. That the latter appeared to be a prearranged situation whereby an FCP supporter would ask the question from the floor is irrelevant. Without an FCP candidate present, the political legitimacy of the questions would have been diminished and cadre party candidates would not have had a difficult time dismissing them.

13 BCTV News covered a fundraising dinner for Jim Kelly and conservative *Vancouver Sun* columnist Trevor Lautens devoted a column to Kelly's candidacy. See *BCTV Late News,* 17 May 1996; Trevor Lautens, *Vancouver Sun,* 18 May 1996.

14 Family Coalition Party of BC, "Family," Newsletter no. 8 (May 1997), 1.

15 The BC Libertarian Party and the Common Sense, Community, Family Party were deregistered for non-compliance with the Election Act. Effectively, they were banned from participating in the next provincial election unless a $10,000 fine was paid. After taking the BC government to court when the Chief Electoral Officer fined and threatened to ban three candidates from the next provincial election, the BC Green Party received a favourable ruling from the court. The ruling overturned the fines and permitted the candidates to run in the 2001 election. See Jim Beatty, "Parties Want Election Act Overhauled,"

Vancouver Sun, 19 March 1997, A1, A16; Canadian Press, "Judge Quashes Election Act Fines, Allowing Green Leader to Seek Seat," *Vancouver Sun,* 8 April 1997, A6.

16 The first of these meetings was held in May, 1997. Among the parties invited were the FCP, the Greens, the Communist Party, the Libertarian Party, the Progressive Conservative Party of BC, the Progressive Democratic Alliance, the Reform Party of BC, and the Social Credit Party. Apart from that of making compliance easier, other topics for reform included candidates' election expense limits, constituency deregistration procedures, and accounting procedures.

17 Jim Beatty, "Parties Want Election Act Overhauled," *Vancouver Sun,* 19 March 1997, A1, A16.

18 Germany has a mixed electoral system in which half the seats in the Bundestag, the German national Parliament, are elected according to the rules of a plurality system (a first-past-the-post system like Canada's) and half are selected on the basis of the percentage of popular votes won by a particular party. To avoid the potentially destabilizing effects of minor parties inundating the Bundestag, a restriction requires that a minor party must receive a 5 percent minimum of the popular vote to be eligible to sit in the legislature. For descriptions of the German electoral system, see Braunthal (1996). For a discussion on other types of proportional representation, see Seidle (1996). For a discussion of British Columbia's use of the single transferable vote, see Elkins (1976).

19 Ironically, Vander Zalm's premiership has been identified as one of the worst for concentrating power in the hands of the premier and a few select personnel. Terence Morley writes that Vander Zalm "concentrated all significant political and administrative power in his own hands and then let it be used by only one other person [David Poole]" (1996, 161).

20 Newspaper headlines have generally supported the idea of switching to a proportional representation system, but it was reported in one article that "a recent opinion poll showed that a majority of New Zealand voters regretted their referendum decision to opt for change." See April Lindgren, "Proportional Representation Fairer System, Advocates Say," *Vancouver Sun,* 2 June 1997, A4; Jonathon Manthorpe, "Voting Reform in New Zealand, Japan, Taking Opposite Paths," *Vancouver Sun,* 27 September 1996, A17; Brad Evans, "19th-Century System Distorts Division of Seats," *Vancouver Sun,* 3 June 1997, A5; Norm Ovenden, "Referendum Urged on Proposed New Way to Elect MPs," *Vancouver Sun,* 4 April 1997, A6.

21 Initial signatories to the coalition included the FCP, the Green Party, the Libertarian Party, the Social Credit Party, the Progressive Conservative Party of BC, the Reform Party of BC, the Communist Party, and the Natural Law Party.

22 The Enterprise League of British Columbia was formed in 1996 with the stated goal of creating "a single unified organization that meets the objectives of all those British Columbians wanting an enterprise-minded government for the province. The League was formed to act as a catalyst and parent body for the merging of these political parties into a single organization." The Liberal, Reform, Progressive Democratic Alliance, Libertarian, Social Credit, and Family Coalition parties were all invited to participate in the venture. The FCP initially became involved with this effort but withdrew its support after the league's directors turned down its request to adopt the FCP's two founding principles. The creation of the Unity Party was the product of a second effort in this regard (see Chapter 1).

23 Wilson was the lone MLA for the Progressive Democratic Alliance with a seat he won in the 1996 provincial election.

Chapter 5: The Tensions of Form

1 There appears to be some discrepancy as to when the NDP actually became formally affiliated with the CLC. Penner (1996) says it was 1961, while Thorburn (1991b) cites 1958.

2 Phillips explicitly uses only the term "traditional" in her analysis. "Derivational" refers to her second observation, that minor parties such as the Greens and the Feminist Party were produced directly out of previously existing social movements, and "complementary" identifies her third argument, which stresses the benefit of viewing parties and movements as working in complement with one another. The term "traditional," referring as it does to the common perspective of parties and movements as antagonists in the political sphere, is perhaps less accurate than the term "competitive," but it is Phillips's choice and I will retain it.

3　The CCF/NDP was most frequently cited as a party that rose out of a social movement. Perhaps surprisingly, given the religious conservative backgrounds of the respondents, the Social Credit Party and League were not cited. Two respondents also commented that parties can influence social movements. Governmental or party policies, they observed, can spur an existing movement into oppositional or supportive action for the policy, or even give rise to a movement as a result of people banding together to oppose the particular governmental initiative.

4　Prior to this merger, Braunthal notes, a "group of radical fundamentalists ... split off from the party [the Greens] because it had become too pragmatic" (1996, 155). These were some of the more militant and purposely committed movement activists within the Greens, who were commonly referred to as the "Fundis," as opposed to the more politically pragmatic and conventional "Realos" (Boggs 1986).

5　For an analysis of social movements and the media, see, for instance, Gitlin (1980).

6　McLintock and Kristianson (1996) note that until the 1940s, the *Victoria Times* and *Vancouver Sun* were identified as Liberal newspapers, while the *Victoria Times-Colonist* and the *Vancouver Province* were Conservative. They also point out that until BC had a full Hansard in 1972, the province's newspapers acted as the official recorders of legislative activity and "the legislative library regularly clipped and pasted newspaper reports into red binders that became the official 'memory' of legislative proceedings" (1996, 124). Although BC did have Journals of the House, which officially recorded motions debated and passed, through to 1970, it was not until 1972 that the complete Hansard report was instituted.

7　The first BCTV report covered West Vancouver–Capilano candidate Jim Kelly's fundraising dinner at Holy Trinity Church in North Vancouver (*BCTV Late Newshour*, 17 May 1996). The second was a report on minor parties running in the election and included the FCP and the Green Party (*BCTV Weekend Newshour*, 26 May 1996). The *Vancouver Sun* article included a photo of FCP leader Heather Stilwell and her husband, Bill, holding an FCP election sign. See Douglas Todd, "Taking a Stand on Moral Issues: Family Party Vows to Live up to Principles," *Vancouver Sun*, 14 May 1996, B3.

8　This can also be seen with political parties. Mike Harcourt, ex-premier and leader of the NDP in British Columbia, complained bitterly about the media bias against him during his political tenure, while federally, Val Meredith of the Reform Party complained in an editorial that the media were biased against her party. See Tom Barrett, "It's Gloves off with Media in Harcourt Book," *Vancouver Sun*, 9 October 1996, A3; Stan Persky, "How the Scrum of the Earth Drove Harcourt into the Ground," *Vancouver Sun*, 1 November 1996, A23; Tom Barrett, "Harcourt Blasts 'Biased' BC Media," *Vancouver Sun*, 12 October 1996, A1; Val Meredith, "Why Reform Gets the Press It Gets," *Vancouver Sun*, 7 May 1997, A13.

References

Abbott, Pamela, and Claire Wallace. 1992. *The Family and the New Right*. London: Pluto Press.

Adam, Barry D. 1995. *The Rise of a Gay and Lesbian Movement*. New York: Twayne Publishers.

Amyot, G. Grant. 1996. "Democracy without Parties: A New Politics." In *Canadian Parties in Transition: Discourse, Organization, and Representation*, edited by A. Brian Tanguay and Alain-G. Gagnon, 2nd ed. Scarborough, ON: Nelson Canada.

Anderson, Gillian, and Tom Langford. 2001. "Pro-Family Organizations in Calgary, 1998: Beliefs, Interconnections and Allies." *Canadian Review of Sociology and Anthropology* 38 (1): 37-56.

Ashford, Nigel. 1981. "New Conservatism and Old Socialism." *Government and Opposition* 16 (3): 353-78.

Barrett, Michele, and Mary McIntosh. 1991. *The Anti-Social Family*. 2nd ed. London: Verso.

Bates, Vernon L. 2000. "The Decline of a New Christian Right Social Movement Organization: Opportunities and Constraints." *Review of Religious Research* 42 (1): 19-40.

Bell, Daniel, ed. 1963. *The Radical Right*. Garden City, NY: Doubleday.

Bendroth, Margaret Lamberts. 1999. "Fundamentalism and the Family: Gender, Culture, and the American Pro-Family Movement." *Journal of Women's History* 10 (4): 35-54.

Benford, Robert D. 1992. "Social Movements." In *Encyclopedia of Sociology,* edited by Edgar F. Borgatta and Marie L. Borgatta. Vol. 4. New York: MacMillan.

–. 1993. "You Could Be the Hundredth Monkey: Collective Action Frames and Vocabularies of Motive within the Nuclear Disarmament Movement." *The Sociological Quarterly* 34 (2): 195-216.

Berger, Brigitte, and Peter L. Berger. 1983. *The War over the Family: Capturing the Middle Ground*. New York: Anchor Press/Doubleday.

Berlet, Chip, and Matthew N. Lyons. 2000. *Right Wing Populism in America: Too Close for Comfort*. London: Guilford Press.

Bibby, Reginald W. 1993. *Unknown Gods: The Ongoing Story of Religion in Canada*. Toronto: Stoddart.

Bickerton, James. 1996. "Parties and Regions: Alternative Models of Representation." In *Canadian Parties in Transition: Discourse, Organization, and Representation*, edited by A. Brian Tanguay and Alain-G. Gagnon, 2nd ed. Scarborough, ON: Nelson Canada.

Blake, Donald E. 1996. "The Politics of Polarization: Parties and Elections in British Columbia." In *Politics, Policy, and Government in British Columbia*, edited by R. Kenneth Carty. Vancouver: UBC Press.

Boggs, Carl. 1986. *Social Movements and Political Power: Emerging Forms of Radicalism in the West*. Philadelphia: Temple University Press.

–. 1995. "Rethinking the Sixties Legacy: From New Left to New Social Movements." In

Social Movements: Critiques, Concepts, Case-Studies, edited by Stanford Lyman. Toronto: Macmillan.

Braunthal, Gerard. 1996. *Parties and Politics in Modern Germany*. Boulder: Westview Press.

Brodie, Janine, Shelley A.M. Gavigan, and Jane Jenson. 1992. *The Politics of Abortion*. Toronto: Oxford University Press.

Buechler, Steven M. 1993. "Beyond Resource Mobilization: Emerging Trends in Social Movement Theory." *The Sociological Quarterly* 34 (2): 217-35.

Burke, Edmund. 1955 [1790]. *Reflections on the French Revolution*. London: Dent.

Burkinshaw, Robert K. 1995. *Pilgrims in Lotus Land: Conservative Protestantism in British Columbia 1917-1981*. Montreal and Kingston: McGill-Queen's University Press.

Burris, Val. 1987. "Business Support for the New Right: A Consumer's Guide to the Most Reactionary American Corporations." *Socialist Review* 91 (January/February): 33-63.

Burstein, Paul. 1991. "Reverse Discrimination Cases in the Federal Courts: Legal Mobilization by a Countermovement." *The Sociological Quarterly* 32 (4): 511-28.

Butcher, John. 1985. "Restraint Economics and the Social Safety Net in British Columbia: The Political Economy of the Post Welfare State in British Columbia's New Reality." Paper presented at the Canadian Association of Geographers Conference, Trois-Rivières, Quebec, May.

Cairns, Alan C., and Daniel Wong. 1991. "Socialism, Federalism and the BC Party Systems 1933-1983." In *Party Politics in Canada*, edited by Hugh G. Thorburn, 6th ed. Scarborough, ON: Prentice-Hall Canada.

Calhoun, Craig. 1993. "New Social Movements of the Early Nineteenth Century." *Social Science History* 17 (3): 385-421.

Canada, Royal Commission on Electoral Reform and Party Financing (RCERPF). 1991. *Reforming Electoral Democracy*. Volumes 1 and 2. Ottawa: Supply and Services Canada.

Canavan, Francis P. 1960. *The Political Reason of Edmund Burke*. Durham: Duke University Press.

–. 1987. *Edmund Burke: Prescription and Providence*. Durham: Carolina Academic Press.

Canel, Eduardo. 1992. "New Social Movement Theory and Resource Mobilization: The Need for Integration." In *Organizing Dissent: Contemporary Social Movements in Theory and Practice: Studies in the Politics of Counter-Hegemony*, edited by William K. Carroll. Toronto: Garamond Press.

Carlin, George. 1996. *George Carlin: Back in Town*. TV Special. HBO.

Carroll, William K., and R.S. Ratner. 1989. "Social Democracy, Neo-Conservatism and Hegemonic Crisis in British Columbia." *Critical Sociology* 16 (1): 29-53.

–. 1999. "Media Strategies and Political Projects: A Comparative Study of Social Movements." *The Canadian Journal of Sociology* 24 (1): 1-34.

Carter, Stephen L. 1993. *The Culture of Disbelief: How American Law and Politics Trivialize Religious Devotion*. New York: Basic Books.

Carty, R. Kenneth. 1991. *Canadian Political Parties in the Constituencies*. Toronto: Dundurn Press.

–. 1996. "Party Organization and Activity on the Ground." In *Canadian Parties in Transition: Discourse, Organization, and Representation*, edited by A. Brian Tanguay and Alain-G. Gagnon, 2nd ed. Scarborough, ON: Nelson Canada.

–. 2001. "What Place for British Columbia in Federal Politics." *BC Studies*, no. 129 (Spring): 5-9.

Chandler, William M., and Alan Siaroff. 1991. "Parties and Party Government in Advanced Democracies." In *Canadian Political Parties: Leaders, Candidates and Organization*, edited by Herman Bakvis. Toronto: Dundurn Press.

Chorney, Harold, and Phillip Hansen. 1985. "Neo-Conservatism, Social Democracy and 'Province Building': The Experience of Manitoba." *The Canadian Review of Sociology and Anthropology* 22 (1): 1-29.

Cohen, Jean L. 1983. "Rethinking Social Movements." *Berkeley Journal of Sociology* 28: 99-112.

Converse, Philip E. 1964. "The Nature of Belief Systems in Mass Publics." In *Ideology and Discontent*, edited by D.E. Apter. London, UK: Free Press of Glencoe.

Cooke, Murray E. 2000. "The Pressure of Electoralism: Successes and Limitations of Movement Parties." *Socialist Studies Bulletin,* no. 60 (April-June): 27-70.

Covell, Maureen. 1991. "Parties as Institutions of National Governance." In *Representing Integration and Political Parties in Canada,* edited by Herman Bakvis. Toronto: Dundurn Press.

Crawford, Alan. 1980. *Thunder on the Right: The "New Right" and the Politics of Resentment.* New York: Pantheon Books.

Cuneo, Michael W. 1989. *Catholics against the Church: Anti-Abortion Protest in Toronto, 1969-1985.* Toronto: University of Toronto Press.

Dalton, Russell J., Manfred Kuechler, and Wilhelm Bürklin. 1990. "The Challenge of New Movements." In *Challenging the Political Order: New Social Political Movements in Western Democracies,* edited by Russell J. Dalton and Manfred Kuechler. Cambridge: Polity Press.

David, Miriam. 1986. "Moral and Maternal: The Family in the Right." In *The Ideology of the New Right,* edited by Ruth Levitas. London: Polity Press.

Diamond, Sara. 1989. *Spiritual Warfare: The Politics of the Christian Right.* Boston: South End Press.

–. 1995. *Roads to Dominion: Right Wing Movements and Political Power in the United States.* New York: Guilford Press.

–. 1998. *Not by Politics Alone: The Enduring Influence of the Christian Right.* London: Guilford Press.

Donzelot, Jacques. 1979. *The Policing of Families.* New York: Pantheon.

Dorrien, Gary. 1993. *The Neoconservative Mind: Politics, Culture and the War of Ideology.* Philadelphia: Temple University Press.

Durham, Martin. 2000. *The Christian Right, the Far Right and the Boundaries of American Conservatism.* Manchester: Manchester University Press.

Duverger, Maurice. 1959. *Political Parties: Their Organization and Activity in the Modern State.* Translated by Barbara North and Robert North. London: Methuen.

Dyck, Rand. 1991. *Provincial Politics in Canada.* 2nd ed. Scarborough, ON: Prentice-Hall Canada.

Eagles, Munroe. 1996. "The Franchise and Political Participation in Canada." In *Canadian Parties in Transition: Discourse, Organization, and Representation,* edited by A. Brian Tanguay and Alain-G. Gagnon, 2nd ed. Scarborough, ON: Nelson Canada.

Eatwell, Roger. 1989. "Right or Rights? The Rise of the 'New Right.'" In *The Nature of the Right: European and American Politics and Political Thought since 1789,* edited by Roger Eatwell and Noel O'Sullivan. London: Pinter Publishers.

Eder, Klaus. 1985. "The New Social Movements: Moral Crusades, Political Pressure Groups, or Social Movements." *Social Research* 52 (4): 869-90.

Eichler, Margrit. 1986. *The Pro-Family Movement: Are They for or against Families?* Ottawa: Canadian Research Institute for the Advancement of Women.

–. 1988. *Families in Canada Today: Recent Changes and Their Policy Consequences.* 2nd ed. Toronto: Gage Educational Publishing Company.

Eisinger, Peter K. 1973. "The Conditions of Protest Behavior in American Cities." *American Political Science Review* 67: 11-28.

Elkins, David J. 1976. "Politics Makes Strange Bedfellows: The BC Party System in the 1952 and 1953 Provincial Elections." *BC Studies,* no. 30 (Summer): 3-26.

–. 1991. "Parties as National Institutions: A Comparative Study." In *Representing Integration and Political Parties in Canada,* edited by Herman Bakvis. Toronto: Dundurn Press.

Erwin, Lorna. 1993. "Neoconservatism and the Canadian Pro-Family Movement." *The Canadian Review of Sociology and Anthropology* 30 (3): 401-20.

Etzioni, Amitai. 1977. "The Neoconservatives." *Partisan Review* 4 (3): 431-37.

Eulau, Heinz, and John C. Wahlke. 1978. "The Role of the Representative: Some Empirical Observations on the Theory of Edmund Burke." In *The Politics of Representation: Continuities in Theory and Research,* Heinz Eulau and John C. Wahlke, with Alan Abramowitz. London: Sage.

Freeman, Jo. 1979. "Resource Mobilization and Strategy: A Model for Analyzing Social Movement Organization Actions." In *The Dynamics of Social Movements: Resource Mobilization,*

Social Control and Tactics, edited by Mayer N. Zald and John D. McCarthy. Cambridge, MA: Winthrop.

Freeman, Michael. 1980. *Edmund Burke and the Critique of Political Radicalism*. Oxford: Basil Blackwell.

Gagnon, Alain-G., and A. Brian Tanguay. 1996. "Minor Parties in the Canadian Political System: Origins, Functions, Impact." In *Canadian Parties in Transition: Discourse, Organization, and Representation*, edited by A. Brian Tanguay and Alain-G. Gagnon, 2nd ed. Scarborough, ON: Nelson Canada.

Gairdner, William D. 1990. *The Trouble with Canada: A Citizen Speaks Out*. Toronto: Stoddart Publishing Co.

–. 1992. *The War against the Family: A Parent Speaks Out*. Toronto: Stoddart.

–. 1998. "Democracy against the Family." In *After Liberalism: Essays in Search of Freedom, Virtue and Order*, edited by William D. Gairdner. Toronto: Stoddart.

Gale, Richard P. 1986. "Social Movements and the State." *Sociological Perspectives* 29 (2): 202-40.

Galipeau, Claude. 1996. "Political Parties, Interest Groups, and New Social Movements: Toward New Representations." In *Canadian Parties in Transition: Discourse, Organization, and Representation*, edited by A. Brian Tanguay and Alain-G. Gagnon, 2nd ed. Scarborough, ON: Nelson Canada.

Gamson, William A. 1975. *The Strategy of Social Protest*. London: Dorsey Press.

Gamson, William A., and David S. Meyer. 1996. "Framing Political Opportunity." In *Comparative Perspectives on Social Movements: Political Opportunities, Mobilizing Structures, and Cultural Framings*, edited by Doug McAdam, John D. McCarthy, and Mayer N. Zald. Cambridge: Cambridge University Press.

Gamson, William A., and Gadi Wolfsfeld. 1993. "Movements and Media as Interacting Systems." *Annals of the American Academy of Political and Social Science* 528: 114-25.

Gentles, Ian, ed. 1995. *Euthanasia and Assisted Suicide: The Current Debate*. Toronto: Stoddart.

Gerhards, Jurgen, and Dieter Rucht. 1992. "Mesomobilization: Organizing and Framing in Two Protest Campaigns in West Germany." *American Journal of Sociology* 98 (3): 555-95.

Gerlach, Luther P. 1999. "The Structure of Social Movements: Environmental Activism and Its Opponents." In *Waves of Protest: Social Movements since the Sixties*, edited by Jo Freeman and Victoria Johnson. Lanham, MD: Rowman and Littlefield.

Gerth, H.H., and C. Wright Mills. 1946. *From Max Weber: Essays in Sociology*. New York: Oxford University Press.

Gilder, George. 1988. *Men and Marriage*. Gretna: Pelican Publishing Co.

Girvin, Brian. 1988a. "Introduction: Varieties of Conservatism." In *The Transformation of Contemporary Conservatism*, edited by Brian Girvin. London: Sage Publications.

–. 1988b. "The United States: Conservative Politics in a Liberal Society." In *The Transformation of Contemporary Conservatism*, edited by Brian Girvin. London: Sage Publications.

Gitlin, Todd. 1980. *The Whole World Is Watching: Mass Media in the Making and Unmaking of the New Left*. Berkeley: University of California Press.

Goffman, Erving. 1974. *Frame Analysis: An Essay on the Organization of Experience*. New York: Harper and Row.

Gottfried, Paul, and Thomas Fleming. 1988. *The Conservative Movement*. Boston: Twayne Publishers.

Gramsci, Antonio. 1971. *Selections from the Prison Notebooks*. Translated and edited by Quintin Hoare and Geoffrey Nowell Smith. New York: International Publishers.

Green, John C. 2000. "The Christian Right and the 1998 Elections: An Overview." In *Prayers in the Precincts: The Christian Right in the 1998 Elections*, edited by John C. Green et al. Washington, DC: Georgetown University Press.

Green, John C., Mark L. Rozell, and Clyde Wilcox. 2001. "Social Movements and Party Politics: The Case of the Christian Right." *Journal for the Scientific Study of Religion* 40 (3): 413-26.

Guppy, Neil, Sabrina Freeman, and Shari Buchan. 1987. "Representing Canadians: Changes in the Economic Backgrounds of Federal Politicians, 1965-1984." *The Canadian Review of Sociology and Anthropology* 24 (3): 417-29.

Gurr, Ted. 1970. *Why Men Rebel*. Princeton: Princeton University Press.

Guth, James L. 1983. "The New Christian Right." In *The New Christian Right: Mobilization and Legitimation*, edited by Robert C. Liebman and Robert Wuthnow. New York: Aldine Publishing.

Habermas, Jürgen. 1981. "New Social Movements." *Telos* 49: 33-37.

–. 1989. "Neoconservatism." In *The New Conservatism: Cultural Criticism and the Historians' Debate*, edited by Sherry Weber Nicholsen. Cambridge: MIT Press.

Haiven, Judith. 1984. *Faith, Hope, No Charity: An Inside Look at the Born Again Movement in Canada and the United States*. Vancouver: New Star Books.

Hammond, Phillip E. 1983 [1980]. "Another Great Awakening." In *The New Christian Right: Mobilization and Legitimation*, edited by Robert C. Liebman and Robert Wuthnow. New York: Aldine Publishing.

Harrison, Trevor. 1995. *Of Passionate Intensity: Right-Wing Populism and the Reform Party of Canada*. Toronto: University of Toronto Press.

Hatt, Ken, Tullio Caputo, and Barbara Perry. 1990. "Managing Consent: Canada's Experience with Neoconservatism." *Social Justice* 17 (4): 30-48.

Hauerwas, Stanley. 1993 [1981]. "Why Abortion Is a Religious Issue." In *The Ethics of Abortion: Pro-Life vs. Pro-Choice*, edited by Robert M. Baird and Stuart E. Rosenbaum. New York: Prometheus Books.

Havemann, Paul. 1986. "Marketing the New Establishment Ideology in Canada." *Crime and Social Justice* 26: 11-37.

Heberle, Rudolf. 1968. "Types and Functions of Social Movements." In *International Encyclopedia of the Social Sciences*, edited by David Sills. New York: Macmillan and Free Press.

Heinz, Donald. 1983. "The Struggle to Define America." In *The New Christian Right: Mobilization and Legitimation*, edited by Robert C. Liebman and Robert Wuthnow. New York: Aldine Publishing.

Herman, Didi. 1994. "The Christian Right and the Politics of Morality in Canada." *Parliamentary Affairs* 47 (2): 268-79.

–. 1997. *The Antigay Agenda: Orthodox Vision and the Christian Right*. Chicago: University of Chicago Press.

Hirsch, Joachim. 1998. "A Party Is Not a Movement and Vice Versa." In *The German Greens: Paradox between Movement and Party*, edited by Margit Mayer and John Ely. Translated by Michael Schatzschneider. Philadelphia: Temple University Press.

Hoffman, Helga, and David Orton. 1989. "Canadian Greens: On the Political Margins." *Canadian Dimension* 23, 8 (November/December): 21-23.

Holmes, Mark. 1998. "A Conservative Education." In *After Liberalism: Essays in Search of Freedom, Virtue and Order*, edited by William D. Gairdner. Toronto: Stoddart.

Holy See. 1983. *Charter of the Rights of the Family*. Quebec: Editions Paulines.

Honderich, Ted. 1990. *Conservatism*. London: Hamish Hamilton.

Hoover, Dennis R. 1997. "The Christian Right under Old Glory and the Maple Leaf." In *Sojourners in the Wilderness: The Christian Right in Comparative Perspective*, edited by Corwin E. Smidt and James M. Penning. Lanham: Rowman and Littlefield Publishers.

Howlet, Michael, and Keith Brownsley. 1988. "The Old Reality and the New Reality: Party Politics and Public Policy in British Columbia 1941-1987." *Studies in Political Economy* 25 (Spring): 141-76.

Howlett, Dennis. 1989. "Social Movement Coalitions: New Possibilities for Social Change." *Canadian Dimension* 23, 8 (November/December): 41-47.

Humphry, Derek, and Ann Wickett. 1986. *The Right to Die: Understanding Euthanasia*. New York: Harper and Row Publishers.

Hynes, Maureen. 1980. "Feminist Party of Canada: Entering the Electoral Mainstream." *Branching Out* 7 (1): 8.

Inglehart, Ronald. 1977. *The Silent Revolution: Changing Values and Political Styles among Western Publics*. Princeton: Princeton University Press.

Irvine, William P. 1991. "Explaining the Religious Basis of the Canadian Partisan Identity: Success on the Third Try." In *The Ballot and Its Message: Voting in Canada*, edited by Joseph Wearing. Toronto: Copp Clark Pitman.

Jenkins, J. Craig. 1983. "Resource Mobilization Theory and the Study of Social Movements." *Annual Review of Sociology* 9: 527-53.

Jenkins, J. Craig, and C. Perrow. 1977. "Insurgency of the Powerless Farm Workers Movements." *American Sociological Review* 42: 249-68.

Jenkins, J. Craig, and Teri Shumate. 1985. "Cowboy Capitalists and the Rise of the 'New Right': An Analysis of Contributors to Conservative Policy Formation Organizations." *Social Problems* 33 (2): 131-46.

Jenson, Jane. 1976. "Party Systems." In *The Provincial Political Systems: Comparative Essays*, edited by David J. Bellamy, Jon H. Pammett, and Donald C. Rowat. Toronto: Methuen.

John Paul II. 1994. *Letter to Families*. Magisterium 19. Sherbrooke, QC: Editions Paulines.

–. 1995. *The Gospel of Life: Evangelium Vitae*. Toronto: Random House.

Johnson, Victoria. 1999. "The Strategic Determinants of a Countermovement: The Emergence and Impact of Operation Rescue Blockades." In *Waves of Protest: Social Movements since the Sixties*, edited by Jo Freeman and Victoria Johnson. Lanham, MD: Rowman and Littlefield.

Johnston, Hank, Enrique Larafia, and Joseph R. Gusfield. 1994. "Identities, Grievances, and New Social Movements." In *New Social Movements: From Ideology to Identity*, edited by Enrique Larafia, Hank Johnston, and Joseph R. Gusfield. Philadelphia: Temple University Press.

Johnston, Richard. 1991. "The Reproduction of the Religious Cleavage in Canadian Elections." In *The Ballot and Its Message: Voting in Canada*, edited by Joseph Wearing. Toronto: Copp Clark Pitman.

Kauffman, L.A. 1990. "The Anti-Politics of Identity." *Socialist Review* 20 (1): 67-79.

Kelly, Christine A. 2001. *Tangled Up in Red, White, and Blue: New Social Movements in America*. Lanham, MD: Rowman and Littlefield.

Kendall, Willmoore, and George W. Carey. 1964. "Towards A Definition of 'Conservatism.'" *Journal of Politics* 26: 406-22.

King, Anthony. 1969. "Political Parties in Western Democracies: Some Skeptical Reflections." *Polity* 2 (2): 111-41.

Kitschelt, Herbert P. 1986. "Political Opportunity Structures and Political Protest: Anti-Nuclear Movements in Four Democracies." *British Journal of Political Science* 16: 57-85.

–. 1989. *The Logics of Party Formation: Ecological Politics in Belgium and West Germany*. London: Cornell University Press.

–. 1990. "New Social Movements and the Decline of Party Organization." In *Challenging the Political Order: New Social Political Movements in Western Democracies*, edited by Russell J. Dalton and Manfred Kuechler. Cambridge: Polity Press.

Klandermans, Bert. 1984. "Mobilization and Participation: Social-Psychological Expansions of Resource Mobilization Theory." *American Sociological Review* 49 (October): 583-600.

–. 1992. "The Social Construction of Protest and Multiorganizational Fields." In *Frontiers in Social Movement Theory*, edited by Aldon D. Morris and Carol McClurg Mueller. London: Yale University Press.

Klandermans, Bert, and Sidney Tarrow. 1988. "Mobilization Into Social Movements: Synthesizing European and American Approaches." *International Social Movement Research* 1: 1-38.

Klotzsch, Lilian, Klaus Könemann, Jörg Wischermann, Bodo Zeuner. 1998. "What Has Happened to Green Principles in Electoral and Parliamentary Politics?" In *The German Greens: Paradox between Movement and Party*, edited by Margit Mayer and John Ely. Translated by Michael Schatzschneider. Philadelphia: Temple University Press.

Kornberg, Allan, William Mishler, and Harold D. Clarke. 1982. *Representative Democracy in the Canadian Provinces*. Scarborough, ON: Prentice-Hall Canada.

Kriesi, Hanspeter. 1996. "The Organizational Structure of New Social Movements in a Political Context." In *Comparative Perspectives on Social Movements: Political Opportunities, Mobilizing Structures, and Cultural Framings*, edited by Doug McAdam, John D. McCarthy, and Mayer N. Zald. Cambridge: Cambridge University Press.

Laclau, Ernesto, and Chantal Mouffe. 1985. *Hegemony and Socialist Strategy: Towards a Radical Democratic Politics*. London: Verso.

Latus, Margaret Ann. 1983. "Ideological PACs and Political Action." In *The New Christian Right: Mobilization and Legitimation,* edited by Robert C. Liebman and Robert Wuthnow. New York: Aldine Publishing.

Lawson, Kay. 1988. "When Linkage Fails." In *When Parties Fail: Emerging Alternative Organizations,* edited by Kay Lawson and Peter H. Merkl. Princeton: Princeton University Press.

Laycock, David. 1994. "Reforming Canadian Democracy? Institutions and Ideology in the Reform Party Project." *Canadian Journal of Political Science* 27 (2): 213-47.

–. 2001. "Saying No: BC Voters and the Canadian Alliance in the 2000 Federal Election." *BC Studies,* no. 129 (Spring): 15-20.

Leslie, Graham. 1991. *Breach of Promise: Socred Ethics under Vander Zalm.* Madeira Park, BC: Harbour Publishing.

Liebman, Robert C., and Robert Wuthnow, eds. 1983. *The New Christian Right: Mobilization and Legitimation.* New York: Aldine Publishing.

Lienesch, Michael. 1993. *Redeeming America: Piety and Politics in the New Christian Right.* North Carolina: University of North Carolina Press.

–. 1997. "The Origins of the Christian Right: Early Fundamentalism as a Political Movement." In *Sojourners in the Wilderness: The Christian Right in Comparative Perspective,* edited by Corwin E. Smidt and James M. Penning. Lanham, MD: Rowman and Littlefield Publishers.

Lipset, Seymour Martin. 1988. "Neoconservatism: Myth and Reality." *Society* 25 (5): 30-37.

Lo, Clarence Y.H. 1982. "Countermovements and Conservative Movements in the Contemporary U.S." *Annual Review of Sociology* 8: 107-34.

Luker, Kristin. 1984. *Abortion and the Politics of Motherhood.* Berkeley: University of California Press.

Lyon, Vaughan. 1983. "The Future of Parties: Inevitable ... Obsolete?" *Journal of Canadian Studies* 18 (4): 108-31.

–. 1992. "Green Politics: Political Parties, Elections, and Environmental Policy." In *Canadian Environmental Policy: Ecosystems, Politics, and Process,* edited by Robert Boardman. Toronto: Oxford University Press.

–. 1996. "Parties and Democracy: A Critical View." In *Canadian Parties in Transition: Discourse, Organization, and Representation,* edited by A. Brian Tanguay and Alain-G. Gagnon, 2nd ed. Scarborough, ON: Nelson Canada.

Macpherson, C.B. 1953. *Democracy in Alberta: The Theory and Practice of a Quasi-Party System.* Toronto: University of Toronto Press.

–. 1980. *Burke.* Toronto: Oxford University Press.

Magnusson, Warren. 1990. "Critical Social Movements: De-Centring the State." In *Canadian Politics: An Introduction to the Discipline,* edited by Alain-G. Gagnon and James P. Bickerton. Toronto: Broadview Press.

Manning, Preston. 1992. *The New Canada.* Toronto: Macmillan Canada.

Marchak, Patricia. 1985. "The New Right and the New Economic Reality" (abridged version). Paper presented at Queen's University, January.

–. 1986. "The Rise and Fall of the Peripheral State: The Case of British Columbia." In *Regionalism in Canada,* edited by Robert J. Brym. Toronto: Irwin Publishing.

Marx, Gary T., and Douglas McAdam. 1994. *Collective Behavior and Social Movements: Process and Structure.* Englewood Cliffs: Prentice-Hall.

Mayer, Margit, and John Ely, eds. 1998. *The German Greens: Paradox between Movement and Party.* Philadelphia: Temple University Press.

McAdam, Doug. 1982. *Political Process and the Development of Black Insurgency: 1930-1980.* Chicago: University of Chicago Press.

–. 1988. "Micromobilization Contexts and Recruitment to Activism." *International Social Movement Research* 1: 125-54.

–. 1996. "Conceptual Origins, Current Problems, Future Directions." In *Comparative Perspectives on Social Movements: Political Opportunities, Mobilizing Structures, and Cultural Framings,* edited by Doug McAdam, John D. McCarthy, and Mayer N. Zald. Cambridge: Cambridge University Press.

McAdam, Doug, John D. McCarthy, and Mayer N. Zald. 1988. "Social Movements." In *Handbook of Sociology*, edited by Neil J. Smelser. London: Sage.

–. 1996. "Introduction: Opportunities, Mobilizing Structures, and Framing Processes – Toward a Synthetic, Comparative Perspective on Social Movements." In *Comparative Perspectives on Social Movements: Political Opportunities, Mobilizing Structures, and Cultural Framings*, edited by Doug McAdam, John D. McCarthy, and Mayer N. Zald. Cambridge: Cambridge University Press.

McAdam, Doug, Sidney Tarrow, and Charles Tully. 2001. *Dynamics of Contention*. Cambridge: Cambridge University Press.

McBride, Stephen. 1992. *Not Working: State, Unemployment, and Neo-Conservatism in Canada*. Toronto: University of Toronto Press.

McBride, Stephen, and John Shields. 1993. *Dismantling a Nation: Canada and the New World Order*. Halifax: Fernwood.

McCaffrey, Dawn, and Jennifer Keys. 2000. "Competitive Framing Processes in the Abortion Debate: Polarization-Vilification, Frame Saving, and Frame Debunking." *The Sociological Quarterly* 41 (1): 41-61.

McCarthy, John D. 1987. "Pro-Life and Pro-Choice Mobilization: Infrastructure Deficits and New Technologies." In *Social Movements in an Organizational Setting: Collected Essays*, edited by Mayer N. Zald and John D. McCarthy. New Brunswick, NJ: Transaction Books.

–. 1996. "Constraints and Opportunities in Adopting, Adapting, and Inventing." In *Comparative Perspectives on Social Movements: Political Opportunities, Mobilizing Structures, and Cultural Framings*, edited by Doug McAdam, John D. McCarthy and Mayer N. Zald. Cambridge: Cambridge University Press.

McCarthy, John D., and Mayer N. Zald. 1973. *The Trend of Social Movements in America: Professionalization and Resource Mobilization*. Morristown: General Learning Press.

–. 1977. "Resource Mobilization and Social Movements: A Partial Theory." *American Journal of Sociology* 82 (6): 1212-41.

–. 1987. "Resource Mobilization and Social Movements: A Partial Theory." In *Social Movements in an Organizational Setting: Collected Essays*, edited by Mayer N. Zald and John D. McCarthy. New Brunswick, NJ: Transaction Books.

McClurg Mueller, Carol. 1992. "Building Social Movement Theory." In *Frontiers in Social Movement Theory*, edited by Aldon D. Morris and Carol McClurg Mueller. London: Yale University Press.

McLintock, Barbara, and Gerry Kristianson. 1996. "The Media and British Columbia Politics." In *Politics, Policy, and Government in British Columbia*, edited by R. Kenneth Carty. Vancouver: UBC Press.

McMenemy, John. 1976a. "Fragment and Movement Parties." In *Political Parties in Canada*, edited by Conrad Winn and John McMenemy. Toronto: McGraw-Hill Ryerson.

–. 1976b. "Parliamentary Parties." In *Political Parties in Canada*, edited by Conrad Winn and John McMenemy. Toronto: McGraw-Hill Ryerson.

–. 1976c. "Party Organization." In *The Provincial Political Systems: Comparative Essays*, edited by David J. Bellamy, Jon H. Pammett, and Donald C. Rowat. Toronto: Methuen.

Meisel, John. 1991 [1985]. "Decline of Party in Canada." In *Party Politics in Canada*, edited by Hugh G. Thorburn, 6th ed. Scarborough, ON: Prentice-Hall Canada.

–. 1991. "The Dysfunctions of Canadian Parties: An Exploratory Mapping." In *Party Politics in Canada*, edited by Hugh G. Thorburn, 6th ed. Scarborough, ON: Prentice-Hall Canada.

Melucci, Alberto. 1980. "The New Social Movements: A Theoretical Approach." *Social Science Information* 19 (2): 199-226.

–. 1989. *Nomads of the Present: Social Movements and Individual Needs in Contemporary Society*, edited by John Keane and Paul Mier. Philadelphia: Temple University Press.

Meyer, David S., and Suzanne Staggenborg. 1994. "Movements, Countermovements, and the Structure of Political Opportunity." Paper presented at Annual Meeting of the American Sociological Association, Los Angeles.

–. 2000. "Social Movements: Creating Communities of Change." In *Conscious Acts and the Politics of Social Change*, edited by Robin L. Teske and Mary Ann Tétrault. Columbia: University of South Carolina Press.

Miliband, Ralph M. 1989. *Divided Societies: Class Struggle in Contemporary Capitalism.* Oxford: Clarendon Press.

Mishler, William. 1979. *Political Participation in Canada: Prospects for Democratic Citizenship.* Toronto: Macmillan.

Moen, Matthew C. 1992. *The Transformation of the Christian Right.* Tuscaloosa: University of Alabama Press.

Mooers, Colin, and Alan Sears. 1992. "The New Social Movements and the Withering Away of State Theory." In *Organizing Dissent: Contemporary Social Movements in Theory and Practice: Studies in the Politics of Counter-Hegemony,* edited by William K. Carroll. Toronto: Garamond Press.

Morley, Terence. 1996. "The Government of the Day: The Premier and Cabinet in British Columbia." In *Politics, Policy, and Government in British Columbia,* edited by R. Kenneth Carty. Vancouver: UBC Press.

Morris, Aldon D., and Carol McClurg Mueller, eds. 1992. *Frontiers in Social Movement Theory.* New Haven: Yale University Press.

Mottl, Tahi L. 1980. "The Analysis of Countermovements." *Social Problems* 27 (5): 620-35.

Mount, Ferdinand. 1982. *The Subversive Family: An Alternative History of Love and Marriage.* London: Unwin Paperbacks.

Murray, Charles A. 1988. *In Pursuit of Happiness and Good Government.* New York: Simon and Schuster.

Nelkin, Dorothy, and Michael Pollak. 1981. *The Atom Besieged: Extraparliamentary Dissent in France and Germany.* London: MIT Press.

Nisbet, Robert. 1981. "The Conservative Renaissance in Perspective." *The Public Interest* 81 (Fall): 128-41.

Noel, S.J.R. 1976. "Leadership and Clientelism." In *The Provincial Political Systems: Comparative Essays,* edited by David J. Bellamy, Jon H. Pammett, and Donald C. Rowat. Toronto: Methuen.

Oakeshott, Michael. 1997 [1962]. "On Being Conservative." In *Twentieth Century Political Theory: A Reader,* edited by Stephen Eric Bronner. New York: Routledge.

Offe, Claus. 1985. "New Social Movements: Challenging the Boundaries of Institutional Politics." *Social Research* 53 (4): 817-68.

–. 1990. "Reflections on the Institutional Self-Transformation of Movement Politics: A Tentative Stage Model." In *Challenging the Political Order: New Social Political Movements in Western Democracies,* edited by Russell J. Dalton and Manfred Kuechler. Cambridge: Polity Press.

–. 1998. "From Youth to Maturity: The Challenge of Party Politics." In *The German Greens: Paradox between Movement and Party,* edited by Margit Mayer and John Ely. Translated by Michael Schatzschneider. Philadelphia: Temple University Press.

Oliver, Pamela E., and Gerald Marwell. 1992. "Mobilizing Technologies for Collective Action." In *Frontiers in Social Movement Theory,* edited by Aldon D. Morris and Carol McClurg Mueller. New Haven: Yale University Press.

Palmer, Bryan D. 1987. *Solidarity: The Rise and Fall of an Opposition in British Columbia.* Vancouver: New Star Books.

Paltiel, Khayyam Zev. 1996. "Political Marketing, Party Finance, and the Decline of Canadian Parties." In *Canadian Parties in Transition: Discourse, Organization, and Representation,* edited by A. Brian Tanguay and Alain-G. Gagnon, 2nd ed. Scarborough, ON: Nelson Canada.

Peele, Gillian. 1988. "British Conservatism: Ideological Change and Electoral Uncertainty." In *The Transformation of Contemporary Conservatism,* edited by Brian Girvin. London: Sage Publications.

Pelletier, Réjean. 1996. "The Structures of Canadian Political Parties." In *Canadian Parties in Transition: Discourse, Organization, and Representation,* edited by A. Brian Tanguay and Alain-G. Gagnon, 2nd ed. Scarborough, ON: Nelson Canada.

Penner, Norman. 1996. "The Past, Present, and Uneasy Future of the New Democratic Party." In *Canadian Parties in Transition: Discourse, Organization, and Representation,* edited by A. Brian Tanguay and Alain-G. Gagnon, 2nd ed. Scarborough, ON: Nelson Canada.

Persky, Stan. 1989. *Fantasy Government: Bill Vander Zalm and the Future of Social Credit.* Vancouver: New Star Books.

Petchesky, Rosalind. 1981. "Antiabortion, Antifeminism, and the Rise of the New Right." *Feminist Studies* 7 (2): 207-46.

Phillips, Susan D. 1996. "Competing, Connecting, and Complementing: Parties, Interest Groups, and New Social Movements." In *Canadian Parties in Transition: Discourse, Organization, and Representation,* edited by A. Brian Tanguay and Alain-G. Gagnon, 2nd ed. Scarborough, ON: Nelson Canada.

Pinard, Maurice. 1971. *The Rise of a Third Party: A Study in Crisis Politics.* Montreal and Kingston: McGill-Queen's University Press.

–. 1973. "Third Parties in Canada Revisited: A Rejoinder and Elaboration of the Theory of One-Party Dominance." *Canadian Journal of Political Science* 6 (3): 439-60.

Pitsula, James M., and Kenneth A. Rasmussen. 1990. *Privatizing a Province: The New Right in Saskatchewan.* Vancouver: New Star Books.

Piven, Francis Fox, and Richard A. Cloward. 1977. *Poor People's Movements: Why They Succeed, How They Fail.* New York: Vintage.

Platt, Gerald M., and Rhys H. Williams. 1988. "Religions, Ideology and Electoral Politics." *Society* 25 (5): 38-45.

Plotke, David. 1990. "What's So New about New Social Movements?" *Socialist Review* 20 (1): 81-102.

Prince, Michael J. 1996. "At the Edge of Canada's Welfare State: Social Policy-Making in British Columbia." In *Politics, Policy, and Government in British Columbia,* edited by R. Kenneth Carty. Vancouver: UBC Press.

Ratner, R.S., and J.L. McMullan. 1985. "Social Control and the Rise of the 'Exceptional' State in Britain, the United States, and Canada." In *The New Criminologies in Canada: State, Crime and Control,* edited by T. Fleming. Toronto: Oxford University Press.

Reed, Ralph E., Jr. 1994a. "What Do Religious Conservatives Really Want?" In *Disciples and Democracy: Religious Conservatives and the Future of American Politics,* edited by Michael Cromartie. Grand Rapids, MI: William B. Eerdmans Publishing.

–. 1994b. *Politically Incorrect: The Emerging Faith Factor in American Politics.* Vancouver: Word Publishing.

–. 1996. *Active Faith: How Christians Are Changing the Soul of American Politics.* Toronto: Free Press.

Resnick, Phil. 2001. "The Two British Columbias." *BC Studies,* no. 129 (Spring): 21-25.

Rochon, Thomas R., and Daniel A. Mazmanian. 1993. "Social Movements and the Policy Process." *Annals of the American Academy of Political and Social Science* 528: 75-87.

Rohrschneider, Robert. 1993. "Impact of Social Movements on European Party Systems." *Annals of the American Academy of Political and Social Science* 528: 157-70.

Rose, Susan D. 1989. "Gender, Education and the New Christian Right." *Society* 26 (2): 59-66.

Roth, Roland, and Detlef Murphy. 1998. "From Competing Factions to the Rise of the Realos." In *The German Greens: Paradox between Movement and Party.* Philadelphia: Temple University Press.

Ruether, Rosemary Radford. 2000. *Christianity and the Making of the Modern Family.* Boston: Beacon Press.

Sandilands, Kate. 1992. "Ecology as Politics: The Promise and Problems of the Ontario Greens." In *Organizing Dissent: Contemporary Social Movements in Theory and Practice: Studies in the Politics of Counter-Hegemony,* edited by William K. Carroll. Toronto: Garamond Press.

Scott, Alan. 1990. *Ideology and the New Social Movements.* London: Unwin Hyman.

Scruton, Roger. 1984. *The Meaning of Conservatism.* 2nd ed. Toronto: MacMillan.

–. 1986. *Sexual Desire: A Moral Philosophy of the Erotic.* New York: Free Press.

Seidle, F. Leslie. 1996. "The Canadian Electoral System and Proposals for Reform." In *Canadian Parties in Transition: Discourse, Organization, and Representation,* edited by A. Brian Tanguay and Alain-G. Gagnon, 2nd ed. Scarborough, ON: Nelson Canada.

Shields, John. 1986. "The Solidarity Experience: Challenges for BC Labour in the 1980's." Paper presented at the Fourth BC Studies Conference, Victoria, BC, November.

Simpson, John H. 1983. "Moral Issues and Status Politics." In *The New Christian Right:*

Mobilization and Legitimation, edited by Robert C. Liebman and Robert Wuthnow. New York: Aldine.

Smelser, Neil. 1962. *Theory of Collective Behavior.* New York: Free Press.

Smidt, Corwin E., and James M. Penning. 1997. "Conclusion." In *Sojourners in the Wilderness: The Christian Right in Comparative Perspective,* edited by Corwin E. Smidt and James M. Penning. Lanham, MD: Rowman and Littlefield.

Snow, David A., and Robert D. Benford. 1988. "Ideology, Frame Resonance, and Participant Mobilization." *International Social Movement Research* 1: 197-217.

–. 1992. "Master Frames and Cycles of Protest." In *Frontiers in Social Movement Theory,* edited by Aldon D. Morris and Carol M. Mueller. New Haven: Yale University Press.

Snow, David A., E. Burke Rochford Jr., Steven K. Worden, and Robert D. Benford. 1986. "Frame Alignment Processes, Micromobilization, and Movement Participation." *American Sociological Review* 51 (August): 464-81.

Snow, David A., Louis A. Zurcher Jr., and Sheldon Ekland-Olson. 1980. "Social Networks and Social Movements: A Microstructural Approach to Differential Recruitment." *American Sociological Review* 45 (October): 787-801.

Soper, Christopher J. 1994. *Evangelical Christianity in the United States and Great Britain: Religious Beliefs, Political Choices.* London: MacMillan Press.

Stackhouse, John G., Jr. 1993. *Canadian Evangelicalism in the Twentieth Century: An Introduction to Its Character.* Toronto: University of Toronto Press.

Steuter, Erin. 1992. "Women against Feminism: An Examination of Feminist Social Movements and Anti-Feminist Countermovements." *The Canadian Review of Sociology and Anthropology* 29 (3): 288-306.

Taggart, Paul. 2000. *Populism.* Philadelphia: Open University Press.

Tanguay, A. Brian. 1992. "Canadian Party Ideologies in the Electronic Age." In *Canadian Political Party Systems: A Reader,* edited by R. Kenneth Carty. Toronto: Broadview Press.

Tanguay, A. Brian, and Alain-G. Gagnon. 1996. "Introduction." In *Canadian Parties in Transition: Discourse, Organization, and Representation,* edited by A. Brian Tanguay and Alain-G. Gagnon, 2nd ed. Scarborough, ON: Nelson Canada.

Taras, David. 1996. "Political Parties as Media Organizations: The Art of Getting Elected." In *Canadian Parties in Transition: Discourse, Organization, and Representation,* edited by A. Brian Tanguay and Alain-G. Gagnon, 2nd ed. Scarborough, ON: Nelson Canada.

Tarrow, Sidney. 1983. *Struggling to Reform: Social Movements and Policy Change during Cycles of Protest.* Western Societies Paper No. 15. Ithaca, NY: Cornell University.

–. 1988. "National Politics and Collective Action: Recent Theory and Research in Western Europe and the United States." *Annual Review of Sociology* 14: 421-40.

–. 1989. *Struggle, Politics, and Reform: Collective Action, Social Movements, and Cycles of Protest.* Western Societies Program Occasional Paper No. 21. Ithaca, NY: Center for International Studies, Cornell University.

–. 1994. *Power in Movement: Social Movements, Collective Action and Politics.* Cambridge: Cambridge University Press.

–. 1996. "States and Opportunities: The Political Structuring of Social Movements." In *Comparative Perspectives on Social Movements: Political Opportunities, Mobilizing Structures, and Cultural Framings,* edited by Doug McAdam, John D. McCarthy, and Mayer N. Zald. Cambridge: Cambridge University Press.

Tedin, Kent L. 1978. "Religious Preference and Pro/Anti Activism on the Equal Rights Amendment Issue." *Pacific Sociological Review* 21 (1): 55-65.

Teske, Robin L., and Mary Ann Tétrault, eds. 2000. *Feminist Approaches to Social Movements, Community and Power.* Columbia, SC: University of South Carolina Press.

Thorburn, Hugh G. 1991a. "Interpretations of the Canadian Party System." In *Party Politics in Canada,* edited by Hugh G. Thorburn, 6th ed. Scarborough, ON: Prentice-Hall Canada.

–. 1991b. "The Development of Political Parties in Canada." In *Party Politics in Canada,* edited by Hugh G. Thorburn, 6th ed. Scarborough, ON: Prentice-Hall Canada.

Tilley, Charles. 1978. *From Mobilization to Revolution.* Reading, MA: Addison-Wesley.

Touraine, Alain. 2001. *Beyond Neoliberalism.* Translated by David Macey. Cambridge: Polity.

Tucker, Kenneth II. 1991. "IIow New Are the New Social Movements?" *Theory, Culture and Society* 8 (2): 75-98.

Unity Party of British Columbia. 2002. "Foundational Principles." *Constitution.* <www.unityparty.bc.ca/constitution/php>.

Vanwoudenberg, Ed. 1989. *A Matter of Choice.* Vancouver: Premier Printing.

Warnock, John W. 1988. *Free Trade and the New Right Agenda.* Vancouver: New Star Books.

Werum, Regina, and Bill Winders. 2001. "Who's 'In' and Who's 'Out': State Fragmentation and the Struggle over Gay Rights, 1974-1999." *Social Problems* 48 (3): 386-410.

Whitehorn, Alan. 1991. "The CCF-NDP and the End of the Broadbent Era." In *Party Politics in Canada,* edited by Hugh G. Thorburn, 6th ed. Scarborough, ON: Prentice-Hall Canada.

Wilcox, Clyde, and Mark J. Rozell. 2000. "Conclusion: The Christian Right in Campaign '98." In *Prayers in the Precincts: The Christian Right in the 1998 Elections,* edited by John C. Green, et al. Washington, DC: Georgetown University Press.

Wilkinson, Paul. 1971. *Social Movement.* London: Macmillan.

Willetts, David. 1992. *Modern Conservatism.* London: Penguin.

Winkler, Earl R. 1984. "Abortion and Victimisability." *Journal of Applied Philosophy* 1 (2): 305-18.

Wolfe, David. 1989. "The Canadian State in Comparative Perspective." *The Canadian Review of Sociology and Anthropology* 26 (1): 95-126.

Woliver, Laura L. 1998. "Social Movements and Abortion Law." In *Social Movements and American Political Institutions,* edited by Anne N. Costain and Andrew S. McFarland. Lanham, MD: Rowman and Littlefield.

Wuthnow, Robert. 1983. "The Political Rebirth of American Evangelicals." In *The New Christian Right: Mobilization and Legitimation,* edited by Robert C. Liebman and Robert Wuthnow. New York: Aldine Publishing.

Young, Walter. 1992. "A Party-Movement: The CCF and the Rejection of Brokerage Politics." In *Canadian Political Party Systems: A Reader,* edited by R. Kenneth Carty. Toronto: Broadview Press.

Zald, Mayer N. 1988. "The Trajectory of Social Movements in America." *Research in Social Movements, Conflicts and Change* 10: 19-41.

–. 1996. "Culture, Ideology, and Strategic Framing." In *Comparative Perspectives on Social Movements: Political Opportunities, Mobilizing Structures, and Cultural Framings,* edited by Doug McAdam, John D. McCarthy, Mayer N. Zald. Cambridge: Cambridge University Press.

Zald, Mayer N., and Roberta Ash. 1966. "Social Movement Organizations: Growth, Decay and Change." *Social Forces* 44 (March): 327-41.

Zald, Mayer N., and Bert Useem. 1987. "Movement and Countermovement Interaction: Mobilization, Tactics and State Involvement." In *Social Movements in an Organizational Setting: Collected Essays,* edited by Mayer N. Zald and John D. McCarthy. New Brunswick, NJ: Transaction Books.

Zirakzadeh, Cyrus Ernesto. 1997. *Social Movements and Politics: A Comparative Study.* New York: Longman Publishing.

Zurcher, Louis, and David A. Snow. 1981. "Collective Behavior: Social Movements." In *Social Psychology, Sociological Perspectives,* edited by Morris Rosenberg and Ralph Turner. New York: Basic Books.

Index

Printed and bound in Canada by Friesens

Set in Stone by Brenda and Neil West, BN Typographics West

Copy editor: Susan Wawanash

Proofreader: Deborah Kerr

Indexer: Noeline Bridge